THE CORRESPONDENCE OF SPINOZA

SPINOZA

(*From the original portrait at Wolfenbüttel*)

THE
CORRESPONDENCE
OF
SPINOZA

Translated and Edited with Introduction
and Annotations by

A. WOLF

NEW YORK
RUSSELL & RUSSELL · INC
1966

FIRST PUBLISHED IN 1928
BY GEORGE ALLEN & UNWIN LTD.

REISSUED, 1966, BY
RUSSELL & RUSSELL, DIVISION OF ATHENEUM HOUSE, INC.
BY ARRANGEMENT WITH FRANK CASS & CO. LTD., LONDON
L.C. CATALOG CARD NO: 66-15948

Printed in Great Britain

DEDICATED

TO

THE MEMORY OF

MY MOTHER

THERESA WOLF

PREFACE

MANY years ago I proposed as the subject of my thesis for a higher degree " Some Aspects of the Philosophy of Spinoza." Two eminent scholars who were consulted about it were of opinion that everything worth saying about Spinoza had already been said. So I turned my attention to other fields of research. But when at last I was done with university examinations and degrees, I returned to Spinoza, only to find that, so far from the last word having been said, the very spade-work had not yet been done properly. Since then it has been my endeavour to do the necessary spade-work whenever I could snatch the time from other, more immediate duties. So far I have published in this connection the *Short Treatise on God, Man and His Well-being* and *The Oldest Biography of Spinoza*, both edited with introductions and annotations. I have also indicated in special papers on the subject some radical errors in the current interpretations of Spinoza's philosophy. The present volume carries the spade-work a stage farther. And I hope that circumstances may prove sufficiently favourable to enable me to complete the translation and annotation of Spinoza's complete works during the next three or four years, in time for the celebration of the tercentenary of his birth in 1932.

It has been my endeavour to make the translation at once as easily intelligible and as thoroughly reliable as possible. The translation is based on the recent Heidelberg edition of the original Latin and Dutch texts of the complete works of Spinoza ; but I have used my own discretion in the choice of alternative texts and in amending a few of the readings.*

* A list of these will be found at the end of the volume, after the Annotations.

Apart from the occasional difficulties of the subjects discussed in the letters—difficulties that could only be dealt with, and are dealt with, either in the Introduction or in the Annotations—there are naturally also difficulties of translation. There are minor difficulties relating to the use of stops and of capitals, which, in all languages, was very different in the seventeenth century from what it is now; and there are more serious difficulties presented by words which have either gone out of use or have entirely changed their meaning. Wherever it could be done without risk of bewildering the reader, something of the flavour of the seventeenth century has been retained in the translation.

The irregular use of capitals can do no harm. Sometimes even unusual punctuation is harmless; but to have followed it throughout, and to have retained extremely long and complicated sentences without some simplification, could only have ended in bewildering the average reader. A few of Bacon's and Boyle's terms have been retained here and there. It would, for instance, have been a pity to drop Boyle's *icicles* in favour of the modern chemist's " dirt." But this kind of thing could only be done sparingly. Except in a few safe contexts it would have been risky to translate *affectio* by " affection," instead of by " state " or " condition." The term *accidens* having no exact English equivalent is translated by *accident* (always in italics), and explained in the Annotations. The verb *determinare* is usually translated by " limit," instead of by the ambiguous " determine," and is likewise explained in the Annotations. The expression *intellectus* is in most cases rendered by the traditional " understanding," but occasionally by " intellect," partly because it seemed somehow preferable, and partly because it seems a pity to let " intellect " go out of use.

The Introduction and the Annotations will, it is

PREFACE

hoped, be found to elucidate all that needs elucidation in the *Correspondence*. Everything of historical and scientific interest is discussed fairly fully. The comments on the more philosophical problems are limited to the immediate needs of the *Correspondence*—the fuller discussion of the most important problems being reserved for subsequent volumes devoted to the *Ethics*, etc.

The preparation of this volume has entailed much labour and research. But for the kind help of a number of friends the publication of the *Correspondence* would have been delayed considerably. I gladly avail myself of this opportunity to express my best thanks to Mr. A. Armitage, Mr. F. W. Chapman, Professor P. Geyl, Mr. D. McKie, Miss I. V. Scowby, and Mr. W. G. van der Tak.

A. WOLF

UNIVERSITY OF LONDON,
November, 1927.

CONTENTS

* The square brackets, throughout these *Contents*, give approximate dates of
undated letters.

CORRESPONDENCE OF SPINOZA

CONTENTS

ILLUSTRATIONS

Table Showing the Present Number of each Letter and its Former Number in the "Posthumous Works" and other Editions before 1882.

Present No.	Former No.	Present No.	Former No.	Present No.	Former No.
I	I	XXX	—	LVIII	LXII
II	II	XXXI	XIV	LIX	LXIII
III	III	XXXII	XV	LX	LXIV
IV	IV	XXXIII	XVI	LXI	XVII
V	V	XXXIV	XXXIX	LXII	XVIII
VI	VI	XXXV	XL	LXIII	LXV
VII	VII	XXXVI	XLI	LXIV	LXVI
VIII	XXVI	XXXVII	XLII	LXV	LXVII
IX	XXVII	XXXVIII	XLIII	LXVI	LXVIII
X	XXVIII	XXXIX	XLIV	LXVII	LXXIII
XI	VIII	XL	XLV	LXVIIA	—
XII	XXIX	XLI	XLVI	LXVIII	XIX
XIII	IX	XLII	XLVIII	LXIX	—
XIV	X	XLIII	XLIX	LXX	—
XV	—	XLIV	XLVII	LXXI	XX
XVI	XI	XLV	LI	LXXII	—
XVII	XXX	XLVI	LII	LXXIII	XXI
XVIII	XXXI	XLVII	LIII	LXXIV	XXII
XIX	XXXII	XLVIII	LIV	LXXV	XXIII
XX	XXXIII	XLVIIIA	—	LXXVI	LXXIV
XXI	XXXIV	XLIX	—	LXXVII	XXIV
XXII	XXXV	L	L	LXXVIII	XXV
XXIII	XXXVI	LI	LV	LXXIX	—
XXIV	XXXVII	LII	LVI	LXXX	LXIX
XXV	XII	LIII	LVII	LXXXI	LXX
XXVI	XIII	LIV	LVIII	LXXXII	LXXI
XXVII	XXXVIII	LV	LIX	LXXXIII	LXXII
XXVIII	—	LVI	LX	LXXXIV	Pref. to
XXIX	—	LVII	LXI		Pol. Tr.

Former No.	Present No.	Former No.	Present No.	Former No.	Present No.
I	I	XXVI	VIII	LI	XLV
II	II	XXVII	IX	LII	XLVI
III	III	XXVIII	X	LIII	LXVII
IV	IV	XXIX	XII	LIV	LXVIII
V	V	XXX	XVII	LV	LI
VI	VI	XXXI	XVIII	LVI	LII
VII	VII	XXXII	XIX	LVII	LIII
VIII	XI	XXXIII	XX	LVIII	LIV
IX	XIII	XXXIV	XXI	LIX	LV
X	XIV	XXXV	XXII	LX	LVI
XI	XVI	XXXVI	XXIII	LXI	LVII
XII	XXV	XXXVII	XXIV	LXII	LVIII
XIII	XXVI	XXXVIII	XXVII	LXIII	LIX
XIV	XXXI	XXXIX	XXXIV	LXIV	LX
XV	XXXII	XL	XXXV	LXV	LXIII
XVI	XXXIII	XLI	XXXVI	LXVI	LXIV
XVII	LXI	XLII	XXXVII	LXVII	LXV
XVIII	LXII	XLIII	XXXVIII	LXVIII	LXVI
XIX	LXVIII	XLIV	XXXIX	LXIX	LXXX
XX	LXXI	XLV	XL	LXX	LXXXI
XXI	LXXIII	XLVI	XLI	LXXI	LXXXII
XXII	LXXIV	XLVII	XLIV	LXXII	LXXXIII
XXIII	LXXV	XLVIII	XLII	LXXIII	LXVII
XXIV	LXXVII	XLIX	XLIII	LXXIV	LXXVI
XXV	LXXVIII	L	L		

INTRODUCTION

INTRODUCTION

THE correspondence of Spinoza is deeply interesting in many ways. It presents a pageant of the leading types of seventeenth-century mentality. It affords contemporary glimpses of important scientific researches and discoveries. It brings us into touch with some of the social and political events and tendencies of the period. It throws a flood of light on the pains and vicissitudes which accompanied the birth of the modern spirit and the emancipation of Western thought from the chains of authority and tradition, to which it had grown so accustomed as almost to dread to venture on the uncharted sea of Freedom. The letters contain things of first-rate importance for the correct interpretation of the philosophy of Spinoza; and, above all, they help one to realize something of the greatness and strength of his character—one of the greatest in the whole history of mankind.

It is well known that the study of Spinoza's writings left a profound and lasting impression on great men like Lessing, Goethe, Huxley, and many others. But the correctness or justification of that impression has sometimes been challenged. It has been suggested that the impression may have been due in large measure to the impressionable phantasy of the recipients. Spinoza's correspondence, however, taken in conjunction with his *Oldest Biography* by Lucas, conclusively refutes the challenge. They show that it was precisely such a profound impression that personal contact with Spinoza left on the minds of lesser and less imaginative people like Oldenburg, De Vries, Jelles, Schuller, and Lucas. The letters, moreover, not only show *that* such an impression was produced by personal intercourse with

Spinoza, they also help to explain *how and why* it was produced. For they reveal, not only his wisdom and tact and unselfish devotion to the pursuit of knowledge, but also his amazing patience with the most trying bores, his calm indifference to the tactlessness or vulgarity of others, his painstaking endeavours to enlighten some of his superstitious correspondents, his constant readiness to help all who avowed an interest in the search for Truth, and withal his outspoken candour and his dislike of all prevarication, even at the risk of estranging some of his oldest friends. These things help one to appreciate the remark which Goethe made to Lavater about a hundred years after the death of Spinoza. "His correspondence," said Goethe, "is the most interesting book one can read in the world of uprightness and of humanity." *

* *Goethe's Gespräche*, Woldemar Frhr. von Biedermann. Ed. 1909, vol. i, pp. 35 f.

§ 1. THE SEVENTEENTH CENTURY

THE seventeenth century marked the climax of that revolt against mere authority and tradition which the Reformation and the Renaissance had initiated. Descartes (1596–1650) was in many ways typical of that century, both in its strength and in its weakness. He voiced its battle-cry of universal doubt—*de omnibus dubitandum*—and his scientific and mathematical achievements hold a place of honour in that golden age of the revival of science. For many centuries the spirit of man had been at once guided and restrained by the reins of authority and tradition, and would not believe its own eyes unless confirmed by some authority, religious or secular. Gradually, however, there arose a succession of adventurous spirits who escaped from the leading-strings and restraints of tradition and authority, and endeavoured to see things for themselves, and to make their orientation in the light of their own capacities. In this way Galilei accepted the reality of sunspots because he saw them with his own eyes aided by the telescope, and was not shaken in his belief merely because it was not confirmed by the authority of Scripture or of Aristotle. In this way likewise he embraced the heliocentric hypothesis, in spite of Scripture and tradition, though the Church was sufficiently powerful to extort a lip-recantation, and to enforce exile and silence. In this way also many people, prompted by their inner conscience, forsook powerful and authoritative Churches, Roman and Protestant, in order to follow the guidance of their own inner light.

But the revolt had its limitations—serious limitations. Descartes' summons to universal doubt was a flourish rather than a serious call to arms. It is almost pathetic to witness how easily his doubts were satisfied. It is almost comical to see how he strains at a gnat and swallows a camel; how he declines to believe in the reality of observed objects, yet readily accepts the reality of a supernatural Deity whom he promptly burdens with the responsibility for all Cartesian beliefs and fancies. No Church dignitary ever exploited God as a very ready help in time of trouble more than Descartes did. If his scientific endeavours require the existence of bodies or of souls, he makes God create them out of nothing. If the bodies need motion and rest to account for their appearances, he makes God endow them with motion and rest. If he finds it convenient to assume the constancy or conservation of motion and rest, he makes God constant or consistent in His relation to motion and rest; and so on. For Descartes the phenomena of Nature are essentially miraculous—that is, the result of the incessant interference of a supernatural Deity. When we have given him all the credit that is due to him for his great achievements in mathematics, in optics, etc., it remains true that fundamentally he remained the loyal disciple of his Jesuit College—his ultimate philosophic orientation is essentially the same as that of the miracle-mongering Church. And Descartes' real achievements were in the domain of Science rather than in that of Philosophy.

Some people may feel tempted to vindicate Descartes the philosopher at the expense of Descartes the Roman Catholic. They may argue (as indeed some people have argued) that Descartes' profession of faith in the three miracles—namely, creation out of nothing, free-will, and the God-man—and his other Christian professions were but lip-professions intended to save his skin from an all-powerful and none too scrupulous Church—in short, they were of the same order as his escape to Holland. They may point out that it was in Descartes' lifetime that Giordano Bruno was burned at the stake and Galileo Galilei was humiliated, imprisoned, and exiled for intellectual boldness, and that the moral of these tragedies was probably not lost on Descartes. But there is little or no evidence in support of this contention. We can only deal with his writings as he left them. And there are other cases in which initial or tentative sceptics and other bold thinkers soon flagged in spirit at sight of uncharted seas, and gladly returned to the sheltered and familiar havens of authority and tradition. Some of Spinoza's correspondents, as we shall see presently, were men of this type, even if they were not all as distinguished as Descartes.

It is a serious disadvantage resulting from the great outward triumph of Christianity that the thinkers of Christendom rarely come into vital contact with other religions and other modes of world orientation. The consequence of this inexperience is that Christian ways of looking at the world are assumed to be true as a matter of course, at all events after a little doctoring by means of the various specifics furnished by Christian apologetists and other dilettante philosophers. Custom is mistaken for conviction, and conviction for demonstration. Add to this the fact that really independent and plausible world-views are very rare, because they are so difficult, and that scepticism (or the refusal to take one's orientation, or to embrace some existing world-view or other) is not a bed of roses, but a bed of thorns for most people, and it becomes sufficiently intelligible why born Christians mostly remain Christians willy-nilly. The philosophy of Christendom is thus prejudiced, more or less, from the start, and its acrobatics are in some ways truly amazing. Earlier, less sophisticated Christians, who still had confidence in human capacity for knowledge, regarded Faith (that is, of course, Christian Faith) as a means to Knowledge; they professed to believe in order that they might know. But modern, more sophisticated Christians find it necessary to shatter Knowledge in order to save Christian Faith. The modesty of this scepticism only veils the conceit of an exclusive revelation. From the " critical " Kant to our " sceptical " Lord Balfour, to say nothing of the army of professional, professorial philosophers at the universities of Christendom, the customary slogan is not " have Faith that you may attain to Knowledge," but " shatter Knowledge that you may lie at ease in Faith."

The slogan, of course, is much older than Kant. We shall find it set out at great, tedious length in the letters of Burgh and of Steno. Both Burgh and Steno appear to have been stirred in their early years by the new spirit of the age. They, too, had set out in search of undiscovered truth. But the buffetings of the open sea were too much for them, and both sought refuge in the Roman Catholic Church. There they found peace (though we do not know for how long), and no doubt it was a kindly thought which prompted each of them to write to Spinoza, their former captain, in a vain attempt to persuade him to seek salvation after their fashion. They had no idea of the mettle of a rare, independent spirit like Spinoza. There were others, of course, somewhat hardier characters than Burgh and Steno. There were people like Boyle and Oldenburg, Velthuysen and Blyenbergh, who wished to make the best of both worlds, and wanted to be at once philosophers and Christians, but Christians first of all. This was stated explicitly by Blyenbergh, who was less intelligent but more candid than the others.

Such, in brief, was the Christian atmosphere in which the philosophy and the science of the seventeenth century breathed. The mentality of that century is much misunderstood when its science and its philosophy are divorced from its theology. It is easy enough to praise and to extol the scientific work of talented investigators like Boyle, or of geniuses like Kepler and Newton, and, of course, they do, indeed, deserve all praise for their achievements; but to understand them adequately and justly it is necessary also to study their theological writings, and then one realizes the exaggerations in the usual accounts of the boldness and daring and originality of seventeenth-century thought.

It would be no exaggeration to say that Huxley's ideal of a man of science, as one who sceptically scrutinizes the credentials of all beliefs before embracing them, was but rarely realized even approximately in the seventeenth century. The Cartesian proclamation of universal doubt (*de omnibus dubitandum*), as will be explained presently, was not really meant, or taken, very seriously. Much more characteristic of the period was the attitude of a man like Hugo Boxel, a statesman and man of the world who believed in ghosts and spooks, and considered himself fully justified in believing in them until their existence could be *disproved*. The question asked, by those who asked questions at all, was not why they *should* believe this or that, but why they *should not* believe it. In all matters within the Christian universe of discourse, in all matters which (like ghosts, evil spirits, witches, etc.) seemed to be sanctioned by the Scriptures, even comparatively enlightened people felt justified in believing in them so long as others could not absolutely disprove them.

The boldest and most original thinker in the seventeenth century was Spinoza, who stood above the theological prejudices from which the others could not entirely extricate themselves.

Needless to say, in speaking of the Christian atmosphere of the seventeenth century, the reference is to Christian dogmas, not to Christian charity, of which, alas! there was as little in the seventeenth century as there is in the twentieth.

§ 2. DESCARTES AND SPINOZA

By proclaiming universal doubt to be the first step to
a genuine philosophy, and by insisting on clear and
distinct ideas as the condition of real knowledge,
Descartes certainly rendered a great service to the
revival of philosophy. But his importance in the
history of philosophy has been grossly exaggerated.
The exaggeration is due to a variety of reasons, only
some of which need detain us here.

In the first place, he was held in high esteem by many
of his contemporaries. This was natural and right.
For the seventeenth century did not yet distinguish
between science and philosophy as we do nowadays.
In the seventeenth century all that is now called science
was just part and parcel of philosophy, and so long as
Descartes the philosopher included Descartes the man
of science, Descartes deserved all the praise he received
as the hero of " the new philosophy." The moment,
however, his contributions to science are divorced
from his contributions to philosophy, as, of course,
they are when we speak of philosophy in the
present-day sense of the term, the position is greatly
altered. However much we may praise his contributions to science, it is really impossible to rank
very highly his contributions to philosophy properly
so called.

In the second place, the exaggeration of Descartes'
merits as a philosopher is due to a natural Christian bias.
The very fact that he set out, or at least professed to set
out, with a thoroughgoing methodological scepticism,
and nevertheless ended as a loyal Christian, made him
especially dear to the philosophers of Christendom,
obsessed as nearly all of them have been and still

are with Christian ideas, as was explained in the preceding section. Hence this attempt to make him the very source and inspiration of all modern philosophy. Spinoza, a Jew, and an excommunicated Jew to boot, Spinoza the reputed atheist and what not, was under the circumstances not likely to be treated as anything but a Cartesian oddity or aberration.

In the third place, under the influence of Hegel and of the magic of Hegelian dialectic, it became the fashion to present the later phases of modern philosophy as a mere unfolding of its earlier phases. And so it came about that the philosophy of Spinoza, like that of Malebranche and of others, was regarded merely as a form of Cartesianism. Look at the earlier editions of Kuno Fischer's great *History of Modern Philosophy*, and you will find that Spinoza was included in the school of Descartes. In the *Encyclopædia Britannica* as late as the thirteenth edition the philosophy of Spinoza was described under Cartesianism. And these works are typical of most works dealing with the history of modern philosophy. It was not very difficult to represent Spinozism as a transformation of Cartesianism. Historians of philosophy, trained in the subtleties of Christian theology, had no misgivings about representing Spinozism as the transubstantiation of Cartesianism. Philosophers skilled in the tricks of Hegelian dialectic readily perceived in the Spinozistic antithesis to Cartesianism the crowning phase thereof.

Another factor which helped to perpetuate the exaggerated estimate of Cartesianism at the expense of Spinozism is the easy intelligibility of Descartes' *Discourse on Method* and his *Meditations*, in contrast with the difficulty of Spinoza's writings. Students of philosophy and even others had no difficulty in reading, and more or less understanding, the *Method* and the *Medita-*

tions; but the vast majority found, and still find, it very difficult to know Spinoza at first hand, so they rely on second or even fifth-hand information, and in this way help to maintain old superstitions.

But let anyone take a simple inventory of the fundamental notions in the philosophy of Descartes and in that of Spinoza; let him compare them frankly and candidly, without theological subtleties or dialectical sophistications, and he will be amazed at the impertinence of the old legend. What was Descartes' idea of God but that entertained by any ordinary Christian and by many others? What were his notions of Extension and of Thought but the ordinary ideas of two classes of realities, namely, bodies and souls, arbitrarily created out of nothing by a supernatural God, and arbitrarily controlled by Him? How entirely different is the Spinozistic conception of God as identical with the infinite Universe, in which nothing ever happens arbitrarily, and of which Extension and Thought are Attributes whose finite modes or modifications are the bodies and souls of ordinary thought and experience! These differences are palpable, and there are others just as palpable, as may be seen from some of the letters which follow.

Moreover, as is clear from his correspondence, Spinoza himself and many of his contemporaries were fully aware of these antagonisms between his philosophy and that of Descartes. Spinoza's letters to Meyer and to Oldenburg show this, and so, in a very remarkable manner, does the letter from Steno, who addressed Spinoza, not as the follower or teacher of the " new philosophy " (that is, Cartesianism), but as the " Reformer " thereof—a term not suggestive of an amicable relationship when used by a fervent Catholic in the seventeenth century. And the earliest biographer of Spinoza, too, refers to the hostility of the Cartesians against Spinoza.* The subtle juggling by which Spinozism has been read out of Cartesianism, by suitable adjustments of both, has only resulted in a misinterpretation of both these systems.

* See *The Earliest Biography of Spinoza*, edited and translated by A. Wolf, pp. 74 f., and Letter LXVIII.

§ 3. OLDENBURG, BOYLE, AND SPINOZA

ABOUT a third of all the existing correspondence of Spinoza consists of letters which passed between him and Oldenburg. It is obvious, moreover, that many more letters, now unfortunately lost, must have passed between them. Oldenburg must therefore be regarded as Spinoza's principal correspondent, as well as the first whose letters have come down to us. For this and for other reasons, he is clearly entitled to special consideration in connection with the study of the correspondence of Spinoza.

HENRY OLDENBURG (? 1615–77) was born in Bremen, where he also studied, graduating as Master in Theology in 1639. His degree thesis dealt with the problem of the relation between Church and State. He came to England about 1640, and appears to have stayed here until 1648. He then travelled about on the Continent, and returned to Bremen about 1652. During the war between England and Holland, following England's enforcement of the Navigation Act in 1651, the ship-owners of Bremen suffered in various ways. So in the summer of 1653 the Council of Bremen sent Oldenburg to negotiate with Cromwell and make arrangements whereby the neutrality of Bremen should be respected. Oldenburg stayed in England, engaged partly in diplomatic work and partly in teaching. One of his pupils was Robert Jones, nephew of Robert Boyle, with whom he thus became acquainted. From 1657 till 1660 he travelled with his pupil on the Continent, and made the acquaintance of many scholars. In 1661 he visited his native town, and from there he went to Leyden, where he looked up his fellow-townsman, Johannes Coccejus,

OLDENBURG

(*From the portrait at the Royal Society*)

Professor of Theology at the University there. Spinoza at that time was living at Rhynsburg, near Leyden, and Oldenburg's eagerness to get to know men of promise may be gathered from the fact that he specially sought out Spinoza in his humble out-of-the-way lodging, and had a long talk with him. Oldenburg's early letters to Spinoza show what a deep impression the much younger man had made on him. In this way Spinoza was brought into touch with the work of the Royal Society, and more especially with the work of Robert Boyle, of which more will be said presently.

When the Royal Society received its Charter of Incorporation in July 1662 Oldenburg was appointed secretary (jointly with Dr. J. Wilkins), and he promptly set about mobilizing " a commerce in all parts of the world with the most philosophical and curious persons to be found everywhere," in order to carry out the design of the members of the Royal Society, who (to quote his own words again) " have taken to task the whole universe." This involved an enormous amount of correspondence for those days. Our present abundance or superabundance of learned and scientific periodicals was unknown in the seventeenth century. The function which they perform now was carried out in those days by letters, which were frequently not letters in the modern sense, but dissertations, " epistolary dissertations " (to use Malpighi's phrase). Some of the letters which passed between Oldenburg and Spinoza were obviously such " epistolary dissertations." They concerned, however, Boyle rather than Oldenburg, who acted as intermediary between Boyle and Spinoza.

In view of subsequent events it must be said that Oldenburg's early letters to Spinoza are remarkable for their impetuous devotion to new discoveries as well as for their homage to Spinoza. They display a curious reversal of rôles, inasmuch as they show us the much older man urging the younger man boldly to spread the sails of the new learning, to cease humouring ignorance and pedantry, and to defy the pigmy theologians. But the spirit of Oldenburg soon flagged after his sad experiences during the plague of London in 1665, the great fire in 1666, and his imprisonment in the Tower of London in 1667. The atmosphere of suspicion, distrust, and hatred which war produces is too well known to need description. Even in the twentieth century the Churches could not or would not seriously attempt to drive out the evil spirits let loose by war, so why expect the seventeenth century to have coped more successfully with the loathsome progeny of Mars? The war between England and Holland (1665-67), coupled with the plague and the great fire of London, certainly tended to upset people's mental equilibrium. Oldenburg's vast foreign correspondence was naturally suspected at Court. The king was himself too great an adept at intrigue not to distrust everybody else. So in June 1667 Oldenburg was clapped into the Tower, where he stayed two terrible months, and might have stayed much longer but for the termination of the war. Oldenburg left his prison a sadder and much more cautious, indeed a very nervous, man, and when, after a break of about ten years, he wrote again to Spinoza, he had changed almost entirely from his former self, partly perhaps under the reactionary influence of Boyle.

ROBERT BOYLE (1627-91) was the seventh son of the Earl of Cork. He was born in Ireland, studied at Eton, and then travelled on the Continent. He was in Italy in the year in which Galilei died and Newton was born (1642), and he returned to England in 1644, just about the time when the Philosophical or " Invisible " College was started. About his important contributions to science something will be said in the next section and in the Annotations. Here we are more concerned with the less meritorious side of his personality.

Like Oldenburg, Boyle was at least as much interested in theology as in science, perhaps even more so. Some of his early experiences are rather significant in this connection. At the age of fourteen he passed through the experience of religious "conversion," or re-birth, in consequence of an awful thunderstorm which he witnessed. His escape from this thunderstorm he attributed to the direct interposition of Providence. Nay, more, already at the age of ten he had actually imposed on himself some disciplinary tasks in arithmetic and in algebra as a penalty for the restless feelings stirred in him when, during his convalescence, he had read the romance *Amadis de Gaula*! Later on he never missed an opportunity of spreading a knowledge of the Gospels, and he spent much money in getting them translated and printed in various languages. Eventually he founded and endowed the "Boyle Lectures"—courses of lectures to be delivered annually for proving the truth of Christianity against "notorious infidels, namely, atheists, theists, pagans, Jews, and Mohammedans." He also stipulated that no reference should be made in these lectures to controversies between Christians. Such was the spirit of Christian charity and candour as Boyle understood it. What understanding could he possibly have for Spinoza? No wonder that, notwithstanding all the external shows of courtesy, Boyle never wrote directly to Spinoza. It is even possible that the foundation of the Boyle Lectures was partly due to Boyle's conception, or rather misconception, of Spinoza's philosophy, especially of his *Tractatus Theologico-Politicus*, coupled, however, with "the shades of doubt," which, as Boyle admitted, "did sometimes cross his mind." It is certainly a fact that at least two series of Boyle Lectures were directed against Spinoza, namely, Samuel Clark's *Demonstration of the Being and Attributes of God : More Particularly in Answer to Mr. Hobbs, Spinoza, and their Followers* (1704), and B. Guerdon's *Boyle Lectures* (1721, 1722).

Boyle and Oldenburg were so steeped in Christian prejudices that they seemed utterly incapable of understanding Spinoza's thought, let alone sympathizing with it. And with the increasing conservatism characteristic of increasing age their estrangement from him increased likewise. When after a great deal of beating about the bush Oldenburg was at length brought to express explicitly his real objections to Spinoza's philosophy, it turned out that he had actually expected Spinoza to write a philosophic defence of orthodox Christianity—in other words, to deliver advance " Boyle Lectures " ! Enlightened Christians, as well as cynics, may find food for thought in this utter incapacity of two good and able men like Boyle and Oldenburg to understand a still better and abler man like Spinoza.

§ 4. THE SCIENTIFIC BACKGROUND OF SPINOZA'S CORRESPONDENCE

ALREADY before Descartes the revolt against mere authority and tradition in the realm of Knowledge had been voiced eloquently and persuasively by Francis Bacon (1561–1626), who elaborated a comprehensive scheme of experimental research worthy of a Lord Chancellor. His plea bore fruit eventually in the shape of a " Philosophical College," which was started, about 1645, for the promotion of experimental science. Its members met frequently in the City of London, or in Oxford, to carry out experiments and to discuss their significance. This somewhat nebulous society, sometimes called the " Invisible College," assumed more definite shape in 1660, became known as the " Royal Society " in the following year and received its Charter of Incorporation on July 15, 1662. Robert Boyle was one of its original and most influential members, and Henry Oldenburg its first Secretary.

The primary aim of the Royal Society was the improvement of natural knowledge by experiments, as distinguished from airy scholastic discussions based on authorities. But the significance of the stress on experiment must not be exaggerated. The divisions between what are now regarded as distinct sciences were few and vague then. Even the present distinction between science and philosophy was very nebulous at that time, a fortiori the difference between experimental and non-experimental science, or between the experimental and the non-experimental sides of the same science. The very ambition of the society tended to leave all such differences on one side. Like its patron-saint Bacon, who had taken all knowledge for his province, the Royal Society took the whole universe to task, and did not at first trouble much about mapping out different fields of inquiry, according to the different nature of the phenomena concerned and of the methods applicable.

As already stated, it fell to Oldenburg to " purchase and entertain a commerce in all parts of the world with the most philosophical and curious persons to be found everywhere." In fact, he had done so already before the Royal Society was fully constituted—and that was probably the reason why he was appointed its secretary in 1663. Thus it came about that, like many others, Spinoza was drawn into the activities of the society, sending lengthy criticisms on Boyle's experiments, communicating information about the scientific activities of Christian Huygens in connection with dynamics, optics, horology, etc., or about continental views on the comets, and so on. It is one of the minor ironies of history that while Oldenburg was searching the whole Continent for new light on Boyle's experiments on nitre, etc., highly relevant facts nearer home were entirely overlooked. If properly appreciated, Mayow's experiments on oxygen, which were carried out in Oxford, would have put a new complexion on Boyle's experiments with nitre ; but they passed unnoticed. In fact, Boyle did not appreciate in this connection the bearing even of his own experiments on the function of air in combustion.

The discussions between Boyle and Spinoza are of some interest for the student of the history of science. They throw no little light on the scientific tendencies of the seventeenth century and on the intellectual attitude of some of its leaders in the domain of science. Boyle may well be described as the scientific executor of Bacon's last will and testament. To some considerable extent he certainly did help to give practical effect to Bacon's designs. And Boyle's own work at once shows the strength and betrays the weakness of the Baconian method—its strength, as an aid to methodical observation and experiment, its weakness in not appreciating sufficiently the supreme importance of illuminating ideas. Like that incomparably greater genius, his younger contemporary, Newton, Boyle fought shy of ideas which were not immediately forced upon him by direct observations. Both were orthodox Christians, quite content to draw upon Scripture for all their more comprehensive cosmic thoughts. Fortunately for them, and for science generally, a great deal of physical, chemical, and astronomical research has no direct bearing on religious problems or philosophical world-views. Boyle's services are strictly confined to this region. His excursions into wider questions were few and clumsy. Spinoza, on the other hand, was a philosopher first and foremost. He was certainly interested also in science, in the narrower sense of the term. He did valuable work in applied optics, and, as his letters show, he carried out various chemical and physical experiments, as far as his very limited time and means allowed. He also dealt with the problem of the rainbow, and with that of probability, or the calculation of chances. But his interests were mainly directed to the wider issues involved—issues for which Boyle had little understanding and less appreciation. So the two were not likely to pull well together. Spinoza, indeed, recognized and appreciated the importance of such detailed observations and experiments as Boyle was carrying out and recording. But he also realized their shortcomings, and was candid enough to express his thoughts. Boyle, like so many people who invite criticism and only expect praise, appears to have been somewhat irritated by Spinoza's comments.

The most important aspect of the discussion between Boyle and Spinoza was that concerning the problem of

the mechanical interpretation of natural phenomena—
a problem of perennial interest. Boyle professed to be
a firm believer in what he called " the tenets of mechanical philosophy." By the mechanical philosophy Boyle
meant the attempt to explain the phenomena of Nature
" by little bodies variously figured and moved "—hence
also the name " Corpuscular (or Corpuscularian) Philosophy." This point of view, according to Boyle, was
common both to the Atomists and the Cartesians.
The Cartesian conception of the ultimate constitution
of matter (extension) was indeed very different from that
of the Atomists. But these remoter questions were of
no interest to Boyle. So far as the immediate needs
of scientific explanation were concerned both schools
of thought were in essential agreement. And Boyle
believed that Chemists and Mechanical (or Corpuscularian) Philosophers ought to come to a mutual
understanding, for they could help each other: the corpuscular philosophy could help to explain plausibly
many chemical phenomena, while chemists could furnish
many experiments in illustration and in confirmation
of the corpuscular philosophy. It was in this spirit that
Boyle carried out the experiments described in *Certain
Physiological Essays* (1661). Spinoza with his thorough-
going naturalism was, of course, in favour of this
method of explaining material phenomena, but he saw
its implications better than Boyle did. Boyle was
quite content to employ mechanical and teleological
explanations side by side. To Spinoza it quite rightly
appeared to be incongruous to explain physical phenomena by reference to their alleged purposes, or ends,
while professing the tenets of a thoroughgoing mechanical philosophy, which should explain them only by
means of corpuscles, figures, and motions. Here
already we see at a glance the difference between the
broader outlook of Spinoza and the more limited or
restricted outlook of Boyle.

INTRODUCTION

The mechanical tendency in modern science owed its vogue, in large measure, to Galilei, the father of modern dynamics. He insisted on explaining physical phenomena by means of primary or mechanical qualities (that is, the geometrical qualities and motion); and he regarded the secondary or sensible qualities of things (colour, sound, etc.) as subjective effects of primary qualities. One important result of this whole movement was a certain enlightenment of science, its emancipation from more or less mysterious forms, occult qualities, chemical principles, etc., which facilitated pseudo-explanations of natural phenomena, and so discouraged methodical, intelligent research. Boyle's adhesion to the mechanical philosophy meant no more than that he was opposed to the aforementioned pseudo-scientific explanations and mystifying hocus-pocus; and his work as a chemist was perhaps all the better just because he did not fully realize the implications of a thorough-going mechanical philosophy, and so did not endeavour to carry it through consistently. It has taken more than two centuries for men of science to realize that it is impossible to explain even simple chemical phenomena, let alone extremely complex biological ones, on strictly and purely mechanical lines. The conception of the "creative evolution" or "emergence" of results incapable of a purely mechanical explanation has become a commonplace now, thanks to the influence of Professor Bergson and of Professor Lloyd Morgan, and Boyle may claim some credit for originating this conception, which is implicit in his distinction between a (mechanical) mixture and a (chemical) compound. Methodologically, however, the regulative notion of a mechanical explanation may still perform the same useful function which it had in the seventeenth century, namely, to exorcise sheer hocus-pocus and to prevent mere mystification from masquerading as scientific explanation.

43

§ 5. HUDDE, BOXEL, BURGH, LEIBNIZ, TSCHIRNHAUS

OTHER correspondents, besides Boyle and Oldenburg, with whom scientific interests brought Spinoza into touch, were Hudde, Leibniz, and Tschirnhaus. Evidently Spinoza had early acquired a reputation for his knowledge of optics and his skill in grinding and polishing lenses, by which he gained his daily bread. Since Galilei's use of the telescope for astronomical observation, interest in optics had become widespread and fashionable. Not only scientists like Galilei, Descartes, and Christian Huygens wrote treatises on optics, but even statesmen like Sir Constantyn Huygens and Burgomaster Hudde were sufficiently interested in the subject to write about it. Possibly Spinoza's acquaintance with Hudde was mediated by Christian Huygens (1629–85), famous in the history of science as the discoverer of the rings of Saturn, as the originator of the undulatory theory of light, and the inventor of the pendulum clock. During the years 1664–66 Spinoza lived within easy walking distance of Huygens, and the two must have got to know each other fairly well, for Huygens in his subsequent letters to his brother referred to Spinoza several times, and wanted to be informed of Spinoza's doings.

JOHAN HUDDE was born in Amsterdam in 1628, and died there in 1704. He entered the University of Leyden in 1654 as a medical student. In 1667 he joined the governing body of his native city; in the following year he became Sheriff; and in 1672 he was elected Burgomaster, or Mayor, an office to which he was subsequently re-elected no less than eighteen times.

44

He is known to have been interested in physics and mathematics, more particularly in optics and in the calculus of probability. These interests probably brought him into touch with Huygens, and through him with Spinoza. As a member of the States of Holland, Hudde would frequently visit The Hague, which was the seat of government, and so would have frequent opportunity of meeting Spinoza, who lived in Voorburg, near The Hague, from 1663 till 1670, and in The Hague itself from 1670 until his death in 1677. Hudde, unlike Huygens, was interested in philosophy as well as in science, and the extant three letters which Spinoza addressed to him deal mainly with the conception of God.

Spinoza's letter to Oldenburg, written in July 1663, shows how necessary Spinoza found it to secure the protection of influential statesmen before venturing to publish his own views on philosophy and religion, which were sure to arouse the hostility of the Calvinist clergy. Maybe Hudde supplied the need, and obtained for Spinoza the friendly interest of ex-Burgomaster Coenraad van Beuningen and of Jan de Witt, the ill-fated Grand Pensionary of Holland.

HUGO BOXEL was another of Spinoza's correspondents who belonged to the governing classes of Holland. In 1655 he was appointed Secretary to his native city Gorkum. Four years later he was elected Pensionary thereof, and held this responsible office until 1672. In that year, in consequence of the murder of the De Witts and the connected political changes, Boxel was deprived of his post. It is not known how he became acquainted with Spinoza, but he probably had something to do with Spinoza's visit to the French camp at Utrecht in 1673. For Boxel is known to have favoured the policy of a Dutch understanding with France. His firm belief in ghosts, evidenced by his letters to Spinoza, is a potent reminder of the character of his age. Even a worldly, enlightened man like Boxel considered it perfectly reasonable to believe things so long as no conclusive evidence could be brought against them. Even men of science were no better then in such matters, and were very remote from Huxley's ideal of a man of science. Spinoza was one of the very few men of his time who asked to know the reasons why he *should* believe what was not evident, instead of waiting for others to submit reasons why he should *not* believe it. The fact that Scripture appeared to sanction the belief in the existence of spirits, etc., was sufficient for most people to confirm their belief in such things.

CONRAAD BURGH was another influential member of the governing classes whom Spinoza got to know somehow. He was one of the wealthiest citizens of Amsterdam, and in 1666 held office as Treasurer General of the United Netherlands. ALBERT BURGH, Spinoza's correspondent, was the son of Conraad. He studied philosophy in Leyden from 1668 onwards, and travelled in Italy in 1673, and became a Catholic. His parents were much upset by this, and apparently persuaded Spinoza to write to him. But in vain. Albert Burgh joined the Franciscan Order, and died in a monastery in Rome.

GOTTFRIED WILHELM LEIBNIZ (1646–1716), as is evident from his first letter to Spinoza, turned to him in the first instance as an authority on optics. In 1671 Leibniz, who was then in the service of the Elector of Mainz, was sent to Paris to save Germany from the aggressive policy of Louis XIV by turning his thoughts to the conquest of Egypt. During the next few years he visited Paris several times on various missions, and there, in 1675, met Tschirnhaus, who sought Spinoza's

permission to show Leibniz his manuscript copy of
Spinoza's *Ethics*. Spinoza's reply shows his suspicion
of Leibniz. This was not unfounded. He had reason
to suspect that Leibniz was working for the reunion
of Protestants and Catholics, which could only result
in their joint suppression of all freedom of thought
and speech. But when, in the following year, Leibniz
visited Spinoza in The Hague, his distrust melted away.
Leibniz, according to his own account, visited Spinoza
frequently, and " conversed with him often and at great
length." He studied Spinoza's *Ethics*, and was much
impressed by it ; but such a Christian crusader could not
be expected to have a lasting sympathy with Spinozism,
and notwithstanding his great reputation as an idealist
philosopher and as a mathematician (he was, with Newton,
one of the discoverers of the differential and integral
calculus), his character does not compare favourably
with that of Spinoza.

EHRENFRIED WALTHER VON TSCHIRNHAUS (1651–
1708) was a German Count who studied at the University
of Leyden during the years 1668–75, but served part
of the time as a volunteer with the Dutch army in the
war with France. In 1674 he became acquainted with
Schuller, of Amsterdam, who told him about Spinoza.
Having studied Descartes, he became interested in
Spinoza, started a correspondence with him, and
visited him in the same year. In the summer of the
following year he visited London, and met Boyle and
Oldenburg. This led to the resumption of the correspondence between Oldenburg and Spinoza, which had
been dropped apparently since 1665. In 1683 Tschirnhaus published his *Medicina Mentis*, the idea of which
had been suggested to him by Spinoza's unfinished
Treatise on the Improvement of the Understanding, from which
he also derived some of his thoughts. His corre-

spondence with Spinoza gives us incidentally the first intimation of his discovery of the tangential measurement of curves. His practical interests embraced the manufacture of large burning-glasses, lenses, mirrors, etc.; and, together with J. L. Böttger, he invented porcelain, the oldest factory for which was started in Meissen, near Dresden, in 1710.

FABRITIUS

THE HON. ROBERT BOYLE

JOANNES HUDDE

GOTTFRIED WILHELM LEIBNIZ

§ 6. DE VRIES, MEYER, BALLING, BOUWMEESTER, JELLES, SCHULLER

OF his other correspondents, some belonged to what may be termed Spinoza's intimate circle. They were De Vries, Meyer, Balling, Bouwmeester, Jelles, and Schuller. Most of them belonged to the Collegiant sect, who, in consequence of the persecuting zeal of the dominant Calvinist clergy, had to dispense with an official clergy of their own, and held private prayer-meetings after the manner of the Quakers. Spinoza got to know them all while he was still in Amsterdam, where some of them, together with others unnamed, held a reading circle for the study of philosophy. This circle was conducted at first by Spinoza, but continued to meet even after his departure from Amsterdam, in 1660, and he sent them various philosophical essays for discussion and criticism, as is clear from the letters of De Vries and also from the concluding paragraph of the *Short Treatise*.*

SIMON JOOSTEN DE VRIES (? 1633–67) was an Amsterdam merchant. He studied under Spinoza, and his warm regard for his teacher shines through his letters. It is also borne out by practical proofs reported by the early biographers of Spinoza. Colerus relates that De Vries once offered Spinoza a present of two thousand florins to enable him to live more comfortably, but Spinoza declined it. On another occasion De Vries wanted to appoint Spinoza his heir, as he was a bachelor himself; but Spinoza dissuaded him from it, and made him leave all his property to his brother.

* See Spinoza's *Short Treatise on God, Man, etc.*, translated by A. Wolf, pp. 149 f., or the Annotations to Letter XV.

De Vries, however, stipulated that his brother should in that case pay Spinoza an annuity of five hundred florins. When the time came Spinoza would not accept more than three hundred.

LODEWIJK MEYER (1630–81) was born in Amsterdam, of Lutheran parents, but like Spinoza he moved in Collegiant circles, and was devoted to the cause of a simple universal religion. From an early age he showed strong literary interests. He wrote poems and plays, brought out an improved edition of a dictionary of foreign terms, helped in the compilation of a Dutch grammar, and did all he could to improve the knowledge of the Dutch language and literature. In 1654 Meyer went to the University of Leyden, where he studied philosophy and medicine, and in 1660 obtained both degrees, M.D. and Ph.D. Possibly he had once taken private lessons from Van den Enden when Spinoza was still with him as assistant master, and so the two young men became friendly. It is noteworthy that his Ph.D. thesis dealt with *Matter and its States, Motion and Rest*. In 1663, as is clear from Spinoza's letters, Meyer saw through the press Spinoza's geometric version of Descartes' *Principles*, and wrote a preface to it. In 1665 he was appointed Director of the Amsterdam Theatre, where he did much to improve the tone of the dramas played and the artistic quality of the performances. But he still found time for philosophy, for in the same year there appeared a book *On the Right of Ecclesiastics*, by a certain Lucius Antistius Constans, a pseudonym of Meyer's, according to Colerus and others. This book foreshadowed certain ideas of Spinoza's *Tractatus Theologico-Politicus*, and may have been the outcome of discussions between the two friends. It was at one time attributed to Spinoza. At all events, in 1666 Meyer published anonymously his *Philosophy the Interpreter of the Holy Scriptures*, which contained Spinozistic allusions, was also at one time ascribed to Spinoza, and was actually published in one volume with the *Tractatus Theologico-Politicus* in 1674. The two friends certainly had many liberal thoughts in common. In 1669 Meyer ceased to be Director of the Amsterdam Theatre, though he was several times appointed by the magistrates as censor thereof. Shortly afterwards he founded a Society of Arts which had for its motto *Nil volentibus arduum* (Where there is a will there is a way). When Spinoza died in 1677, Meyer was almost certainly one of the friends who prepared for publication the *Opera Posthuma*, as is evidenced by the lavish use of capitals and accents, to which Meyer was much addicted. It appears that we are also indebted to Meyer for the best existing portrait of Spinoza, now in the library at Wolfenbüttel. It was bought from the executors of Professor Francius, Meyer's co-Director of the Amsterdam Theatre, and probably belonged to Meyer originally (see the frontispiece).

PIETER BALLING was a Mennonite, and an enemy of dogmatism. By calling he was an agent, the Amsterdam representative of various Spanish merchants. It is possible that Spinoza's knowledge of Spanish first brought them together. In 1662 Balling published his *Light on the Candlestick*, in which he attacked dogmatism and advocated a simple religion based on the inward light of the soul. In 1664 he translated into Dutch Spinoza's version of Descartes' *Principles*.

JOHAN BOUWMEESTER (1630–80) was born in Amsterdam, studied philosophy and medicine in Leyden, and qualified as a doctor in 1658. He was an intimate friend of L. Meyer, and in 1663 he wrote a laudatory poem prefixed to Spinoza's version of Descartes' *Principles*, to which Meyer wrote the preface. He also co-operated with Meyer in the Society *Nil volentibus arduum*, and was his co-Director of the Amsterdam Theatre in 1677. It is interesting to note that the Society *Nil volentibus arduum* once commissioned Bouwmeester to translate, from the Arabic, Ibn Tophail's *Improvement of Human Reason, exhibited in the Life of Hai Ibn Yokdan*. A Dutch translation actually appeared in 1672. The translator is indicated by the initials S. D. B., which some people regard as those of Spinoza (B. D. S.) slightly disguised.

JARIG JELLES (?–1683) was a spice merchant in Amsterdam, but in 1653 he entrusted his business to a manager, in order that he might be free to devote himself to the pursuit of knowledge, which he considered to be " better than choice gold," according to his biographer. He was one of the friends who persuaded Spinoza to publish his geometric version of Descartes' *Principles*, in 1663. He even defrayed the cost of its publication. It was probably at his instigation that Jan H. Glazemaker translated into Dutch the *Tractatus Theologico-Politicus* soon after its anonymous appearance in 1670. Spinoza's letter to Jelles shows that he only heard incidentally and vaguely about the impending appearance of the Dutch translation, and that he feared, rightly of course, that it might result in the prohibition of the Latin original as well as of the Dutch version. Jelles respected Spinoza's wish, and the Dutch translation of the *Tractatus Theologico-Politicus* was not published until 1693. According to a note written by Leibniz in 1676, Jelles was said to support Spinoza financially at the time. When Spinoza died, in 1677, Jelles was one of the small band of friends who took in hand the publication of the *Posthumous Works* both in Latin and in Dutch. The preface to the *Posthumous Works* is said to have been written in Dutch by Jelles, and translated into Latin by L. Meyer. Glazemaker was responsible for the Dutch version of the *Opera Posthuma* (*De Nagelate Schriften van B. D. S.*). Jelles died in 1683, and the following year witnessed the publication of his *Confession of Faith*, with a biographical introduction which says that Jelles " strove unremittingly to penetrate more and more deeply into the knowledge and love of God, and he made such progress therein that there are few people who have worked their way up to such a high level of spiritual insight." This we may well believe. In his relations with other men he was so little estranged by differences of origin that in his long and important preface to the *Posthumous Works* of Spinoza he did not even mention the fact that Spinoza was a Jew by birth.

GEORG HERMANN SCHULLER (1651–79) was born in Wesel, studied medicine in the University of Leyden, and settled down in Amsterdam as a medical practitioner. It is not known how Spinoza got to know him. His letters betray a certain immaturity, but his enthusiasm appears to have impressed Spinoza, who consulted him medically on various occasions, and sent for him during his last illness. Schuller was the only person present at his bedside when the great philosopher passed away. For a long time it used to be supposed that L. Meyer had performed this last office, but Schuller's name appears among the signatories to the official inventory of Spinoza's property made immediately after the philosopher's death, and there is no evidence of any contact between Meyer and Spinoza during the last years of the latter's life. Immediately after the death of Spinoza, Schuller, who, as we have seen, knew both Leibniz and Tschirnhaus, wrote to Leibniz, who was then Librarian in Hanover, to offer him the manuscript of Spinoza's *Ethics* for one hundred and fifty florins, but withdrew the offer immediately afterwards. Schuller died at the early age of twenty-eight.

§ 7. BLYENBERGH, OSTENS, VELTHUYSEN, FABRITIUS, GRAEVIUS, STENO

WE may now deal briefly also with the remaining correspondents of Spinoza, namely, Blyenbergh, Ostens, Velthuysen, Fabritius, Graevius, and Steno.

WILLEM VAN BLYENBERGH (?–1696) was a grain broker of Dordrecht. He had a taste for theology, and regarded philosophy merely as the handmaid to theology. His attitude was sufficiently clear from the long title of a small book which he published in 1663, *Theology and Religion defended against the views of Atheists, wherein it is shown by natural and clear arguments that God has implanted and revealed a Religion, that God wants to be worshipped in accordance with it, and that the Christian Religion not only agrees with the Religion revealed by God but also with the Reason which is implanted in us.* Could anything be simpler! Unfortunately, Spinoza did not know of this book, or he might have spared himself much annoyance and trouble. But perhaps it is as well to know this correspondence between them, if only as evidence of Spinoza's extraordinary patience with such a bore. Poor Blyenbergh simply could not get away from his limited circle of ideas. He went round and round his barren patch like one possessed, and all Spinoza's endeavours to elucidate matters were wasted on him. In 1674 he published a *Refutation of the blasphemous Book called Tractatus Theologico-Politicus*, and, in 1682, a polemic against Spinoza's *Ethics*. Having thus distinguished himself as a defender of the faith, Blyenbergh was elected Burgomaster of Dordrecht in 1695.

JACOB OSTENS (1625–78) was a Collegiant, born probably at Utrecht. He settled as a surgeon in

Rotterdam, and seems to have become acquainted with Spinoza as an advocate of a simple, universal faith. Very little is known about him, and he is of interest to Spinoza students mainly as a link between Spinoza and Velthuysen.

LAMBERT VAN VELTHUYSEN (1622–85) was born in Utrecht, and studied philosophy, theology, and medicine at the University of his native city, where he subsequently practised medicine. In comparison with the clergy of the dominant Church, he was so liberal as to come into conflict with them on various occasions. But Spinoza's views were beyond him, and he regarded the *Tractatus Theologico-Politicus* as atheistic and fatalistic. This annoyed Spinoza, but did not shake his faith in Velthuysen's sincerity and devotion to truth. After the death of Spinoza and the publication of his *Posthumous Works*, Velthuysen attacked his *Ethics* in a treatise *On Natural Religion and the Origin of Morality*.

JOHANN LUDWIG FABRITIUS (1632–97) was born in Schaffhausen, and studied in Cologne and Utrecht. In 1660 he was appointed Professor of Philosophy and of Theology in the University of Heidelberg. He appears to have been in close touch with the Prince Palatine, to whose son he acted as tutor. In 1674 the French seized Heidelberg and closed the University. Fabritius fled, and wandered from place to place until he settled in Frankfurt, where he died in 1697. In connection with the invitation which he sent to Spinoza in 1673, it is interesting to note that the University of Heidelberg recently commissioned the publication of a sumptuous edition of the complete works of Spinoza, which was published in 1926.

JOHAN GEORG GRAEVIUS (1632–?) was born in Naumburg. In 1661 he was appointed Professor of Rhetoric in the University of Utrecht. How he got to know Spinoza is not known, nor does he appear to have deserved Spinoza's confidence. It was through Graevius that Stoupe, a Swiss adventurer in the service of France against Holland, persuaded Spinoza in 1673 to visit the French camp at Utrecht, and soon afterwards slandered him in a book called *The Religion of the Dutch* (1673). As Graevius himself was violently opposed to Spinoza's *Tractatus Theologico-Politicus*, his share in Stoupe's design may not have been innocent.

NICHOLAS STENO (Nils Stensen in Danish) was born in Copenhagen in 1638. He took his medical degree at the University of Copenhagen, and then spent three years at the University of Leyden, carrying on researches in physiology. It must have been during this period that Steno became friendly with Spinoza, who lived in Rhynsburg, near Leyden, from 1660 till 1663. Steno then travelled for some time, and went to Paris in 1664. Here he came under the influence of Bossuet, and forsook Lutheranism for Roman Catholicism in 1667, while in Florence, where he had settled in 1666, and had been appointed physician to the Grand Duke. In 1668 Steno was elected Professor of Anatomy at Copenhagen, but, owing to friction because of his change of faith, he soon returned to Florence. In 1669 he published the *Program* of a treatise *On Solids Naturally contained within Solids*, dealing with gems, minerals, and fossils enclosed in rocks. Oldenburg published an English version of it in 1671. Steno also made important contributions to anatomy. Among his earliest discoveries in this field was that of the parotid gland and its ducts, one of which is still called " Steno's Duct " (*Ductus Stenonianus*).

INTRODUCTION

In 1677 Pope Innocent XI made him Bishop of Titopolis and Vicar Apostolic for Northern Europe. For some time Steno lived in Hanover, then in Schwerin, where he died in 1687. He was buried at Florence, in the Basilica of S. Lorenzo.

§ 8. THE PHILOSOPHICAL IMPORTANCE OF SPINOZA'S CORRESPONDENCE

THE importance of Spinoza's correspondence for the adequate understanding of his philosophy is very great. Not only does it give us a more homely and less formidable account of various philosophical conceptions (such as Freedom, Duration and Time, Infinity, the Unity of Nature, etc.) than is to be found in his other writings, but some of his fundamental ideas are explained more adequately in his letters than elsewhere, at least in the sense that they are presented in a manner less liable to misinterpretation, if one studies them with an open mind and does not approach them with a mind already steeped in prejudice. It is not too much to say that some of the most mischievous misinterpretations of the philosophy of Spinoza are mainly due to an insufficient study of his letters, or at least to an insufficiently impartial study of them. In illustration of this contention I propose to deal briefly with three basic problems in the interpretation of Spinozism, namely, (*a*) the question of the relation of the Attributes to Substance ; (*b*) the question of the significance of the frequent use of geometrical illustrations by Spinoza; and (*c*) the question of the nature of the Attributes.

(*a*) The prevalence of the so-called critical philosophy of Kant during the nineteenth century, and its tendency towards the epistemological interpretation of all philosophical problems, and even of systems of philosophy, led to what may be described as a Kantian interpretation of the relation of the Attributes to Substance in the system of Spinoza. In other words, the Attributes were alleged to have been regarded by Spinoza not as real, objective characters or constituents of Substance, but merely as our subjective ways of conceiving Substance—Substance being the thing-in-itself (*noumenon*) of which Attributes are but the appearances (phenomena). This sort of interpretation was put forward by J. E. Erdmann (*Grundriss der Geschichte der Philosophie*, Band II) and others, who justified themselves by reference to *Ethics* I, Definition iv, which states: " By attribute I mean that which the intellect apprehends of substance as constituting its essence." Spinoza's Letters (II, IV, IX), however, make it quite clear that this quasi-Kantian interpretation is wrong, and that Spinoza regarded Attributes as having the same objective reality as Substance itself. Substance (or God, or Nature) is, for Spinoza, the unified totality of Attributes. The only difference between Substance and its Attributes is that each Attribute can be thought of separately, whereas in reality all the Attributes are inseparably together in Substance. Moreover, according to Spinoza, the intellect gives us a knowledge of the real and not of mere appearances. It is, consequently, illegitimate to read into Spinoza the distinction between what Substance is in reality and what it is to the intellect, except for the difference between the number of the Attributes conceived

(*b*) The significance almost universally attached to Spinoza's frequent use of geometrical or other mathematical illustrations is based on the assumption that Spinoza agreed with the common conception of the nature of geometrical figures and their properties. The common conception dates at least from the time of Plato, if it is not even older. According to this conception, geometrical figures as studied in geometry are the nearest perceptible or imaginative approach to Ideas as Plato conceived them—eternal, rational entities beyond the vicissitudes of time and change. The most important feature of the common conception, so far as we are at present concerned, is the way in which the properties of a geometrical figure are usually conceived to be interrelated. They are, namely, held to be related to one another in a purely rational or logical manner, to which time is simply irrelevant; they are not, it is maintained, related causally to one another, because the causal relation involves time-sequence and change, which do not concern geometrical figures. Such, briefly, is the usual idea about geometrical figures and their properties; and the idea is so widespread that it does not appear to have occurred to anybody even to put the question whether Spinoza shared this view. It has simply been assumed all along that he did entertain this view, and the fact that he sometimes employed the expression *causa seu ratio* (cause or reason) has given rise to the view that for Spinoza there was only one kind of relationship in the universe, namely, the purely rational or logico-mathematical relationship, for, so it was alleged, he reduced *causes* to *reasons*. And so it has come about that the most usual description of Spinoza's philosophy is that it is a " *mathematical* pantheism." The phrase is due to W. Windelband (*Präludien zur Philosophie*), but the interpretation which it expresses is much older and is very widely accepted.

Now I do not propose to raise here the question whether the current conception of geometrical figures and their properties is correct or not. This does not directly concern us here. What does concern us very much is whether Spinoza held such a view, and the answer to this is quite definitely No. Letter LX makes it very clear that Spinoza regarded geometrical figures as effects produced by certain movements. Thus, for example, he defines a circle as " a figure described by a line one point of which is fixed while the other is revolving." Moreover, he explicitly adds that he prefers this definition to other possible definitions of the same figure just because it expresses the *efficient cause* of the figure defined. Similarly, we may rightly suppose, he regarded a rectilinear triangle as a figure produced when three straight lines are moved about and joined in such a way as to enclose a space. And similarly with other figures. Really, therefore, Spinoza's frequent use of geometrical illustrations is so far from confirming the usual conception of Spinoza's world as a purely mathematical, or logico-mathematical, system, that *prima facie* it rather suggests a causal or dynamic system.

(*c*) Spinoza's conception of the Attributes (or their organic totality, Substance) was essentially dynamic, not static like the Eleatic and Platonic views of the nature of ultimate reality. The unprejudiced student of Spinoza's writings cannot possibly overlook the dynamic terminology which Spinoza employs throughout his writings. Activity is for him an essential character of reality, if not identical with it. This is clear from such statements as the following : " The more essence a thing has, so much more has it also of activity " (*Short Treatise*, p. 146 of my translation) ; " the more perfect a thing is, the more reality it possesses, and consequently acts more " (*Ethics*, V, xl). And he does not say this of finite objects or modes only. He maintains this view with regard also to Attributes and Substance. In the *Short Treatise*, pp. 34 and 120, and again in his *Ethics*, II, i, vii and xxi, he describes the Attributes Thought and Extension as *powers*. And in *Ethics* I, xvii, II, iii, etc., Substance, or God Himself, is identified with *power*, and we are told that it is as impossible for us to think that God does not *act* as that He does not exist.

The accuracy of this dynamic interpretation of Spinoza finds interesting confirmation in his correspondence (Letters LXXXI and LXXXIII). In answer to Tschirnhaus's inquiry about the Cartesian conception of matter as mere inert extension, Spinoza says that from matter or extension so conceived, natural phenomena could not possibly be derived. And when Tschirnhaus reminded him that Descartes had supposed that God had added the necessary motion and rest to set things going, he only betrayed his own confusion of a rational philosophy with a miracle-dealing theology. The use of the same term Extension by Spinoza and by Descartes has unfortunately obscured for most people the enormous difference between the Cartesian and the Spinozistic conception of the ultimate nature of matter. For Spinoza Extension or Matter is essentially Physical Energy. It expresses itself in the infinite mode of motion and rest, which consequently need not be introduced miraculously from the outside, as was the case in Descartes' scheme of things. Extension, says Spinoza very explicitly (*Short Treatise*, p. 120), is " the power to produce " motion and rest, or kinetic and potential energy, as we may say.

The history of science since the seventeenth century has fully justified Spinoza's conception of the dynamic or kinetic character of matter, as against the view of Descartes and all his contemporaries as well as many distinguished successors. Descartes, for example, could only account for the movements of the planets by invoking, as is usual with him, a *Deus ex machina* and inventing the machinery of aether vortices to carry the planets. Even Newton clung to the aether, and for much the same reason, namely, because matter was conceived as inert. But after Newton's formulation of the law of universal gravitation a marked change came about. In spite of Newton's opposition to it, the view which gradually prevailed was that gravitation is inherent in matter as such; and the kinetic conception of matter has grown so much in favour that " matter " has almost been displaced by energy or "fields of force." *

Enough, it is hoped, has been said to show the need of an impartial revision of the common interpretations of Spinozism in the light of a thorough study of all the writings of Spinoza, including especially his correspondence.

* A fuller discussion of the problem will be found in " Spinoza's Conception of the Attributes of Substance," by A. Wolf (*Proceedings of the Aristotelian Society*, 1927).

§ 9. BIBLIOGRAPHICAL

THE *Correspondence* of Spinoza was first published in the year of his death, 1677, in a volume entitled *Opera Posthuma*, which also contained the *Ethica*, the *Tractatus Politicus*, the *Tractatus de Intellectus Emendatione*, and the *Compendium Grammatices Linguae Hebraeae*. In this first edition the correspondence consisted of seventy-four letters, while another letter was given in the place of a preface to the *Political Treatise*. So of all his actual correspondence only seventy-five letters were published altogether by the friends who edited the *Posthumous Works*. It is known that the editors and the publishers had more letters than were printed, but they were mostly destroyed for various reasons.

The principal reason was the fear lest the editors got themselves or others into trouble with the Dutch authorities. Hence, also, the omission of all the names of Spinoza's Dutch correspondents from such letters as were published. Considering the persecuting zeal of the Calvinist preachers, and their increased influence with the civic authorities after the fall of the De Witt regime, it was no doubt dangerous for people to have their names associated in any friendly way with Spinoza or with the De Witts. The oldest biographer of Spinoza laments that he had to observe as much secrecy, when writing his account of the life of the philosopher, as if he had been committing a crime.[1] The absence of any letters to or from Jan de Witt may be due to their destruction caused by such fear ; and the same may be said of many other letters, such as the correspondence which must have passed between Spinoza and various people in Holland before he visited the French camp

---

[1] See *The Oldest Biography of Spinoza*, p. 41.

in Utrecht, in 1673, on the invitation of Prince Condé and at the instigation of Colonel Stoupe.

Another reason is suggested by the separate title-page of the *Correspondence* in the *Posthumous Works*. This title-page lays stress on the fact that the letters contribute not a little to the elucidation of Spinoza's other works. The editors of the *Opera Posthuma*, as appears from the preface thereto, were not deeply interested in the personal history of Spinoza, but only in his teachings. Letters which were mainly of personal interest, we may accordingly assume, were regarded as " of no importance "—to use the phrase actually used by the son of the publisher of the *Opera Posthuma* (Rieuwertsz) with reference to some Spinoza letters once in his or in his father's possession.* It is known that in some cases the editors of the *Opera Posthuma* deliberately omitted from the letters which they published passages of purely personal interest, such as the concluding paragraphs of Letter VI. It was the same lack of interest in the personal history and development of Spinoza that was responsible for their failure to publish the *Apology* or Defence which he had written at the time of his excommunication, in 1656, and his *Short Treatise on God, Man, and his Well-Being*, which he had written between 1656 and 1660. From their point of view, these works had been superseded by the *Tractatus Theologico-Politicus* and the *Ethica* respectively, and had no further interest.

However, during the past hundred years or so another ten letters have been recovered and a fragment of an eleventh letter. So that altogether, including the fragment, the extant correspondence of Spinoza consists at present of eighty-six letters. Of this total, forty-nine were written by Spinoza and thirty-seven by his corre-

* See Dr. Halmann's report of a conversation with Rieuwertsz, in 1704, in J. Freudenthal's *Die Lebensgeschichte Spinoza's* (1899).

spondents. In recent years diligent search has been made, in many European libraries and elsewhere, in the hope of discovering more of Spinoza's correspondence, but in vain so far. Still, all hope has not been abandoned, especially in view of the fact that as recently as 1900 the late Mr. Meno Haas, at that time a partner in the London firm of booksellers, David Nutt & Co., informed Mr. Nijhoff, the Hague publisher, that he had seen some unpublished Spinoza letters in a private collection in England.

The eleven letters not included in the *Posthumous Works*, but published since then, are those numbered XV, XXVIII, XXIX, XXX, XLVIIIA, XLIX, LXVIIA, LXIX, LXX, LXXII, and LXXIX.

Of Spinoza's own letters twelve are still extant either in autograph or in facsimile. They are the letters numbered VI, IX, XV, XXIII, XXVII, XXVIII, XXXII, XLIII, XLVI, XLIX, LXIX, and LXXII. They have been published in facsimile, with transliterations, translations, and notes, by the late Dr. Willem Meyer.*

A few words of explanation are necessary regarding the numerical order of the letters. The editors of the *Opera Posthuma* had arranged the correspondence in an order which attempted to combine the chronological arrangement with that according to correspondents. Thus, for example, all the letters to and from Oldenburg were grouped together, and arranged chronologically within the group ; similarly with the letters which passed between Spinoza and other correspondents. On this plan the letters were numbered from I to LXXIV in the first edition. The discovery of hitherto unpublished letters inevitably upset this numerical order to some extent, and when the memorial edition of Spinoza's

---

* *Nachbildung der im Jahre 1902 noch erhaltenen eigenhändigen Briefe des Benedictus de Spinoza* . . . Herausgegeben von W. Meyer, im Haag, 1903.

works was published, in 1882, the editors, Van Vloten and Land, decided to rearrange the letters in a strictly chronological sequence without regard to the correspondents. At that time only nine additional letters had been discovered. Adding the letter which had been used as preface to the *Political Treatise*, there was a total of eighty-four letters, which were numbered accordingly. The new numbers were, of course, in most cases different from the old ones. Since 1882 the new numbers have come into general use among Spinoza scholars in place of the old ones; and in order to avoid the need of upsetting the new numerical order, the two letters discovered since 1882 have been put in their proper place and numbered XLVIIIA and LXVIIA respectively. To facilitate cross-reference between the older and the present numerical designations of the various letters, two comparative tables are given to enable the reader to identify the letters according to either system of enumeration. And, of course, it is open to anybody to read the letters in any other order, such as the order according to the nature of the problems discussed, etc.

Something must be said, next, about the different versions of Spinoza's correspondence. In the *Opera Posthuma* the correspondence, like everything else contained in that edition, appeared in Latin. Some of the letters, however, had originally been written in Dutch, and had been translated into Latin either by Spinoza himself, or by the editors, or by other friends of Spinoza. In every such case the letter was described as a translation (*Versio*). On the other hand, there appeared in the same year, 1677, a Dutch version of the *Opera Posthuma* (except the Hebrew Grammar), namely, *De Nagelate Schriften*. In this edition, of course, all the letters are in Dutch. Those originally written in Latin, or which were only available in Latin versions, had to be translated into Dutch for this edition, while letters originally written in Dutch and then still extant in Dutch were in some cases, at all events, printed from the Dutch originals, which occasionally contained passages omitted from the Latin versions printed in the *Opera Posthuma*. In some cases there are also extant two Latin versions of the same letter, usually the original letter and either an amended copy, or the first draft of it, retained by Spinoza. Volume IV of the Heidelberg edition of *Spinoza Opera* contains all the extant versions of Spinoza's correspondence, as well as detailed information relating to the history of each letter. Some information of this kind will be found in the Annotations.

The present translation is based on the Heidelberg edition, and the version followed is the original one, if still extant, whether in Latin or in Dutch, while deviations of any importance, found in other extant versions, are indicated in the Annotations. Letters XVIII, XIX, XX, XXII, XXIII, XXIV, XXVII, XXVIII, XXIX, XL, XLI, XLIV, L, LII, and LIII have been translated from the Dutch; all the others from the Latin.

With regard to the special literature on the subject there is little to be said, as Spinoza's correspondence has not hitherto received very much attention. The best French version is contained in *Oeuvres de Spinoza* traduites par Emile Saisset (3 vols., Paris, Charpentier, 1872). The best German translation is *Spinozas Briefwechsel* übertragen von Carl Gebhardt (Leipzig: Meiner, 1914). Selections from Spinoza's correspondence were first translated (or rather very freely rendered) into English by R. Willis in his *Benedict de Spinoza : His Life, Correspondence and Ethics* (London, Trübner, 1870), and again by R. H. M. Elwes in *Spinoza's Chief Works* (2 vols., London, Bohn, 1883-4). The present translation is the only complete English translation. It is more complete than any other translation in any language, and, it is believed, also the most accurate. Of books about Spinoza's correspondence the only one worth mention is *Spinozas Entwicklungsgang, besonders nach seinen Briefen geschildert,* von A. Baltzer (Kiel : Lipsius Tischer, 1888). But, of course, all modern books on the life and philosophy of Spinoza contain some allusions to his correspondence.

THE LETTERS
OF CERTAIN LEARNED MEN
To B. D. S.
AND THE AUTHOR'S REPLIES
CONTRIBUTING NOT A LITTLE TO
THE ELUCIDATION OF HIS OTHER WORKS.

LETTER I   HENRY OLDENBURG

Very illustrious Sir, honoured Friend,

    So reluctantly did I tear myself away from your side recently when I was with you in your retreat at Rhynsburg, that no sooner am I back in England than I strive, as far as possible, to rejoin you at least by an exchange of letters. Solid learning combined with humanity and refinement of character (with all of which Nature and Industry have most amply endowed you) provide such charms of their own that they win the love of all men who are open-minded and liberally educated. Come, then, most excellent Sir, and let us join our right hands in unfeigned friendship, and let us diligently cultivate it with every kind of devotion and service. If anything from my slender store can be of service to you, consider it yours. As to the gifts of mind which you possess, allow me to claim a share of them, since this can be done without detriment to you.

    At Rhynsburg we conversed about God, about infinite Extension and Thought, about the difference and the agreement of these attributes, about the nature of the union of the human soul with the body ; also about the Principles of the Cartesian and the Baconian Philosophy. But as we then discoursed about problems of such moment as through a lattice and only in a hurry, and they continue to crucify my mind, let me venture to plead with you by right of the friendship begun between us, and to ask you very cordially to set forth your ideas on the above-mentioned subjects somewhat more fully, and especially not to mind instructing me in the following two points, namely, first, wherein you place the true distinction between Extension and

Thought, and secondly, what defects you observe in the Philosophy of Descartes and of Bacon, and how you consider that these defects may be removed from their midst, and sounder views be substituted for them. The more freely you write to me on these and similar subjects, the more closely will you bind me to you, and you will strongly put me under an obligation to render equivalent services, if only I can.

Here there are already in the press *Certain Physiological Essays*, written by a certain English Noble, a man of excellent erudition. They treat of the nature of air and of its Elastic property, established by forty-three experiments; also of Fluidity and Firmness, and the like. As soon as they are printed I will see to it that they are delivered to you by a friend who is probably crossing the sea shortly.

Meanwhile farewell, and keep in memory your friend who is

Yours in all love and devotion,
HENRY OLDENBURG

LONDON, $\frac{16}{26}$ *August* 1661.

LETTER II   B. D. S.

TO THE VERY NOBLE AND LEARNED
MR. HENRY OLDENBURG

Reply to the Preceding.

VERY ILLUSTRIOUS SIR,

How pleasant your friendship is to me you will be able to judge for yourself if only you can prevail upon your modesty to allow you to consider the excellent qualities which you have in abundance, and although, when I consider them, I seem to myself to be not a little bold because assuredly I dare to enter into friendship with you, especially when I consider that all the possessions of friends, particularly those that are spiritual, ought to be shared, yet this step will have to be attributed to your humanity and benevolence rather than to me. From the height of this humanity you have been willing to lower yourself and to enrich me with the abundance of your benevolence to such an extent that I do not fear to enter into that close friendship which you steadfastly offer me, and which you deign to ask from me in return, and I will make it my earnest care to cultivate it diligently. With regard to my mental endowments, if I possess any, I should most willingly allow you to make a claim upon them, even if I knew it would be to my great detriment. But lest I seem in this way to wish to decline what you ask of me by right of our friendship, I will try to set forth what I think about the subjects of which we spoke, although I do not think that this will be a means of binding you more closely to me without the intervention of your kindness.

I will begin, then, to speak briefly of God, whom I define as a Being consisting of infinite attributes of which each is infinite, or in the highest degree perfect of its kind. Here it should be noted that I understand by attribute all that which is conceived through itself, and in itself; so that its conception does not involve the conception of some other thing. For example, Extension is conceived through itself, and in itself; but not so motion. For it is conceived as in something else, and its conception involves Extension. That this is, indeed, the true definition of God is clear from the fact that we understand by God a Being supremely perfect, and absolutely infinite. That such a Being exists, it is easy to prove from this definition; but, since this is not the place for it, I will omit the proof.

But what I ought to prove here in order to satisfy

75

your first enquiry, most illustrious Sir, are the following. First, that in nature there cannot exist two substances, unless they differ in their whole essence. Secondly, that a substance cannot be produced ; but that existence pertains to the essence thereof. Thirdly, that every substance must be infinite or supremely perfect of its kind. When these points have been proved you will easily be able, most illustrious Sir, to see my trend of thought, if only you will also pay attention to my definition of God, so that there is no need to speak more clearly on these matters. But in order to prove these points clearly and briefly I could think of nothing better than to submit for your consideration such proofs after the manner of Geometry, and so I send them* here separately, and await your verdict on them.

You ask me, secondly, what errors I observe in the Philosophy of Descartes and of Bacon. In this matter, although it is not my custom to expose the errors of others, I am nevertheless willing to gratify you. The first, then, and greatest error, is that they have strayed so far from the knowledge of the First Cause and of the origin of all things. The second is that they did not know the true nature of the human Mind. The third is that they never arrived at the true cause of Error. The extreme necessity of a true knowledge of these three things is only ignored by those who are utterly destitute of learning and training. That they have strayed from the knowledge of the First Cause and of the human Mind is easily gathered from the truth of the three propositions mentioned above : wherefore I turn to the demonstration of the third error alone. I will say little of Bacon who speaks quite confusedly on this subject, and proves almost nothing, but only makes assertions. For, first, he supposes that, besides

* See *Ethics*, Part I, from the beginning up to Proposition IV.

the deception of the senses, the human intellect is fallible by its very nature, and imagines everything after the analogy of its own nature, and not after the analogy of the universe, so that it is like an uneven mirror [turned] to the rays of things, which mingles its own nature with the nature of the things, etc. Secondly, that the human intellect on account of its peculiar nature is prone to make abstractions, and imagines things to be stable which are in flux, etc. Thirdly, that the human understanding is unquiet, it cannot stop or rest. And such other causes as he assigns can easily all be reduced to the single one of Descartes, namely, because the human will is free and wider in scope than the intellect, or, as Verulam * himself more confusedly says (Aphorism 49), because the intellect is no dry light, but receives an infusion from the will. (Here it should be noted that Verulam often uses Intellect for Mind, in which respect he differs from Descartes.) Therefore, taking little notice of the other reasons which are of no moment, I will show that this reason is false, a fact which they, too, would easily have seen if they had only paid attention to this, namely, that will differs from this or that volition in the same way as whiteness differs from this or that white thing, or humanity from this or that man ; so that it is just as impossible to conceive that will is the cause of this or that volition as that humanity is the cause of Peter and Paul. Since, therefore, will is nothing but a thing of reason and cannot be said to be in any way the cause of this or that volition, and particular volitions, since they need a cause in order to exist, cannot be said to be free, but are necessarily what they are determined to be by their causes, and, lastly, since, according to Descartes, these very errors are particular volitions, it necessarily follows that errors, that is, particular volitions,

* See *Novum Organum*, Book I, Aphorisms 48-51.

are not free, but are determined by external causes, and in no way by will. This is what I promised to prove. Etc.

[RHYNSBURG, *September* 1661.]

LETTER III   HENRY OLDENBURG

To the Very Illustrious Mr. B. d. S.

Reply to the Preceding.

EXCELLENT SIR, AND DEAREST FRIEND,

Your very learned letter has been delivered to me, and read with great pleasure. I warmly approve your geometric method of proof : but, at the same time, I blame my own dullness in that I do not so promptly grasp what you so accurately teach. Permit me, I pray, to present the evidence of this stupidity of mine, as I put forward the following questions, and seek from you their solutions.

The first is, do you understand clearly and without doubt that from the mere definition which you give of God, it can be demonstrated that such a Being exists ? I, indeed, when I consider that definitions contain nothing but conceptions of our Mind, moreover that our Mind conceives many things which do not exist, and is very fruitful in the multiplication and augmentation of things once conceived, I do not see yet how from the conception that I have of God I can infer the existence of God. To be sure, from the mental store of all the perfections which I observe in men, animals, vegetables, minerals, etc., I can conceive and fashion some single substance which may fully possess all these excellences, nay more, my Mind is capable of multiplying and augmenting them to infinity, and so of feigning by itself some most perfect and most excellent Being ; yet the existence of such a Being cannot by any means be inferred from that.

The second question is, have you no doubt that Body is not limited by Thought, nor Thought by Body? since it is still an open question what thought is, whether it is a corporeal motion, or a certain spiritual act entirely different from the corporeal.

The third question is, whether you hold those axioms, which you communicated to me, as indemonstrable Principles, recognised by the light of Nature, and standing in no need of proof? It may be that the first Axiom is of such a kind; but I do not see how the remaining three can be included in the number of such principles. For the second axiom supposes that there exists nothing in Nature besides substances and *accidents*, whereas many assert that time and place have the character of neither. Your third Axiom, namely, that *Things which have different attributes have nothing in common*, is so far from being clearly conceived by me that the whole universe seems rather to prove the contrary. For all the things known to us both differ in some respects, and also agree in certain respects. Lastly, the fourth axiom, namely, *Things which have nothing in common cannot be one the cause of the other* is not so obvious to my dull intellect as to need no further light for its illumination. For God has nothing essentially in common with created things, yet is He held by almost all of us to be their cause.

Since, then, these axioms do not seem to me to be placed beyond all risk of doubt, you will easily conjecture that your Propositions which are based on them cannot but be shaky. And the more I consider them, the more I am overwhelmed with doubts about them. For against the first proposition I submit that two men are two substances, and have the same attribute, since both are endowed with reason; whence I conclude that there do exist two substances with the same attribute. With regard to the second, I consider that, since nothing can be the cause of itself, it can hardly be grasped by us how it can be true that *a substance cannot be produced, not even by any other substance.*

For this Proposition declares that all substances are causes of themselves, and that they are all and sundry independent of each other, and thus makes them so many Gods, and in this wise denies the First Cause of all things. This conclusion I willingly confess that I cannot grasp, unless you do me the favour of disclosing to me somewhat more clearly and more fully your opinion on this high subject, and of teaching me the origin and production of Substances, the dependence of things on one another, and their mutual subordination. I adjure you by that friendship into which we have entered, to deal with me freely and faithfully in this matter, and I beg you most earnestly to be fully persuaded that all these matters which you deign to impart to me will remain inviolate and safe, and that I will not do anything to let them become public so as to cause you harm or injury.

In our Philosophical Society we indulge, as far as our powers allow, in diligently making experiments and observations, and we spend much time in preparing a History of the Mechanical Arts, feeling certain that the forms and qualities of things can best be explained by the principles of Mechanics, and that all the effects of Nature are produced by motion, figure, texture, and the varying combinations of these, and that there is no need to have recourse to inexplicable forms and occult qualities, as to a refuge for ignorance.

The book, which I promised, I will send to you as soon as your Dutch Ambassadors, who are acting here, send some messenger to the Hague (as they are often wont to do), or as soon as some other friend, to whom I can safely entrust it, goes to you.

I beg your forgiveness for my prolixity and frankness, and especially I pray you that what I have freely said without any disguise, or courtly elegance, in answer to your letter, you should take in good part as friends are wont to do, and believe me to be without pretence and artfulness

Your very devoted
HENRY OLDENBURG.

LONDON, 27 *Sept.* 1661.

LETTER IV   B. D. S.

TO THE VERY NOBLE AND LEARNED
MR. HENRY OLDENBURG

Reply to the Preceding.

VERY ILLUSTRIOUS SIR,

While preparing to go to Amsterdam, there to spend a week or two, I received your extremely welcome letter and saw your objections to the three Propositions which I sent; I will try to satisfy you on these points only, omitting the rest for want of time.

And so I say, in reply to the first objection, that the existence of the thing defined does not follow from the definition of every kind of thing: but follows only (as I showed in the Scholium which I appended to the three Propositions) from the definition or idea of some attribute, that is, (as I explained clearly with regard to the definition of God) of a thing which is conceived through itself and in itself. Unless I am mistaken I have in the said Scholium set out the ground of this difference clearly enough, especially for a Philosopher. For he is supposed to know the difference which exists between a fiction and a clear and distinct conception, and also the truth of this Axiom, namely, that every definition, or clear and distinct idea, is true. Having noted these points, I do not see what more is required for the solution of the first question.

Therefore I proceed to the solution of the second. Here you seem to concede that if Thought does not pertain to the nature of Extension, then Extension cannot be limited by Thought; to be sure you are only in doubt about the example. But please note, if anyone says that Extension is not limited by Extension but by Thought, is not that the same as saying that Extension is not infinite absolutely but only in so far as it is Extension? That is, he does not allow that Extension is infinite absolutely, but only in so far as it is extension, that is in its own kind? But you say, Thought is, perhaps, a corporeal act. So be it, although I make no such concession; but this at least you will not deny, that Extension, in so far as it is Extension, is not Thought; which is sufficient to explain my definition and to prove my third Proposition.

You proceed in the third place to object to my assertions that the Axioms are not to be reckoned among common Notions. Over this, however, I will not dispute. But you doubt their truth, or rather you seem to want to show that their contrary is more like the truth. But, pray, observe the definition I gave of Substance and of *Accident*, from which all these things are inferred. For I understand by substance that which is conceived through itself and in itself, that is, something the conception of which does not involve the conception of some other thing, and by modification, or by *Accident*, that which is in something else, and is conceived through that in which it is. It clearly follows, therefore, first that substance is by nature prior to its *Accidents*. For without substance these can neither exist nor be conceived. It follows, secondly, that besides Substances and *Accidents* nothing exists in reality, or outside the intellect. For whatever exists, is conceived either through itself or through some other thing, and the conception of it either does or does not involve the conception of some other thing. It follows, thirdly, that things which have different attributes have nothing in common between them. For by attribute I described that the conception of which does not involve the conception of some other thing. Fourthly and lastly, it follows that things which have nothing in common between them cannot be one the cause of the other. For when the effect has nothing in common with its cause, then whatsoever it might have, it would have from nothing. As to your contention that God has nothing essentially in common with created things, etc., I stated the exact opposite in my definition. For I said that God is a Being consisting of infinite attributes, of which each is infinite, or supremely perfect of its kind. With regard to your argument against the first Proposition, I pray you, my Friend, to consider that men are not created but only begotten, and that their bodies existed already before, although in another form. This, however, is inferable, as I freely confess, namely, that if one part of matter were destroyed, then all Extension would vanish at the same time. The second Proposition, however, does not make many Gods, but one only, that is, one God consisting of infinite attributes, etc.

[RHYNSBURG, *October* 1661.]

LETTER V   HENRY OLDENBURG

To the Very Illustrious Mr. B. d. S.

Reply to the Preceding.

MUCH HONOURED FRIEND,
       Receive the little book which I had promised you, and send me in return your opinion of it, and

especially of the experiments it gives on Nitre, and Fluidity, and Firmness. My best thanks for your second learned letter which I received yesterday. I am extremely sorry, however, that your journey to Amsterdam prevented you from answering all my doubts. I beg you to send me what was then omitted as soon as you have the leisure. You have, indeed, afforded me much light in this last letter; but not so much as to remove the darkness completely; which I believe, will happily come to pass when you shall have instructed me distinctly and clearly about the true first origin of things. For as long as it is not clear to me through what cause and in what manner things began to be and by what bond they depend on the First Cause, if there be such a thing, so long all that I hear or read seems to me disconnected. Therefore, very learned Sir, I earnestly beg you to hold forth the torch before me in this matter, and not to doubt of my loyalty and gratitude, who am

Your very devoted

HENRY OLDENBURG.

LONDON, $\frac{11}{21}$ Oct. 1661.

LETTER VI   B. D. S.

TO THE VERY NOBLE AND LEARNED

MR. HENRY OLDENBURG.

Reply to the Preceding.

CONTAINING COMMENTS ON THE BOOK OF THE MOST NOBLE ROBERT BOYLE, ON NITRE, FLUIDITY, AND FIRMNESS.

VERY ILLUSTRIOUS SIR,

I have received the book of the very talented Boyle and I have read it as much as my leisure allowed. I thank you very much for this gift. I see that, already when you first promised me the book, I made no vain conjecture in thinking that you would not be interested in anything unless it was of great moment. Meanwhile, most learned Sir, you wish me to send you my humble opinion on what he has written : this I will do according to my modest capacity, noting, namely, those points which seem to be obscure or insufficiently demonstrated ; but owing to other occupations I have not yet been able to go through, much less to examine, it all. Receive therefore in what follows what I find to comment about Nitre, etc.

On Nitre.

First he infers from this experiment on the redintegration of Nitre that Nitre is something heterogeneous, consisting of fixed and of volatile parts. Its nature, however, (at least as regards its manifestations) certainly differs from the nature of the parts of which it is composed, although it arises solely from the mere mixture of these parts. I remark that, in order that this conclusion may be pronounced valid, yet another experiment is required by which it would be shown that the Spirit of Nitre is not really Nitre, and without salt of lye cannot be reduced to a state of coagulation, or be crystallized; or at least it was necessary to inquire whether the quantity of fixed salt which remains in the crucible is always found to be the same from the same quantity of Nitre, and whether it is proportionate when there is more Nitre. As to what the very illustrious author says (section 9) he has discovered with the aid of the scales, and also that the Phenomena of the Spirit of Nitre are so different from, indeed some of them contrary to, the Phenomena of Nitre itself, in my opinion at least they do nothing to confirm his conclusion. In order to make this clear I will explain in a few words what occurs to me as the simplest explanation of this redintegration of Nitre; and at the same time I will add two or three very easy experiments by which this explanation may to some extent be confirmed.

In order, then, to explain this phenomenon in the simplest possible way, I will posit no other distinction between Spirit of Nitre and Nitre itself than that which is sufficiently manifest, namely that the particles of the latter are in a state of rest, while those of the former agitate each other with no little vehemence. With regard to the fixed salt I shall suppose that this has nothing to do with the constitution of the essence of Nitre; but I shall consider it as the dregs of Nitre, from which even the Spirit of Nitre (as I find) is not free; although reduced to fine powder they float about in it in large quantities. This salt or these dregs have pores or spaces hollowed out commensurably with the size of the particles of Nitre. But when by the action of fire the Nitric particles were driven out of the pores, some of these became narrower, and others were consequently forced to become dilated, and the substance itself, or the walls of these pores, were made rigid and at the same time very brittle; therefore when the Spirit of Nitre was allowed to trickle thereon, certain of the particles of the Spirit began to penetrate impetuously into these narrower pores, and since their thickness is not uniform (as has been well shown by Descartes) they first bent the rigid walls like an arc and then broke them; and when they broke them they compelled the fragments to spring back, and, since they retained their previous motion, they remained as incapable as they were before of being coagulated or crystallized; parts, indeed, of the Spirit which penetrated into the larger pores, since they did not touch the walls, were necessarily surrounded by some very fine matter, and were expelled by it again, in the same way that bits of wood are expelled by a flame or by heat, and were given off in smoke; but if they were sufficiently numerous, or had united with the fragments of the walls and with the particles which had entered into the narrower passages, they would form drops which fly upwards. If, however, the fixed salt is loosened by means of water * or air, and is rendered more inert, then it becomes sufficiently capable of stopping the rush of the particles of Nitre, and forcing them to lose the motion which they had, and again to come to rest, like a cannon-ball when it strikes the sand or mud. It is just this consistency of the particles of Spirit of Nitre that constitutes the redintegration of Nitre, to effect which fixed salt (as appears from this explanation) is employed as a kind of instrument. So much about the redintegration.

Let us now see, if you please, first why Spirit of Nitre and Nitre itself are so different from each other in taste ; secondly why Nitre is inflammable, whereas Spirit of Nitre is not at all so.

In order that we may understand the first question, we must notice that bodies which are in motion never come into contact with other bodies along their largest surfaces ; but bodies which are at rest touch other bodies with their largest surfaces : and so if particles of Nitre are put on the tongue when they are at rest, they will lie upon it on their largest surfaces, and in this way they block its pores, which causes cold ; add to this the fact that Nitre cannot be dissolved by the saliva into sufficiently small particles. But if these particles are placed on the tongue when they are in excited motion, they will touch it with their sharp-pointed surfaces and will penetrate into its pores, and the more excited their motion, the more sharply will they prick the tongue ; in the same way a needle will give rise to different sensations according as it touches the tongue with its point or lies flat upon it.

* If you ask why from the infiltration of Spirit of Nitre into the dissolved fixed salt there arises an effervescence, then read the note on § 24.

The reason, however, why Nitre is inflammable whereas its Spirit is not, is that when the particles of Nitre are in a state of rest, it is more difficult for them to be carried upwards by the fire than when they have their own motion in all directions, and for this reason so long as they are at rest they will resist the fire, until the fire separates them from each other, and encompasses them on all sides ; but when the fire does encompass them, it carries them hither and thither along with it until they acquire their own motion and go up in smoke. But the particles of the Spirit of Nitre, since they are already in motion, and are separate from one another, are dilated in every direction within a larger compass by a little heat from a fire, and in this way some go off in smoke, others make their way into the matter which supplies the fire, before they have been entirely encompassed by the flame ; and so they extinguish rather than feed the fire.

I will proceed now to the experiments which seem to confirm this explanation. The first is that I discovered that the particles of Nitre, which go off in smoke amid a crackling noise, are pure Nitre ; for once or twice when I liquefied Nitre until the crucible was sufficiently hot, and then set fire to it with a live coal, I collected the smoke in a cold glass flask until it was moist with the smoke, and afterwards I made the flask still more moist by breathing on it, and then * I put it out into the cold air to dry. When I had done this there appeared here and there in the flask small icicles of Nitre, and in order to remove the suspicion that this was obtained not from the volatile particles only, but perhaps because the flame carried with it whole parts of Nitre (as I say, according to the opinion of the very illustrious Mr. Boyle) and gave off together with the volatile parts also the fixed parts before they were dissolved : in

* When I made this experiment the air was very clear.

88

order, I repeat, to remove this suspicion I made the smoke
go up through a tube, like A, more than a foot long,
as through a chimney, so that the heavier parts
might adhere to the tube, and I should only
collect the more volatile parts passing through
the narrower opening at B; and the experiment succeeded as I have said. I did not,
however, wish to stop there, but, in order to
examine the matter further I took a larger
quantity of Nitre, liquefied it, and set fire to
it with a live coal; and, as before, I placed
a tube A over the crucible, and near the opening B, so long as the flame lasted, I held a small
piece of looking glass to which some matter adhered
which became liquid on being exposed to the air,
and, although I waited for several days, I could
observe none of the effects of Nitre; but when I added
Spirit of Nitre it was turned into Nitre. From this, it
seems to me, I can conclude, first, that the fixed parts
are separated from the volatile in the process of lique-
faction, and that the flame drives the separated parts
upwards; secondly that after the fixed parts have been
separated from the volatile amid a crackling noise they
cannot unite with them again: from which it may be
concluded, in the third place, that the parts which
had adhered to the flask and had coagulated into
icicles were not the fixed parts but only the volatile
parts.

The object of the second experiment is to
show that the fixed parts are only the dregs
of Nitre; because I find that the more Nitre
is filtered, the more volatile it is, and the more
apt to crystallize. For when I placed crystals
of purified or filtered Nitre in a glass goblet
like A, and poured in a little cold water, it partly
evaporated with the cold water, and these fugitive

particles adhered to the rim of the glass at the top and coagulated into small icicles.

The third experiment is one which seems to show that the particles of Spirit of Nitre, when they lose their own motion, are rendered inflammable. I trickled drops of Spirit of Nitre into a moist paper bag, and then sprinkled sand over it, through the pores of which the Spirit of Nitre continuously penetrated, and when the sand had absorbed all, or nearly all, the Spirit of Nitre, I dried it thoroughly in the same paper bag over the fire. This done, I removed the sand and placed the paper against a live coal, and the moment it caught fire it gave off sparks in the way it usually does when it has absorbed Nitre itself. If I had had the opportunity of making further experiments I would have added to these others, which perhaps would have made the matter clearer; but as I am much distracted by other matters, I shall, if you will forgive me, put this off until some other occasion, and proceed now to other considerations.

§ 5. Where the very illustrious Mr. Boyle treats in passing of the shape of the particles of Nitre, he blames modern writers because they have given a wrong account of it. I do not know whether he means to include Descartes among these. If he does, then he is perhaps blaming him because of what others have said about him. For Descartes does not speak about such particles as can be seen with the eyes. And I do not think that the very illustrious Mr. Boyle means that, if the flakes of Nitre were to be rubbed down until they were changed to parallelepipeds, or some other shape, they would then cease to be Nitre; but perhaps he is referring to some other Chemists who admit nothing but what they can see with their eyes and touch with their hands.

§ 9. If this experiment could be carried out accurately,

it would entirely confirm what I wished to conclude from the first experiment mentioned above.

In §§ 13 to 18 the very illustrious Mr. Boyle is trying to show that all tactile qualities depend only on motion, shape, and the remaining mechanical states. But, since these proofs are not put forward by the very illustrious Mr. Boyle, as mathematical, there is no need to see whether they are completely convincing. But in the meanwhile I do not know why the very illustrious Mr. Boyle is so anxious to conclude this from this experiment of his ; for this has already been proved sufficiently and more than sufficiently by Verulam and afterwards by Descartes. And I do not see that this experiment provides us with any clearer proofs than other experiments which are sufficiently common. For, as far as heat is concerned, is not this equally clear from the fact that if two pieces of wood, although cold themselves, are rubbed together, they produce a flame simply as a result of the motion ? or from the fact that lime sprinkled with water becomes hot ? With regard to sound, I do not see that anything more remarkable is to be found in this experiment than is found in the boiling of ordinary water, and in many other things. But with regard to colour, to adduce only what can be proved, I will say nothing except that we see all green plants change into so many and such different colours. Moreover, if bodies which emit an evil odour are shaken, then they emit a worse odour, especially so if they become somewhat hot. Lastly sweet wine is turned into vinegar, and so with many other things. All these things, therefore * (if I may speak with philosophical candour) I should consider superfluous. This I say because I fear lest others, who esteem the very illustrious author less than is his due, should judge him wrongly.

§ 24. Of the cause of this phenomenon I have already

* In the letter which I sent I omitted this advisedly.

spoken : here I will only add that I also have found by experience that particles of fixed salt float about in these saline drops. For when they flew upwards they touched a plate of glass which I held ready for the purpose, and which I had warmed a little so that whatsoever volatile particle adhered to the glass should fly off ; when this had happened I perceived a coarse white matter adhering here and there to the glass.

§ 25. In this section the very illustrious Mr. Boyle seems to want to show that the alkaline parts are carried hither and thither by the impact of the salt particles, but that the salt particles lift themselves into the air by their own force. In my explanation of the phenomenon I also said that the particles of Spirit of Nitre acquire a more violent motion because when they enter into the wider pores, they are necessarily surrounded by some very fine matter, and are driven off by it as particles of wood are driven off by fire ; but the alkalised particles received their motion from the impact of those particles of Spirit of Nitre which had penetrated into the narrower pores. Here I add that pure water cannot so easily dissolve and soften the fixed parts : wherefore it is not surprising that when Spirit of Nitre is added to a solution of this fixed salt dissolved in water, there should begin such an ebullition as the very illustrious author describes in § 24 ; I even think that this ebullition will be more violent than if Spirit of Nitre were to be added to the fixed salt while it is still intact. For in water it is dissolved into very minute molecules, which can be more easily broken up, and more freely moved than when all parts of the salt lie on each other, and adhere firmly to one another.

§ 26. Of the taste of the acid of Spirit of Nitre I have already spoken ; wherefore it only remains to speak of the alkali. When I placed this on the tongue, I felt a sensation of heat followed by a prick. This shows me that it is a kind of lime : for in the same way that lime is heated by means of water so this salt is heated by means of the saliva, or of perspiration, or of Spirit of Nitre, and perhaps even of moist air.

§ 27. It does not immediately follow that a particle of matter acquires a new shape because it is joined to another : it only follows that it becomes larger, and this is sufficient to produce the effect which the very illustrious author seeks in this section.

§ 33. What I think of the Philosophical Method of the very illustrious Mr. Boyle I will say when I have seen the Dissertation of which mention is made here and in the Introductory Note, page 23.

On Fluidity.

§ 1. *It is manifest enough that they are to be reckoned amongst the most general affections, etc.* . . . I should think that notions which are derived from popular usage, or which explain Nature not as it is in itself, but as it appears to human sense, should by no means be numbered among the highest generic terms, nor should they be mixed up (not to say confounded) with notions which are pure and which explain Nature as it is in itself. Of this kind are motion, rest, and their laws ; of the former kind are the terms visible and invisible, hot, cold and, to say it at once, fluid and firm, etc.

§ 5. *The first is the littleness of the bodies that compose it, for in bigger parcels of matter, etc.* Even if bodies are small they have (or can have) uneven and rough surfaces. Therefore if large bodies move in such a proportion that their motion is related to their mass as the motion of minute bodies is related to their mass, then they ought to be called fluid if the name fluid did not signify something extrinsic, and were not merely appropriated from popular use to mean those moving bodies whose minuteness and intervening spaces escape human sense. Therefore to divide bodies into fluid and firm will be the same as to divide them into visible and invisible.

The same §. *If we were not able to confirm it by chemical experiments.* One will never be able to prove this by chemical or by other experiments, but only by reasoning and calculation. For by reasoning and calculation we divide bodies infinitely; and consequently also the Forces which are required to move them; but we shall never be able to prove this by experiment.

§ 6. *Great bodies are too unwieldy to constitute fluid ones, etc.* Whether by fluid is to be understood what I said just now, or not, the thing is obvious of itself. But I do not see how the very illustrious author proves this by the experiments brought forward in this section. For (since we want to doubt what is uncertain) however unsuitable bones may be for the formation of chyle and similar fluids, they may perchance be suitable enough for the formation of some new kind of fluid.

§ 10. *And this by making them less pliant than formerly, etc.* Without any change of the parts, but only because the parts which are forced into the receiving body are separated from the rest, they could coagulate so as to form another body more solid than oil. For bodies are lighter or heavier according to the kinds of fluid in which they are immersed. So particles of butter when floating in milk form part of the liquid; but when the milk is stirred and acquires a new motion to which all the parts composing the milk cannot equally accommodate themselves, the result is simply this, that certain of the heavier parts separate themselves and force the lighter ones to the surface. But since these lighter particles are so much heavier than air that they cannot form a liquid with it, they are forced down by it, and as they are unsuitable for motion, and cannot form a liquid by themselves, they lie on one another and adhere to each other. Vapours, too, when they are separated from the air are changed into water which may be said to be firm in comparison with air.

§ 13. *And I choose an instance in a bladder distended with water rather than in a bladder filled with air, etc.* Since the particles of water are always moving hither and thither unceasingly, it is clear that, if they are not prevented by surrounding bodies, they will make it expand in all directions ; further I confess I am not yet able to see how the distention of a bladder full of water helps to confirm his opinion about the small spaces : for the reason why the particles of water do not yield when the sides of the bladder are pressed with the finger as they other-

wise would do, if they were free, is because there is no equilibrium or circulation such as there is when some body, say our finger, is surrounded by a fluid or by water. But however much the water is pressed by the bladder, yet its particles would yield to a stone which was also enclosed in the bladder, in the same way as they usually do outside the bladder.

The same §. *Whether there may not be a portion of matter, etc.* We must answer affirmatively unless we prefer to progress to infinity or (and nothing can be more absurd) to grant the existence of a vacuum.

§ 19. *That the particles of the liquid find admittance into those pores, and are detained there (by which means, etc.).* This must not be affirmed absolutely of all liquids which find admittance into the pores of others. For the particles of Spirit of Nitre if they enter into the pores of white paper make it rigid and friable ; which may be observed if a few drops are poured into a glowing iron evaporator, like A, and the smoke sent up through a paper bag, like B. Moreover, even Spirit of Nitre softens leather yet does not really make it moist, but, on the contrary, makes it shrink, just as fire does.

The same §. *Whom Nature having designed to fly sometimes in the air and to live sometimes in the water, etc.* He seeks the cause in the purpose.

§ 23. *Though their motion be but seldom perceived by us. Take then, etc.* Without this experiment and without any ado the matter is sufficiently clear from the fact that our breath, which in winter time is clearly perceived to move, in summer time or in heated rooms cannot be perceived by us. Moreover, if in summer time the breeze cools suddenly, the vapours rising from water, which, because of the new density of the air, cannot be as easily dispersed throughout the air, as they could before it cooled, are gathered together again over the surface of the water in such quantities that we can see them clearly. Again a movement is often too slow to be perceived by us, as we can learn from the gnomon and the shadow of the sun, and very often it is too fast to be perceived by us, as may be seen in the case of lighted kindling-wood when it is moved with some speed in a circle ; here, certainly, we imagine the lighted part to be at rest at all the places of the circumference which it describes by its motion. I would give the reasons for these things here, if I did not think it unnecessary. Lastly, let me say in passing that, for the understanding of the nature of a fluid in general, it is enough to know that we can move our hand about in it in all directions, with a motion proportionate to the fluid, without any resistance, as is sufficiently clear to those who pay due attention to those notions which explain Nature as it is in itself, and not indeed as it is presented to human sense. But I do not therefore look down upon this account as useless ; but on the contrary, if of every liquid there were an account given as accurately as possible with the highest trustworthiness, I should consider it of the greatest service for the understanding of the special features which differentiate them : which is to be most earnestly desired by all Philosophers as something very necessary.

OF FIRMNESS.

§ 7. *It seems consonant to the universal laws of Nature.* This is Descartes' proof; I do not see that the very illustrious Mr. Boyle adduces any genuine proof derived from his experiments or observations.

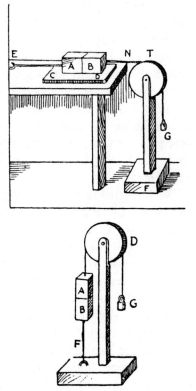

I had made many notes on this and on what follows ; but afterwards I saw that the very illustrious author corrects himself.

§ 16. *And once four hundred and thirty two* [ounces]. If it is compared with the weight of the quicksilver enclosed in the tube it comes near to the real weight. But I considered it worth while to examine this, in order as far as possible to ascertain both the proportion between the lateral or horizontal pressure of the air and the perpendicular pressure, and I think it can be done in this way

Let C D, in Figure 1, be a plane mirror, very accurately smoothed, A B two pieces of marble immediately touching one another; let the piece of marble A be attached to a hook E, but B to a cord N, T is a pulley, G a weight which will show the force that is required to pull apart the piece of marble B from the piece A in the horizontal direction.

In Figure 2, let F be a sufficiently strong silk thread by which the piece of marble B is tied to the floor, D a pulley, G the weight which may show the force which is required to pull apart the piece of marble A from the piece of marble B in the perpendicular direction. It is not necessary to explain these things more fully.

Here you have, my friend, what I find to be remarked about the experiments of Mr. Boyle. With regard to your first questions, when I look through my answers to them I do not see that I have omitted anything. And if perchance I have stated something obscurely (as I often do for want of words) I pray you to be kind enough to point it out to me. I will take pains to explain it more clearly.

With regard to your new question, namely, how things began to be and by what bond they depend on the first cause, I have written a whole booklet on this subject and also on the Improvement of the Understanding, and I have been engaged on copying it out and improving it. But sometimes I leave the work since I have not yet any definite plan for its publication. I am naturally afraid lest the theologians of our time take offence and with their usual hatred attack me, who utterly loathe quarrels. I shall await your advice on this matter, and in order that you may know what is contained in this work of mine that might be some small cause of offence to the preachers, I say that many attributes which they and all others at least who are known to me attribute to God, I regard as things created; and on the other hand, things which they, on account of their prejudices, regard as created, I contend to be attributes of God, and as misunderstood by them; and also that I could not separate God from Nature as all of whom I have any knowledge have done. And so I await your advice; for I look to you as to a most faithful friend of whose good faith it would be wrong to doubt. In the meanwhile fare well and as you have begun so continue to love me who am

Yours entirely
BENEDICTUS SPINOZA.

[RHYNSBURG, *April* 1662.]

LETTER VII   HENRY OLDENBURG

TO THE VERY ILLUSTRIOUS MR. B. D. S.

Reply to the Preceding.

Many weeks ago already, very illustrious Sir, I received your very welcome letter, with its learned comments on Boyle's book. The Author himself joins me in thanking you very much for the reflections which you have communicated to us: he would have signified his gratitude sooner had he not entertained the hope that he might in a short time be relieved from the mass of business with which he is burdened, and so be able at the same time to send you his answer together with his thanks. But he feels that so far his hope has deceived him, for he has been so disturbed with both public and private affairs that this time he can do no more than express his grateful feeling to you, and must put off until some other time the communication of his opinion on your Notes. It happens also that on the publication of his writings two Adversaries attacked him, and he feels himself bound to answer them at the very first opportunity. These writings, indeed, are not directed against his Treatise on Nitre, but against his other little book which contains his Pneumatic Experiments proving the Elasticity of Air. As soon as he has completed these labours he will make known to you his views about your objections; but in the meantime he asks you not to put an unfavourable construction on this delay.

The Society of Philosophers of which I have spoken to you has now, by the King's grace, been converted into the Royal Society, and has been presented with a public Charter, whereby special Privileges are granted to it, and great hope is held out that it will be endowed with the necessary revenues.

I would by all means advise you not to begrudge to scholars the results at which with your mental sagacity and learning you have arrived both in Philosophical and Theological matters; let them be published, however much the Theological quacks may growl. Your commonwealth is the freest, in it philosophy should be pursued with the greatest freedom: but your own prudence will suggest to you that you should express your ideas and your opinion with as much moderation as possible; for the rest, leave the issue to Fate. Come then, excellent Sir, and banish all fear of stirring up the pygmies of our time; long enough have sacrifices been made to ignorance and absurdity; let us spread the sails of true knowledge, and search more deeply into the innermost parts of Nature than has been done hitherto. I should think that your reflections could be printed in your country with impunity, and there is no need to fear that any of them will cause offence among the wise. If you find such for your patrons and supporters (and such, I answer for it, you will certainly find) why should you dread an ignorant Momus? I will not let you go, honoured Friend, until I have persuaded you; and, as far as it is in my power, I will never be content to let your thoughts, which are so weighty, be suppressed in eternal silence. I pray you urgently that you will not mind letting me know, as soon as you conveniently can, what decision you will adopt about this matter.

Maybe such things will happen here as will not be unworthy of your cognizance. For the afore-mentioned Society will now strive more eagerly to fulfil its purpose, and maybe, so long as peace lasts in these shores, will grace the Republic of Letters in no common manner.

Farewell, distinguished Sir, and believe me
Your very devoted and very friendly
HENRY OLDENBURG.

[LONDON, *July* 1662.]

LETTER VIII   SIMON DE VRIES

TO THE VERY ILLUSTRIOUS MR. B. D. S.

MOST UPRIGHT FRIEND,

I have already long wished to be with you once but the weather and the hard winter have not been sufficiently favourable to me. Sometimes I complain of my fate in being removed from you by a distance which keeps us so long from one another. Happy indeed, very happy, is your companion Casearius who lives under the same roof, and can converse with you on the best subjects at breakfast, at dinner, and on your walks. But although our bodies are so widely separated from one another, yet you have been very often in my mind, especially when I am occupied with your writings, and hold them in my hands.

But since everything is not sufficiently clear to the members of our society (and that is why we have resumed our meetings) and also in order that you may not think that I have forgotten you, I made up my mind to write this letter.

As to the society, this is how it is conducted ; one member (but each takes his turn) reads through, explains according to his conception, and, moreover, proves everything, following the sequence and order of your propositions ; then, if it happens that we cannot satisfy one another, we think it worth while to make a note of it, and to write to you, so that, if possible, the matter may be made clearer to us, and that under your leadership we may be able to defend the truth against those who are superstitiously religious or even Christian, and to stand firm against the onslaught of the whole world.

So, since, on our first reading them through and explaining them, the definitions did not all seem clear to us, we did not all hold the same opinion about the nature of definition. In your absence we consulted meanwhile a certain author, namely, a mathematician called Borellus ; when he states the nature of a definition, of an axiom and of a postulate, he also cites the opinions of others on this subject. His own opinion reads as follows : *Definitions are employed in a proof as premises. Therefore they must be known clearly, otherwise scientific or the clearest knowledge cannot be derived from them.* In another place he says : *The ground of a construction or the essential first and best known phenomenon of any subject must not be chosen at random but with the greatest care. For if the construction and the said phenomenon be impossible, then the result will not be a scientific definition, as for instance, if some one were to say : " Let any two straight lines enclosing a space be called figurals." They would be definitions of the non-existent, and impossible ; and consequently ignorance rather than knowledge would be derived from them. Again, if the construction, or the said phenomenon, be something possible and true, but yet unknown to us or doubtful, then also it will not be a good definition ; for conclusions which are derived from something unknown and doubtful will themselves be uncertain and doubtful, and will therefore produce conjecture and opinion, but not sure knowledge.*

Tacquet seems to differ from this opinion: he asserts, as you know, that it is possible to proceed directly from a false proposition to a true conclusion. Clavius, however, whose view he also introduces, is of this opinion: *Definitions are arbitrary expressions, and it is not necessary to adduce a reason why something is defined in this way or that; but it is enough that the thing defined should never be asserted to correspond with some [real] thing, unless it can first be proved that the given definition does correspond with it.* Thus Borellus will have it that the definition of anything ought to consist of a relation or construction which is first, essential, very well-known to us, and true. Not so Clavius: whether it be the first or the best known, or true or not, is of no importance so long as the definition we have given is not asserted to correspond with something [real], unless the given definition is first proved to correspond with it. We would rather follow the opinion of Borellus; but we do not really know with which of the two you, Sir, agree, or whether you agree with neither.

Therefore, since such various conflicting views are put forward about the nature of definition, which is included among the principles of demonstration, and since our thought is not relieved from the difficulties of this subject nor from those which result from it, we should very much wish that you, Sir, would write to us (if we are not causing you too much trouble, and if you have leisure to do so) what you yourself think about this subject, and also what is the distinction between axioms and definitions. Borellus does not admit any real difference between them, except in name: but I believe you maintain another difference.

Further, the third Definition is not sufficiently clear to us; I adduced as an example what you, Sir, said to me at the Hague, namely, that a thing can be considered in two ways, either as it is in itself, or as it is in relation to something else. For instance the Understanding, for it can be considered either under Thought or as consisting of ideas. But we do not see clearly what this distinction is ; for we suppose that if we conceive thought rightly, then we ought to reckon it with ideas, for if all ideas were removed from thought, we should destroy thought itself. With regard to this thing, since this example is not sufficiently clear to us, the thing itself is to some extent obscure and we need further explanation.

Finally, in the Third Scholium to Proposition 8, in the beginning, occurs the following statement : *Hence it appears that although two attributes are conceived as really distinct (that is, one without the help of the other) yet they do not therefore constitute two entities or two different substances ; the reason is because it is of the nature of a substance that all its attributes, I mean each one of them, should be conceived through itself, because they all existed in it at the same time.* Thus you, Sir, seem to suppose that the nature of a substance is so constituted that it can have many attributes, which you have not yet proved, unless you refer to the fifth definition of the absolutely infinite substance, or God ; otherwise, if I may say that each substance has only one attribute and if I had the idea of two attributes, then I could rightly conclude that where there are two different attributes there are also two different substances. We entreat you to give a clearer explanation also with reference to this.

Further, I thank you very much for your writings, which were conveyed to me by P. Balling, and gave me much pleasure. But especially the Scholium to Proposition 19.

If I can serve you here in anything that is in my power, then I am at your service ; you have only to let me know.

I have joined a course on anatomy, and I am about half-way through ; when it is finished I shall begin a course on chemistry, and, as you advise, go through the whole medical course.

I stop and look forward to your answer. Accept greetings from me who am
Your very devoted
S. J. D'VRIES.

1663 GIVEN AT AMSTERDAM
24th February

SR. BENEDICTUS SPINOZA
AT
RHYNSBURG
1663.

LETTER IX   B. D. S.

TO THE VERY LEARNED YOUNG MAN SIMON DE VRIES.

Reply to the Preceding.

(ON THE NATURE OF DEFINITION AND AXIOM.)

HONOURED FRIEND,
I have received your letter which I have so long desired, and I thank you very much for it and for your affection towards me. Your long absence has been no less disagreeable to me than to you ; meanwhile however I am glad that my night-work is of use to you and to our friends. For in this way I speak with you from afar while you are absent. You have no reason to envy Casearius. Indeed, there is no one whom I find more disagreeable, or with whom I have been more careful to be on my guard than with him ; so that I should like you and all our acquaintances to be warned not to communicate my opinions to him until he shall have attained to a riper age. He is too boyish as yet, rather unstable, and more eager for novelty than for

truth. Yet I hope that he will cure himself of these puerile faults in a few years. Indeed I am almost sure of it, as far as I can judge from his nature; and so his character makes me fond of him.

With regard to the questions which have been propounded in your society (which is organized quite wisely) I see that you are perplexed by them because you do not distinguish between different kinds of definition. You do not distinguish between a definition which serves to explain a thing whose essence only is sought, and concerning whose essence alone there is doubt, and a definition which is put forward only to be examined. For the former, since it has a determinate object, ought to be true; the latter need not be. For instance, if someone were to ask me for a description of the Temple of Solomon, then I ought to give him a true description of the temple unless I want to talk nonsense. But if I have constructed in my mind some temple which I wish to build, and from the description of it I conclude that I must buy such and such land, so many thousand stones, and a certain quantity of other materials, would any sane man say that my conclusion is wrong because I have perhaps made use of a false definition? Or will any one ask me to prove my definition? This would be equivalent to telling me that I have not conceived what I have conceived, or demanding a proof that I have conceived what I have conceived: which is sheer trifling.

Therefore, a definition either explains a thing as it exists outside the understanding, and then it ought to be true, and does not differ from a proposition, or an axiom, except in so far as it deals only with the essences of things or of states, whereas an axiom is wider since it extends to eternal truths. Or else a definition explains a thing as it is conceived or can be conceived by us: and then, indeed, it differs from an axiom and a proposition because all that is required of it is merely that it should be conceived, and not, like an axiom, that it should be conceived as true. Therefore that definition which is not conceivable is bad. In order to make this clear to you let me take the example given by Borellus, that is, if some one were to say, let any two straight lines which enclose a space be called figurals. If he understands by straight line what all other people understand by curved line, then his definition is good (for by that definition will be understood a figure such as ⬭ *a* or similar figures), provided he does not afterwards mean by it squares and other figures. If, however, he understands by straight line what we commonly understand by it, the thing is clearly inconceivable, and therefore it is not a definition. All these things are thoroughly confused by Borellus, whose opinion you are inclined to embrace.

I add another example, namely, that which you adduce at the end. If I say that each substance has only one attribute, that is a mere assertion and needs demonstration. But if I say, by substance I understand that which consists of only one attribute, it will be a good definition, only after that I must call entities consisting of more attributes than one by some other name than substance.

As to your remark that I have not proved that substance (or being) can have more attributes than one, perhaps you did not pay sufficient attention to the proofs. For I have adduced two. The first is that there is nothing more evident to us than the fact that every entity is conceived by us under some attribute, and that the more reality or being an entity has the more attributes there must be attributed to it. So that the absolutely infinite being must be defined, etc. The second, to which I award the prize, is that the more attributes I attribute to any entity the more I am compelled to attribute existence to it, that is, the more do I conceive it as true. Quite the contrary would happen if I had imagined a Chimæra or something similar.

As to your remark that you do not conceive of Thought except under ideas, because when you take away ideas you destroy thought, I believe that this happens to you because while you, who are a thinking being, do this, you set aside all your thoughts and conceptions. Therefore it is not to be wondered at that when you have set aside all your thoughts there remains nothing for you to think about. As regards the main thing, I think I have sufficiently plainly and clearly proved that intellect, even though infinite, pertains to created Nature, not to creating Nature.

But I do not yet see what this has to do with the understanding of the third definition, nor even why it should cause difficulty. For the definition as I gave it you, unless I am mistaken, reads as follows : *By substance I mean that which is in itself and is conceived through itself, that is, whose conception does not involve the conception of some other thing. I mean the same by attribute, except that it is called attribute with respect to the intellect, which attributes such and such a nature to substance.* This definition, I say, explains clearly enough what I wish you to understand by substance or attribute. You however wish me to explain by means of an example, which it is very easy to do, how one and the same thing can be called by two names. But, not to seem niggardly, I will supply two examples. First, I say that by the name Israel I mean the third Patriarch, I also mean the same Patriarch by the name Jacob, since the name Jacob was given to him because he had seized his brother's heel. Secondly by plane I mean that which reflects all the rays of light without any change ; I mean the same by white, except that it is called white in relation to a man who is looking at the plane [surface].

With this I think I have fully answered your questions.

Meanwhile I shall wait to hear your judgment; and if there is yet anything which you do not consider to be well or clearly enough demonstrated, then be not shy to point it out to me, etc.

[RHYNSBURG, *March* 1663.]

LETTER X

B. D. S.

To the Most Learned Young Man SIMON DE VRIES.

HONOURED FRIEND,

You ask me whether we need experience to know whether the Definition of some Attribute is true. To this I reply, that we only need Experience in the case of whatever cannot be deduced from the definition of a thing, as, for instance, the existence of Modes : for this cannot be deduced from the definition of a thing. But we do not need experience in the case of those things whose existence is not distinguished from their essence, and therefore follows from their definition. Indeed, no experience will ever be able to teach us this : for experience does not teach us the essence of things ; the utmost which it can effect is to determine our mind so that it only thinks of certain essences of things. Therefore, since the existence of attributes does not differ from their essence, we shall not be able to apprehend it by any kind of experience.

You ask furthermore whether even things or the states of things are eternal truths ? I answer certainly. If you continue, why do I not call them eternal truths ? I answer, in order that I may distinguish them, as all usually do, from those which do not explain any thing or any state of a thing, as, for instance, *nothing is produced from nothing*. This I say, and similar propositions, are called absolutely eternal truths, by which they wish to indicate nothing else than that such things have no place outside the mind, etc.

[RHYNSBURG, *about March* 1663.]

LETTER XI   HENRY OLDENBURG

To the Very Illustrious Mr. B. d. S.

Reply to Letter VI.

Most excellent Sir, dearest Friend,
        I could produce many excuses for my long
silence ; but I shall reduce my reasons to two, the illness
of the most Noble Boyle and the pressure of my own
affairs. The former hindered Boyle from answering
your observations on Nitre sooner ; the latter have so
occupied me for several months that I scarcely seemed
to be my own master, and so could not discharge the
obligation which I confess that I owed you. I rejoice
that, for the time at least, both obstacles are removed,
so that I can resume my intercourse with so great a
friend. I do so indeed with the utmost pleasure ; and
I am determined (with Heaven's help) to exercise the
greatest care that in future our correspondence shall
not suffer so long an interruption.

But before I turn to those matters which concern
you and me alone, let me deliver what is due to you in
the name of Mr. Boyle. He has received the notes,
which you made on his Chemico-Physical Treatise,
with his usual kindliness, and he sends you his best
thanks for your criticism. Meanwhile he desires you
to be warned that the object that he had set before
himself was not so much to show that this was a really
philosophic and perfect analysis of Nitre, but rather to
explain that the common Doctrine of Substantial Forms
and Qualities which is also accepted in the Schools,
rests on a weak foundation, and that what they call
the specific differences of things can be reduced to the
magnitude, motion, rest and position of their parts.
After this preliminary remark, the Author says further
that his experiment with Nitre was enough and more

than enough to show that by chemical analysis the whole mass of Nitre broke up into parts which differed from one another and from the original whole ; afterwards, however, it was so re-compounded out of these parts and reconstituted again that it fell little short of its original weight. He adds, too, that he has shown that this is the actual fact ; he did not deal with the process of the thing, with which your conjecture seems to be concerned, nor did he determine anything about it, since to do so would have been beyond his design. Meanwhile, he thinks that your suppositions about the process, your view that the fixed salt of Nitre is as it were its dregs, and other similar suppositions, are gratuitous and unproved. As to your assertion that these dregs, or this fixed salt, has pores hollowed to the size of the particles of Nitre, on this point the Author remarks that the salt of potash combined with Spirit of Nitre produces Nitre just as much as Spirit of Nitre does when combined with its own fixed salt. Hence he thinks it clear that similar pores are to be found in bodies of that kind from which Nitric spirits are not given off. The Author does not see that the necessity of that very fine matter, which you set up in addition, is proved by any phenomena : it is assumed simply from the hypothesis that a vacuum is an impossibility.

What you assert about the causes of the difference in taste between Spirit of Nitre and Nitre itself, the Author says, does not affect him : but what you relate about the inflammability of Nitre and the non-inflammability of Spirit of Nitre he says presupposes Descartes' theory of fire, with which he declares he is not yet satisfied.

As to the Experiments by which you seek to confirm your explanation of the Phenomenon, the Author replies, first, that with regard to its matter, Spirit of Nitre is indeed Nitre, but by no means so with regard to its form, since they differ very much in their qualities and virtues, namely, in taste, smell, volatility, the power of dissolving metals, and of changing the colours of vegetables, etc. Secondly, as to your remark that certain particles which are carried upwards combine into Crystals of Nitre, he maintains that this happens because Nitric particles are pushed out together with Spirit of Nitre through the action of fire, just as happens in the case of soot. Thirdly, to your observation on the effect of purification, the Author replies that in this purification, Nitre is, for the most part, freed from a certain kind of salt which is like common salt; and that the ascending and forming into icicles is common to this and to other salts, and depends on the pressure of the air and certain other causes, which must be discussed elsewhere, and have nothing to do with the present question. Fourthly, with regard to what you say about your third experiment, the author says that the same happens also with certain other salts; he asserts that the paper when it is actually alight agitates the rigid and solid particles which composed the salt, and in this way produces a scintillation with them.

Again, with regard to your idea that in Section 5 the noble Author is blaming Descartes, he believes that it is you who are to blame in this matter, and he says that he was in no way referring to Descartes, but to Gassendi and others, who attribute to the particles of Nitre a cylindrical form whereas it is really prismatic; nor was he speaking of other than visible forms.

To your notes on Sections 13–18 he merely replies that he wrote them in the first place in order to show and to make known the use of chemistry for confirming the Mechanical Principles of Philosophy, and he has not found these matters conveyed and discussed so clearly by other writers. Our Boyle belongs to the number of those who have not so much confidence in their reason as not to wish that the Phenomena should agree with their reason. Moreover, he says that there is a great difference between common experiments, where we do not know what Nature contributes and what other factors intervene, and those experiments in which it is known for certain what the additional factors are. Pieces of wood are much more composite bodies than the thing with which the Author deals. And in the boiling of ordinary water fire is added from outside which is not applied in our production of sound. Again, the reason why green plants change into so many and such different colours is still being sought. That this, however, is brought about by the change of the parts is shown by this experiment, from which it is clear that the colour was changed by the pouring on of Spirit of Nitre. Lastly, he says that Nitre has neither an offensive nor a sweet odour, but acquires an offensive odour merely in consequence of its dissolution, and loses it when it is re-compounded.

To your notes on Section 25 (the rest, he says, does not touch him) he replies that he has made use of the Epicurean principles, which will have it that motion is innate in the particles ; for it was necessary to use some Hypothesis to explain the Phenomenon ; yet he does not, on that account, make it his own, but uses it to maintain his own opinion against the Chemists and the Schoolmen, while showing that the fact can be well explained on the said hypothesis. To your comment on the powerlessness of pure water to dissolve the fixed parts our Boyle replies that chemists here and there observe and assert that pure water dissolves alkalised salts more rapidly than others.

The Author has not yet had time to devote to your notes on Fluidity and Firmness. I am sending you these things which I have noted down, so as not to be any longer deprived of learned intercourse and discussion with you.

But I do most earnestly beg you to take in good part these very disconnected and disjointed replies which I am sending to you ; you must ascribe this to my haste rather than to the mind of the illustrious Boyle. For I have put them together from friendly talk with him on this subject rather than from any dictated and methodical answer of his. Hence it happens, no doubt, that many of his remarks have escaped me which were perhaps more sound and better expressed than what I have here reported. I therefore take the whole blame upon myself, and absolve the Author entirely from it.

Now let me turn to our own affairs. And here at the very threshold let me ask you whether you have finished that very important essay in which you treat of the origin of things and of their dependence on the first cause as well as of the Improvement of our Understanding. Certainly, dearest Sir, I believe that nothing can be published that will be more welcome or more acceptable, to men who are really learned and wise, than a Treatise of that kind. This is what a man of your intelligence and genius should put before his eyes rather than the things that please the Theologians of our time and fashion : for they do not look for truth so much as for their own advantage. Therefore I adjure you by the bond of our friendship and by every duty of augmenting and spreading the truth, not to grudge or refuse us your writings on these subjects. If, however, there is some reason of greater moment than any I can foresee which may hinder you from publishing the work, I most earnestly beg you not to mind communicating to me a summary of it by letter ; and for this service you will find me a grateful friend.

Other works by the very learned Boyle will shortly be published, which I will send you instead of a reward. To these I will also add others which will give you an account of the whole organization of our Royal Society, of the Council of which I am a member together with twenty others, and of which I am one of the Secretaries together with one other.

On this occasion I am prevented by shortage of time from being able to digress further. I promise you all the loyalty which can come from an honest mind, and every readiness for any services which can be rendered by my slender powers, and I am from my heart,

Most excellent Sir,

Yours entirely

HENRY OLDENBURG.

LONDON, 3 *April* 1663.

LETTER XII   B. D. S.

To THE VERY LEARNED AND VERY EXPERT

LUDOVICUS MEYER, P.M.Q.D.

(ON THE NATURE OF THE INFINITE.)

DISTINGUISHED FRIEND,

I have received two letters from you, one dated 11 January, and delivered to me by our friend N. N.; the other dated 26 March, and sent to me by some friend, I do not know by whom, from Leyden. Both were most welcome; particularly because I gathered from them that all is very well with you and that you frequently think of me. I give you, then, my best thanks, such as I owe you, for your kindness towards me, and for the honour which you have ever deigned to do me; and I beg you at the same time to believe that I am no less devoted to you, which I shall always endeavour to show, as much as my slender powers will allow, when the opportunity is given me. And to begin, I shall be careful to reply to the question which you ask me in your letters.

You ask me, then, to communicate to you the results

of my thoughts about the Infinite, which I shall most gladly do.

The question concerning the Infinite has always seemed most difficult, or rather insoluble, to all, because they did not distinguish between what must be infinite because of its own nature, or in virtue of its definition, and that which has no limits, not indeed in virtue of its essence, but in virtue of its cause. And also because they did not distinguish between that which is called infinite because it has no limits, and that whose parts we cannot equate with or explain by any number, although we know its maximum and minimum. And lastly because they did not distinguish between that which we can only understand but cannot imagine, and that which we can also imagine. I say that if they had paid attention to these distinctions, then they would not have been overwhelmed by such a vast crowd of difficulties. For they would then have clearly understood which kind of infinite cannot be divided into parts, or can have no parts, and which, on the contrary, [has parts] and that without contradiction. Moreover, they would also have understood which kind of Infinite can be conceived as greater than another Infinite, without any complication, and which cannot be so conceived; as will become clearly apparent from what I shall soon have to say.

But, first, let me in a few words explain these four, namely, Substance, Mode, Eternity, and Duration. The things that I should like to be noted about Substance are the following—First, that existence pertains to its essence, that is, that its existence follows from its mere essence and definition: this, unless my memory deceives me, I have already proved to you some time ago by word of mouth without the help of other propositions. The second point, which follows from this first one, is that substance is not one of many, but that there exists only one of the same nature. Thirdly and lastly, no substance can be conceived as other than infinite. I call the states of substance Modes, whose definition, in so far as it is not the definition of Substance, cannot involve existence. Therefore, although they exist, we can conceive them as non-existent, from which it also follows that when we are considering only the essence of Modes, and not the whole order of Nature, we cannot from the fact that they now exist deduce that they will exist or will not exist in the future, or that they existed or did not exist in the past. Hence it is clear that we conceive the existence of Substance as entirely different from the existence of Modes. Hence arises the difference between Eternity and Duration : for by means of Duration we can only explain the existence of Modes, but we can only explain the existence of Substance by means of Eternity, that is, the infinite enjoyment of existence or (in awkward Latin) *essendi*.

From all this it is clear that we can at will determine the existence and duration of Modes and conceive it as greater or less, and divide it into parts, when, as most frequently happens, we are considering their essence only and not the order of Nature. Indeed we can do so without thereby in any way destroying the conception which we have of them. But Eternity and Substance, since they cannot be conceived as other than infinite, cannot be treated thus without our destroying our conception of them at the same time. Therefore those who think that Extended Substance consists of parts, or of bodies really distinct from one another, are talking foolishly, not to say madly. For this is just as if one endeavoured, by merely adding together and accumulating many circles, to form a square, or a triangle, or something else different in its whole essence. Therefore that whole medley of arguments, by which Philosophers generally try to show that Extended Substance is finite, collapses of its own accord : for they all suppose that corporeal substance is composed of parts. In the same way others, who have persuaded themselves that a line is composed of points, could also find many arguments by which they would prove that a line is not divisible to infinity.

If however you ask why, by some natural impulse we are so prone to divide extended substance, I reply, because we conceive quantity in two ways, namely, abstractly or superficially, in so far as we have it in our imagination by the help of the senses ; or as substance, which happens only through the intellect alone. And so if we consider quantity as it is in the imagination, as happens most frequently and more easily, it will be found to be divisible, finite, composed of parts, and one of many. But if we consider it as it is in our intellect, and if the thing is apprehended as it is in itself, which is very difficult to do, then, as I have sufficiently proved to you before now (if I remember rightly) it will be found to be infinite, indivisible and unique.

Moreover, because we can determine Duration and Quantity as we please, namely, when we conceive the latter abstracted from Substance and we separate the former from the mode whereby it flows from eternal things, there arise Time and Measure ; Time to determine Duration and Measure to determine Quantity in such a way that, as far as possible, we may imagine them easily. Then because we separate the states of Substance from Substance itself, and reduce them to classes, so that, as far as possible, we may imagine them easily, there arises Number by which we determine them. Hence one can see clearly that Measure, Time and Number are nothing but Modes of thought or rather of imagination. Therefore it is not to be wondered at that all who have tried to understand the course of Nature by such Notions, and these moreover ill understood, should have so marvellously entangled themselves that at length they could not extricate themselves except by breaking up everything and committing even the most absurd absurdities. For since there are many things which we cannot grasp with the imagination, but only with the intellect, such as Substance, Eternity, and others—if any one tries to explain such things by Notions of this kind, which are merely aids to the imagination, he does nothing more than take pains to rave with his imagination. And even the Modes of Substance themselves can never be rightly understood if they are confused with such things of Reason or with aids of the imagination. For when we do this we separate them from Substance and from the mode by which they flow from Eternity, without which, however, they cannot be rightly understood.

In order that you may see this still more clearly take this example : if anyone conceived Duration abstractly, and, confusing it with Time, began to divide it into parts, he would never be able to understand how, for instance, an hour can pass. For in order that the hour may pass it will be necessary for the half of it to pass first, and then a half of what is left, and then a half of what remains of this remainder ; and if you thus go on indefinitely, subtracting the half of what is left, you will never be able to reach the end of the hour. Therefore, many who have not got used to distinguishing the things of reason from real things, have dared to declare that Duration is composed of moments, and so have rushed upon Scylla in their desire to avoid Charybdis. For to say that Duration is composed of moments is the same as to say that Number is obtained from the mere addition of noughts.

Moreover, as is sufficiently clear from what has just been said, neither Number, nor Measure, nor Time, inasmuch as they are only aids of the imagination, can be infinite. For otherwise Number would not be number, nor Measure measure, nor Time time. Hence one may see clearly why many who confused these three with real things, because they did not know the true nature of things, actually denied that there is an Infinite. But how lamentably they have argued let the mathematicians judge, whom arguments of this kind could not put off in matters which were clearly and distinctly perceived by them. For they have not only discovered many things which cannot be expressed by any number, which shows sufficiently the inadequacy of numbers to determine everything, but they also have many things which cannot be equated with any number but exceed any number that can be given. But they do not conclude that such things exceed every number because of the multitude of their parts, but because the nature of the thing cannot admit number without

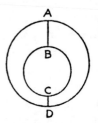

manifest contradiction. For instance, all the inequalities of the space A B C D between the two circles and all the variations which matter moving therein must undergo, exceed every number. This conclusion is not drawn because of the excessive size of the intervening space. For however small a portion of it we take, yet the inequalities of this small portion will exceed every number. Nor is this conclusion reached because, as happens in other cases, we do not know the maximum and minimum—for we have both in this example of ours, namely, the maximum A B, and the minimum C D. The conclusion is only reached because the nature of the space interposed between two circles having different centres cannot be so treated. And so if any one wishes to determine all these inequalities by some definite number, then he will, at the same time, have to bring it about that a circle should not be a circle.

Similarly, to return to our point, if any one wishes to determine all the motions of matter which have taken place hitherto, namely, by reducing them and their Duration to a definite number and time, he will be attempting nothing else than to deprive corporeal Substance, which we cannot conceive except as existing, of its states, and to bring it about that it should not have the nature which it has. This, as also many other things on which I have touched in this letter, I could clearly prove here, did I not think it superfluous.

From all that has now been said one can clearly see that certain things are infinite in their own nature, and can in no wise be conceived as finite ; that some, how-ever, are so in virtue of the cause on which they depend, yet when they are considered abstractly, they can be divided into parts and viewed as finite ; lastly, that some are said to be infinite or, if you prefer, indefinite, because they cannot be equated with any number, yet they can be conceived as greater or less. For it does not follow that those things which cannot be equated with any number are necessarily equal, as is sufficiently clear from the example adduced and from many others.

I have at last put briefly before your eyes the causes of the errors and confusions which have arisen about the question of the Infinite, and, unless I am mistaken, I have thus explained them all in such a way that I do not think that there remains any question about the Infinite on which I have not touched here, or which cannot be very easily answered from what has been said. Therefore I do not think it worth while to detain you any longer with these things.

But here I should like it to be noted in passing that the more recent Peripatetics, as I at least think, misunder-stood the argument of the Ancients by which they strove to prove the existence of God. For, as I find it in the works of a certain Jew, named Rab Chasdai, it reads as follows. If there is an infinite regression of causes, then all things which exist will be things that have been caused. But it cannot pertain to anything that has been caused that it should necessarily exist in virtue of its own nature. Therefore there is in Nature nothing to whose essence it pertains that it should exist necessarily. But this is absurd : and therefore also that. Therefore the force of the argument lies not in the idea that it is impossible for the Infinite actually to exist, or that a regression of causes to infinity is impossible, but only in the impossibility of supposing that things which do not exist necessarily in virtue of their own nature, are not determined to existence by something which does exist necessarily in virtue of its own nature, and which is a Cause, not an Effect.

Since time forces me to hasten, I should now like to turn to your second letter : but I shall more easily be able to reply to its contents when you have deigned to visit me. Therefore, I beg you, if it can be done, to come as soon as possible : for the time of my removal is rapidly approaching.

That is all. Farewell and remember me, who am, etc.

RHYNSBURG, 20 *April* 1663.

LETTER XIII   B. D. S.

To the Very Noble and Learned
Mr. HENRY OLDENBURG.

Reply to Letter XI.

Most Noble Sir,
Your letter, which I have long desired, I have at last received, and I am also free to answer it. But before I begin, I will briefly relate the reasons which hindered me from replying sooner.

When I transferred my household furniture here in

the month of April, I went to Amsterdam. There certain friends asked me to prepare for them a copy of a certain Treatise containing a summary of the second Part of the *Principles* of Descartes, proved in the geometrical manner, and the most important problems which are discussed in Metaphysics, which I had dictated some time ago to a certain young man to whom I did not wish to teach my own opinions without reserve. Then they asked me to prepare as soon as I could also the first Part in the same method. Not to oppose my friends I immediately set myself to do this work, and finished it within two weeks, and gave it to my friends, who asked me finally to allow them to publish them all. This they were easily able to obtain, though on the condition that one of them should, in my presence, clothe them in more elegant style, and add a short Preface, in which he should warn Readers that I do not acknowledge as my own views all that is contained in this Treatise,* *for I have written therein many things which are the very contrary of the views I embrace ;* and this he should show by means of an example or two. A certain friend of mine who is responsible for the publication of this little book, promised to do all these things, and for this reason I remained some time in Amsterdam.

Since my return to this village, in which I now live, I have scarcely been able to be my own master, because of the friends who deigned to visit me. Now at last, my very delightful Friend, I have some time over in which to tell you this, and at the same time to give you the reason why I allow the publication of this Treatise. Perhaps, on this occasion, there will be found some who hold the first places in my country, who will desire to see the other things which I have written and which I acknowledge as my own ; and they will make it

---

* In the letter which I sent I omitted this and everything else that is expressed in other letters [of the alphabet = italics].

their business that I should be able to publish them without any risk of trouble. Should this indeed happen, then I have no doubt that I shall publish some things immediately; but if not, I shall be silent rather than obtrude my opinions on men against the wishes of my country, and make them my enemies. Therefore, my honoured Friend, I pray you not to mind waiting till then : for then you shall have either a printed copy of the Treatise or the summary of it for which you asked me. And if, meantime, you would like to have a copy or two of the work which is now in the press, I will comply with your wish when I know it, and when I also know of some intermediary by whom I shall be able to send them conveniently.

I now return to your letter. I send you and the very Noble Boyle many thanks, as I ought, for your very clearly shown kindness towards me, and for your goodwill : for although the affairs with which you are occupied are so many, so important, and so weighty, they could not make you forget your Friend, nay you even kindly promise to take care in every way that our correspondence shall not in future be interrupted so long. I also give many thanks to the very learned Mr. Boyle for having deigned to reply to my Notes, in however cursory and preoccupied a manner. For my part, I confess that they are not of such importance that the very learned Mr. Boyle should spend time in answering them which he can devote to higher thoughts. I, indeed, did not think, I could not even have persuaded myself, that the very learned Mr. Boyle had set before himself in his Treatise on Nitre no other end than merely to show that the puerile and trivial doctrine of Substantial Forms, Qualities, etc., rests on a weak foundation ; but since I persuaded myself that the very illustrious Mr. Boyle wished to explain the nature of Nitre, namely, that it is a heterogeneous body, consisting of fixed and volatile parts, I wished to show in my explanation (as I think I showed sufficiently and more than sufficiently) that we can explain all the Phenomena of Nitre, at least all those that I know, very easily, even if we do not admit that Nitre is a heterogeneous body, but regard it as homogeneous. Therefore it was not necessary for me to show that the fixed salt was the dregs of Nitre, but only to suppose it, in order that I might see how the very illustrious Mr. Boyle could show me that this salt was not the dregs but was absolutely necessary to make up the essence of Nitre, which could not be conceived without it; since, as I say, I thought that the very illustrious Mr. Boyle wished to show this.

When, however, I said that the fixed salt has pores hollowed out according to the dimensions of the particles of Nitre, I did not need this to explain the redintegration of Nitre. For, as clearly appears from what I have said, namely, that its redintegration consists simply in the coagulation of the Spirit of Nitre, any calx, whose pores are too narrow to be able to contain the particles of Nitre and whose walls are weak, is able to resist the motion of the particles of Nitre, and therefore, according to my Hypothesis, to redintegrate the Nitre itself. Therefore it is no wonder that other salts, for instance salt of tartar and of potash, can be found, by whose help Nitre can be redintegrated. But I only said that the fixed salt of Nitre has pores hollowed out to the dimensions of the particles of Nitre, in order to give a reason why the fixed salt of Nitre is better suited to redintegrate the Nitre in such a way that it falls but little short of its original weight. Moreover, from the fact that there are found other salts by which Nitre can be redintegrated, I thought I could show that the calx of Nitre was not necessary for the essence of Nitre, had not the very illustrious Mr. Boyle said that there is no salt which is more general (namely, than Nitre) : and so it could be hidden in tartar and in potash. When I further said that the particles of Nitre in the larger pores are surrounded by a finer matter, I inferred this, as the very illustrious Mr. Boyle notes, from the impossibility of a vacuum ; but I do not know why he calls the impossibility of a vacuum an Hypothesis, since it clearly follows from the fact that nothing has no properties. And I am surprised that the very illustrious Mr. Boyle should doubt this, since he seems to declare that there are no real *accidents* : but, I ask, will there not be a real *accident* if there be Quantity apart from Substance ?

With regard to the causes of the difference in taste between Spirit of Nitre and Nitre itself, I was obliged to put them forward in order to show how I could very easily explain its Phenomena from the sole difference which alone I am prepared to admit between Spirit of Nitre and Nitre itself, without taking account of the fixed salt.

What I communicated about the inflammability of Nitre and the non-inflammability of Spirit of Nitre supposes no more than that in order to produce a flame in any body there is required a matter which separates the parts of that body and sets them in motion ; both of which I think daily experience and reason teach sufficiently.

I pass on to the experiments which I adduced to confirm my explanation, not absolutely, but, as I expressly said, *to a certain extent*. And so the very illustrious Mr. Boyle advances against the first experiment which I submitted nothing but what I myself expressly said : but as for the rest, namely, about my attempt to save from suspicion that which the very illustrious Mr. Boyle and I have both remarked, he says absolutely nothing. As to what he then says about my second experiment, namely, that through purification

Nitre is for the most part freed from a certain salt like common salt, this he only says, but does not prove. For I, as I expressly said, did not bring forward these experiments completely to confirm by them the things which I had asserted, but only because those experiments, which I had asserted and shown to be consistent with reason, seemed to confirm them to a certain extent. As to his remark that the fact of rising to form icicles is common to it and to other salts, I do not see what that has to do with the matter : for I admit that even other salts have dregs, and are rendered more volatile when they are freed from them. Against the third experiment I do not see that anything is adduced that touches me. In the fifth section I thought that the noble author blamed Descartes, as he did even in other places, relying on the liberty of philosophizing which is conceded to anyone, and which does not hurt the dignity of either party ; so even others will probably think with me, if they have read the writings of the very illustrious Mr. Boyle and the *Principles* of Descartes, unless they are expressly warned. I do not yet see that the very illustrious Mr. Boyle explains his opinion clearly : for he does not yet say whether Nitre ceases to be Nitre if its visible icicles, of which alone he says he is speaking, are rubbed until they are changed into parallelepipeds, or into another figure.

But I leave these questions and turn to what the very illustrious Mr. Boyle sets down in Sections 13–18, and I say that I willingly admit that this redintegration of Nitre is indeed an excellent experiment for investigating the very nature of Nitre, that is, when we have learnt first the Mechanical principles of philosophy, and that all variations in bodies come about in accordance with the laws of Mechanics; but I deny that this follows any more clearly and more evidently from the experiment just mentioned than from many other common

experiments, *from which, however, this does not follow.*
When the very illustrious Mr. Boyle says that he has not
found these views of his so clearly explained and discussed
by others, perhaps, he has something, which I cannot
see, to urge against the arguments of Verulam and
Descartes, by which he thinks he can refute them. I
do not cite these arguments here, because I do not think
that the very illustrious Mr. Boyle does not know them :
this, however, I will say, that they too wished that the
phenomena should agree with their Reason ; if nevertheless they were mistaken in some things, they were
men, and I think that nothing human was alien to them.

He says, further, that there is a great difference
between those experiments (that is, the common and
doubtful experiments which I adduced) about which
we do not know what Nature contributes to them, and
what other factors intervene, and those experiments
wherein it is quite certain what the contributory factors
are. But I do not yet see that the very illustrious Mr.
Boyle has explained to us the nature of the things which
are employed in this thing, that is, the nature of the calx
of Nitre or of Spirit of Nitre ; so that these two seem
to us no less obscure than the things which I instanced,
namely common lime and water, from the mixture of
which heat results. With regard to wood, I admit that
this body is more composite than Nitre ; but as long as
I do not know the nature of either and the way in which
heat arises in either of them, what, I ask, does it matter ?
Then I do not know on what ground the very illustrious
Mr. Boyle ventures to assert that, in this thing of which
we are speaking, he knows what Nature contributes.
*How, I pray, will he be able to show us that this heat did not
arise from some very fine matter?* Perhaps because so
little was lost of the original weight ? But if nothing
had been lost, I do not think that any conclusion could
be drawn. For we see how easily things can be dyed

a certain colour from a very small amount of matter, without becoming thereby sensibly heavier or lighter. Therefore, I can doubt, and not without reason, whether certain things may not perhaps have been present which could not be observed by any sense ; especially so long as it is not known how all those variations, which the very illustrious Mr. Boyle observed when experimenting, could arise from the said bodies. Indeed, I hold it for certain that the heat and that effervescence which the very illustrious Mr. Boyle describes arose from adventitious matter. Then I think that I can more easily conclude from the ebullition of water (I say nothing now of its agitation) that the disturbance of the air is the cause from which sound arises, than from this experiment, where the nature of the concurring factors is entirely unknown, and in which heat is indeed observed, but it is not known how or from what causes it has originated. Lastly, there are many things which give off no odour whatsoever, yet if their parts are shaken in some way and grow hot, an odour is perceived immediately, and if they grow cold again they again have no odour (at least as far as human sense is concerned) as, for example, amber and other things of which I do not even know whether they are more composite than Nitre.

My notes on the twenty-fourth section show that Spirit of Nitre is not pure spirit, but abounds in calx of Nitre and other things ; and that I therefore doubt whether the very illustrious Mr. Boyle could have observed with sufficient care what he says that he has discovered with the help of the scales, namely, that the weight of the Spirit of Nitre, which he dropped in, approximately equalled the weight of that which was lost during the detonation.

Lastly, although, as far as the eye is concerned, pure water can dissolve alkalised salts more rapidly, yet, since it is a more homogeneous body than air is, it cannot, as air can, have so many kinds of corpuscles which can find their way into the pores of every kind of calx. Therefore, since water consists principally of definite particles of one kind, which can dissolve calx up to a certain point, whereas air cannot do so, it follows that water will dissolve calx up to that point far sooner than air will. But since, on the other hand, air consists of grosser as well as of much finer particles, and of all kinds of particles, which can penetrate far narrower pores than those which the particles of water can penetrate, the particles of air can find an entry in many ways. Hence it follows that air, although it cannot do so as quickly as water can (which does not consist of so many particles of every kind), can dissolve calx of Nitre far better and more finely, and make it more inert and therefore more able to resist the motion of the particles of Spirit of Nitre. For I am not so far compelled by the experiments to recognize any difference, between Spirit of Nitre and Nitre itself, other than that the particles of the latter are in a state of rest, whereas those of the former jostle against each other in great agitation. So that there is the same difference between Nitre and its Spirit as there is between ice and water.

But I dare not detain you longer on these matters : I fear I have been too prolix, although I have tried to be as brief as I could : if nevertheless I have been wearisome I pray you to overlook it, and at the same time to take in good part the free and sincere utterances of a Friend. For I judged it ill-advised to keep absolute silence on these matters when replying to you. Yet to praise those things which pleased me little would be sheer flattery, than which I consider nothing is more dangerous and more pernicious in Friendship. I therefore determined to open my mind to you very frankly ; and I thought that nothing would be more welcome to philosophers than this. Meanwhile if you think it more advisable to consign these thoughts to the fire than to communicate them to the very learned Mr. Boyle, they are in your hands ; do as you please, only believe me most devoted and most friendly to you and to the very noble Boyle. I am sorry that owing to my slender means I am unable to show this except in words : however, etc.

VOORBURG, $\frac{17}{27}$ *July* 1663.

LETTER XIV   HENRY OLDENBURG

To THE VERY ILLUSTRIOUS MR. B. D. S.

MOST ILLUSTRIOUS SIR, MUCH HONOURED FRIEND,

I find in the renewal of our correspondence a great deal of happiness. And so you may know that it was with extraordinary joy that I received your letter addressed to me on $\frac{17}{27}$ July, especially so for the double reason, that it gave evidence of your well-being and because it makes me more certain of the constancy of your friendship for me. To crown it all there is added your announcement that you have sent to the press the first and second parts of the *Principles* of Descartes demonstrated in the geometric manner, and your very generous offer to me of one or two copies of it. I accept the gift most willingly, and I pray you, if you please, to send the Treatise, which is already in the press, to Mr. Peter Serrarius, who lives at Amsterdam, for transmission to me. For I have commissioned him to receive a small packet of this kind, and to forward it to me by a friend who is crossing shortly. For the rest, allow me to say that I bear it with impatience that you should even now suppress those writings which you acknowledge as yours, especially in a Commonwealth that is so free that you are allowed there to think what you like and to say what you think. I should like you to break through those barriers, especially when you can conceal your name, and in this way place yourself beyond all chance of danger.

The very noble Boyle has gone away : as soon as he has returned to town I will communicate to him that part of your very learned letter which concerns him, and will write to you his opinion on your views as soon as I have obtained it. I think you have already seen his *Sceptical Chymist*, which was published some time ago in Latin, and has been widely circulated abroad : it contains many Chemico-Physical paradoxes, and subjects to a severe examination the Hypostatical Principles (as they call them) of the Spagyrists.

He has lately published another little book which perhaps has not yet reached your booksellers : therefore I am sending it to you enclosed herewith, and I warmly pray you to accept this small gift kindly. The little book, as you will see, contains a defence of the elasticity of the air against a certain Francis Linus, who makes a great to-do to explain the Phenomena mentioned in Mr. Boyle's *New Physico-Mechanical Experiments* in a subtle manner which eludes all understanding and sense. Read through and consider the little book and communicate to me your views about it.

Our Royal Society is diligently and earnestly pursuing its purpose, confining itself within the limits of experiments and observations, and avoiding all the intricacies of Disputations.

Recently an excellent experiment was undertaken which gives much concern to those who believe in a vacuum, but very much pleases those who believe that space is a plenum. However, it is this. Let a glass phial A, filled to the brim with water, and placed with its opening turned down in a glass jar B, containing water, be placed in the Receiver of Mr. Boyle's New Pneumatic engine; next let the air be exhausted from the Receiver: bubbles will be seen to ascend in great quantities from the water into the phial A, and to force down the water from thence into the jar B, under the surface of the water contained therein. Let the two small vessels be left in this state for a day or two, the air being pumped out of the said Receiver repeatedly by means of frequent pumpings. Then let them be removed from the Receiver, and the Phial A be filled again with this water freed from air, and again inverted in the jar B, and let both vessels be again enclosed in the Receiver. The Receiver again being exhausted by means of the requisite amount of pumping, perhaps a small bubble will be perceived to ascend from the neck of the Phial A, which, emerging at the top and expanding itself by reason of the continual pumping, again forces down all the water out of the Phial, as before. Then let the Phial again be taken from the Receiver, and be filled again to the brim with water from which the air has been exhausted, and be again inverted as before, and placed in the Receiver. Then let the Receiver be thoroughly emptied of air, and when it is duly and completely empty, the water will remain suspended in the Phial in such a way as not to descend at all. In this experiment the cause, which, according to Boyle, is believed to sustain the water in the Torricellian experiment (that is, the air which presses upon the water in the vessel B) clearly seems to be removed, and yet the water in the Phial does not descend.

I had intended to add more here but my friends and affairs call me away. I will only add this. If you like to send me the things which you are having printed, please address your letters and parcels in the following way, etc.

I cannot conclude the letter without urging on you again and again the publication of those things which you yourself have thought out. I shall never cease to exhort you until you satisfy my request. Meanwhile if you were willing to disclose to me certain chapters of their contents, oh! how I should love you and how closely bound to you I should consider myself. Fare well, very well, and continue to love me as you do.

Your most devoted and most friendly
HENRY OLDENBURG.

LONDON, 31 *July* 1663.

LETTER XV   B. DE SPINOZA

OFFERS CORDIAL GREETINGS TO MR. LUDOVICUS MEYER.

DEAREST FRIEND,
    The Preface which you have sent to me by our friend de Vries, I return through him. As you yourself will see, I have made a few notes in the margin, but there remain a few things which I thought it more advisable to point out to you by letter.

Namely, first, when on page 4 you inform the reader of the occasion on which I wrote the first part, I should like you, either there or wherever you please, also to inform him that I wrote it within two weeks. Thus fore-warned, no one will think that these matters are so clearly presented that they cannot be explained more clearly, and they will not be held up by one or two small words here and there which they may perhaps find obscure.

Secondly, I should like you to warn people that I

prove many things in a way that is different from that in which they were proved by Descartes, not in order to correct Descartes, but only the better to retain my own order, and not to increase the number of axioms, and that for the same reason I prove many things which Descartes merely asserts without any proof, and that I have had to add other things which Descartes omitted.

And, lastly, I want to ask you most earnestly, my dearest friend, to omit what you wrote at the end against that petty man and to delete it entirely. And although there are many reasons which urge me to ask you this, I will mention only one. I should like all men to be able easily to persuade themselves that these are published for the good of all men, and that you, in publishing this little book, are mastered simply by a desire to spread the truth, and that you are doing all in your power to make this little work welcome to everyone, and to induce men, in a kindly and friendly way, to take up the study of true philosophy, and to pursue the good of all. This everyone will easily believe when he sees that no one is hurt, and that nothing is put down which can be even slightly offensive to anyone. If, however, afterwards that man or any other choose to show his malevolent mind, then you will be able to depict his life and character, not without approval. Therefore I ask you not to mind waiting till then and to allow yourself to be persuaded, and to believe me your most devoted and

in all affection yours

B. DE SPINOZA.

VOORBURG, 3 *August* 1663.

Our friend de Vries had promised to take this with him, but since he does not know when he will return to you, I am sending it by someone else.

Together with this letter I send you a part of the Scholium to Proposition 27 of Part 2, where page 75 begins, in order that you may give it to the printer, to be printed anew.

These things which I send herewith must necessarily be printed anew, and 14 or 15 lines must be added, which can easily be inserted.

LETTER XVI   HENRY OLDENBURG
To the Very Illustrious Mr. B. d. S.

EXCELLENT SIR AND MOST HONOURED FRIEND,
     Scarcely three or four days have elapsed since I sent you a letter through the ordinary post. In that letter I mentioned a certain little book written by Mr. Boyle, which was to be sent to you. At that time there appeared to be no hope of finding a friend so soon who would deliver it. Since that time some one has come forward sooner than I had thought. So you may now receive what could not be sent to you then, along with the most dutiful greetings of Mr. Boyle who is now returned to Town from the country. He asks you to consult the preface which he wrote to his Experiments on Nitre, and you will then understand what was the real aim which he set before himself in this work; namely, to show that the doctrines of the new and more solid Philosophy are elucidated by clear experiments, and that these [experiments] can be excellently explained without the forms, qualities, and trivial elements of the Schools; but he by no means took it upon himself to teach what is the nature of Nitre, or even to disprove what can be said by anyone about the homogeneity of matter, or about the differences of bodies which arise merely from motion and figure, etc. This only, he says, he wished to show, that the various textures of bodies produce their various differences, and that from these proceed very different effects, and that therefore so long as analysis into primary

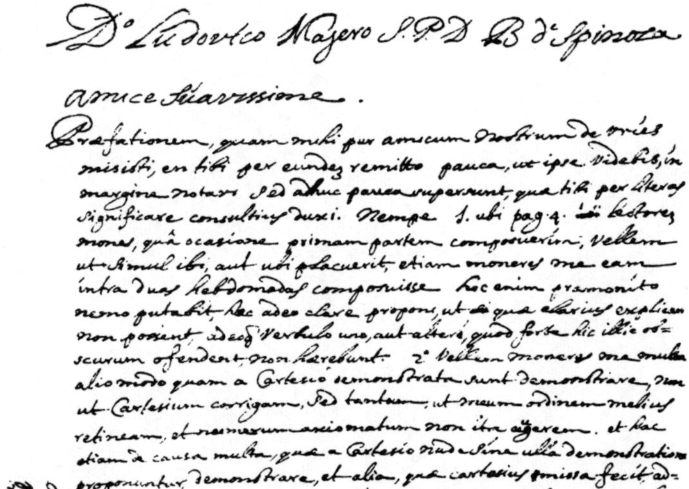

Dº Ludovico Mayero S.P.D. B. d'Spinoza

Amice suavissime.

Praefationem, quam mihi per amicum nostrum de Vries misisti, en tibi per eundem remitto. pauca, ut ipse videbis, in margine notavi. sed adhuc pauca supersunt, quae tibi per literas significare consultius duxi. Nempe 1. ubi pag. 4. lectores mones, quâ occasione primam partem composuerim, vellem ut simul ibi, aut ubi placuerit, etiam moneres me eam intra duas hebdomadas composuisse. hoc enim praemonito nemo putabit, haec adeo clare proponi, ut si qua clarius explicari non possent, adeoque verbulo uno, aut altero, quod forte hic illic obscurum offendent, non haerebunt. 2º Vellem moneres me multa alio modo quam a Cartesio demonstrata sunt demonstrare, non ut Cartesium corrigam, sed tantum, ut meum ordinem melius retineam, et numerum axiomatum non ita augerem. et hac etiam de causa multa, quae a Cartesio nude sine ulla demonstratione proponuntur, demonstrare, et alia, quae Cartesius omissa fecit, addere debuisse. denique enixissime te rogare volo, amice charissime, ut illa, quae in fine scripsisti, in illum homunculum missa faceres, et ipsa prorsus deleres. et quamvis ad hoc te rogandum multae me moveant rationes, unam tantum reddam. vellem enim, ut omnes sibi facile persuadere possint, haec in omnium hominum gratiam evulgari, teque in hoc libello edendo solo veritatis propagandae desiderio teneri, teque adeo maxime curare, ut hoc opusculum omnibus gratum sit, homines que ad vera philosophiae studium benevole, atque benigne invitare omniumque utilitati studere. quod facile unusquisque credet, ubi neminem laedi videbit. nec aliquid proponi, quod alicui offendiculo esse potest. quod si tamen postea vir iste, aut alius suum malevolum animum ostendere velit: tum ejus vitam, et mores non sine applausu depingere poteris. peto igitur, ut eousque expectare non graveris, teque exorari sinas, et me tibi addictissimum credas, atque

Omni studio tuum

B. de Spinoza

Voorburgi 3 augusti 1663

Amicus de Vries haec secum ferre promiserat, sed quia nescit quando ad vos reversurus est per alium mitto.

FACSIMILE OF LETTER XV WITHOUT THE P.S.

matter has not been made, a certain heterogeneity is rightly inferred by Philosophers and by others. I should not think that there is any disagreement between you and Mr. Boyle on the fundamental question.

But as to what you say that any calx whose pores are too narrow to hold particles of Nitre and whose walls are weak is able to resist the motion of the particles of Nitre and therefore the redintegration of Nitre itself, Boyle answers that if Spirit of Nitre is mixed with other kinds of calx it will not for all that combine with them to form real Nitre.

As regards the Argument which you use to disprove the existence of a vacuum, Boyle says that he knows it, and has seen it before, but by no means assents to it : he says that there will be an opportunity to discuss the matter elsewhere.

He requested me to ask you if you can supply him with an example in which two odorous bodies, when combined into one, compose an entirely odourless body (namely Nitre). He says that such are the parts of Nitre : for its Spirit spreads a most offensive smell, and fixed Nitre is not destitute of odour.

Moreover, he asks you thoroughly to consider whether the comparison which you have instituted of ice and water with Nitre and its Spirit, is a proper one : for all ice is only resolved into water, and odourless ice, when it has turned again into water, remains odourless : but as between Spirit of Nitre and its fixed salt their qualities will be found to be different, as the printed Treatise fully teaches.

These and similar things I gathered from the illustrious Author in the course of conversation about this subject; but I am sure that owing to the weakness of my memory I reproduce them in a manner likely to do him harm rather than to do him credit. Since you are in agreement on the principal point of the matter, I will not enlarge on it any further : rather I would bring it about that you should unite your mental gifts to cultivate earnestly a genuine and solid philosophy. Be it permitted to me especially to advise you to continue to pursue with energy the principles of things with the keenness of your mathematical mind : as I incessantly urge my Noble friend Boyle to confirm and elucidate them by experiments and observations frequently and accurately made. You see, my dearest Friend, what I am aiming at, what I am striving to attain. I know that our native philosophers in this Realm will in no way abandon their experimental gifts ; and I am no less convinced that you will act strenuously in your province, however much the mob of Philosophers or of Theologians may howl or complain. As I have already exhorted you to this end in several previous letters I restrain myself now lest I make you weary. I only make this further request, that you will deign to send me as quickly as possible by Mr. Serrarius whatever has already been committed to print, whether it be your commentary on Descartes or something drawn from your intellect's own stores. You will hold me so much more closely bound to you and you will understand that whatever opportunity may present itself

   I am
    Your most devoted
     HENRY OLDENBURG.

LONDON, 4 *August* 1663.

LETTER XVII   B. D. S.

To THE VERY LEARNED AND PRUDENT
MR. PETER BALLING.

MY DEAR FRIEND,
  Your last letter written, if I am not mistaken, on the 26th of last month has come into my hands

safely. It has caused me no little sadness and anxiety, although this has certainly diminished now that I dwell on your good sense and strength of mind, by which you know how to despise the adversities of fortune, or rather of fancy, at the very time when they are assailing you with their strongest weapons. But my anxiety daily grows more; and therefore I beseech and adjure you by our friendship not to mind writing to me fully.

As to the omens of which you make mention, namely, that while your child was still well and strong you heard sobs like those it uttered when it was ill and just before it died, I should think that this was not a real sobbing but only your imagination; since you say that when you raised yourself and adjusted yourself to listen, you did not hear them as clearly as before, or afterwards, when you had fallen asleep again. Surely this shows that those sobs were nothing but pure imagination, which being unfettered and free, was able to imagine certain sobs in a more distinct and vivid manner than at the time when you raised yourself and directed your attention to the particular place of the sound.

I can confirm and at the same time explain what I have just said by something which happened to me at Rhynsburg last winter. When I awoke one morning, when the sky was already growing light, from a very heavy dream, the images which had come to me in my dream remained as vividly before my eyes as if they had been real things, especially the image of a certain black and scabby Brazilian whom I had never seen before. This image for the most part disappeared when, in order to divert myself with something else, I fixed my eyes on a book or some other object: but as soon as I again turned my eyes away from such an object and fixed them on something inattentively, the image of the same Ethiopian again appeared with the same vividness, and that again and again until gradually it disappeared from my presence. I say that what happened to me with my inner sense of sight happened also with your hearing. But since the cause was very different, your case was an omen, but mine was not. The matter will be clearly understood from what I will now describe.

The effects of the imagination arise from the constitution either of the Body or of the Mind. This, in order to avoid all prolixity, I will for the present prove only from experience. We find that fevers and other physical changes are the causes of delirium, and that those who have thick blood imagine nothing but quarrels, troubles, murders, and the like. But we see that the imagination is also determined to a great extent by the constitution of the soul; for, as we know from experience, in all things it follows the traces of the intellect and concatenates its images and words in a certain order, and interconnects them, just as the intellect does with its demonstrations; so much so that there is almost nothing that we can understand of which the imagination does not form some image from the trace thereof. Since this is so, I say that all the effects of the imagination that proceed from physical causes can never be *omens* of future events; because their causes involve no future thing. But the effects of imagination, or images that derive their origin from the constitution of the Mind can well be *omens* of some future event; since the Mind can confusedly have a presentiment of something yet to come. Therefore this can be as firmly and vividly imagined as if something of that kind were present.

Thus a father (to take an example similar to your case) so loves his son that he and his beloved son are like one and the same being. And since (according to what I have proved on another occasion) there must necessarily exist in Thought the idea of the states of the essence of the son, and their consequences, and since the father, because of this union with his son, is a part of the said son, the soul of the father must necessarily participate in the ideal essence of the son, and in its states and their consequences, as I have proved elsewhere more fully. Further, since the soul of the father participates ideally in those things which follow from the essence of the son, he (as I said) can now and then imagine one of the things which result from the son's essence as vividly as if he had it before him, that is, if the following conditions are fulfilled. I. If the event which happens to the son in the course of his life is important. II. If it is such that we can very easily imagine it. III. If the Time at which the event will occur is not too remote. IV. Lastly, if the body is not only of a sound constitution as regards health, but if it is also free, and exempt from all those cares and affairs which, coming from outside, confuse the senses. In this matter it may also be useful to think of such things as excite ideas very similar to these. For example, if while we are speaking with this or that man we hear sobs, it will often happen that when we think of the same man again, then these sobs, perceived with our ears when we spoke with him, will come into our memory again.

This, my dear Friend, is my view about your question. I confess I have been very brief; but I have taken pains to supply you with material for writing to me at the first opportunity. Etc.

VOORBURG, 20 *July* 1664.

LETTER XVIII WILLIAM VAN BLYENBERGH

To THE VERY ILLUSTRIOUS MR. B. D. S.

SIR AND UNKNOWN FRIEND,

I have already given myself the honour of reading through your Treatise, which has recently been published, pretty frequently and attentively, as also its Appendix. It will be more fitting for me to tell others rather than yourself of the very great solidity which I found in it, and of the pleasure which I derived from it: but I cannot refrain from saying this much, that the more frequently I read it with attention the more I am pleased with it, and that I continually observe something which I had not noticed before. But in this letter (lest I appear to be a Flatterer) I will not express too much admiration for the Author: I know that the Gods sell all things at the price of toil. But not to keep you wondering too long who it is and how it happens that someone who is unknown to you ventures to take such a great liberty as to write to you, I will tell you that he is one who, impelled by the sheer desire for pure truth, endeavours in this brief and transitory life, as far as human intelligence permits, to set his feet firmly in knowledge: one who, in his search for truth, sets before himself no other object than truth itself; one who seeks to obtain for himself through science neither honours nor riches, but truth alone, and peace of mind as a result of truth: and one who, among all truths and sciences, does not find more pleasure in any of them than in Metaphysics, at least in certain parts of it, if not in all of it, and finds his whole joy of life in devoting thereto the hours of leisure which he has to spare. But not everyone is so fortunate, or not everyone applies so much diligence as, I imagine, is the case with you, and therefore not everybody attains to the degree of perfection which I observe already in your work. In a word, it is one whom you may get to know better, if you will kindly so greatly oblige me as to help to open a way and penetrate through my tangled thoughts.

But to return to your Treatise. Just as I found many things therein that pleased my taste very much, so also I encountered some things which I could not very well digest. It would not be right for me, who am a

stranger to you, to complain thus, the more so as I do
not know whether it will please or displease. This is
the reason why I send you this first, with the request
that, in case you have time and inclination in these
winter evenings to oblige me to the extent of answering
the difficulties which I still find in your book, you will
let me send you some of them, though with the proviso
that you should not be hindered thereby from doing
anything that is more necessary or more pleasant. For
I desire nothing more strongly than the fulfilment of
the promise made in your Book to publish a fuller
development of your views. What I at last entrust to
my pen I would have put to you orally, when coming to
greet you, but since I was prevented first [by not know-
ing] where you were living, and then by the contagious
disease, and lastly by my business, this was postponed
time after time.

However, in order that this letter may not be entirely
empty, and because I hope that you will welcome it,
I will here submit this one thing only : namely, in several
places, in the *Principles* as well as in the *Metaphysical
Thoughts*, in order to explain either your own opinion
or that of Monsieur Descartes, whose philosophy you
were teaching, you assert that to create and to preserve
are one and the same thing (which is so self-evident
to those who have directed their thoughts to it that it
is a fundamental notion), and that God not only created
substances, but also the motions in the substances, that
is, that God not only maintains the substances in their
state, by a continuous creation, but also preserves their
motions and strivings. For instance, God by His immediate volition or action (whichever one may like to call
it) not only makes the soul continue to exist, and per-
severe in its state, but He also causes it to be related in
such a way to the motions of the Soul. That is, just as
God's continuous creation makes things continue to

exist, so also within the things the strivings or the motions of the things arise from the same cause, seeing that except God there is no cause of Motion. And so it follows that God is not only the cause of the Substance of the Soul, but also of every motion or striving of the Soul, which we call will, as you usually assert everywhere. From this statement it also necessarily seems to follow either that there is no evil in the movement or will of the Soul, or that God Himself is the immediate cause of evil. For even the things which we call evil come about through the soul, and consequently through such an immediate influence and coöperation of God. For instance, the soul of Adam wants to eat of the forbidden fruit. According to the above statement the volition of Adam occurs as the result of the influence of God, not merely in so far as he wills, but also, as we shall immediately show, in so far as he wills thus. So that the forbidden act of Adam is either no evil in itself in so far as God not only stirred his will but also in so far as He stirred it in that way, or else God Himself appears to do that which we call evil. And methinks that neither you nor Monsieur Descartes solves this difficulty by saying that evil is something unreal, in which God does not concur. For whence, then, came the will to eat, or the Devil's will to pride? For since (as you rightly remark) will is not something other than the Soul itself, but is this or that motion or striving of the Soul, it has as much need of God's coöperation in the one case as in the other. Now the coöperation of God, as I understand from your writings, is nothing else than the determination of a thing by His will in this or that manner. And so it follows that God concurs in, that is, determines, the evil will in so far as it is evil, as well as the good will. For His will, which is an absolute cause of all that is both in the substance and in the strivings, seems then also to be a first cause of the evil will, in so far as it is evil. Moreover, in that case, there is either no determination of an evil will in us of which God did not know from eternity, or we ascribe to God an imperfection. But how does God know it except through His decrees? Therefore His decrees are the cause of our determinations, and so again it seems to follow either that a bad will is no evil, or else that God is the immediate cause of that evil. And it is not valid to apply here the Theologians' distinction about the difference between the deed and the evil adhering to the deed, for God decreed not only the action but also the manner of the action, that is, God not only decreed that Adam should eat, but also that he should necessarily eat in violation of the command, so that it again seems to follow either that Adam's eating contrary to the command was no evil or else that God Himself caused it.

Worthy Sir, this much only, for the present, of what I cannot penetrate in your Treatise; for it is hard to maintain both extremes. But I shall expect from your penetrating judgment and diligence such an answer as will give me complete satisfaction, and I hope to show you in the future under what obligation you will have put me thereby. Worthy Sir, be assured that I ask this for no other reason than the desire for truth. I am disinterested, as I am a free person, not dependent on any profession, but I earn my living by honest trading, and devote my spare time to these matters. I also humbly beg you to be pleased with my difficulties; and whenever it please you to write an answer, which I shall await with a very longing heart, then please write to W. v. B., etc.

Meanwhile I shall be and remain, Sir,
Your devoted servant
WILLIAM VAN BLYENBERGH.

DORDRECHT, 12 *December* 1664.

LETTER XIX   B. D. S.

To the Very Learned and Prudent
Mr. WILLIAM VAN BLYENBERGH.

Reply to the Preceding.

SIR AND VERY WELCOME FRIEND,

Your letter of the 12th December, enclosed in another of the 21st December, I only received on the 26th of the same month, while I was at Schiedam. I gathered from them your great love of truth, and that it alone is the aim of all your endeavours. This made me, who also have nothing else in view, decide not only fully to grant your request, namely, that I should be willing to answer, according to my understanding, the questions which you send me now or will send me in the future, but also on my side to do all that can promote our closer acquaintance and sincere friendship. For, of all the things which are beyond my power nothing is more esteemed by me than to be allowed to have the honour of entering into the bonds of friendship with people who sincerely love truth. For I believe that of the things beyond our power, there is nothing in the world which we can love with tranquillity except such men. For it is as impossible to dissolve the love which such bear one another, since it is founded on the love which each has for the knowledge of truth, as it is to refuse to embrace the truth once it has been grasped. Moreover, it is the greatest and most pleasant which can be found among things which are not within our power; since nothing but truth can unite together different views and dispositions. I pass over the very great advantages which follow from it, that I may not detain you longer with things which no doubt you know yourself. I have done so thus far in order the better to show you how pleasant it is to me, and will be in future, to be allowed to have an opportunity of being able to show my ready service.

And, in order to seize the present opportunity, I will agree to answer your question which turns on this point, namely, that it seems clearly to follow from God's Providence, which is the same as His will, as well as from God's coöperation and the perpetual creation of things, either that there are no sins and no evil, or that God causes the sins and the evil. But you do not explain what you mean by evil: and, as far as I can see from the example of Adam's determined will, you seem to mean by evil the will itself in so far as it is conceived to be so *determined, or to be such as to be opposed to the command of God;* and therefore (as I should also admit, if that were so) there seems a great absurdity in asserting either of these two, namely, that God Himself brings to pass things opposed to His will, or that they are good although opposed to God's will. But I for my part cannot admit that *sins and evil are something positive, much less that anything can exist or come to pass against the will of God. On the contrary, I say that not only is sin not something positive, but also that only improperly and when speaking in human fashion can we say that we sin against God, just as when we say that men make God angry.*

For, as to the first point, we know well that everything that is, considered in itself and without regard to anything else, includes perfection, which always extends in each thing as far as does the essence of the thing itself. For it is indeed nothing different. I also take, for example, the resolution or the determined will of Adam to eat of the forbidden fruit; this resolution or determined will, considered in itself, includes as much perfection as it expresses essence. This we may understand from the fact that we cannot conceive imperfection in things unless we consider other things which have more essence. And therefore we shall be able to find no imperfection in the decision of Adam when we consider it in itself, and do not compare it with other things which are more perfect, or show a more perfect state. Yes, one can compare it with countless other things which in comparison with it are much more imperfect, such as stones, logs of wood, etc., and this everyone also admits in fact, for everyone observes with admiration and delight in animals the very things which he detests and regards with aversion in men. For example, the wars of bees, the jealousy of doves, etc., things which we detest in men and for which we nevertheless consider animals more perfect. This being so, *it clearly follows that sins, seeing that they signify nothing but imperfection, cannot consist in anything which expresses essence, like the decision of Adam or the execution thereof.*

Moreover, we also cannot say that the will of Adam opposed the will of God, and that it was evil because it displeased God. For besides the fact that it would argue a great imperfection in God if something were to happen against His will and if He were to desire something which He could not obtain, and if His nature were so determined that, like His creatures, He would have sympathy with some things and antipathy toward others, it would also be entirely opposed to the nature of God's will. For since this is not something different from His understanding, it is as impossible for anything to happen contrary to His will as it is for it to happen contrary to His understanding, that is, whatever should happen contrary to His will, would have to be by nature such as to be contrary to the understanding, like a square circle. Since, then, the will or the decision of Adam, considered in itself, was not evil, nor, properly speaking, against the will of God, so it follows that God can be, or rather, according to the argument which you mention, must be its cause, not indeed *in so far as it was evil, for the evil in it was no more than a privation of a more perfect state,* which Adam had to lose through that action. It is certain that Privation is not something positive, and that the term is only used in relation to our understanding, and not in relation to God's understanding. This comes about thus, namely, because we express by one and the same definition all individuals of the same kind, for example, all who have the external shape of men, and therefore we consider that they are all equally capable of the highest perfection which we can deduce from such a Definition, and when we find one whose deeds are incompatible with that perfection, then we consider that he is deprived thereof and that he deviates from his nature. *This we should not do, had we not brought him under such a definition, and attributed to him such a nature.* But since God neither conceives things abstractly nor makes such general definitions, and no more essence belongs to things than the Divine Understanding and power imparts to them and actually gives them, it clearly follows *that one can only speak of this privation in relation to our understanding, but not in relation to God.*

Herewith, methinks, the question is completely answered. But in order to make the path smooth and to remove every obstacle, I must still answer the following two questions, namely, first, why Scripture says that God desires the wicked to repent, and also why He forbade Adam to eat of the tree, when He had ordained the contrary ; secondly, what seems to follow from what I have said, that the ungodly by their pride, avarice, desperation, etc., serve God as well as do the pious by their generosity, patience, love, etc., because they also carry out the will of God.

However, in answer to the first question I say that Scripture, since it especially serves the common people, continually speaks in human fashion, for the people are not capable of understanding high matters. And therefore, I believe that all those things which God revealed to the Prophets as necessary to salvation, are written in the form of laws, and so the Prophets composed a whole Parable, namely, first they described God as a King and Lawgiver because He revealed the means of salvation and of perdition, of which He was the cause. The means, which are no more than causes, they then called Laws, and wrote them down in the form of Laws. Salvation and perdition, which are no more than the effects which necessarily follow from these means, they represented as reward and punishment. And they adapted all their words to this parable rather than to the truth. And everywhere they described God as a man, now angry, now merciful, now desiring the future, now seized by jealousy and suspicion, and even deceived by the Devil. So that Philosophers, and with them all those who are above the Law, that is, who follow virtue not as a Law but from love of it because it is the best thing, need not trouble about such words.

The prohibition to Adam, then, consisted solely in this, namely that God revealed to Adam that the eating of the fruit of the tree brought death, just as He reveals also to us through our natural understanding that poison is deadly. But if you ask to what end He revealed this to him, I answer, in order to make him thus much more perfect in knowledge. Therefore to ask God why He did not give him also a more perfect will, is just as absurd as to ask why He did not give to the circle all the properties of a sphere. This follows clearly from what was said above, and I have proved it also in the Scholium to Proposition 15 of the First Part [of the *Principles* of Descartes proved geometrically].

With regard to the second difficulty, it is indeed true that the ungodly express the will of God according to their measure, but they are not therefore to be in any way compared to the pious. For the more perfection anything has, the more does it participate also in Deity, and the more does it express the perfection of God. Therefore since the pious have incalculably more perfection than the ungodly, their virtue cannot be compared with that of the ungodly because the ungodly lack the love of God which springs from the knowledge of Him, and whereby alone we, according to our human understanding, are said to be the servants of God. Indeed, since they know not God, they are no more than a tool in the hand of the master which serves unconsciously, and perishes in the service ; on the other hand, the pious serve consciously, and become more perfect by their service.

This, Sir, is all that I can now submit in answer to your question. I wish nothing more than that it may satisfy you. But if you still find difficulty, then I beg you to let me know, in order to see if I can remove it. You on your side need not have any scruples, but as long as you do not consider yourself satisfied, I would like nothing better than to know the reasons thereof, so that truth may dawn at last. I do indeed wish that I might write in the language in which I was brought up. I might possibly express my thoughts better. But please take it in good part, and yourself correct the mistakes, and consider me

Your devoted Friend
and servant
B. DE SPINOZA.

THE LONG ORCHARD,
5 *January* 1665.

I shall stay in this Orchard another three or four weeks, and then I propose to return to Voorburg. I believe that I shall receive an answer from you before this time is up. If your business affairs do not permit of it, then please write to Voorburg with this address, To be delivered in the Church lane at the house of Mr. Daniel Tydeman, painter.

LETTER XX   WILLIAM VAN BLYENBERGH
To the Very Illustrious Mr. B. d. S.
Reply to the Preceding.

Sir and worthy Friend,
          When first I received your letter and read it
through hurriedly I not only meant to reply immediately
but also to repudiate many things. But the more I read
it, the less I found matter for objection therein. And
great as was my longing to see it, so great was the
pleasure I derived from reading it.

But before I proceed to make the request that you
would solve some more difficulties for me, it is necessary
that it should be known that I have two General Rules
in accordance with which I always endeavour to philoso-
phize. One is the clear and distinct apprehension of
my understanding, the other is the revealed Word or
the will of God. In accordance with the one I endeavour
to be a lover of the truth, but in accordance with both
I endeavour to be a Christian Philosopher. And whenever it happens that, after long consideration, my natural
knowledge either seems to conflict with this Word, or
cannot very well be made to harmonize with it, then this
Word has so much authority with me that I rather suspect
the conceptions which I imagine to be clear, than place
them above, and in opposition to, that truth which I
think I find prescribed for me in that book. And what
wonder, since I want steadfastly to continue to believe
that that Word is the Word of God, that is, that it has
come forth from the highest and most perfect God, who
possesses more perfections than I can grasp, who perhaps
wished to declare more perfections of Himself and His
works than I with my finite understanding can grasp
to-day. I say *can grasp to-day*, for it may be that I am
by my own doing deprived of greater perfections, and

so if, perchance, I had the perfection whereof I am deprived through my own doing, I should be able to understand that all that is stated and taught us in that Word agrees also with the soundest conceptions of my Mind. But since I now suspect myself of having, by my continual error, deprived myself of a better state, and since, as you assert in [your *Principles*], Part I, Proposition 15, our knowledge even when most clear, still contains imperfection, I rather turn towards that Word, even without a reason, merely on the ground that it has proceeded from the most perfect Being (this I take for granted now, because the proof of it is not in place here or would take too long) and therefore must be accepted by me. If, now, I were to judge of your letter only under the guidance of my first rule to the exclusion of the second, as though I had it not, or it did not exist, I should be obliged to admit very many things, as I also do, and I should admire your lucid conceptions, but my second rule compels me to differ from you more widely. However, within the limits of a letter I shall examine them somewhat more extensively under the guidance of one or of the other.

First, in accordance with the first stated rule, I had asked : since, following your assertions, creation and preservation are one and the same thing, and God makes not things only, but also the motions and modes of things, to continue in their own state, that is, concurs in them, does it not seem to follow *that there is no evil* or *that God Himself causes evil?* I relied on this rule, that nothing can happen against the will of God, since otherwise it would involve an imperfection, or the things which God brings to pass (among which there appear also to be included the things which we call evil) must also be evil. But since this too involves a contradiction, and however I turned it I could not free myself from the contradiction, I had recourse to you who should be the best interpreter of your own conceptions. You say in your reply that you persist in your first presupposition, namely, that nothing happens or can happen against the will of God. But when an answer has to be given to the problem whether God, then, does not do evil you say that *sin is not something positive, and also that we cannot except very improperly be said to sin against God*, and in the Appendix, Part I, Chapter VI, you say that there *is no absolute evil as is self-evident : for whatever exists, considered in itself, without reference to another thing, includes perfection which in each thing extends as far as does the essence of that thing itself, and therefore it clearly follows that sins, which denote no more than imperfections, cannot consist in anything which expresses essence.* If sin, evil, error, or whatever name one may be pleased to give it, is nothing but the loss or privation of a more perfect state, then by all means it seems to follow that to exist is not an evil or an imperfection, but that evil can arise in something existing. For that which is perfect cannot be deprived of a more perfect state by an equally perfect action, but only by the fact that we turn to something imperfect, because we do not make the best use of the powers given to us. This you seem to call *no evil but merely a lesser good, because things considered in themselves include perfection. Secondly, because, as you say, no more essence belongs to things than the divine understanding and power assigns and actually gives to them : therefore they cannot show more reality in their actions than they have received essence.* For if I can render neither greater nor less results than I have received essence, it is impossible to think of a privation of a more perfect state ; for if nothing happens against the will of God, and if only so much comes to pass as there is essence for, then in what conceivable way can there be evil, which you call privation of a better state ? How can anyone suffer the loss of a more perfect state through an action so constituted and dependent ?

Therefore, methinks, you cannot but assert one of two things, either that there is something evil, or, if there is no evil, that there can be no privation of a better state. For it seems to me to be contradictory that there should be no evil and yet that there should be a privation of a better state.

But you will say, through the privation of a more perfect state we relapse into a lesser good, but not into an absolute evil. But (Appendix, Part I, Chapter 3) you have taught me that one must not quarrel over words. Therefore I do not dispute now whether it may be called an absolute evil or not ; but only whether the fall from a better to a worse state is not what is called by us and may also be rightly called, a more evil state, or a state which is evil. But should you say that this evil state still contains much good, I ask whether the man cannot be called evil who by his careless action has brought about the privation of his more perfect state, and is consequently now less than he was before.

But in order to escape these foregoing arguments, since you still seem to have some difficulties with this matter, you say that *evil indeed exists and that evil did indeed exist in Adam, but that it is not something positive, and is only called such with respect to our understanding and not with respect to God's understanding, and that with respect to our understanding it is Privation (but only in so far as we deprive ourselves of the best liberty, which concerns our nature, and is in our power) but that with respect to God it is Negation.* But now let us examine here whether what you call evil, if it is evil only in relation to us, would not be evil : and next whether evil, regarded as what you assert it to be, must be called mere *Negation* with respect to God.

I seem to a certain extent to have answered the first question above : and even though I admitted that my being less perfect than another being cannot posit any evil in me, because I cannot demand a better state from my creator, and it makes me only different in degree, yet I cannot but admit that if I am less perfect now than I was in the past, and have brought about my imperfection by my own fault, I must then confess that I am so much worse. I mean if I consider myself as I was before ever I fell into imperfection, and compare myself with others who have greater perfection than I have, then this lesser perfection is no evil, but a good of a lower grade. But if I compare myself as I am after I have fallen from a more perfect state, and when deprived of it through my own carelessness, with my former nature with which I issued from my creator's hand, and was more perfect, then I must consider myself to be worse than before ; for it is not the creator but I myself who have brought myself to this, for I had, as you too admit, the power of keeping myself from error.

As to the second point, namely whether evil, which, as you assert, consists in the privation of a better state which not only Adam but also we all have lost by a too hasty and disorderly action, whether this evil is simply *Negation* in relation to God. But in order to examine this point thoroughly, we must see how you regard man and make him dependent on God before he fell into error, and how the same man is regarded after this error. Before the error you describe him as one to whom no more perfection pertains than the Divine under-standing and power imparts and in fact gives him, that is, (unless I mistake your meaning) that man can show no more and no less perfection than God has put essence into him, and this makes man depend on God in the same way as the Elements, stones, plants, etc. But if this is your opinion, then I cannot understand the remark in the *Principles*, Part I, Proposition 15 : *But since the will is free to determine itself, it follows that we have the power of restraining the faculty of assent within the limits of our understanding, and hence of acting so that we do not fall into error.* Does it not seem a contradiction to make the will so free that it can keep itself from error, and at the same time to make it so dependent on God that it cannot show either more or less perfection than God has given it essence ?

As to the other point, namely, how you regard man after his error, on this you say that man by a too hasty action, namely, by not restraining his will within the limits of his understanding, deprives himself of a more perfect state. But it seems to me that both here and also in the *Principles* you should have shown somewhat more fully the two extremes of this Privation, what he possessed before the privation, and how much he retained after the loss of this perfect state (as you call it). Something is indeed said about what we have lost but not about what we have retained. *Principles*, Part I, Proposition 15 : *Therefore the whole imperfection of error consists simply in the privation of the best liberty, and this is called error.* Let us, however, examine these two remarks, just as they have been asserted by you. You will have it not only that there are in us such different modes of thinking, some of which we call willing and others understanding, but also that there exists between them such an order that we ought not to will things before we have clearly understood them, and if we always keep our will within the limits of our understanding we shall never err, and lastly that it is in our power to be able to keep our will within the limits of our understanding. When I consider this earnestly, surely one of two things must be true : either all this that has been asserted is mere fancy, or God has impressed on us this very order. But if God has imprinted in us this very order, would it not be beside the mark to say that this has been done without any purpose, and that God does not desire that we should observe and follow this order? For that would posit a contradiction in God. And, if we must observe the order implanted in us, how can we be and remain so dependent on God? For if no one shows either more or less perfection than he has received essence, and if these forces must become known from their effects, then he who lets his will go beyond the limits of his understanding has not received so much power from God, otherwise he also would have exercised it, and consequently he who errs could not have received from God the perfection of not erring, or he would never err, for according to your assertion there is always given as much essence as there is exercised perfection.

Secondly, if God has given us so much essence that we can maintain this order, as you say we can maintain it ; and if we always produce as much perfection as we have essence, how does it come about that we transgress this order, how comes it that we can transgress it, and that we do not always restrain our will within the limits of our understanding ?

Thirdly, if I am so dependent on God, as I have above shown you to assert, that I can control my will neither within nor without the limits of my understanding, unless God has previously given me just sufficient essence, and has by His will pre-determined one or the other, if we look into this more closely, how can the freedom of the will avail me at all ? Indeed does it not seem to argue a contradiction in God to give an order that we should keep our will within the limits of our understanding, and not to give us so much essence or perfection that we may be able to carry it out ? And if, according to your assertion, He had given us so much perfection, surely we should never be able to err : for we must produce as much perfection as we have essence, and must always show in our works the power that was given us. But our errors are a proof that we have no such power that is so dependent on God (as you will have it). So that one of these alternatives must be true, either we are not so dependent on God, or we have not in ourselves the power of being able not to err. But, according to your assertion, we have the power of not erring. Therefore we cannot be so dependent.

From these remarks I think it is now clear that it is impossible that evil, or the being deprived of a better state, should be negation in relation to God. For what is meant by privation, or the loss of a more perfect state? Is it not a transition from a greater to a lesser perfection, and consequently from a greater to a lesser essence, and being placed by God in a certain degree of perfection and essence? Is not that to will that we cannot attain to another state without His perfect knowledge unless He had resolved and willed otherwise? Is it really possible that this creature, the creature brought forth by that omniscient and perfect Being, who wished it to retain such a state of essence, indeed a creature with which God is continually concurring in order to preserve it in that state of being, is it possible that it should decline in essence, that is be diminished in perfection, without the knowledge of God? This seems to me to involve an absurdity. Is it not absurd to say that Adam lost a more perfect state, and consequently was incapable of carrying out the order which God had placed in his soul, and that God had no knowledge of that loss and of the imperfection and to what extent and how much perfection Adam had lost? Is it really conceivable that God should constitute a being that should be so dependent that it could produce only such action and that then it should through that action lose a more perfect state (to say nothing of His being alleged to be an absolute cause thereof) and that God should have no knowledge of it?

I admit that there is a difference between the action and the evil adhering to the action; but I cannot understand your remark *But evil in relation to God is Negation.* That God should know the action, determine it, and concur in it, and yet have no cognizance of the evil which is in the action, nor know what the outcome of it would be, all this seems to me to be impossible in the case of God. For observe with me that He concurs in my act of begetting children by my wife, for that is something positive, and consequently God has clear knowledge of it ; but in so far as I misuse this action with another woman contrary to my promise and vow there is evil concurrently with this action. Now what is there in this which is negative in relation to God ? Not the fact that I perform an act of procreation, for God concurs in this in so far as it is positive. The evil, then, which occurs with the action must consist only in the fact that I do it contrary to my own vow, or else the command of God, with such a woman as I ought not to have intercourse with. But now is it conceivable that God should know our actions, that He should concur in our actions, and yet not know with whom we commit the actions, the more so because God also concurs in the action of the woman with whom I had to do. Methinks it is difficult to believe this of God. Consider the act of killing. In so far as it is a positive act, God concurs in it. But according to you He is ignorant of the effect of the action, namely the destruction of a being and the dissolution of God's creature. As if God did not know His own work. (I fear that I cannot well understand your meaning here, for your conceptions seem to me too penetrating for you to commit such a gross error.) But perhaps, you will reply here that the actions, such as I represented them, are all quite good and that no evil accompanies them. But then I cannot understand what it is that you call evil, which follows the privation of a more perfect state. Moreover, the whole world would then be put in lasting confusion, and we human beings should be made like unto the beasts. See now what profit such a view would bring to the world.

You also reject the common description of man, but ascribe to each man as much perfection of action as God in fact gives him to exercise. But this I can only take to mean that the ungodly serve God by their action just as well as the godly do. Why? Because neither can produce works more perfect than the amount of essence that has been given to each of them, and which they show through their works. And I do not think that you answer this question satisfactorily in your second answer when you say *the more perfection a thing has, the more it has of Deity, and the more it expresses the perfection of God. Therefore, since the pious have incalculably more perfection than the ungodly, their virtue cannot be compared with that of the ungodly. For these are as a tool in the hand of the master which serves unconsciously, and perishes in the service; but the pious on the contrary serve consciously [and become more perfect by their service].* Of both, however, it is true that they cannot do more, for as much more perfection as these produce beyond the others, so much more essence have they received beyond the others. Do not the ungodly, then, with their little perfection, serve God as much as the godly? For according to your assertion, God wants no more from the ungodly, otherwise He would have given them more essence. But He did not give them more essence, as appears from their works. Therefore He wants no more from them. And if each after his kind does what God wants, no more and no less, why should he who does less, but still does just as much as God desires from him, not please God as much as the godly does?

Moreover as we, according to your assertion, lose a more perfect state through the evil which by our

---

* The Dutch original misquotes : "and perish in the service." Corrected in the Latin version.

carelessness accompanies the act, so here also you seem to want to state that, by keeping our will within the limits of our understanding, we not only remain as perfect as we are, but that we even become more perfect from our service. This seems to me to involve a contradiction if while we are alleged to be so dependent on God that we can produce neither more nor less perfection than we have received essence, that is, than God has willed, we should yet be able to become either worse, by our carelessness, or better, by our prudence. So I can only suppose that if man is such as you describe him, the ungodly by their actions serve God as much as do the godly by their actions, and so we are made as dependent on God as the elements, plants and stones, etc. Of what use, then, is our understanding? Of what use our power of keeping our will within the limits of our understanding? Why is this order impressed upon us?

And see too, on the other side, of what we deprive ourselves, namely anxious and earnest considerations to make ourselves perfect according to the law of God's perfection, and according to the order which He has impressed on us to make ourselves perfect. We deprive ourselves of prayer and sighing to God, from which we have so often felt that we derive an extraordinary increase of strength. We deprive ourselves of all religion, and of all the hopes and all the joys which we expect from prayers and religion.

For, surely, if God has no knowledge of evil, it is still less credible that He should punish evil. What reasons are there, then, why I should not eagerly commit all villainies (if only I can escape the condemnation of the judge)? Why not enrich myself by horrible means? Why not do whatever pleases us indiscriminately, and whatever the flesh prompts us to do? But you will say, because we must love virtue for its own sake. But how can I love virtue? I have not been endowed with so much essence and perfection. And if I can derive as much pleasure from the one as from the other why should I make the exertion to keep my will within the limits of my understanding? Why not do whatever my passions lead me to? Why not secretly kill the man who is in my way in anything? etc. See what an opportunity we give to all the ungodly and to ungodliness. We make ourselves like logs of wood and all our doings just like the movements of a clock.

From what has been said it seems to me very difficult to allege that we can only improperly be said to sin against God. For otherwise of what significance is the power given us of being able to keep our will within the limits of our understanding by exceeding which we sin against the command? But you will probably say that this is no sin against God but only concerns ourselves; for if we were properly to be said to sin against God then it would also have to be said that something happens against God's will. But that, according to your opinion, is impossible, therefore also sin. But anyway one of two things must be true, either God wills it, or does not will it. If God wills it, how can it be evil in relation to us? And if He does not will it, then, according to your opinion, it should not come to pass. But although this, according to your opinion, involves some absurdity, yet it seems to me very dangerous to admit therefore the absurdities mentioned above. Who knows whether, if we bestow much thought, some expedient might not be found by us to reconcile these matters to some extent?

With this I will conclude my examination of your letter under the guidance of my first general rule. But before I proceed to examine it in accordance with my second rule, I will state two things which concern this thought of your letter. Both are stated by you in your *Principia*, Part I, Proposition 15. The first is your assertion *that we can keep our power of willing and of judging within the limits of our understanding.* To this I cannot yet assent absolutely. For if this were true, surely we should be able to find one man, out of the countless many, who would show by results that he had this power. Yet every one can find very clearly from his own experience that, however much strength he may exert, he cannot reach that goal. And if anyone has a doubt about it let him examine himself and see how often in spite of his understanding his passions overcome his Reason, even when he exerts his utmost strength. But you will say, the reason why we do not achieve it is not that it is beyond our power, but that we do not apply sufficient diligence. I reply to this that if it were possible, surely one would be found out of so many thousands. But of all men there has not been, nor is there, one who would dare to boast that he has not fallen into error. And what surer proof can we adduce for these things than examples ? If there were a few at least, that would be one [proof], but now there is not one, and so there is no proof. But you will be able to make objection and say : If it is possible that I, by suspending my judgment and keeping my will within the limits of my understanding, can once bring it to pass that I do not err, why should I not always be able to realize this effect when I exercise the same diligence ? I reply that I cannot see that we have to-day as much strength as to be able always to continue to do so. Once, by exerting all my strength, I can walk two miles in one hour, but I cannot do that always. So I can for once, by great exertion, refrain from error, but I have not sufficient strength to be able to do so always. It seems clear to me that the first man as he issued from the hand of that perfect master worker had these powers, but that (and in this I agree with you) either by not making sufficient use of this power or by misusing it, he lost the perfect state of being able to do what was before then quite in his power. This I could confirm with many arguments, did I not fear to be too lengthy. And herein I think lies the whole essence of Holy Scripture, and therefore we must hold it in great respect, since it teaches us what is so clearly confirmed by our natural understanding, namely, that our fall from our first perfection came about and was caused by our carelessness. What is there more necessary than to remedy this fall as much as possible? And it is the sole aim of Holy Scripture to bring fallen man back to God.

The second point concerns *Principles*, Part I, Proposition 15, which asserts that *to understand things clearly and distinctly is opposed to the nature of man.* From this you conclude finally that *it is much better to give our assent to things even though they are confused, and to exercise our freedom than to remain indifferent always, that is, on the lowest rung of freedom.* I do not find this clear enough for me to assent to it. For a suspension of our judgment preserves us in the state in which we were created by the creator, but to assent to what is confused is to assent to what we do not understand, and, when we do this, it is as easy to assent to the false as to the true. And if (as Monsieur Descartes somewhere teaches us) we do not, when assenting, comply with the order which God has given concerning our understanding and our will, namely, that we should only assent to what we clearly understand, then even if we sometimes by chance discover the truth, yet we are sinning since we do not embrace the truth according to that order with which God willed that we should embrace it. Consequently just as the withholding of an assent preserves us in that state in which God has put us, so confused assent puts us in a worse condition than we are. For it lays the foundation of errors through which we then lose our perfect state. But I hear you say, is it not better to make ourselves more perfect by assenting to things even when confused rather than, by not assenting, to remain always on the lowest rung of perfection and freedom? But, apart from the fact that we have denied this, and have to some extent shown that we have made ourselves not better but worse, it also seems to us impossible and a contradiction that God should extend the knowledge of things determined by Him further than the knowledge which He has given us, indeed, that God should include an absolute cause of our errors. This is not inconsistent with the fact that we cannot complain against God that He should grant us more than He has granted, since He was not bound to do so. It is indeed true that God was not bound to give us more than He has given us, but God's supreme perfection also posits that a creature proceeding from Him should involve no contradiction, such as would otherwise appear to follow. For nowhere in created Nature do we find knowledge except in our own understanding. To what other end could this have been given us but that we might contemplate and know the works of God? And what then seems also to follow more evidently than that there must be agreement between the things which must be known and our understanding?

But if I should examine your letter under the guidance of my second general rule, then we should have to differ more than we do under the guidance of the first. For I think (please inform me if I am wrong) that you do not ascribe to the Holy Scriptures that infallible truth and divinity which I believe exist therein. It is true that you say you believe that God has revealed the things of Holy Scripture to the Prophets, but in such an imperfect manner that, if it happened as you state, it would imply a contradiction in God. For if God has revealed His Word and His will to men, then He has revealed it to them for a definite purpose, and clearly. If, now,

the Prophets have composed a Parable out of that
Word which they have received, then God must either
have willed that also, or He did not will it. If God
did will that they should compose a Parable from His
Word, that is, that they should stray from His meaning,
then God was the cause of the error, and then God
willed something self-contradictory. If God did not
will it, then it is impossible that the Prophets should
have been able to compose a Parable therefrom. Moreover, it seems credible, if we suppose that God communicated his Word to the Prophets, that He communicated
it to them in such a way that they should not err in
receiving it. For God must have had a definite purpose
in communicating His Word, but God's purpose could
not have been to lead men into error thereby, for that
would be a contradiction in God. Also man could
not err contrary to the will of God, for this, according
to your opinion, is impossible. In addition to all this,
one cannot believe of this most perfect God that He
should permit a meaning other than He wished to be
given by the Prophet to His Word communicated to
the Prophets in order they should explain it to the
common people. For if we state that God has communicated His Word to the Prophets, we state also that God
appeared to the Prophets, or spoke with them, in some
extraordinary manner. If, now, the Prophets make
a Parable of this communicated Word, that is, give it
a sense other than God wished them to give it, then
God would certainly have told them so. Also it is as
impossible with respect to the Prophets, as it is a contradiction with respect to God, to hold that the Prophets
could have understood something different from what
God had willed that they should understand.

I see also very little proof that God has revealed His
Word as you state, namely, that He revealed only salvation and perdition, and appointed sure means to that end,

and that salvation and perdition are no more than the effects of the appointed means. For, surely, if the Prophets had received the Word of God in this sense what reasons could they have had for giving it another meaning ? But I do not see you produce a single proof capable of convincing us that these views should be set above the views of the Prophets. But if you think that the proof consists in this, that otherwise this Word would include many imperfections and contradictions, then I say that this is merely an assertion and not a proof. And who knows, if both meanings were examined, which would contain the fewer imperfections ? Lastly, the supremely perfect Being knew well what the common people could understand, and consequently what was the best method by which the common people must be taught.

As to the second part of your first question, you ask yourself why God forbade Adam to eat of the fruit of the tree when He had nevertheless ordained the contrary, and you answer that the prohibition addressed to Adam consisted solely in this, namely, that God revealed to Adam that the eating of the fruit of this tree caused death just as He reveals to us through our natural understanding that poison is deadly for us. If it is established that God forbade something to Adam, what reasons are there to compel me to place more belief in the account of the manner of the prohibition stated by you than in that stated by the Prophets to whom God Himself revealed the manner of the prohibition ? You will say : My manner of prohibition is more natural, and therefore more like the truth, and more becoming to God. But I deny all this. Nor do I conceive that God has revealed to us through our natural understanding that poison is deadly ; and I see no reason whereby I should know that anything is poisonous, if I had seen no evil effects of poison in the case of others, or heard of them. Daily experience teaches us how many men, because they do not know poison, eat it unwittingly and die. But you will say, if people knew that it was poison they would know that it is evil. But I answer that no one knows poison, or can know it, unless he has seen and heard that someone has hurt himself by using it. And if we suppose that up to this day we have never heard or seen that anyone has been hurt by the use of this kind of thing, we should not only not know it now, but we should fearlessly use it to our hurt. Suchlike truths are taught us every day.

What can give greater delight to an upright intellect in this life than the contemplation of the perfect Deity? For, just as it is concerned with the most perfect, so it must also include the most perfect that can come to our finite understanding. And, indeed, I have nothing in my life for which I would exchange this pleasure. In this I can pass much time with heavenly joy; but all at once I can be also sad at heart, when I realize that my finite understanding is wanting in so much. This sorrow, however, I comfort with the hope which I have, and which is dearer to me than life, that I shall exist again and continue to exist, and shall contemplate this Deity more perfectly than I do to-day.

When I consider this brief and fleeting life, in which I expect my death any moment, if I were bound to believe that I should cease to be, and that I should be cut off from this holy and glorious contemplation, I should certainly be much more miserable than all creatures who have no knowledge that they will come to an end. For then, before my death, the fear of death would make me unhappy, and after my death, I should be nothing, and I should therefore be unhappy since I should be deprived of that divine contemplation. And your opinions seem to lead me to this, that when I cease to be here, I shall also cease to be for ever. The Word and the will of God, on the contrary, give me strength by their inner testimony in my soul that after this life I shall at some time enjoy myself in a more perfect state in the contemplation of the most perfect Deity. Surely, even if this hope should eventually be found to be false, yet it makes me happy so long as I hope. This is the only thing that I desire of God, and shall desire with prayers, sighs and earnest wishes (would that I could contribute more to it) as long as there is breath in this body, namely, that it may please Him through His Divinity to make me so fortunate that, when this body is dissolved, I may then still remain a thinking being, so that I may continue to contemplate the perfect Deity. And if only I can obtain this, it is a matter of indifference to me what people here believe, of what views people persuade each other here, whether there is anything that is founded on the natural understanding and can be grasped, or not. This and this alone is my wish, my desire and my constant prayer, that God may confirm this certainty in my soul. And if I have this (and, oh! if I have it not, then I am the most wretched) my soul shall cry out with longing, *As the hart panteth after the water brooks, so panteth my soul after thee, O living God. Oh when will the day come that I shall be with you and behold you?* * And if only I attain to this I have every aim and desire of my soul. But these hopes do not appear to me in your doctrine that our service is not pleasing to God. Nor can I grasp why God (if at least I may speak of Him in this human fashion) should bring us forth and sustain us, if He takes no pleasure in our service and our praise. But if I am mistaken about these opinions of yours I wish to have your explanation.

But I have detained myself and perhaps also you too long, and as I see that my time and paper are exhausted, I will finish. This is what I would still like to see solved

* [Psalm xlii, 1, 2, misquoted.]

in your letter.   Perhaps here and there I have drawn from your letter some conclusion which perchance you do not intend, but on this I should like to hear your explanation.

I have recently occupied myself with the consideration of certain attributes of God, in which your *Appendix* has given me no little help, and in fact I have only paraphrased your views which seem to me to present nothing but proofs.   Therefore I am very much surprised that L. Meyer says in the Preface that this does not yet give your views, but that you were bound thus to teach your pupil whom you had promised to teach the Philosophy of Descartes, but that you have a totally different opinion both about God and the soul and especially about the will of the soul.   I see also that it is said in this Preface that you will shortly publish the *Metaphysical Thoughts* in an amplified form.   Both these I long for very much, for I expect something special from them.   It is not, however, my habit to praise anyone to his face.

This is written in sincere friendship, as requested in your letter, and in order that the truth may be discovered. Forgive me for writing at such length, more than I intended.   If I may receive a reply to this, you will oblige me very much.   As to writing in the language in which [you] were brought up, I can have no objection, if at least it is Latin or French ; but I beg to be allowed to receive this answer still in this same language as I have understood your meaning in it quite well, and maybe I should not understand so clearly in Latin.   By doing so, you will lay me under such an obligation that I shall be and remain,

Sir, your most devoted and dutiful
WILLIAM VAN BLYENBERGH.

DORDRECHT, 16 *Jan.* 1665.

I should like to be informed more fully in your reply what you really mean by a Negation in God.

LETTER XXI   B. D. S.

To the Very Learned and Eminent
Mr. WILLIAM VAN BLYENBERGH.

Reply to the Preceding.

SIR AND FRIEND,

When I read your first letter I believed that
our opinions almost coincided; but I understand from
your second letter, which was delivered to me on the
21st of this month, that this is far from being so. I
can see that we differ not only about the conclusions
which may be ultimately derived from first principles,
but also about those principles themselves. So much
so that I hardly believe that our correspondence can be
for our mutual instruction. For I perceive that no
proof, however sound according to the Laws of Proof,
avails with you, unless it agrees with that explanation
which you, or other Theologians known to you, give
to Holy Scripture. But if you hold that God speaks
more clearly and effectively through Holy Scripture
than through the light of the natural understanding,
which He also gave us, and in His Divine Wisdom
continually preserves firm and uncorrupted, you have
strong reasons for moulding your understanding to the
opinions which you attribute to Holy Scripture. I
myself could not do otherwise. But as far as I am
concerned, since I openly and unambiguously confess
that I do not understand Holy Scripture although I have
spent some years in the study of it, and since it has not
escaped my notice that when I have a strong proof
no such thoughts can occur to me that I can ever entertain any doubt about it, I acquiesce wholly in that which
my understanding shows me, without any suspicion
that I may be deceived, or that Holy Scripture, although
I do not search it, can contradict it : for truth does not

conflict with truth, as I have already clearly shown before in my *Appendix* (I cannot indicate the chapter, for I have not the book here with me in the country). Even if I were once to find untrue the fruits of my natural understanding, they would make me happy, since I enjoy them, and I endeavour to pass my life not in sorrow and sighing but in peace, joy and cheerfulness, and thereby I ascend a step higher. Meanwhile I know (and this gives me the greatest satisfaction and peace of mind) that all things come to pass as they do by the power of the most perfect Being, and His immutable decree.

But to return to your letter. I sincerely express my best thanks to you for having laid bare to me in time your method of philosophizing. But I give you no thanks for attributing to me such opinions as you wish to deduce from my letter. What material, I pray, did my letter provide for imputing to me these opinions, namely, that men are like unto beasts, that men die and perish after the manner of beasts, that our works are displeasing to God, etc.? (It may be that we differ entirely on this last point, since I cannot but think that you conceive God as taking pleasure in our works as one who has achieved His end, inasmuch as something has succeeded according to His wish.) As far as I am concerned, I have assuredly said clearly that the upright serve God, and by their continual service they become more perfect, and love God. Is this to make them like beasts, or to declare that they perish like beasts, or, lastly, that their works do not please God?

If you had read my letter with greater attention, you would have clearly perceived that our difference lay in this alone, namely, whether the perfections which the upright receive, are conferred upon them by God as God, that is, absolutely, without our attributing to Him any human attributes (as I understand), or whether they are conferred on them by Him as a judge, which last is what you assert. Therefore you urge in defence of the wicked that they serve God as much as do the good, since they do what they can in accordance with the decree of God. But this by no means follows from my remarks: for I do not introduce God as a judge, and therefore I estimate works according to the quality of the work, and not according to the capacity of the workman, and the reward which follows the work follows on it as necessarily as it follows from the nature of a triangle that its three angles must be equal to two right angles. And this everyone will understand if he only considers that our greatest blessedness consists in love toward God, and that this love necessarily flows from the knowledge of God, which is so strongly commended to us. This can be easily proved in general if we will only pay attention to the nature of God's Decree, as I have explained in my *Appendix*. But I admit that all those who confuse the Divine nature with human nature are quite unable to understand this.

I had intended to end this letter here, lest I should weary you further with matters which (as is clear from the very devout addition appended at the end of your letter) serve for jest and laughter and are of no real use. But not entirely to decline your request, I will proceed further to the explanation of the words Negation and Privation, and briefly bring out what is necessary to make the meaning of my preceding letter more lucid.

I say, then, in the first place, that Privation is not an act of depriving, but only a simple and mere lack, which in itself is nothing: for it is only a thing of Reason, or a way of thinking, which we form when we compare things with each other. We say, for example, that a blind man is deprived of sight because we easily imagine him as seeing. This imagination comes about either because we compare him with others who see, or because we compare his present state with a past state when he did see. And when we consider this man in this way, that is by comparing his nature with that of others or with a former nature of his own, we affirm that sight belongs to his nature and therefore we say that he is deprived of it. But when the decree of God and His nature are considered, we cannot say of that man any more than of a stone, that he is deprived of sight, for at that time sight pertains to that man no less inconsistently than to a stone; *for to that man there pertains and belongs nothing more than the Divine understanding and will attributed to him.* And therefore God is no more the cause of his not seeing than of the stone's not seeing, which is mere Negation. *So also when we consider the nature of the man who is led by his desire for pleasure, and when we compare his present desire with that which is felt by the upright, or with that which he himself had on another occasion, we assert that the man is deprived of a better desire, because we judge that the desire of virtue then pertains to him. This we cannot do if we consider the nature of God's decree and His understanding. For in this respect the better desire belongs no more to that man's nature at that time than it does to the Nature of a Devil or of a stone,* and therefore in this respect the better desire is not Privation but Negation. So that Privation is nothing else than denying of a thing something which we judge to pertain to its nature, and Negation is nothing else than denying something of a thing because it does not belong to its nature. Hence it is clear why the desire of Adam for earthly things was evil only in relation to our understanding and not in relation to that of God. *For although God knew both the past and the present state of Adam He did not therefore conceive Adam as deprived of a past state, that is, conceive the past state as pertaining to his nature.* For then God would conceive something contrary to His will, that is, contrary to His own understanding.

If you had rightly perceived this, and also that I do not admit that liberty which Descartes ascribes to the Mind, as L. M., in my name, testified in the Preface, you would not find even the smallest contradiction in my words. But I see that I should have done much better if, in my first letter, I had replied in the words of Descartes, saying that we cannot know how our liberty, and whatever depends on it, agrees with the foresight and freedom of God (as I have done in various places in the *Appendix* to Descartes' *Principia*) so that we can find in the creation by God nothing inconsistent with our liberty, since we are unable to understand in what way God has created things, and (what is the same thing) how He preserves them. But I thought you had read the Preface and that I should be sinning against the duty of friendship, which I offered heartily, if I did not answer according to the thought that was really in my mind. But this is of no consequence.

Since, however, I see that you have not hitherto rightly grasped the Mind of Descartes, I pray you to pay attention to these two points.

First, that neither Descartes nor I have ever said that it pertains to our nature to confine our will within the limits of our understanding, but only that God has given us a limited understanding and an unlimited will yet in such a way that we do not know to what end He has created us ; moreover that an unlimited will of this kind, or a perfect will, not only makes us more perfect, but is also very necessary for us, as I will show in what follows.

Secondly, that our liberty is placed not in a certain contingency or in a certain indifference, but in the mode of assertion or denial, so that the less indifferently we affirm or deny something the more free we are. For instance, if the nature of God is known to us, then the assertion that God exists follows as necessarily from our own nature as it follows necessarily from the nature of a triangle that its three angles are equal to two right angles. And yet we are never more free than when we assert a thing in this way. But since this necessity is nothing else than the decree of God, as I have clearly shown in my *Appendix* to Descartes' *Principles*, it may to a certain extent be understood how we do something freely, and are the cause of it, notwithstanding the fact that we do it necessarily, and according to the Decree of God. This, I say, we can understand to a certain extent, when we affirm something which we clearly and distinctly perceive; but when we assert something which we do not clearly and distinctly grasp, that is, when we suffer our will to roam beyond the limits of our understanding, then we cannot thus perceive this necessity and the Decrees of God, but only our liberty, which is always included in our will (in which respect only our actions are called good or evil). And if we then try to reconcile our liberty with God's Decree and His continual creation, we are confusing that which we clearly and distinctly understand with that which we do not perceive, and therefore our effort is vain. It is enough for us, therefore, that we know that we are free, and that we can be thus free, notwithstanding the decree of God, and that we are the cause of evil, because no action can be called evil except only in relation to our freedom. So much, then, with regard to Descartes, so that I might show that his words in this connection contain no contradiction.

I will now turn to what concerns myself, and first I will briefly call to mind the advantage which comes from my opinion, and which especially consists in this, namely, that our understanding offers Mind and Body to God without any superstition. I do not deny that prayers are very useful to us : for my understanding is too small to determine all the means which God has to lead men to the love of Him, that is, to salvation. So far is my opinion from being harmful that, on the contrary, for those who are not prepossessed by prejudices and childish superstition, it is the sole means of attaining to the highest degree of blessedness.

As to what you say, that I make men so dependent on God that I make them like the elements, plants and stones, this shows sufficiently that you most perversely misunderstand my opinion, and confuse things which concern the understanding with imagination. For if you had grasped with your pure understanding what dependence upon God is, you would certainly not think that things in so far as they depend on God, are dead, corporeal and imperfect (who ever dared to speak in so vile a fashion of the most perfect Being ?). On the contrary, you would understand that for that reason, and in so far as they depend on God, they are perfect—so much so, that we best understand this dependence and necessary operation through God's decree when we consider not logs and plants, but the most intelligible and most perfect created things, as appears clearly from what I have said before, in the second place, about the meaning of Descartes which you should have noticed.

And I cannot refrain from saying that I am very much surprised that you say : if God did not punish crime (that is, as a judge with such a punishment as the offence itself does not bring with it : for only this is in question) what consideration could restrain me from eagerly perpetrating all sorts of crimes ? Surely he who only abstains from this from fear of punishment (which I hope is not so with you) in no way acts from love, and embraces virtue as little as possible. So far as I am concerned, I avoid or endeavour to avoid crimes because they are expressly repugnant to my special nature, and would make me stray from the love and the knowledge of God.

Further, if you had paid a little attention to human nature and grasped the nature of the decree of God, as I explained in my Appendix, and finally, if you had known how inference should proceed before a conclusion is reached, then you would not have said so boldly that this opinion makes us like logs, etc., nor would you have imputed to me the many absurdities which you imagine.

With regard to those two points which, before you proceed to your second rule, you say that you cannot understand, I reply first that Descartes is enough to enable you to arrive at your conclusion, namely, that if you will only pay attention to your own nature you will have the experience that you can suspend your judgment. But if you say that you do not find in your own experience that we have so much power over Reason to-day that we can always continue to do so, this for Descartes would be the same as saying that we cannot see to-day that as long as we exist we shall always be thinking things, or retain the nature of a thinking thing, which surely involves a contradiction.

To your second point, I say, with Descartes, that if we could not extend our will beyond the limits of our very limited understanding, we should be most wretched. It would not be in our power to eat a piece of bread, or to move a step, or to exist. For all things are uncertain and full of dangers.

I pass on now to your second Rule, and I assert that I do indeed believe that I do not attribute to Scripture that Truth which you believe to be therein, and yet I believe that I ascribe to it as much, if not more, authority, and that, far more cautiously than others, I take care not to impute to it certain childish and absurd views; and this no one can do better unless he understands Philosophy well, or has Divine revelations. So the explanations of Scripture which ordinary Theologians offer have very little influence with me, especially when they are of that kind which always take Scripture according to the letter and the external meaning. And yet I have never seen any Theologian except the Socinians, who was so dense as not to perceive that Holy Scripture very frequently speaks of God in human fashion, and expresses its meaning in Parables. As to the contradiction which you endeavour to show, in vain (in my opinion at least), I believe that you mean by Parable something entirely different from what is commonly meant. For who has ever heard that he who expresses his ideas in Parables strays from his meaning? When Micah said to King Ahab that he had seen God sitting on His throne, and the heavenly hosts standing on the right and on the left, and that God asked them who would deceive Ahab, this was certainly a Parable, by which the Prophet sufficiently expressed the chief point which he had to reveal in God's name on that occasion (which was not one for teaching sublime dogmas of Theology), so that he in no way strayed from His meaning. So also the other Prophets, at the command of God, revealed the Word of God to the people in this way, as the best means, though not as that which God enjoined, of leading the people to the primary object of Scripture, which according to the word of Christ himself consists, of course, in loving God above all things and one's neighbour as oneself. High speculations, I believe, concern Scripture least. As far as I am concerned, I have learned none of the eternal attributes of God from Holy Scripture, nor could I learn them.

As to your fifth argument (namely, that the Prophets have made manifest the Word of God in such a manner), since truth is not opposed to truth, it only remains for me to show (as anyone may judge who understands the method of proof) that Scripture, just as it is, is the true, revealed Word of God. Of this I can have no Mathematical Proof, except by Divine Revelation. For this reason I said, *I believe*, but not *I know mathematically, that all things which God revealed to the Prophets, etc.*, since I firmly believe, but I do not know mathematically, that the Prophets were the intimate counsellors and the faithful messengers of God; so that in all that I have asserted there is no contradiction whatsoever, whereas on the contrary not a few may be found on the other side.

As to the rest of your letter, namely, where you say *Lastly, the supremely perfect Being knew, etc.*, and what you then adduce against the example about the poison, and, lastly, what concerns the *Appendix*, and what follows, I say that they do not concern the present question.

As to the Preface by L. M., it is therein certainly shown what points Descartes should still have proved in order to construct a sound proof of the Freedom of the Will, and it is added that I favour the contrary opinion, and how I do so. This perhaps I shall explain in its proper time but I have no mind for it now.

But I have not thought about the work on Descartes, since the time when it appeared in the Dutch language, nor have I given it further consideration : and this not without a reason, which it would take long to recount here. So there remains nothing more to say but that I am, etc.

[SCHIEDAM, 28 *Jan.* 1665.]

LETTER XXII   WILLIAM VAN BLYENBERGH

To the Very Illustrious Mr. B. d. S.

Reply to the Preceding.

SIR AND WORTHY FRIEND,

I received your letter of the 28th January in due course, but affairs other than my studies prevented me from answering it sooner. And as your letter was sprinkled here and there with very touchy reproofs, I hardly knew what to think of it. For in your first letter of the 5th January you offered me your friendship resolutely and heartily, with the assurance that not only was my letter of that time very welcome to you but that subsequent letters would be so too. Indeed I was requested in a friendly way to bring forward freely any other difficulties which I might be able to raise. This I did somewhat more extensively in my letter of the 16th January. To this I expected a friendly and instructive answer in accordance with your own request and promise. But I received on the contrary one which does not savour of too much friendship, stating *that no proofs, however clear they may be, avail with me, that I do not understand Descartes' meaning, that I confuse material with spiritual things too much, etc., so much so, indeed, that our correspondence could no longer serve for our mutual instruction.* To all which I answer very friendly that I certainly do believe that you understand the above mentioned things better than I do, and that you are more accustomed to distinguish the corporeal things from the spiritual. For in Metaphysics, which I am only now beginning, you have already climbed to a high rung, and therefore I sought to insinuate myself in your favour so that I might receive instruction. But I never thought of giving offence by candid objections. I thank you heartily for the trouble you have taken with both letters, and especially with the second, from which I grasped your meaning more clearly than from the first. Nevertheless, I cannot give it my assent, unless the difficulties which I think I still find therein are removed for me. And this neither need be, nor can be, a ground for offence. For it is a great defect in our understanding to assent to a truth without having such grounds for our assent as are necessary.

Even if your conceptions are true, I may not assent to them, as long as I still have reasons for obscurity or doubt, even if these doubts arise, not from the thing as you present it, but from the imperfection of my understanding.   And since you know this fully, let it not be taken amiss if I again formulate some objections, as I am obliged to do as long as I cannot clearly grasp the thing.   For I do so with no other object than that of discovering the truth, and not with the intention of distorting your meaning against your intention.   And therefore I beg you to give me a friendly answer to these few questions.

You say that *nothing has more essence than the Divine will and power allow, and in fact give to it, and when we consider the nature of a man who experiences the desire for pleasure and we compare his present desires with those of the pious or with those which he himself had another time, then we assert that the man is deprived of a better desire, because we judge then that the desire of virtue pertains to him.   This we cannot do if we consider the nature of God's decree and understanding. For in relation to this the better desire belongs no more to that man's nature at that time than it does to the nature of the Devil or of a stone, etc.   For although God knew both the past and the present state of Adam, God did not therefore conceive that Adam was deprived of the past condition, that is, that the past condition belonged to his present nature, etc.* From these words it seems to me to follow clearly, though subject to correction, that according to your opinion, nothing else pertains to a being but what it has at the moment when it is apprehended.   That is, if I have a desire for pleasure, then this desire belongs to my essence at that time, and if I have no desire for pleasure then the not-desiring belongs to my essence at the time when I do not desire.   Consequently also it must follow without fail that in relation to God I include as much perfection (different only in degree) in my actions when I have a desire for pleasures as when I have no desire for pleasure, when I practise all sorts of rascalities as when I practise virtue and righteousness. For at that time there belongs to my essence only as much as I do since, according to your assertion, I can do neither more nor less than corresponds to the essence which I have in fact received. Now since the desire for pleasure and villainy belongs to my essence at the time when I practise them, and at that time I receive that essence and no more from the Divine power, so the Divine power only requires of me such actions. Therefore it seems to me to follow clearly from your statement that God desires villainies in one and the same way as He desires these actions which you call virtuous. Let it now be granted that God, as God, and not as judge, gives to the pious and to the ungodly such essence, and only as much essence, as He wishes them to exercise. What reasons are there then that God should not desire the action of the one in the same way as the action of the other ? For, since God gives to each one the quality for his action, it follows undoubtedly that He desires in the same way but also as much from those to whom He has given less, as from those to whom He has given more. Consequently, God in respect of Himself wills in the same way more or less perfection in our actions, the desire for pleasures and the desire for virtues, all alike, so that they who practise villainies must necessarily practise villainies because at that time nothing else pertains to their essence, just as he who practises virtue practises virtue because the power of God has willed it that this should belong to his essence at that time. Again, therefore, I cannot but think that God wills both, and in the same way, villainy as well as virtue. And inasmuch as He wills both, He is the cause of both, of the one as well as of the other, and to that extent, both must please Him. It is too hard for me to conceive this of God.

I see, indeed, that you say that the pious serve God, but from your writings I can only understand that to serve God is merely to do such actions as God has willed us to do, and this, you write, the wicked and the licentious also do. What difference is there, then, in relation to God, between the service of the pious and of the ungodly? You also say that the pious serve God, and by service continually become more perfect, but I cannot grasp what you mean by "becoming more perfect," nor what is meant by "continually become more perfect." For both the ungodly and the pious receive their being, and also their preservation or continual creation of their being, from God as God, not as judge, and both fulfil the will of God in the same way, namely, in accordance with God's decree. What difference can there be, then, between the two essences in relation to God? For "becoming continually more perfect" does not proceed from their action, but from the will of God, so that if the ungodly by their actions become more imperfect, this does not proceed from their actions but solely from the will of God. And both only fulfil the will of God. So there can be no difference between these two beings in respect of God. What reasons are there, then, why these should continually become more perfect by their actions, and the others perish in their service?

But you seem to place the difference between the actions of the one and of the other in this, that the one includes more perfection than does the other. I believe confidently that therein lurks my error or yours, for I cannot find in your writings any rule according to which a thing is called more or less perfect, except in so far as it has more or less essence. Now if this is the standard of perfection, then, in relation to God's will, crimes are always as acceptable to Him as the actions of the pious. For God, as God, that is, in relation to Himself, wills them in the same way, since both proceed from His decree. If this is the only standard of perfection, errors can only improperly be so called, but in reality there are no errors, in reality there are no crimes, and everything only embraces that and such essence as God has given it, which be it what it may, always includes perfection. I confess that I cannot clearly understand this. And you must forgive me when I ask whether murder is as pleasing to God as almsgiving, or whether in relation to God stealing is as good as being righteous. If not, what reasons are there for it? If yes, what reasons can there be which should induce me to do the one action which you call virtuous rather than the other? What law or rule forbids me the one rather than the other? If you say, the law of virtue itself, I must certainly confess that I find in what you say no law according to which virtue can be regulated or recognized. For everything depends inseparably on the divine will and therefore the one action is as virtuous as the other. And I do not understand your remark that one must act from love of virtue, as I cannot grasp what you mean by virtue or the law of virtue. You say, indeed, that you shun vice or villainy because they are repugnant to your special nature, and would lead you astray from the divine knowledge and love. In all your writings, however, I find not a single rule or proof relating to this. Indeed forgive me that I must say that the contrary seems to follow from your writings. You avoid the things which I call wicked because they are repugnant to your special nature, but not because they involve vice. You refrain from doing them just as we refrain from eating food which disgusts our nature. Surely he who avoids evil things merely because they are repugnant to his nature has little to boast of his virtue.

Here again the question arises if there were a mind to the special nature of which the pursuit of pleasures and villainies was not repugnant but rather agreeable, is there any ground for virtue which must induce him to do good and avoid evil ? But how is it possible that a man should be able to relinquish the desire for pleasure when this desire at that time pertains to his essence and he has actually received it from God and cannot relinquish it ?

I also cannot see this conclusion in your writings, that those actions which I call villainies would seduce you from the knowledge and love of God. For you have only done what God willed, and you could not do more because, at this time, nothing more was given to your essence by the divine power and will. How can an action so constituted and dependent make you stray from the love of God ? To stray is to be confused, and not to be dependent, and this, according to your assertion, is impossible. For whether we do this or that, whether we exercise more or less perfection we have received it for our essence, at the time, immediately from God. How then can we go astray ? Or do I not understand what is meant by error ? However here, and here alone, must lurk the cause of my or of your misapprehension.

Here I would say and ask many more things. First, whether thinking substances depend on God in a different way from lifeless substances ? for although the thinking beings include more essence than do the lifeless, still do they not both have God and God's decrees as the source of their motion in general, and of such motions in particular ? And consequently, inasmuch as they are dependent are they not dependent in one and the same way ? Secondly, since you do not allow to the soul the freedom which Descartes has ascribed to it, what difference is there between the dependence of thinking and of soulless substances? And if they have no freedom of will, in what way do you conceive dependence upon God? And how is the soul dependent on God? Thirdly, if our soul has no freedom, is not our action properly God's action and our will really God's will?

And I could ask many other questions but I dare not request so much from you. I await first of all your answer to the foregoing pages only. Perhaps I shall be able by means of it to understand your opinion better, and then discuss this thing with you some time more fully by word of mouth.

For when I have received your answer, then as I shall have to go to Leyden a few weeks hence, I will give myself the honour of greeting you sometime in passing, if it is agreeable to you. Trusting to this, I say, after hearty greetings, that I remain

Your devoted servant,
WILLIAM v. BLYENBERGH.

DORDRECHT, 19 *Feb.* 1665.

If you do not write to me under cover, please write to Willem van Blyenbergh, Grain-broker, near the great Church.

P.S.—I forgot in my great haste to insert the question, whether by our precaution we cannot prevent what would otherwise happen to us.

LETTER XXIII   B. D. S.

TO THE VERY LEARNED AND EMINENT
WILLIAM VAN BLYENBERGH.

Reply to the Preceding.

SIR AND FRIEND,
I have received two letters from you this week: the one, of the 9 March, which served merely

to inform me of the other, of the 19 February, which was sent to me from Schiedam. In this last one I see that you complain about what I had said *that no proof can avail with you, etc.*, as if I had said this in reference to my reasoning because it did not satisfy you immediately. This is far from my meaning. But I had in view your own words, which are as follows : *and if ever it happen that, after long consideration, my natural knowledge seems either to conflict with this word or not fully, etc., this word has so much authority with me that I rather doubt the conceptions which I think are clear than, etc.* Therefore, I did no more than repeat your words briefly, and I do not believe that I gave the smallest ground for offence thereby, especially as I only adduced them as an argument to show our great difference.

Moreover, since at the end of your second letter you wrote that your only wish is to continue in faith and hope, and that you were indifferent to the rest which we persuade ourselves about our natural understanding, I thought as I still think, that my writing could be of no use, and that therefore it was more advisable for me not to neglect my studies (which I must otherwise discontinue for so long) for the sake of things which can be of no use. And this does not contradict my first letter. For then I regarded you as a Philosopher pure and simple, who (as many, who consider themselves Christians, admit) has no other touchstone for truth than the natural understanding, and not theology. But you have taught me differently, and shown me that the foundation on which I meant to build our friendship, was not laid as I had thought.

Lastly, as regards the rest, this happens very commonly in the course of disputation without on that account going beyond the bounds of courtesy, and for this reason I have taken no notice of such things in your second letter and will also do likewise with this one.

So much about your displeasure, in order to show that I have given no ground for it, much less for thinking that I cannot bear contradiction. I will now turn to your objections, in order to reply to them.

First then, I say that God is absolutely and effectively the cause of everything that has essence, be it what it may. Now, if you can show that Evil, Error or Villainy, etc., is something which expresses essence, then I will fully admit to you that God is the cause of villainy, evil, error, etc. I think that I have sufficiently shown that that which gives its form to evil, error, or crimes, does not consist in anything which expresses essence, and that therefore it cannot be said that God is the cause thereof. For example Nero's matricide, in so far as it contained something positive, was not a crime : for Orestes too did the same outward deed and had the same intention of killing his Mother, and yet he is not blamed, at least not in the same degree as Nero. What then was Nero's crime ? Nothing else than that by this deed he showed that he was ungrateful, unmerciful, and disobedient. And it is certain that none of these things expresses any essence, and therefore God was not the cause of them, although He was the cause of the act and the intention of Nero.

Further, I should like to remark here that while we are speaking philosophically we must not use the modes of expression of Theology. For Theology has usually, and not without reason, represented God as a perfect man ; therefore it is quite appropriate in Theology that it should be said that God desires something, that God is affected with weariness at the deeds of the ungodly, and with pleasure at those of the pious. But in Philosophy, where we clearly understand that to apply to God the attributes which make a man perfect, is as bad as to want to apply to a man those which make perfect an elephant or an ass, these and similar words have no place; and we cannot use them here without thoroughly confusing our conceptions. Therefore speaking philosophically we cannot say that God demands something from someone, or that something wearies or pleases Him, for all these are human attributes, which have no place in God.

Lastly, I would like to remark that although the actions of the pious (that is, of those who have a clear idea of God, in accordance with which all their actions and thoughts are determined) and of the ungodly (that is, of those who have no idea of God, but only confused ideas of earthly things, in accordance with which all their actions and thoughts are determined) and lastly, of everything that exists, proceed necessarily from God's eternal laws and decrees, and continually depend on God, nevertheless they differ from one another not only in degree but also in essence. For although a mouse is as dependent on God as an angel is, and sadness as much as joy, yet a mouse cannot therefore be a kind of angel, or sadness a kind of joy. And herewith I think that I have answered your objections (if I have rightly understood them, for I am sometimes in doubt whether the conclusions which you draw do not differ from the Proposition which you undertake to prove).

This however will appear more clearly if, following these fundamental notions, I answer the questions which you proposed to me. The first is whether killing is as agreeable to God as alms-giving. The second is, whether in relation to God stealing is as good as being righteous. The third is whether, if there is a mind to whose especial nature the pursuit of pleasure and of crime is not repugnant but acceptable, there is any ground for virtue which would necessarily persuade it to do good and avoid evil?

To the first I say that (speaking philosophically) I do not know what you mean by *agreeable to God*. If the question is whether God does not hate the one and love the other, or whether the one has not done God harm, and the other a favour, I answer No. And if the question is this, whether men who slay and those who give alms are not equally good or perfect, I again say No.

With regard to your second, I reply, if *good in relation to God* means that the righteous man does some good to God, and the thief some evil, I answer that neither the righteous nor the thief can cause either pleasure or weariness to God. But if the question is whether both actions in so far as they are something real and caused by God, are not equally perfect, then I say that if we consider the actions alone, and in such a way, it may well be that they are equally perfect. If you then ask *whether the thief and the righteous are equally perfect and blessed, I answer No. For by a righteous man I understand one who firmly desires that each shall possess his own. I show in my Ethics (which I have not yet published) that this desire arises necessarily in the pious from the clear knowledge which they have of themselves and of God. And since the thief has no such desire, he necessarily lacks the knowledge of God and of himself, that is, the chief thing which makes us men.* If you also ask what can induce you to do that action which I call virtuous rather than the other, I reply that I do not know which out of the infinite ways that there are, God makes use of in order to determine you to such actions. It may be that God has impressed upon you a clear idea of Himself so that you forget the world for love of Him, and love the rest of mankind as yourself, and it is clear that such a constitution of mind is opposed to everything else which is called evil, and therefore they cannot exist in the same subject. But this is not the place to explain the fundamentals of Ethics, or to prove all that I say, for my present object is simply to answer your objections and to defend myself against them.

Lastly as regards your third question, it supposes

a contradiction, and is just as if somebody asked me if it accorded better with the nature of some one that he should hang himself, would there be any reasons why he should not hang himself? However, suppose it is possible that there is such a nature. Then I say (whether I admit the freedom of the will or not) that if someone sees that he can live better on the gallows than at his own table, he would act most foolishly if he did not go and hang himself. And he who saw clearly that he would in fact enjoy a more perfect or better life or essence by pursuing crimes rather than by following virtue, would also be a fool if he did not pursue them. For in relation to such a perverted human nature crimes would be virtuous.

As to your other question, which you added at the end of your letter, since one could ask an hundred such questions in an hour without arriving at any conclusion about anything, and since you yourself do not press for an answer I will leave it unanswered.

And for the present I will only say that I shall expect you about the time which you appointed with me, and that you will be very welcome. But I should like it to be soon, because I already intend to go to Amsterdam for a week or two. In the meantime, I remain, with cordial greetings,

Your devoted Servant,

B. DE SPINOZA.

VOORBURGH, 13 *March* 1665.

LETTER XXIV   WILLIAM VAN BLYENBERGH

To THE VERY ILLUSTRIOUS MR. B. D. S.

Reply to the Preceding.

SIR AND FRIEND,

When I had the honour of visiting you, time did not permit me to stay longer with you, still less did my memory enable me to retain what was discussed, although, as soon as I had left you, I mustered all my thoughts in order to be able to retain what I had heard. For that purpose, when I reached my next stopping-place, I endeavoured by myself to commit your opinions to paper, but found then that I had not in fact retained even a quarter of our discussions. And therefore you must excuse me, if I weary you once more by asking you something about things concerning which I did not clearly understand your views, or did not retain them well. I wish I could repay you for your trouble by doing you some service. They were these :

First, whenever I read your *Principles and Metaphysical Thoughts* how can I distinguish between what you state according to the views of Descartes and what is stated in accordance with your own views ?

Secondly, is there really such a thing as error, and in what does it consist ?

Thirdly, why do you state that the will is not free ?

Fourthly, why do you let Meyer say in the Preface *that you admit indeed that there exists in Nature a thinking substance ; but yet deny that this constitutes the essence of the human soul ; but think that just in the same way as extension is infinite, so thought also is not finite, and therefore just as the human body is not absolute but is only a finite part of extension existing in a certain way, according to the laws of extended nature through motion and rest, so also the human soul is not absolute, but only a finite part of thought determined in a certain way by ideas, in accordance with the laws of thinking nature, and it is concluded that it must exist as soon as the human body begins to be real.* From these words it seems to me to follow that just as the human body is composed of thousands of small bodies, so also the human spirit is composed of thousands of thoughts : and just as the human body, when it breaks up, returns and is again resolved into the thousands of bodies, of which it was composed, so also our spirit when it leaves the body is resolved into the manifold thoughts of which it is composed. And just as the separated bodies of our human Body do not remain united with each other, but other bodies come between them, so also it seems to follow, that when our spirit breaks up, the innumerable thoughts of which it was composed, are no longer united but separated. And just as our bodies when they disintegrate remain indeed bodies but not human bodies, so also after death our thinking substance is so disintegrated that our thoughts or thinking substances remain, but their essence is not the same as when they were called a human spirit. Hence it continues to appear to me as though you stated that man's thinking substance is changed and is dissolved like corporeal substance, indeed that some even, as you (if I remember rightly) stated of the wicked, are entirely annihilated, and retain no thought whatever. And as Descartes, according to Meyer's statement, only supposes that the soul is an absolutely thinking substance, so it seems to me that both you and Meyer are only making suppositions for the most part. Therefore I do not clearly grasp your meaning in these things.

Fifthly, you stated, both in our conversation and in your last letter of the 13th March, that from our clear knowledge of God and of ourselves there arises our steadfast desire that each should continue to possess his own. But you have still to explain in what way the knowledge of God and of ourselves makes us have a steadfast desire that each should possess his own, that is, in what way the knowledge of God induces or obliges us to love virtue and to avoid those actions which we call wicked, and whence it comes about (since according to your statement, murder and theft contain something positive, just as alms-giving does) that killing does not include as much perfection, blessedness and happiness as does alms-giving. But should you perchance say, as you say in your last letter of the 13th March, that this question belongs to the *Ethics* and that it is discussed there by you, then, indeed, since without an explanation of this question and of the preceding questions I am unable to understand your meaning clearly, and am left with absurdities which I cannot reconcile, I would ask you kindly to give me a fuller answer to them and especially to state some of your principal Definitions, Postulates and Axioms on which your *Ethics*, and especially this question, is based. Perhaps the trouble will alarm you, and you will excuse yourself, but I beseech you to satisfy my request this time, since without the solution of this last question I shall never be able to understand your real meaning. I wish I could offer you some recompense for your service. I dare not limit you to one or two weeks, I only beg you to let me have your answer here before your departure to Amsterdam. By doing so you will put me under the greatest obligation, and I shall show that I am and remain, Sir,

Your most devoted servant,
WILLIAM VAN BLYENBERGH.

DORDRECHT, 27 *March* 1665.

To MR. BENEDICTUS DE SPINOZA,
    Staying in Voorburgh.

Per couverto.

LETTER XXV   HENRY OLDENBURG

TO THE VERY ILLUSTRIOUS MR. B. D. S.

VERY ILLUSTRIOUS SIR AND MY DEAREST FRIEND,
    I rejoiced greatly when I understood from recent letters of Mr. Serrarius that you are alive and well and remember your Oldenburg. But at the same time I strongly blamed my fortune (if it is right to use such a

word) which has brought it about that for a space of so many months I have been deprived of that very pleasant intercourse with you which I enjoyed before. I must blame the great number of my affairs, as well as an excess of domestic calamities, for my very great devotion and loyal friendship for you will always stand on a firm footing, and endure unshaken. Mr. Boyle and I frequently speak of you, your learning and your profound reflections. We should like the fruit of your mind to be brought forth and entrusted to the care of learned men, and we are confident that you will fulfil our expectation in this matter.

There is no reason for printing Mr. Boyle's discussion on Nitre, and on Firmness and Fluidity in your country: for it has already been printed in Latin here, only there is no opportunity of transmitting copies to you. I pray you, therefore, not to allow any printer in your country to attempt such a thing. Boyle, too, has published an excellent Treatise on Colours, both in English and in Latin, and also an Experimental Account of Cold, of Thermometers, etc., wherein there are many excellent things, many new things. Nothing but this unfortunate war prevents the transmission of the books to you. There has appeared also a certain excellent Treatise on Sixty Observations with the Microscope, wherein many things are asserted boldly, but Philosophically (indeed, according to Mechanical Principles). I hope that our Booksellers will find a way of despatching copies of all these to your country. I long to receive from your own hand what you have done recently, or what you have now in hand. I am

Your most devoted and affectionate

HENRY OLDENBURG.

LONDON, 28 *April* 1665.

LETTER XXVI   B. D. S.

To the Very Noble and Learned
MR. HENRY OLDENBURG.

[*Reply to the Preceding.*]

MOST HONOURABLE FRIEND,

A few days ago a certain friend of mine said he had been given your letter of the 28th of April by an Amsterdam Bookseller, who doubtless received it from Mr. Ser. I rejoiced greatly at length to be able to know from you yourself that you are well and as kindly disposed towards me as before. I, for my part, whenever opportunity arose, did not fail to ask Mr. Ser. and Christian Huygens, Z.D., who also told me that he knew you, about you and your health. From the same Mr. Huygens I also understood that the very learned Mr. Boyle is alive and has published in English that excellent Treatise on Colours, which he would lend me if I were versed in English. I rejoice therefore to know from you that this Treatise, together with the other on Cold and on Thermometers, of which I had not yet heard, have been presented with Latin citizenship, and endowed with civic rights. The book on the observations with the Microscope is also in the possession of Mr. Huygens, but unless I am mistaken it is in English. He has told me many wonderful things about these microscopes and also about certain Telescopes, constructed in Italy, with which they could observe eclipses in Jupiter caused by the interposition of his satellites, and also a certain shadow on Saturn, as if made by a ring. On the occasion of these things I cannot wonder sufficiently at the rashness of Descartes, who says that the reason why the Planets next to Saturn (for he thought that its projections were Planets, perhaps because he never saw them touch Saturn) do not move may be because Saturn does not rotate round its own axis. For this does not agree with his principles, and he could very easily have explained the cause of the projections from his principles, if he had not laboured under a prejudice, etc.

[VOORBURG, *May* 1665.]

LETTER XXVII

B. D. S.

To the Very Courteous and Honourable
Mr. WILLIAM VAN BLYENBERGH.

Reply to Letter XXIV.

SIR AND FRIEND,

When I received your letter of the 27th March, I was on the point of starting for Amsterdam, and therefore left it at home but half read, with the intention of answering it on my return; for I thought it only contained things relating to the first questions. But on reading it through afterwards I found its contents to be quite different, and that it asked not only for a proof of the things which I had caused to be stated in the Preface with the sole aim of making known to everybody my opinions and thoughts and not of proving or of explaining them, but also the proof of a large part of Ethics, which as everyone knows, must be based on Metaphysics and Physics. And therefore I could not persuade myself to satisfy the request, but I wished to have an opportunity of asking you orally and in the friendliest way to desist from your request, and then I would at the same time give you the reason for my refusal, and lastly show you that these things do not contribute anything to the solution of your first question, but that, on the contrary, these things for the most part depend on that question. So that it is far from true that my view regarding the necessity of things cannot be understood without the solution of these new questions, since the solution of these and what pertains thereto cannot be grasped without understanding first the necessity of things. For, as you know, the necessity of things touches Metaphysics, and the knowledge of this must always come first. But before I could get the desired opportunity I received this week yet another letter under cover from my host which seems to show some displeasure caused by the long delay, and which has therefore compelled me to write these few lines in order to express briefly my decision and intention, as I have now done. I hope that when you have considered the matter you will willingly desist from your request, and will nevertheless retain your kindly disposition towards me. I for my part will show, in all ways that I can and may, that I am

Your well-disposed Friend and Servant,

B. DE SPINOZA.

To Mr. WILLIAM VAN BLEYEN BERGH,
      GRAIN-BROKER,
         AT DORDRECHT,
    NEAR THE GREAT CHURCH.
Pt.
VOORBURG, 3 *June* 1665.

LETTER XXVIII   B. D. S.

To THE VERY LEARNED AND EXPERT
MR. JOHN BOUWMEESTER.

EXCELLENT FRIEND,

I do not know whether you have entirely forgotten me, but many things concur in suggesting the suspicion. First, when I was on the point of setting out for my journey I wished to say good-bye to you, and thought that, as you yourself had invited me, I should without doubt find you at home. I found you had gone to the Hague. I return to Voorburg nothing doubting but that you would at least visit me in passing. But, if it please the Gods, you have returned home, without having greeted your friend. Lastly, I have been waiting three weeks, and in all this time no letter from you has come into sight. If therefore you wish to remove this opinion of mine, you will do so easily by a letter from you, in which you will also be able to point out a way of arranging our intercourse by letter, of which we once talked in your house. Meanwhile I should like earnestly to ask you, or rather I pray and beseech you by our friendship, to be willing to prosecute some serious work with real eagerness, and to deign to devote the better part of your life to the cultivation of your understanding and your soul. I say this while there is yet time, and before you complain that time or rather you had slipped away.

Moreover, in order to say about our projected correspondence something which may encourage you to write more freely to me, you must know that I have before now suspected, and I am almost certain, that you are rather diffident about your abilities, more indeed than is right, and that you are afraid that you may ask, or assert, something which may not savour of a learned man. But it does not become me to praise you to your face, and to enumerate your endowments. If, however, you are afraid lest I should communicate your letters to others, to whom you might then become a laughing-stock, on this point I give you my word that I will preserve them religiously, and that I will not communicate them to any mortal without your leave. On these conditions you can begin our correspondence, unless perchance you doubt my good faith, which I do not believe. I expect, however, to learn your opinion about this from your first letter. I also expect some of that conserve of red roses which you promised, although

I have for a long time now been better. After my departure from there I opened a vein once, but the fever did not cease (although I was rather more active than before the blood-letting, as I think, because of the change of air). But I have twice or three times been afflicted with the tertian fever, which, however, I have driven off at last with a good diet, and sent to the devil. I know not where it went, but I am taking care that it should not return.

As regards the third part of my philosophy, I will shortly send something of it to you, if you wish to be its translator, or to my friend de Vries. Although I had resolved to send nothing until I had completed it, yet since it is taking longer than I had expected, I do not wish to keep you waiting too long. I will send it to you up to about the eightieth proposition.

I hear much of English affairs, but nothing certain. The populace does not cease to apprehend all things evil, nor can any one find a reason why the fleet does not set sail. Indeed, the matter does not yet seem to be safe. I fear that our people wish to be too wise and far-seeing. But the course of events will itself show at last what they have in mind, and what they will attempt—may the Gods prosper it. I should like to hear what our people there think and what they know for certain, but more, and above all things, that you consider me, etc.

[VOORBURG, *June* 1665.]

LETTER XXIX   HENRY OLDENBURG

To the Very Illustrious Mr. B. d. S.

EXCELLENT SIR, MOST HONOURED FRIEND,

From your last letter, written to me on the 4th of September, it is clear that you have our affairs at heart, and not merely as a passing interest. You have laid under an obligation not only me, but also our most noble Boyle, who joins me in thanking you very much for this, and who will requite your kindness and affection when occasion offers, by every kind of service which can be rendered by him. You will also be able to persuade yourself firmly that the same thing is true of me. As regards that too officious man who, notwithstanding the version of the Treatise on Colours which has already been prepared here, nevertheless wished to provide another, perhaps he will realize that he has ill consulted his own interests by his preposterous eagerness. For what would happen to his Translation if the Author enlarged the Latin version, prepared here in England, with many experiments that are not found in the English version? Necessarily, our version, which is shortly to be distributed, must then be altogether preferable to his, and must be much more highly esteemed by sensible men. But let him revel in his own sense, if he likes ; we shall look after our own affairs as may seem to be most advisable.

Kircher's *Subterranean World* has not yet appeared in our English world on account of the plague, which hinders nearly all traffic. In addition there is this most dreadful war, which brings in its train a very Iliad of evils, and all but wipes out all human kindness from the world.

Meanwhile, however, although our Philosophical Society holds no public meetings in these times of danger, yet here and there its Fellows do not forget that they are such. Hence some are privately occupied with Experiments in Hydrostatics, others with Anatomical, others with Mechanical, and others with other experiments. Mr. Boyle has subjected to examination the problem of the origin of Forms and Qualities as it has been hitherto treated in the Schools and by teachers, and he has composed on this subject a treatise (no doubt excellent), which will shortly go to press.

I see that you are not so much philosophizing as, if I may say so, theologizing; for you are writing down your thoughts about Angels, prophecy and miracles. But perhaps you are doing this in a philosophical manner. However that may be, I am sure that the work is worthy of you, and especially desired by me. Since these very difficult times hinder freedom of intercourse, I ask you at least not to mind telling me in your next letter your plan and object in this work of yours.

Here we are daily expecting news of a second naval battle, unless perhaps your Fleet has again retired into port. The courage with which you hint that your men fight is brutish not human. For if men acted under the guidance of reason, they would not so rend one another in pieces, as is obvious to everybody. But why do I complain? There will be wickedness as long as there are men; but that is not unrelieved, and is counterbalanced by the intervention of better things.

While I am writing this, a letter is delivered which was written to me by that distinguished astronomer of Dantzig, Mr. John Hevelius. In this he tells me, among other things, that his *Cometography*, consisting of twelve books, has already been in the press for a whole year, and that four hundred pages, or the first nine books, are finished. He says, moreover, that he has sent me some copies of his *Prodromus Cometicus*, in which he has fully described the first of the two recent comets. But they have not yet come into my hands. He states, besides, that he is publishing another book on the second comet also, and is submitting it to the judgment of the learned.

What, I pray you, do your people think of the pendulums of Huygens, especially of that kind which is said to show the measure of time so exactly that it can be used for finding out longitudes at sea? Also what is happening about his Dioptrics, and his Treatise on

Motion, both of which we have been expecting for a long time already. I am sure that he is not idle; I only wish to know what he is working at.

Farewell, and continue to love

Your most devoted

H. O.

[LONDON, *September* 1665.]

To MR. BENEDICTUS SPINOSA,
IN THE BAGGYNE STREET
IN THE HOUSE OF MR. DANIEL, PAINTER,
IN ADAM AND EVE
AT THE HAGUE.

LETTER XXX   B. D. S.

TO THE VERY NOBLE AND LEARNED
MR. HENRY OLDENBURG.

Reply to the Preceding.

. . . I rejoice that your philosophers are alive and remember themselves and their republic. I shall expect news of what they have done recently, when the warriors are sated with blood, and rest in order to renew their strength a little. If that famous scoffer were alive to-day, he would surely die of laughter. These disorders, however, do not move me to laughter nor even to tears, but rather to philosophizing, and to the better observation of human nature. I do not think it right for me to laugh at nature, much less to weep over it, when I consider that men, like the rest, are only a part of nature, and that I do not know how each part of nature is connected with the whole of it, and how with the other parts. And I find that it is from the mere want of this kind of knowledge that certain things in Nature were formerly wont to appear to me vain, disorderly, and absurd, because I perceive them only in part and mutilated, and they do not agree with our philosophic mind. But now I let every man live according to his own ideas. Let those who will, by all means die for their good, so long as I am allowed to live for the truth.

I am now writing a Treatise about my interpretation of Scripture. This I am driven to do by the following reasons : 1. The Prejudices of the Theologians ; for I know that these are among the chief obstacles which prevent men from directing their mind to philosophy ; and therefore I do all I can to expose them, and to remove them from the minds of the more prudent. 2. The opinion which the common people have of me, who do not cease to accuse me falsely of atheism ; I am also obliged to avert this accusation as far as it is possible to do so. 3. The freedom of philosophizing, and of saying what we think ; this I desire to vindicate in every way, for here it is always suppressed through the excessive authority and impudence of the preachers.

I have not yet heard that any Cartesian explains the phenomena of the recent comets on Descartes' hypothesis ; and I doubt whether they can rightly be thus explained. . . .

[VOORBURG, *September or October* 1665.]

LETTER XXXI   HENRY OLDENBURG

To the Very Illustrious Mr. B. d. S.

[*Reply to the Preceding.*]

MOST EXCELLENT SIR, HONOURED FRIEND,

You act as befits a wise man and a philosopher, you love good men. And there is nothing to make you doubt that they love you in return and esteem your merits as they should. Mr. Boyle joins with me in sending you hearty greeting, and urges you to go on with your philosophy strenuously and thoroughly. Especially do we warmly beseech you to communicate it to us, if you see any light on that most difficult investigation, which turns on the question of our knowing how each part of Nature accords with the whole of it, and in what way it is connected with all the other parts.

I entirely approve the reasons which you mention as inducements to write your Treatise on Scripture, and I desperately wish already to see your thoughts on that subject with my own eyes. Mr. Serrarius may perhaps shortly send me a small parcel. To him, if you think fit, you may safely entrust what you have already written on this subject, and you may also be sure of our readiness to render services in return.

I have read part of Kircher's *Subterranean World*, and although his reasoning and theories do not evidence a great mind, yet the Observations and Experiments which are given to us in it speak well for the author's diligence, and his desire to deserve well of the Republic of Philosophers. You see therefore that I attribute to him a little more than piety, and you will easily discern the mind of those who sprinkle him with this Holy Water.

When you mention the Treatise on Motion by Huygens, you intimate that Descartes' Laws of Motion are nearly all false. I have not now at hand the little book which you published some time ago on the *Principles of Descartes, proved Geometrically*. I do not recall whether in this you showed that error, or whether you followed Descartes closely for the sake of others. I wish that at length you would bring forth the fruits of your own thought, and entrust them to the philosophical world to cherish and to foster. I remember that you pointed out somewhere that many of the things which Descartes himself said were beyond human comprehension, nay even others more sublime and subtle, can be clearly understood by men and be most clearly explained. Why do you hesitate, my Friend, what do you fear?

Make the attempt, go forward, accomplish this most important task, and you will see that the whole chorus of real Philosophers will defend you. I venture to pledge my word, which I would not do if I doubted my power to redeem it. I cannot believe at all that you entertain the thought of attempting anything against the Existence and Providence of God, and so long as these supports are intact Religion stands on a firm basis, and all Philosophical Reflections can easily be either defended or excused. Therefore make an end of delays, and suffer not your cloak to be rent.

I think you will shortly hear what there is to say about the recent comets. Hevelius of Dantzig and the Frenchman Auzout, both learned men and Mathematicians, are disputing among themselves about the Observations which were made. The controversy is being considered at present, and when the dispute is decided, the whole affair will, I believe, be communicated to me, and by me to you. This much I can already say, that all the Astronomers, at least those who are known to me, hold the view that there were not one but two comets, and that I have not so far met anyone who has tried to explain their Phenomena by means of the Cartesian Hypothesis.

I pray you, if you receive any further news of the studies and doings of Mr. Huygens and of the success of his pendulums in the matter of ascertaining longitude, and of his removing to France, not to mind letting me know as soon as possible. Add, too, I pray you, what is said in your country about the Negotiation of peace, about the plans of the Swedish army which has been sent against Germany, and the progress of the Bishop of Munster. I believe that the whole of Europe will be involved in wars next summer, and all things seem to tend towards an unusual change.

Let us serve the highest Divinity with a pure mind,

and cultivate a Philosophy which is true, sound and useful. Some of our Philosophers who followed the King to Oxford hold frequent meetings there, and are concerned in promoting Physical studies. Among other things they have recently begun to inquire into the nature of sounds. I believe they will make experiments to discover in what proportion weights must be increased to stretch a chord, without the aid of any other force, so that it may be applied to produce the next higher note which makes a certain consonance with the previous sound. More about this another time.

Farewell and remember your most devoted

HENRY OLDENBURG.

LONDON, 12 *October* 1665.

LETTER XXXII   B. D. S.

TO THE VERY NOBLE AND LEARNED
MR. HENRY OLDENBURG.

Reply to the Preceding.

MOST NOBLE SIR,

I thank you and the very Noble Mr. Boyle very much for kindly encouraging me to go on with my Philosophy. I do indeed proceed with it, as far as my slender powers allow, not doubting meanwhile of your help and goodwill.

When you ask me what I think about the question which turns on *the Knowledge how each part of Nature accords with the whole of it, and in what way it is connected with the other parts*, I think you mean to ask for the reasons on the strength of which we believe that each part of Nature accords with the whole of it, and is connected with the other parts. For I said in my preceding letter that I do not know how the parts are really interconnected, and how each part accords with the whole;

for to know this it would be necessary to know the whole of Nature and all its Parts.

I shall therefore try to show the reason which compels me to make this assertion; but I should like first to warn you that I do not attribute to Nature beauty or ugliness, order or confusion. For things cannot, except with respect to our imagination, be called beautiful, or ugly, ordered or confused.

By connection of the parts, then, I mean nothing else than that the laws, or nature, of one part adapt themselves to the laws, or nature, of another part in such a way as to produce the least possible opposition. With regard to whole and parts, I consider things as parts of some whole, in so far as their natures are mutually adapted so that they are in accord among themselves, as far as possible; but in so far as things differ among themselves, each produces an idea in our mind, which is distinct from the others, and is therefore considered to be a whole, not a part. For instance, since the motions of the particles of lymph, chyle, etc., are so mutually adapted in respect of magnitude and figure that they clearly agree among themselves, and all together constitute one fluid, to that extent only, chyle, lymph, etc., are considered to be parts of the blood: but in so far as we conceive the lymph particles as differing in respect of figure and motion from the particles of chyle, to that extent we consider them to be a whole, not a part.

Let us now, if you please, imagine that a small worm lives in the blood, whose sight is keen enough to distinguish the particles of blood, lymph, etc., and his reason to observe how each part on collision with another either rebounds, or communicates a part of its own motion, etc. That worm would live in this blood as we live in this part of the universe, and he would consider each particle of blood to be a whole, and not a part. And he could not know how all the parts are controlled by the universal nature of blood, and are forced, as the universal nature of blood demands, to adapt themselves to one another, so as to harmonize with one another in a certain way. For if we imagine that there are no causes outside the blood to communicate new motions to the blood, and that outside the blood there is no space, and no other bodies, to which the particles of blood could transfer their motion, it is certain that the blood would remain always in its state, and its particles would suffer no changes other than those which can be conceived from the given relation of the motion of the blood to the lymph and chyle, etc., and so blood would have to be considered always to be a whole and not a part. But, since there are very many other causes which in a certain way control the laws of the nature of blood, and are in turn controlled by the blood, hence it comes about that other motions and other changes take place in the blood, which result not only from the mere relation of the motion of its parts to one another, but from the relation of the motion of the blood and also of the external causes to one another : in this way the blood has the character of a part and not of a whole. I have only spoken of whole and part.

Now, all the bodies of nature can and should be conceived in the same way as we have here conceived the blood : for all bodies are surrounded by others, and are mutually determined to exist and to act in a definite and determined manner, while there is preserved in all together, that is, in the whole universe, the same proportion of motion and rest. Hence it follows that every body, in so far as it exists modified in a certain way, must be considered to be a part of the whole universe, to be in accord with the whole of it, and to be connected with the other parts. And since the nature of the universe is not limited, like the nature of the blood, but absolutely infinite, its parts are controlled by the nature of this infinite power in infinite ways, and are compelled to suffer infinite changes. But I conceive that with regard to substance each part has a closer union with its whole. For as I endeavoured to show in my first letter, which I wrote to you when I was still living at Rhynsburg, since it is of the nature of substance to be infinite, it follows that each part belongs to the nature of corporeal substance, and can neither exist nor be conceived without it.

You see, then, in what way and why I think that the human Body is a part of Nature. As regards the human Mind I think it too is a part of Nature : since I state that there exists in Nature an infinite power of thought, which in so far as it is infinite, contains in itself subjectively the whole of Nature, and its thoughts proceed in the same way as Nature, which, to be sure, is its ideatum.

Then I declare that the human mind is this same power, not in so far as it is infinite, and perceives the whole of Nature, but in so far as it is finite and perceives only the human Body, and in this way I declare that the human Mind is a part of a certain infinite intellect.

But it would be too long a business accurately to explain and prove here all these things, and all that is connected with them, and I do not think that you expect me to do so at the moment. Indeed I am not sure that I have rightly understood your meaning, and so have not answered something different from what you asked. This I should like to find out from you.

As to your next remark, that I hinted that the Cartesian Laws of motion are nearly all false, if I remember rightly, I said that Mr. Huygens thinks so. Nor did I say that any law is false except the sixth Law of Descartes, and even about that I said that I think Huygens too is mistaken. On that occasion I begged you to communicate to me the experiment which you have tried according to this hypothesis in your Royal Society. But I gather that you are not allowed to do so, since you give me no answer on that point.

The said Huygens was, and is still, fully occupied in polishing dioptrical glasses. For this purpose he has constructed a machine, in which he can turn tools, and it is indeed sufficiently neat. But I do not yet know what advance he has made thereby, nor, to confess the truth, do I greatly desire to know. For experience has taught me sufficiently that in spherical tools it is safer and better for glasses to be polished with a free hand than by any machine. Of the success of his pendulums, and the date of his moving to France I cannot as yet write anything certain.

The Bishop of Munster after having foolishly entered Frisia, like Aesop's goat entered the well, has made no progress. Indeed, unless the winter begins very early he will not leave Frisia except with great loss. There is no doubt that he dared to attempt this adventure through the persuasions of some traitor or other. But these things are too old to be written as news, and nothing new has happened in this week or two that is worth writing about. There appears no hope of peace with the English. A rumour, however, has lately been spread because of the conjectured significance of a Dutch ambassador having been sent to France, and also because of the people of Overijsel, who are doing their utmost to introduce the Prince of Orange, in order, as many think, to inconvenience the Dutch rather than to benefit themselves, and have dreamed of a plan of sending the said prince to England as a mediator. But the matter is clearly different. The Dutch at present do not think of peace even in their dream, unless matters come to the point where they can buy peace. There is still some doubt about the plans of the Swede. Many think that he is trying for Mainz, others for the Dutch. But these are no more than conjectures.

I wrote this letter last week. But I could not send it, because the wind prevented my going to the Hague. That is the disadvantage of living in the country. It is but rarely that I receive a letter when it is due, for unless there is by chance an opportunity of sending it here at the time, then a week or two passes before I receive it. Then not infrequently there is a difficulty about my being able to send it in due time. Therefore when you see that I do not answer you as promptly as I should, you must not think that this is due to my forgetting you. Meanwhile time urges me to bring this to an end. Of the rest on another occasion. Now I can say no more than that I ask you to give a hearty greeting from me to the very Noble Mr. Boyle, and to remember me who am

In all affection yours

B. DE SPINOZA.

VOORBURG, 20 *November* 1665.

I desire to know whether all astronomers think that there were two comets on the ground of their motion or only in order to maintain Kepler's hypothesis. Farewell.

> *To* MR. HENRY OLDENBURG,
> SECRETARY OF THE ROYAL SOCIETY,
> IN THE PALL MALL,
> IN ST. JAMES'S FIELDS,
> IN LONDON.

LETTER XXXIII HENRY OLDENBURG

TO THE VERY ILLUSTRIOUS MR. B. D. S.

[*Reply to the Preceding.*]

MOST DISTINGUISHED SIR, MUCH HONOURED FRIEND,
Your philosophic reflections on the agreement and connection of the parts of Nature with the whole

give me much pleasure, although I do not follow sufficiently how we can exclude order and symmetry from Nature, as you seem to do; especially as you yourself admit that all its bodies are surrounded by others, and are mutually determined in a definite and constant manner both as to their existence and their action, while the same proportion of motion to rest is always conserved in all things, which seems to me to be itself the sufficient ground of a true order. But perhaps in this I do not understand you sufficiently, any more than I did with regard to what you had written before about the Laws of Descartes. Would that you would undertake the trouble of teaching me wherein you think that both Descartes and Huygens were mistaken about the laws of motion. By doing me this service you would make me very thankful, and with all my might I would strive to deserve well of you.

I was not present when Mr. Huygens performed here in London the Experiments confirming his Hypothesis. I have learned since then that, among other experiments, he suspended a ball, weighing one pound, after the manner of a pendulum, which, when it was released, struck another ball, suspended in the same way but weighing only half a pound, from an angle of forty degrees, that Huygens, by means of a very brief Algebraical Calculation had predicted the effect and that this answered exactly to the prediction. A certain distinguished man who has proposed many such experiments which Huygens is said to have solved, is away. As soon as I am able to meet this man who is now away I will perhaps explain the matter to you more fully and more exactly. Meanwhile I pray you again and again not to decline the above request of mine, and moreover not to mind communicating to me also anything you may have learnt about the success of Huygens in the polishing of Telescopic Glasses. I hope, now that, by the grace of God, the plague is noticeably less violent, our Royal Society will shortly return to London, and resume its weekly meetings. You may be sure that I shall communicate to you any of its proceedings that are worth knowing.

I have mentioned before some Anatomical Observations. Mr. Boyle (who greets you very kindly) wrote to me not so long ago, that certain distinguished Anatomists at Oxford had assured him that they had found the windpipe both of sheep and of oxen filled with grass; and that a few weeks ago the said Anatomists had been invited to look at an ox, which for two or three days had held its neck almost continually stiff and straight up, and had died of a disease quite unknown to its owners. When the parts connected with the neck and throat were dissected, they found to their surprise that its windpipe right inside the very trunk was almost entirely filled with grass, as if someone had rammed it in by force. This furnished a suitable cause for inquiring both how such a great quantity of grass got there, and how, when it was there, the animal could survive for such a long time?

Moreover, the same friend informed me that a certain inquiring Doctor, also of Oxford, had found milk in human blood. He relates about a girl who had had rather a large breakfast at seven in the morning and whose foot was bled at eleven on the same day. The first blood was collected in a dish and after a short interval of time took on a white colour. But the subsequent blood flowed into a smaller vessel which, unless I am mistaken, they call *acetabulum* (in English, a sawcer), and this blood immediately took the form of a cake of milk. Five or six hours later the Doctor returned and inspected both lots of blood. That which was in the dish was half blood, but half chyleform, and this chyle floated in the blood as whey in milk. But the blood which was collected in the saucer was all chyle, without any appearance of blood. When he heated each of the two over the fire separately, both liquids grew hard. The girl, however, was quite well, and was only bled because she had never had her monthly courses although she was well and had a good colour.

But I turn to Politics. Here there is a rumour in everybody's mouth that the Jews, who have been dispersed for more than two thousand years, are to return to their country. Few in this place believe it, but many wish it. You will tell your friend what you hear and think about this matter. For my part I cannot put any confidence in this News so long as it is not reported by trustworthy men from the City of Constantinople, which is concerned in this most of all. I should like to know what the Jews in Amsterdam have heard about the matter, and how they are affected by such an important announcement, which if it were true would seem to bring a crisis on the whole world.

There appears as yet no hope of Peace between England and the Netherlands.

Explain to me, if you can, what the Swede and the Brandenburger are driving at ; and believe me to be

Your most devoted

HENRY OLDENBURG.

LONDON, *8th December* 1665.

P.S.—I will shortly tell you, God willing, what our philosophers think about the recent comets.

LETTER XXXIV   B. D. S.

To the Highly Esteemed and Prudent
Mr. JOHN HUDDE.

MOST ESTEEMED SIR,

The proof of the Unity of God on the ground that His nature involves necessary existence, for which you asked and which I undertook to give, I have been unable to send before this, on account of certain preoccupations. In order to do so I will suppose

I. That the true definition of each thing includes nothing but the simple nature of the thing defined. Hence it follows

II. That no definition involves or expresses a multitude or a definite number of individuals; since it involves and expresses nothing else than the nature of the thing as it is in itself. For instance the definition of a triangle includes nothing else than the simple nature of a triangle, but not a definite number of triangles; just as the definition of Mind, that it is a thinking thing, or the definition of God, that He is a perfect Being, includes nothing else than the nature of Mind and of God; but not a definite number of Minds or of Gods.

III. That of each existing thing there must necessarily be a positive cause through which it exists.

IV. That this cause must be placed either in the nature and the definition of the thing itself (namely because existence belongs to its nature, or this necessarily includes it) or outside the thing.

From these presuppositions it follows that if there exists in Nature a definite number of individuals, there must be one or more causes which could produce just that number of individuals, no greater and no less. If, for instance, there exist in Nature twenty men (in order to avoid confusion I shall suppose them all to exist at the same time and to be the first men to exist in Nature), then in order to give the reason why there exist twenty men, it is not enough to investigate the cause of human nature in general; but we must also investigate the reason why there are no more and no less than twenty men in existence. For (according to the third supposition) a reason and cause must be assigned for the existence of every man. But this cause (according to the second and third supposition) cannot be contained in the nature of man himself: for the true definition of man does not involve the number of twenty men. And so (according to my fourth supposition) the cause of the existence of these twenty men, and therefore of the existence of each individually, must be found outside them. Hence we must absolutely conclude that all things which are conceived as existing many in number are necessarily produced by external causes and not by the force of their own nature. But since (according to supposition) necessary existence belongs to the nature of God, it is necessary that His true definition should also include necessary existence: and therefore His necessary existence must be inferred from the true definition of Him. But from the true definition of Him (as I have already proved before from my second and third supposition) the necessary existence of many Gods cannot be inferred. There follows, therefore, the existence of one God only. This is what was to be proved.

This, most esteemed Sir, seems to me now the best method of proving the proposition. Formerly I proved the same proposition otherwise, by applying the distinction between Essence and Existence; but considering what you pointed out to me, I preferred to send you this proof. I hope it will satisfy you, and I shall await your judgment on it, and meanwhile remain, etc.

VOORBURG, *7th January* 1666.

LETTER XXXV   B. D. S.

To the Highly Esteemed and Prudent
Mr. JOHN HUDDE.

Most esteemed Sir,

In your last letter, written on the 30th of March, you have made quite clear what was somewhat obscure to me in the letter you wrote to me on the 10th of February. Since, then, I now know what you really think, I will put the question in the form in which you conceive it, that is, whether there can only be one Being which subsists in virtue of its own sufficiency or force. I not only affirm this, but also undertake to prove it, namely, from the fact that its nature involves necessary existence. This can be most easily proved from the understanding of God (as I explained in Proposition XI of my *Geometrical Proofs of the Principles of Descartes*), or it can be proved from the other attributes of God. In order, then, to attack this problem, let me first briefly point out what properties must be possessed by a Being that includes necessary existence. These are—

I. It must be eternal : for if a limited duration were attributed to it, then that Being would be conceived as not existing, or as not involving necessary existence, beyond that limited duration. This is inconsistent with its definition.

II. It must be simple, not composed of parts. For in Nature and in our knowledge the component parts of a thing must be prior to that which is composed of them. This is out of place in that which is by its own nature eternal.

III. It cannot be conceived as limited, but only as infinite. For if the nature of this Being were limited, and were also conceived as limited, then beyond those limits that nature would be conceived as non-existent. This again is inconsistent with its definition.

IV. It must be indivisible. For if it were divisible it could be divided into parts either of the same or of a different nature. In the latter case it could be destroyed, and so not exist. This is contrary to the definition. In the former case, each part would contain necessary existence in itself, and thus one part could exist and consequently be conceived apart from another, and therefore that Nature could be understood as finite. This according to the foregoing is contrary to the definition. Hence we may see that if we want to ascribe any imperfection to a Being of this kind, we immediately fall into contradiction. For whether the imperfection which we want to impute to such a Nature consists in some defect, or in certain limitations which a nature of this kind is alleged to possess, or in some change which through lack of strength, it could suffer from external causes, we are always brought back to this, that this Nature, which involves necessary existence, does not exist, or does not exist necessarily. And therefore I conclude,

V. That everything which includes necessary existence can have in itself no imperfection, but must express pure perfection.

VI. Moreover, since it can only be the result of perfection that a Being should exist by its own sufficiency and power, it follows that if we suppose a Being which does not express all perfections to exist by its own nature, then we must also suppose that there exists also that Being which does include in itself all perfections. For if a Being which is endowed with less power exists through its own sufficiency, how much more must that exist which is endowed with the greater power.

Lastly, to come to our problem, I assert that there can only be one Being whose existence belongs to its nature, that is, that Being only which possesses all perfections in itself, and which I shall call God. For if there be assumed a Being to whose nature existence belongs, that Being must contain no imperfection, but (according to note 5) must express every perfection. And therefore the nature of that Being must belong to God (whom, according to note 6, we must also assert to exist), since He possesses in Himself all perfections and no imperfections. And it cannot exist outside God. For if it were to exist outside God, one and the same Nature, which involves necessary existence, would exist as two, which, according to our previous proof, is absurd. Therefore nothing outside God, but God alone, involves necessary existence. This is what was to be proved.

These, most esteemed Sir, are the things which I can at present contribute towards the proof of this matter. I should like to be able to prove also that I am, etc.

B. D. S.

VOORBURG, 10th April 1666.

LETTER XXXVI
B. D. S.

To the Very Honourable and Prudent
Mr. JOHN HUDDE.

MOST HONOURABLE SIR,

I was unable (on account of some obstacle) to reply sooner to your letter written on the nineteenth of May. But since I observe that for the most part you suspend your judgment about my proof which I sent you (I believe on account of the obscurity which you find in it), I will endeavour here to explain its meaning more clearly.

First, then, I enumerated four properties which a Being, existing in virtue of its own sufficiency or force, must possess. These four and the remaining similar properties I reduced to one in the fifth note. Then, in order to deduce all that was necessary for my proof from the single supposition, I endeavoured in the sixth note to prove the existence of God from the given supposition ; and thence, lastly, assuming nothing more to be known than the simple meaning of the words, I came to the conclusion which was sought.

This, briefly, was my intention, this was my aim. Now I will explain the meaning of each link separately, and first I will begin with the assumed properties.

In the first you will find no difficulty. It, as also the second, is nothing else than an Axiom. For by simple I mean no more than that it is not composite or composed of parts which are different by nature, or of others which agree in their nature. The proof is certainly universal.

You have very well understood the meaning of the third (namely, to this purport, that if the Being is Thought it cannot be conceived as limited in Thought, if the Being is Extension, it cannot be conceived as limited in Extension, but only as unlimited). You say however that you do not understand the conclusion based on this, that it is a contradiction to conceive under the negation of existence something whose definition includes existence, or (what is the same thing) affirms existence. And since *limited* denotes nothing positive, but only privation of the existence of the same nature which is conceived as limited, it follows that that the definition of which affirms existence, cannot be conceived as limited. For instance, if the term *extension* includes necessary existence, it will be just as impossible to conceive extension without existence, as extension without extension. If this is granted it will also be impossible to conceive limited extension. For if it is conceived as limited it must be limited by its own nature, that is, by extension; and this extension, by which it would be limited, would have to be conceived under the negation of existence. This, according to supposition, is a manifest contradiction.

In the fourth I wished only to show that such a Being cannot be divided into parts of the same nature or into parts of a different nature, whether those which are of a different nature involve necessary existence, or not. For, I said, if the latter were the case, it could be destroyed, since to destroy a thing is to resolve it into such parts that none of them expresses the nature of the whole;

but if the former were the case, it would be inconsistent with the three properties already formulated.

In the fifth I only presupposed that perfection consists in being, and imperfection in the privation of being. I say *privation* ; for although, for instance, extension negates thought of itself, this in itself is no imperfection in it. But it would argue imperfection in it, if it were to be deprived of extension, as would actually happen if it were limited, similarly if it lacked duration, position, etc.

You entirely admit the sixth : and yet you say your difficulty remains untouched (the difficulty, namely, why there cannot be several beings, existing through themselves, but differing in nature, just as thought and extension are different and can perhaps subsist through their own sufficiency). From this I can only judge that you have understood it in a very different sense from me. I am sure that I see in what sense you understand it, but in order not to lose any time, I will only explain my own meaning. I say, then, with regard to the sixth, that if we assume that something which is only unlimited and perfect of its kind exists by its own sufficiency, then we must also admit the existence of a being that is absolutely unlimited and perfect ; which Being I shall call God. For if, for instance, we wish to assert that extension, or thought (which can be perfect each in its own kind, that is, in a certain kind of being) exist by their own sufficiency, we shall also have to admit the existence of God, who is absolutely perfect, that is, the existence of an absolutely unlimited being.

Here I would have you note what I have just said with regard to the word *imperfection*, namely, that this means that a thing lacks something which nevertheless belongs to its nature. For instance, Extension can only be said to be imperfect in respect of duration, position, or quantity, namely, because it does not last longer, or does not retain its position, or is not greater. But it can never be said to be imperfect because it does not think, since nothing of this kind is required by its nature, which consists only in extension, that is, in a certain kind of being, in respect of which alone it can be said to be limited or unlimited, imperfect or perfect. And since the nature of God does not consist of a certain kind of being but of absolutely unlimited being, His nature also requires all that perfectly expresses *being*; otherwise His nature would be limited and deficient. This being so, it follows that there can only exist one Being, namely God, which exists by its own force. For if, for example, we assume that extension involves existence, so that it is eternal and unlimited, it is also necessary that it should express absolutely no imperfection but only perfection : and so Extension will belong to God, or will be something which in some way expresses the nature of God, since God is a Being that is not only in a certain respect but absolutely unlimited in essence, and omnipotent. And this which is said of Extension (by way of an arbitrary illustration) will also have to be asserted of everything that we may want to set up as having such a nature. I conclude, therefore, as in my former letter, that nothing besides God, but only God, subsists by His own sufficiency. I believe that this is enough to explain the meaning of my former letter, but of this you will be the better judge.

With these words I might end : but since I have a mind to get new tools made for me for polishing glasses, I should like to hear your advice on the matter. I do not see what advantage we obtain by polishing convex-concave glasses. On the contrary, convex-plane lenses must be more useful, if I have made the calculation correctly. For if (for convenience) we put the ratio of refraction at 3 to 2, and in the accompanying figure append letters as you put them in your small Dioptrics, it will be found from the prescribed equation that N I or, as it is called, $z = \sqrt{\frac{9}{4}zz - xx} - \sqrt{1 - xx}$. Whence it follows that if $x = 0$, z will $= 2$, which will then also be the longest. And if $x = \frac{3}{5}$, z will $= \frac{43}{25}$, or a little more; that is, if we suppose that the ray B I does not suffer a second refraction when it turns from the glass towards I. But let us now suppose that this ray on issuing from the glass is refracted at the plane surface B F and that it turns, not towards I, but towards R. When therefore the lines B I and B R are in the same ratio as the refraction, that is (as was here supposed) of 3 to 2, and if we then follow the trend of the equation, we get $N R = \sqrt{zz - xx} - \sqrt{1 - xx}$. And if again, as before, we put $x = 0$, N R will $= 1$, that is, equal to half the diameter. But if $x = \frac{3}{5}$, N R will $= \frac{20}{25} + \frac{1}{50}$.

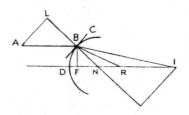

This shows that this focal length is smaller than the other, although the optic tube is less by a whole semi-diameter. So that if we were to make a Telescope as long as D I by making the semi-diameter $= 1\frac{1}{2}$, while the aperture B F remained the same, the focal length would be much less. Moreover, the reason why convex-concave glasses are less satisfactory is that, besides requiring double the labour and expense, the rays, since they are not all directed towards one and the same point, never fall perpendicularly on the concave surface. But as I have no doubt that you have already considered these things before now, and have invoked more accurate calculations, and have finally decided this very question, I ask your opinion and advice on this matter, etc.

[VOORBURG, *about June* 1666.]

LETTER XXXVII   B. D. S.

To the Very Learned and Expert
Mr. JOHN BOUWMEESTER.

Most learned Sir, excellent Friend,

I have been unable to answer sooner your last letter which I received long ago. I have been so hindered by various preoccupations and cares that I could scarcely free myself from them in the end. But, since I can collect my thoughts again to some extent, I do not want to fail in my duty, but wish as soon as possible to give you very many thanks for your love and devotion towards me, which you have very often shown by your actions, but to which you have now borne enough and more than enough witness in your letter, etc.

I now pass to your question which is as follows—*whether there is or can be such a Method that by means of it we can proceed safely and without weariness in the consideration of the most exalted subjects? or whether like our bodies, our minds also are subject to accidents, and our thoughts are governed more by chance than by art?* These questions I think I shall satisfy if I show that there must necessarily be a Method by which we can direct and concatenate our clear and distinct conceptions, and that the understanding is not, like the body, subject to accidents.

This, indeed, follows from this alone, that one clear and distinct conception, or several together, can absolutely be the cause of another clear and distinct conception. Nay, rather, all the clear and distinct conceptions which we form can only arise from other clear and distinct conceptions which are in us ; they acknowledge no other cause outside us. Whence it follows that whatever clear and distinct conceptions we form depend only on our nature and its definite and fixed laws, that is, on our absolute power, and not on chance that is, on causes which, though they also act according to definite and fixed laws, are unknown to us, and are foreign to our nature and power. As regards the other conceptions, I admit that they depend to the greatest extent possible upon chance. Therefore it seems clear what the true Method must be, and in what it especially consists, namely, only in the knowledge of the pure understanding, and of its nature and laws. In order to acquire this, we must first of all distinguish between understanding and imagination, or between true ideas and the rest, namely, the fictitious, the false, the doubtful, and absolutely all those which depend only on the memory. To understand this, at least as far as the Method requires, there is no need to know the nature of the mind through its first cause; it is enough to get together a short account of the mind or of conceptions in the way in which Verulam teaches.

I think I have in these few words explained and proved the true Method, and at the same time indicated the way by which we may attain to it. It remains, however, to warn you that for all these there are required incessant thought and a most constant mind and purpose. To gain these, it is first of all necessary to adopt a definite mode and plan of life, and to set before one a definite end. But enough of these things for the present, etc.

Farewell and love him who sincerely loves you,

BENED. DE SPINOSA.

VOORBURG, 10 *June* 1666.

LETTER XXXVIII   B. D. S.

TO THE VERY ILLUSTRIOUS MR. JOHN VAN DER MEER.

SIR,

While living in solitude here in the country I reflected on the question which you have proposed to me, and found that it was very simple. The Universal

Proof of it is based on this, that the fair player in a game of chance is he who makes his chance of winning or losing equal to that of his opponent. This equality * consists in the prospect and the money which the opponents stake and risk; that is, if the prospect is the same for both sides, then each must stake and risk the same amount of money; but if the prospects are unequal, then one player must stake and put in as much more money as his prospect is greater, and in this way the chances of both sides become equal, and the game will be a fair one. If, for example, A when playing with B, has two prospects of winning and only one of losing, while B, on the other hand, has only one prospect of winning and two of losing, it seems clear that A must risk as much for each prospect as B risks for his, that is, A must risk twice as much as B.

In order to show this still more clearly let us suppose that three persons, A, B, C, play together with equal chances, and that each stakes an equal sum of money. It is clear that, since each stakes an equal sum of money, each also risks only a third in order to gain two-thirds, and that, since each is playing against two, each also has only one prospect of winning thereby against two of losing thereby. If we suppose that one of these three, namely C, withdraws before the game has begun, it is clear that he may only take back what he staked, that is, a third part, and that B, if he wants to buy C's chance, and take his place, must stake as much as C takes back. To this A cannot object: for it makes no difference to him whether he must rely on one chance against two chances of two different men, or of one man. If this is so, then it follows that if anyone holds out his hand for another to guess one out of two numbers in order to win a certain sum of money if he guesses the right number or to lose an equal sum of money if he does not

---

* So the Latin version; the Dutch has " chance."

guess it, then the chance is equal for both sides, namely, for him who invites the guess as well as for him who must make the guess. Again, if he holds out his hand for another to guess at the first attempt one number out of three and win a certain sum of money if he guesses the right number, or lose half that sum if he does not guess it, then both sides will have an equal chance, just as both sides have an equal chance if he who holds out his hand allows the other two guesses, on condition that, if he guesses rightly, he wins a certain sum of money, or if he does not guess rightly, he loses double the amount.

The chance is also equal if he allows him to make three guesses at one of four numbers, in order to win a certain sum of money if he is right, or otherwise to lose three times as much; or if he is allowed four attempts to guess one of five numbers, in order to win one amount or to lose fourfold, and so forth. From all this it follows that it is just the same to him who holds out his hand and allows another to guess, if the other guesses one number out of many as many times as he likes, so long as, in return for the number of his guesses, he also stakes and risks as much money as is proportionate to the number of attempts divided by the sum of the numbers. If, for instance, there are five numbers, and the one is not allowed to make more than one guess, he must stake only $\frac{1}{5}$ against the $\frac{4}{5}$ of the other; if he is to guess twice he must risk $\frac{2}{5}$ against the other's $\frac{3}{5}$; if three times $\frac{3}{5}$ against the other's $\frac{2}{5}$; and so forth, $\frac{4}{5}$ against $\frac{1}{5}$, and $\frac{5}{5}$ against $\frac{0}{5}$. Consequently, it is just the same for him who allows others to guess, if, for example, he only risks $\frac{1}{6}$ of the total stakes in order to win $\frac{5}{6}$, whether one man guesses five times or five men each guess once. Such is the purport of your Question.

[VOORBURG] 1 *October* 1666.

LETTER XXXIX   B. D. S.

To the Very Courteous and Prudent Mr. JARIG JELLES.

WORTHY FRIEND,

Various obstacles have hindered me from answering your letter sooner. I have looked up what you pointed out with regard to Descartes' *Dioptrics*. He mentions no other cause, why the images at the back of the eye become larger or smaller, than the crossing of the rays which come from different points of the object, namely, according as they begin to cross each other nearer to or further from the eye, and he does not consider the size of the angle which these rays make when they cross each other at the surface of the eye. And although this last cause is the most important, which must be considered in the case of telescopes, yet he wanted, it seems, to pass it over in silence, because, as it appears, he knew of no means of gathering the rays coming in parallel lines, from different points, in as many other points. And therefore he could not mathematically determine this angle.

Perhaps he was silent about it in order not to put the circle in any way above the figures which he had introduced. For it is certain that in this matter the circle surpasses all other figures which can be discovered. For the circle being everywhere the same, has everywhere the same property. For instance, the circle A B C D has this property, that all rays parallel to the axis A B or coming from the direction A, are refracted at its surface in such a way that they afterward all come together at the point B. Similarly,

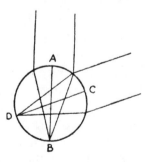

all rays parallel to the axis C D, and coming from the direction C, will be refracted at the surface in such a way that they will all come together at the point D. This can be said of no other figure, although Hyperbolas and Ellipses also have infinite diameters. The fact is, therefore, as you write, namely, if nothing else is taken into consideration except the length of the eye or of the telescope, we should be obliged to make very long telescopes before we could see the objects on the Moon as distinctly as the objects which we have here on the earth. But, as I have said, it turns chiefly on the size of the angle which is formed by the rays coming from different points, at the surface of the eye, when they cross each other there. And this angle also becomes greater or less according as the foci of the glasses put in the telescope are more or less distant. If you desire to see the proof of this, well then, I am ready to send it when you like.

VOORBURG, 3 *March* 1667.

LETTER XL   B. D. S.

To the Very Courteous and Prudent Mr. JARIG JELLES.

Worthy Friend,

I have duly received your last letter written on the fourteenth of this current month, but, owing to various hindrances, I could not answer it sooner. With regard to the matter relating to Helvetius, I have spoken about it with Mr. Vossius who (not to relate in a letter all that we said to each other) ridiculed it greatly, and expressed surprise that I should inquire of him about such a trivial thing. Taking no notice of this I went nevertheless to the silversmith, named Brechtelt, who had tested the gold. But he, speaking very differently from Vossius, said that between smelting and separation the gold had increased in weight and had become heavier by as much as the weight of the silver that he had put into the smelting crucible for the purpose of the separation.   Therefore he firmly believed that this gold which transmuted his silver into gold, contained something uncommon.   He was not the only one who found this so, but various other men who were present at that time did so too.   After this, I went to Helvetius himself, who showed me the gold and the crucible which was still gilded on the inside, and said to me that he had thrown into the melted lead not more than about one-fourth part of a grain of barley or of mustard seed.   He added that within a short time he would publish an account of the whole matter, and further said that at Amsterdam a man (and he thought it was the same man as had called on him) had performed the same operation, of which you will doubtless have heard.   This is all that I was able to learn about this matter.

The writer of the little book about which you write (in which he presumes to show that the arguments in Descartes' third and fifth Meditation, by which he proves the existence of God, are false) is certainly fighting his own shadow, and will harm himself more than others. Descartes' axiom is, I confess, somewhat obscure and confused, as you have also remarked, and he would have expressed it more clearly and truly thus : *That the power of Thought to think about or to comprehend things, is not greater than the power of Nature to exist and to act.*   This is a clear and true axiom, according to which the existence of God follows very clearly and validly from the idea of Him.   The argument of the said author of which you give an account shows clearly enough that he does not yet understand the matter.   It is indeed true that we may go on to infinity if thereby we would solve the question in all its parts : but otherwise it is very silly.   For example, if some one asked by what such a finite body is set in motion, it is possible to answer that it is determined to such a motion by another body, and this body again by another, and so on to infinity. This answer, I say, is possible, because the Question is only about the motion, and by positing each time another body, we assign a sufficient and eternal cause of such motion. But if I see a book containing excellent thoughts which is written beautifully, in the hands of a common man, and I ask him whence he has such a book, and he thereupon answers that he has copied it from another book in the possession of another common man who can also write beautifully, and so on to infinity, then he does not satisfy me. For I am asking him not only about the form and arrangement of the letters, about which alone he answers me, but also about the thoughts and meaning which their arrangement expresses, and this he does not answer by thus going on to infinity. How this can be applied to ideas may easily be understood from what I have explained in the ninth axiom of my *Mathematical Proofs of Descartes' Principles of Philosophy*.

I now proceed to answer your other letter, dated the ninth of March, in which you ask for further explanation of what I wrote in my previous letter about the figure of the circle. This you will easily be able to grasp if you will only please notice that all the rays which are supposed to fall in parallel lines on the anterior glass of a telescope are not really parallel because they all come from one and the same point. But they are considered such, because the object is so far from us that the opening of the telescope, in relation to its distance, may be considered simply as a point. Moreover, it is certain that, in order to see a whole object, we need not only the rays from a single point, but also all the other cones of rays which come from all the other points. And therefore it is also necessary that when they pass through the glass they should come together in as many

other foci. And although the eye is not so exactly
constructed that all the rays which come from different
points of an object come together exactly in so many foci
at the back of the eye, yet it is certain that the figures
which can bring this about, must be ranked above
all others. And since a definite segment of a circle
is able to bring it about that all the rays which come
from one point are (speaking according to Mechanics)
brought together in another point on its diameter, it
will also bring together all the other rays, which come
from the other points of the object, at so many other
points. For from any point in the object a line can be
drawn which passes through the centre of the circle,
although for that purpose the opening
of the telescope must be made much
smaller than it would otherwise be made
if there were no need of more than a
single focus, as you will easily be able
to see.

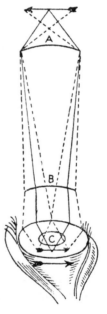

What I say here of the circle cannot be said of the Ellipse, or the
Hyperbola, much less of other more
complex figures, since only from a
single point in the object can a line
be drawn which passes through both
their foci. This is what I wanted to
say in my first letter about this matter.

From the attached diagram you will
be able to see the proof that the angle
formed at the surface of the eye by
the rays coming from various points,
is greater or less according as the foci
are more or less distant. So, after sending you cordial
greeting, there remains nothing but to say that I am, etc.,

B. DE S.

VOORBURG, 25 *of March*, 1667.

To the Very Courteous and Prudent Mr. JARIG JELLES.

SIR,

I will here relate in a few words what I have discovered by experiment in regard to the matter about which you asked me first by word of mouth and then in writing. To this I will add what I now think on the subject.

I had a wooden tube made for me 10 feet long with a bore of 1⅔ inches. To this I fixed three perpendicular tubes as shown in the attached figure.

In order to discover first whether the pressure of

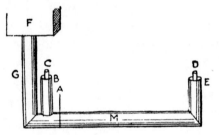

water in tube B was as great as in E, I closed the tube M at A with a small board made for that purpose. I then made the mouth of B so narrow that it could hold a narrow glass tube like C. When I had filled the tube with water by means of the vessel F, I took note of the height to which the water rose in the narrow tube C. I then closed the tube B, and removing the small board A, allowed the water to flow into the tube E, which I had prepared in the same way as B. And after I had refilled the whole tube with water I observed that it rose to the same height in D as it had done in C. This made me believe that the length of the tube was very little or no hindrance.

However, in order to investigate this more closely

I also sought to find out whether the tube E could also fill a vessel of a cubic foot which I had made for the purpose, in as short a time as B did. In order to measure the time, since I had no pendulum clock at hand, I made shift with a bent glass tube like H, whose shorter tube was immersed in water, while the longer hung in the free air. When I had all this ready, I first let the water through the tube B, in a stream as thick as the tube itself, until the vessel of a cubic foot was full. I then weighed with accurate scales how much water had meanwhile flowed into the small basin L, and I observed that it weighed about four ounces. I then closed the tube B, and let the water flow through the tube E, in a stream equally thick, into the vessel of a cubic foot. When this was full I weighed the water again, as before, which had meanwhile flowed into the small basin, and I found that it did not weigh even half an ounce more. But since the streams, from B as well as from E, did not continually flow with the same force, I repeated the operation, and I brought first as much water as we had found it necessary to have at hand from our experience the first time. There were three of us as busy as possible, and we prepared the above-mentioned experiment more accurately than before, though not as accurately as I could wish. I did, however, obtain sufficient evidence to enable me to some extent to come to a decision about this matter, because I found about the same difference on the second as on the first occasion. Considering the matter and these experiments I find myself compelled to conclude that the difference which the length of the tube can produce, takes place only at the beginning, that is, when the water begins its flow; but that when it has continued to flow for a little while, it will flow with as much force

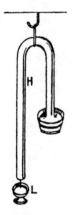

through a very long as through a short tube. The reason for this is that the pressure of the high water always retains the same force, and that all the motion which it communicates, it in turn derives continuously through the action of gravity; and therefore it will continue to communicate this motion to the water in the tube, until, being pushed on, it has acquired as much speed as the higher water can give it gravitational force. For it is certain that if the water in the tube G imparts to the water in the tube M one degree of speed in the first moment, then in the second moment, if it retains its original force, as it is supposed to do, it will communi-

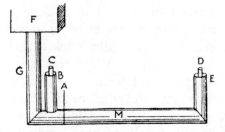

cate four degrees of speed to this water, and so forth, until the water in the long tube M has received just as much velocity as the gravitational force can give the higher water, contained in the tube G. Therefore the water running through a tube forty thousand feet long would after a short time, and solely through the pressure of the higher water, acquire as much velocity as if the tube M were only one foot long. I could have determined the time required by the water in the longer tube to acquire so much speed, if I had been able to obtain more exact instruments. However, I think this is not necessary, because the main point is sufficiently determined, etc.

VOORBURG, 5 *September* 1669.

LETTER XLII   LAMBERT DE VELTHUYSEN, M.Dr.

To the Very Learned and Honoured
Mr. JACOB OSTENS.

MOST LEARNED SIR,

I have at length obtained some free time, and at once applied my mind to satisfying your wishes and requests. Now you ask me to tell you my opinion, and pronounce my verdict, on the book entitled *Discursus Theologico-Politicus*. This I have now decided to do, as far as time and my capacity allow. I will not however go into details, but I will give a compendious account of the author's thought, and of his views on religion.

I do not know of what nationality he is, or what manner of life he follows, I am not even interested to know it. The argument of his book shows sufficiently that he is not dull-witted, and that he has not merely indolently and perfunctorily examined and looked into the religious controversies which are carried on in Europe between Christians. The writer of this book has convinced himself that he will be more favourably placed for examining the opinions through which men break up into factions, and divide into parties, if he lays aside and casts off prejudices. Therefore he has laboured more than enough to free his mind from every superstition. In attempting to show himself immune from this he has gone too far in the opposite direction, and in order to avoid the error of superstition, he seems to me to have cast off all religion. At all events he does not rise above the religion of the Deists, of whom (so evil are the morals of this age) there is a sufficiently large number everywhere, and especially in France. Mersenne published a treatise against them, which I remember reading once. But I think that scarcely any one of the number of the Deists has written on behalf of that thoroughly bad cause with such a malicious mind, and so cleverly and cunningly, as the author of this dissertation. Moreover, unless I am mistaken in my conjecture, this man does not include himself in the ranks of the Deists, and does not allow men to retain the least bit of religious worship.

He acknowledges God and confesses Him to be the maker and founder of the Universe. But he declares that the form, appearance, and order of the world are evidently as necessary as the Nature of God, and the eternal truths, which he holds are established apart from the decision of God. Therefore he also expressly declares that all things come to pass by invincible necessity and inevitable fate. And he asserts that with those who consider matters correctly there is no room for precepts and commands; but that the ignorance of men has introduced names of this kind just as the inexperience of the people has made room for modes of speech whereby feelings are attributed to God. And so God also adapts Himself to man's comprehension when He reveals to men in the form of a command those eternal truths and the other things which must necessarily come to pass. He teaches that it is as necessary that those things, which are governed by laws, and are thought to be remote from the will of men, should come to pass, as that the nature of a triangle is necessary. And therefore those things which are embodied in precepts do not depend on the will of man, and will not, according as they are followed or evaded, procure for men any good or evil, any more than God's will can be influenced by prayers or His eternal and absolute decrees be changed. And so he teaches that the reason of these precepts and decrees is and comes to this, that the inexperience and ignorance of man have moved God to let them be of some use among those who cannot form more perfect thoughts about God, and who need such wretched aids to rouse in them a love of virtue and a hatred of vices. And so we can see that the author makes no mention in his writing of the use of prayer, just as he makes no mention of life or of death, or of any reward or punishment, through which men are influenced by the judge of the universe.

He does this in accordance with his principles. For what room can there be for a last judgment? Or what expectation of reward or of punishment, when all things are attributed to fate, and all things are declared to emanate from God with inevitable necessity, or rather, when he declares that this whole universe is God? For I fear that our author is not very far removed from this opinion; at least there is not much difference between declaring that all things emanate necessarily from the nature of God and that the Universe itself is God.

However, he places man's highest pleasure in the cultivation of virtue, which he says is its own reward, and the sphere of all that is most important. And therefore he thinks that the man who understands things correctly ought to devote himself to virtue not because of the precepts and the law of God, or through hope of reward, or fear of punishment, but because he is attracted by the beauty of virtue, and the joy of mind which man experiences in the exercise of virtue.

And so he declares that only apparently does God, through the Prophets and revelation, exhort men to virtue by the hope of reward and the fear of punishment, which two are always connected in laws, since the mind of ordinary men is so constituted and so badly educated that they cannot be impelled to the exercise of virtue, except by arguments borrowed from the nature of laws, and from the fear of punishment, and from the hope of reward: but men who consider the matter truly, understand that there is no truth or force in arguments of this kind.

He does not think it of any importance, although he is really overthrown by this axiom, that the Seers and holy Teachers, and so God Himself, since God spoke to men through their mouth, used arguments which, if their nature be considered, are in themselves false. For openly and in all sorts of places, when occasion arises, he professes and emphasizes that Holy Scripture is not intended to teach the truth and the nature of the things of which mention is made in it, and which it adduces for its own purpose to lead men to virtue ; and he denies that the Prophets were so learned in these matters as to be altogether immune from the errors of the crowd in preparing arguments and thinking out reasons by means of which they stirred men to virtue, although the nature of moral virtues and vices was perfectly clear to them.

And therefore, moreover, the Author teaches that the Prophets, even when they were admonishing those to whom they were sent of their duty, were not entirely free from errors of judgment, but that their holiness and credibility were not diminished thereby, although they made use of speech and arguments which were not true, but adapted to the preconceived ideas of those to whom they spoke, and by means of them stimulated men to virtues, about which no man is ever in doubt, and over which there is no controversy among men. For the object of sending a Prophet was to promote the cultivation of virtue among men, not the teaching of any truth. And so he considers that this error and ignorance on the part of the Prophet was not harmful to his hearers whom he incited to virtue, since he thinks it matters little by what arguments we are incited to virtue so long as they do not upset the moral virtue to stimulate which they were intended and urged by the Prophet. For he thinks that the truth of other things which is perceived by the mind has no importance for piety, since moral holiness is in fact not contained in that truth : and he thinks that the knowledge of truth and even of mysteries is more or less necessary according as they contribute more or less towards piety.

I think the author is referring to the axiom of those Theologians who distinguish between the discourse of a Prophet when he is enunciating a doctrine, and when he is simply narrating something, and this distinction, unless I am mistaken, is accepted by all Theologians, and he most erroneously believes that his opinion agrees with this doctrine.

Therefore he thinks that all those who deny that Reason and Philosophy are the interpreters of Scripture will follow his view. For since it is agreed by all that in Scripture innumerable things are predicated of God which do not befit Him, but are adapted to men's comprehension, so that men may be moved by them, and the love of virtue may be awakened in them, he thinks it must be asserted that the holy Teacher wished by these untrue arguments to educate men in virtue, or that liberty is allowed to everyone who reads Holy Scripture to judge according to the principles of his Reason of the meaning and purpose of the holy Teacher. This opinion the author entirely condemns and refutes together with those who teach, in agreement with the paradoxical Theologian, that Reason is the interpreter of Scripture. For he thinks that Scripture must be understood literally, and that men must not be allowed the liberty of interpreting arbitrarily and rationalistically what ought to be understood by the words of the prophets, and so decide, according to their reasons and according to the knowledge of things which they have acquired for themselves, when the Prophets spoke literally, and when they spoke figuratively. But there will be occasion for discussing these things in what follows.

To return to the things from which I have digressed

somewhat, the Author, adhering to his principles of the fatalistic necessity of all things,* denies that any miracles come to pass which are contrary to the laws of Nature : since he asserts, as I remarked above, that the natures of things and their order are no less necessary than are the nature of God and the eternal truths. Therefore he teaches that it is just as impossible for anything to depart from the laws of Nature as it is impossible in the case of a triangle that its three angles should not be equal to two right angles ; that God cannot bring it about that the less heavy weight should lift the more heavy, or that a body moving with two degrees of motion should overtake a body moving with four degrees of motion. Therefore he declares that miracles are subject to the ordinary laws of Nature, which, he teaches, are just as immutable as the very natures of things, since the very natures of things are contained in the laws of Nature. He does not admit any other power of God than the ordinary one which is exercised in conformity to the laws of Nature, and he thinks that another cannot be conceived, since it would destroy the natures of things, and would itself be self-contradictory.

A miracle, then, in the mind of the Author, *is that which happens unexpectedly and the cause of which is unknown to the common people.* Thus the common people attribute it to the power of prayer and the special direction of God when, following on duly conceived prayers, some imminent evil seems to have been averted, or some prayed-for good seems to have been obtained, when however, according to the Author's opinion, God had already decreed absolutely from eternity that those things should come to pass which the common people believe to have happened by [special] intervention and efficacy.

---

* Note by B. D. S. to this place : *He says this unjustly : for I have shown expressly that miracles afford no knowledge of God ; but that He is known much better from the steady order of Nature.*

For the prayers are not the cause of the decree, but the decree is the cause of the prayers.

All this about fate and the invincible necessity of things, both as regards the natures and as regards the occurrence of things which happen daily, he bases on the nature of God, or to speak more clearly, on the nature of God's will and understanding, which, although different in name, are in God really identical. Therefore he asserts that God willed this universe, and all that happens in it successively, just as necessarily as He necessarily knows this same universe. But if God necessarily knows this universe and its laws, as also the eternal truths contained in these laws, he concludes that God could no more have created another universe than He could overthrow the natures of things, and make twice three be seven. And as we cannot conceive anything different from this universe and its laws, in accordance with which things come into being and perish, but whatever fiction of this kind that we can imagine overthrows itself, so he teaches that the Nature of the divine understanding, and of the whole universe, and of those laws, according to which Nature proceeds, is so constituted that God can no more conceive with His understanding any things different from these which now are, than it is possible for things to be at the moment different from themselves. And so he concludes that just as God cannot now produce things which are self-destructive, so God cannot conceive or know natures different from those which now exist, since the comprehension and understanding of these natures is as impossible (since, according to the view of the author, it involves a contradiction) as the production of things different from those which now exist, is impossible now : for all those natures, if they are conceived as different from those which now exist, would necessarily also be opposed to those which now exist. For since the natures of things contained in this universe are (according to the view of the Author) necessary, they cannot have that necessity from themselves, but from the nature of God, from which they necessarily emanate. For he will not have it, with Descartes, whose doctrine however he wishes to appear to have accepted, that as the natures of all things are different from the nature and essence of God, so the ideas of them are freely in the divine mind.

With these arguments, of which I have been speaking, the Author has paved the way to those things of which he delivers himself at the end of his book and towards which all the teachings of the preceding chapters are directed. Thus he wishes to instil into the mind of magistrates and of all men this axiom : The right of establishing the divine worship which shall be publicly observed in the state belongs to the Magistrates. Hence it is right for the Magistrates to permit the citizens to think and speak of religion as their mind and disposition bid them, and to allow the subjects that liberty even with regard to acts of external worship, as long as the cultivation of moral virtues or piety can remain intact. For since there can be no controversy about these virtues, and the knowledge and practice of other things contain no moral virtue, he concludes that God cannot be displeased whatever the religious rites which men adopt besides. But the author is speaking of those sacred rites which do not constitute moral virtue nor come into contact with it, which are neither opposed to virtue nor alien from it, but which men adopt and profess as aids to true virtues, so that thus through the love of these virtues they may become acceptable and pleasing to God, for God is not offended by the pursuit and practice of things which, being indifferent, make no difference as regards virtues or vices, though men connect them with the practice of piety, and use them as aids to the cultivation of virtue.

The Author, in order to prepare men's minds to accept these paradoxes, asserts first that the whole religious cult established by God and handed down by the Jews, that is, by the citizens of the Israelite commonwealth, was only directed to this, that they should pass their life happily in their commonwealth; but that the Jews were not dear and acceptable to God above other nations. God, he says, has from time to time communicated this to the Jews through His Prophets, when He reproached them with their ignorance and error, because they identified holiness and piety with the worship established and prescribed for them by God, when it should only have been identified with the love of moral virtues, that is, with the love of God and with the love of one's neighbour.

And since God has imbued the minds of all nations with the principles and as it were with the seeds of virtues so that they may spontaneously and almost without any instruction realize the difference between good and evil, he concludes therefore that God has not left the other nations destitute of those things by means of which true blessedness can be obtained, but has shown Himself equally benevolent to all men.

Moreover he states that in order to put the [other] nations on an equality with the Jews in all the things which may in some way be of assistance and use towards obtaining true felicity, the [other] nations have not been without true prophets. This he sets out to prove by examples. Further he hints that God by His sovereignty ruled the other nations through the agency of good angels, whom, following the usage of the Old Testament, he calls Gods. Therefore the religious rites of the other nations did not displease God as long as they were not so corrupted by men's superstition as to alienate men from true holiness and to impel them to perpetrate in their religion things inconsistent with virtue. But God forbade the Jews, for special reasons peculiar to that people, to worship [other] nations' Gods which by God's ordinance and arrangement were worshipped by the [other] nations as properly as the Angels, the appointed guardians of the commonwealth of the Jews, were counted by the Jews in their way among the number of the Gods, and were treated by them with divine honours.

And since the Author thinks that it is generally admitted that external worship as such is not acceptable to God, he thinks it of very little importance with what ceremonies this external worship is carried out, so long as it is of such a kind that it is so worthy of God as to excite reverence for God in the minds of men, and to incite them to the love of virtue.

Then he thinks that the sum [and substance] of all religion is comprised in the cultivation of virtue, and that all knowledge of mysteries is superfluous that is not naturally adapted to virtue and formed to promote it, and that that knowledge is more potent and more necessary which contributes more effectively to teaching men virtue, and inciting them towards it. From this he concludes that we must approve, or at least not reject, all those opinions about God and His worship, and the things which pertain to religion, which, in the mind of those who hold them, are true and designed to the end that honesty may thrive and flourish. To establish this theory he quotes the Prophets themselves as the authors and witnesses of his view. They were convinced that it does not weigh with God at all what views men hold about religion, but that that worship and those opinions which proceed from a love of virtue and reverence for the Divinity are acceptable to God. And they took such liberties that they even brought forward such arguments to incite men to virtue as were indeed not true in themselves but which, in the opinion of those

whom they addressed, were considered such, and were
naturally adapted to supply a spur to induce them to
devote themselves more eagerly to virtue. And so
he supposes that God left the choice of arguments to
the prophets, so that they might apply those which were
adapted to the times and to the thoughts of persons, and
which they, according to their understanding, thought
good and effective.

Hence he thinks it came to pass that different Divine
Teachers used different, and often mutually conflicting,
arguments, that Paul taught that man was not justified
by works and James inculcated the opposite doctrine.
For James saw, so the Author thinks, that the Christians
were misapplying the doctrine of justification by faith,
and so he shows in many places that man is justified
by faith and by works. For he understood that it was
not to the interest of the Christians of his time to inculcate
and to publish, as Paul had done, that doctrine about
faith, by which men calmly reposed on God's mercy, and
took almost no trouble about good works. For Paul
had to deal with the Jews who erroneously placed their
justification in the works of the Law, especially delivered
to them by Moses, and, thinking that they were thereby
raised above all [other] nations, and had a road to blessedness prepared for them alone, rejected the method of
salvation by faith whereby they were reduced to equality
with the [other] nations and stripped and deprived of
all privileges. Therefore since both propositions, that
of Paul as well as that of James, were, for different
sorts of times and persons, and connected circumstances,
excellent helps towards making men pay regard to piety,
the Author thinks it was part of the Apostolic wisdom to
apply now the one and now the other doctrine.

And this, among many others, is the reason why the
Author thinks it entirely inconsistent with the truth to
want to explain the sacred text with the aid of reason,

and to make this the interpreter of Scripture, or to interpret one holy teacher through another, since they have equal authority, and the words which they used must be explained by the mode of speaking and the rhetorical peculiarity natural to those Teachers. So in the investigation of the true sense of Scripture attention must be paid, not to the nature of the thing itself, but only to the literal meaning.

Since, therefore, Christ himself and the other divinely sent Teachers showed and taught by example and precept that men attain to happiness only by the love of virtue and that the rest is of no importance, the Author wishes to prove that the sole care of the Magistrates should be that justice and honesty may flourish in the state, but scarcely to regard it as their function to consider which religious service and which doctrines are most accordant with the truth; but they must take care that such are not adopted as place an obstacle to virtue, even if they accord with the view of those who profess them.

Thus, without offending the Deity, the magistrates can easily tolerate different religious institutions in their state. And in order to persuade us of this he takes this course. He asserts that there is a kind of moral virtues, practised in social communities and concerned with outward acts, of such a sort that no one ought to exercise them according to his private judgment and decision, but that the cultivation, exercise and modification of these virtues depend on the authority and power of the Magistrates, both because outward acts of virtue derive their nature from circumstances, and because man's duty to perform external actions of this kind is judged according to the advantage or disadvantage which is derived from these actions; so that these external actions if not carried out at the right time lose their character of virtues, and their opposites must be reckoned among the number of virtues. The Author thinks that there is another kind of virtues which exist inwardly in the mind; these always preserve their nature, and do not depend on the changing state of circumstances.

It is never permitted to anybody to show a propensity to cruelty and harshness, and not to love his neighbour and truth. But there can come times in which it may be lawful not indeed to lay aside this disposition of mind and the love of the said virtues, but either to refrain from them as far as external actions are concerned, or even to do things which, as far as external appearance goes, are deemed inconsistent with these virtues. And so it may happen that it may no longer be the duty of an upright man to state the truth openly, and, either by speech or writing, to let the citizens share in that truth, and communicate it to them, if we think that more harm than good will redound to the citizens from that pronouncement. And although individuals should embrace all men in love, and it is never permitted to banish that feeling, yet it happens rather frequently that certain persons may be severely treated by us without our fault, when it is certain that the clemency with which we are prepared to treat them would do us much harm. So, indeed, all think that it is not always opportune to state all truths, whether they pertain to religion or to civic life. And he who teaches that roses should not be thrown before swine, if there is any fear of the swine fiercely attacking those who offer them the roses, likewise holds that it is not the duty of a good man to instruct the multitude in certain chapters of religion for fear that the people, when these things are made public and broadcast among the multitude, will overwhelm the commonwealth, or the Church, and so more harm than good may ensue for the citizens and for the saints.

But since civil societies, from whom the power and authority to pass laws cannot be taken away, have instituted, among other things, that it must not be left to the choice of individuals to decide what is useful for men who together constitute a civic body, but that this must be entrusted to the rulers, the Author argues that therefore it is the right of the Magistrates to decide what kind and what doctrines ought to be taught publicly in the commonwealth, and that it is the duty of the subjects, as far as concerns outward profession, to refrain from teaching and professing dogmas about which the Magistrates have ordained by laws that silence shall be observed in public; since God has no more left this to the judgment of individuals than He has allowed them, in opposition to the intention and decrees of the magistrates or against the verdict of the judges, to do things by which the power of the laws is eluded and the magistrates are thwarted in their aim. For the Author thinks that about matters of this kind, concerning external worship and its profession, men can come to an agreement, and that the external acts of divine worship can as safely be entrusted to the judgment of the Magistrates, as justice is left to it, and the power of estimating injury done to the state, and of punishing it by force. For, just as a private person is not bound to accommodate his judgment of the injury done to the state to the judgment of the Magistrates, but is allowed to have his own opinion, although (if the case requires it) he is bound to contribute his part in putting into execution this decision of the magistrates, even so, the Author thinks that it is indeed the right of private persons in the commonwealth to judge about the truth and the falsity, as also about the necessity, of some dogma, and that the individual cannot be forced by the laws of the state to have the same opinion about religion. But it depends on the judgment of the Magistrates what doctrines ought to be put forward in public, and it is the duty of private persons to keep silent about their opinions on religion when they differ from the view of the Magistrates, and to do nothing whereby the laws enacted by the Magistrates concerning worship might lose their force.

But, since it can happen that the Magistrates, differing from many of the multitude on certain points of religion, wish to have taught in public certain doctrines which are different from the view of the multitude, and that the Magistrates nevertheless hold it to be important for the honour of God that there should be a public profession of these dogmas in their commonwealth, the Author sees that there remains the difficulty that very great harm may be done to the citizens on account of the difference of the judgment of the Magistrates from the judgment of the multitude. Therefore to the preceding consideration the author adds a second, which may appease the minds both of the Magistrates and of their subjects, and preserve liberty in religion intact. This is, that the Magistrates need not fear the wrath of God even if they allow in their Commonwealth religious rites which in their opinion are perverse, so long as these rites are not opposed to the moral virtues, and do not subvert them. The ground of this view cannot escape you since I have given it sufficiently fully in what I have said above. For the Author has stated that God is indifferent and does not care what opinions men hold in their religion, and mentally approve and defend, and what religious rites they practise in public, since all these things must be reckoned among the number of things which have no affinity with virtue and vice; although it is the duty of each so to make his calculations that he may adopt those doctrines and that worship by which he thinks he can make the greatest progress in the love of virtue.

Here, most Honoured Sir, you have a compendious summary of the doctrine of the Political Theologian, which in my opinion abolishes and absolutely subverts all worship and religion, and secretly introduces Atheism, or imagines such a God that men are not affected by reverence for His divinity, since He Himself is subject to fate. No place is left for the divine government and providence, and all distribution of rewards and punishments is abolished. It is easy to see at least from this book of the Author that by his method and arguments the authority of all Holy Scripture is infringed, and is only mentioned by the Author for form's sake, just as it follows from the position which he adopts that the Koran must be put on a level with the word of God. Nor has the Author left himself a single argument with which to prove that Mahomet was not a true Prophet, since even the Turks according to the command of their Prophet cultivate the moral virtues about which all the nations are agreed; and according to the Author's teaching it is not uncommon for God to lead the nations to whom He has not imparted the oracles given to the Jews and to the Christians by other revelations to the path of Reason and obedience.

I think, therefore, that I have not strayed far from the truth, or done any injury to the Author, if I denounce him as teaching pure Atheism with hidden and disguised arguments.

L. v. V.

UTRECHT, 24 *Jan.* 1671, Old Style.

LETTER XLIII   B. D. S.

To the Very Learned and Honoured
MR. JACOB OSTENS.

MOST LEARNED SIR,
         You are doubtless surprised that I have made you wait so long; but I can hardly make up my mind to answer the letter of that man, which you were pleased to send me. Nor do I do so now for any other reason

than because I promised. But in order also to gratify my own mind as far as possible, I will discharge my debt in as few words as I can, and briefly show how perversely he has interpreted my meaning; whether he has done this from malice or from ignorance, I could not say easily. But to the point.

First he says *that it concerns him little to know of what nationality I may be, or what manner of life I follow.* But if he had known this he would not have persuaded himself so easily that I teach Atheism. For Atheists are wont to desire inordinately honours and riches, which I have always despised, as all those who know me are aware. Then, in order to smooth the path to his goal, he says that I am not dull-witted, in order, forsooth, that he may more easily persuade men that I have argued cleverly and adroitly, but with evil intent, for the thoroughly bad cause of the Deists. This shows sufficiently that he has not understood my reasons. For who can be so ingenious and so astute as to give hypocritically so many and such strong reasons in support of something which he considers to be false? Whom, I say, will he believe after this to have written sincerely, if he believes that the fictitious can be proved as soundly as the true? However, I am not surprised at this now. For thus was Descartes once maligned by Voetius, and thus fare generally the best men.

He then continues. *In order to avoid the error of superstition, he seems to me to have cast aside all religion.* What he understands by Religion and what by superstition, I do not know. Does that man, I pray, cast aside all religion who declares that God must be recognized as the Highest Good, and that He must be loved as such with a free spirit? and that in this alone does our highest felicity and supreme liberty consist? that, furthermore, the reward of virtue is virtue itself, and the punishment of folly and weakness is the folly itself?

and, lastly, that everyone ought to love his neighbour, and to obey the commands of the supreme power? I not only said all this explicitly, but also proved it with the strongest arguments. But I think I see in what bog this man sticks. Namely, he finds nothing to please him in virtue itself and in understanding, but would rather live under the impulse of his feelings, if it were not for this single obstacle, that he fears punishment. Thus he abstains from evil deeds and follows the divine commands as a slave, unwillingly, and with a vacillating mind, and for this servitude he expects to be honoured by God with gifts, far pleasanter to him than the divine love itself, and the more so in proportion as the good which he does is repugnant to him, and he does it unwillingly. Hence it comes that he believes that all those, who are not restrained by this fear, lead unbridled lives, and cast aside all religion. But I pass over these things, and turn to his deduction, by which he wants to show that *I teach Atheism by hidden and disguised arguments*.

The basis of his argument is this, that he thinks that I take away God's liberty, and subject Him to fate. This is entirely false. For I assert that all things follow with inevitable necessity from the nature of God, just as all assert that it follows from the nature of God that He understands Himself. Certainly, no one denies that this follows necessarily from the divine nature, and yet no one conceives that God is forced by some fate, but that He understands Himself altogether freely although necessarily. Here I find nothing that cannot be perceived by anybody. If, nevertheless, he believes that these assertions were made with evil intent, what then does he think of his own Descartes, who states that nothing is done by us which has not been pre-ordained by God, or rather that every single moment we are, as it were, created anew by God, and that nevertheless we act with the freedom of our will. This, assuredly, as Descartes himself confesses, no one can understand.

Moreover, this inevitable necessity of things sets aside neither divine nor human laws. For moral precepts, whether they receive the form of law from God Himself, or not, are nevertheless divine, and salutary; and whether we receive the good, which follows from virtue and the divine love, from God as a judge, or whether it emanates from the necessity of the divine nature, it will not therefore be either more or less desirable, just as, on the other hand, the evils which follow from evil deeds are not to be feared any the less because they follow from them necessarily; and, lastly, whether we do what we do necessarily, or freely, we are still led by hope or by fear. Therefore he asserts falsely *that I declare that there is no room left for precepts and commands,* or as he continues later *that there can be no expectation of reward or punishment, when all things are attributed to fate, and it is declared that all things emanate from God with inevitable necessity.*

I do not here inquire why it is the same, or not very different, to assert that all things emanate necessarily from the nature of God, and that the universe is God; but I should like you to note the remarks which he no less spitefully adds. These are *that I mean that man should devote himself to virtue not because of the precepts and law of God, or the hope of reward, or the fear of punishment, but, etc.* This you will certainly not find anywhere in my *Treatise*; on the contrary, in Chapter IV I have expressly said that the sum [and substance] of the divine law (which is divinely inscribed in our mind, as I said in Chapter XII) and its supreme injunction are to love God as the highest good; that is, not from fear of some punishment (for love cannot spring from fear) nor for love of some other object, by which we hope to be gratified, for then we should not so much love God Himself as that which we desire. And I showed in the same chapter that God had revealed this same law to His Prophets; and whether I declare that this law of God received the form of law from God Himself, or whether I conceive it like the rest of God's decrees which involve eternal necessity and truth, it will nevertheless remain the decree of God and a lesson in salvation; and whether I love God freely, or from the necessity of the decree of God, nevertheless I shall love God, and I shall be saved. Therefore I could now say that this man belongs to the class of those about whom I said at the end of my Preface that I would rather that they should entirely neglect my book, than that by misinterpreting it, as they are wont to misinterpret everything, they should become troublesome, and without benefiting themselves should hinder others.

Although I think this is sufficient to show what I intended, I thought it worth while to add a few remarks, namely, that he falsely thinks that I am referring to the Axiom of those Theologians who distinguish between the discourse of a Prophet when he is teaching something and when he is simply narrating something. For if by this axiom he means that one which in Chapter XV I ascribed to a certain Rabbi Judah Alpakhar, how could I think that mine agrees with it when in the same Chapter I rejected it as false? But if he is thinking of something else, I confess that I still do not know of it, and thus I could not be referring to it.

Further I do not see why he says that I think that all those will agree with me who deny that Reason and Philosophy are the interpreters of Scripture, when I have refuted their opinion as well as that of Maimonides.

It would take too long to review everything by which he shows that he has not passed judgment on me with an entirely calm mind. Therefore I proceed to his conclusion. There he says that *I have left myself no argument with which to prove that Mahomet was not a true Prophet.*

This indeed he endeavours to prove from my opinions, whereas really it clearly follows from them that he was an impostor, seeing that he entirely took away that freedom which Universal Religion, revealed by the natural and by prophetic light, allows, and which I have shown ought to be fully allowed. And even if this were not so, am I bound, I pray, to show that a certain Prophet is false? On the contrary, the Prophets were bound to show that they are true. But if he replies that Mahomet also taught the divine law, and gave sure signs of his mission, as the other Prophets did, then there will really be no reason why he should deny that he was a true Prophet.

As regards the Turks and the other Gentiles, if they worship God by the exercise of justice and charity towards their neighbour, I believe that they have the Spirit of Christ and are saved, whatever convictions they may in their ignorance hold about Mahomet and the oracles.

Thus you see, my friend, that this man has strayed far from the truth. Nevertheless, I admit that he does no harm to me but very much to himself when he is not ashamed to say that I teach Atheism by hidden and disguised arguments.

For the rest, I do not think you will find here anything which you can consider too severe an expression against this man. But if you meet with something of this sort, I beg you either to delete it, or to correct it, as you may think fit. I have no mind to irritate him, whoever he may be, and to raise up for myself enemies of my own making; and since this is often the result in disputes of this kind, I could scarcely prevail on myself to reply, and I could not have prevailed, had I not promised.

Farewell. To your prudence I commit this letter, and myself, who am, etc.

[THE HAGUE, *February* 1671.]

LETTER XLIV   B. D. S.

To the Very Courteous and Prudent Mr. JARIG JELLES.

WORTHY FRIEND,

When Professor . . . . . . recently paid me a visit, he told me among other things that he had heard that my *Tractatus Theologico-Politicus* has been translated into Dutch, and that someone, he did not know who, proposed to get it printed. I therefore beg you most earnestly please to find out about this, so as, if possible, to stop the printing of it. This is not my request only, but also that of many of my good friends who would not like to see the book prohibited, as will without doubt happen, if the book is published in Dutch. I firmly trust that you will do me and our cause this service.

A certain friend has sent me, some time ago, a small book called *Homo Politicus*, or *Political Man* of which I had already heard much. I have read it through, and found it the most pernicious book that can be conceived by men. The highest good of the man who wrote it, is money and honours. To this he adapts his teaching, and shows the way whereby to attain them; that is, by inwardly rejecting all religion, and outwardly assuming such as shall best serve his advancement, and also by keeping faith with no one except in so far as it may tend to his own advantage. As regards the rest, he praises most highly simulation, promising without giving, lying, perjury and many other things. When I had read this, the thought occurred to me of writing a little book indirectly against it, in which I would treat of the highest good, and then of the restless and wretched plight of those who are greedy for money and covet honours, and, lastly, show, by clear arguments and many examples, that through the insatiable desire for Honours and Riches commonwealths must perish, and have perished.

How much better and more excellent the thoughts of Thales of Miletus were than those of the above-mentioned writers is assuredly clear from the following consideration. Among friends, he said, all things are in common ; the wise are the friends of the Gods [and all things belong to the Gods] * ; therefore all things belong to the wise. In this way did this very wise man make himself the most rich, by nobly despising riches rather than by greedily hunting after them. Another time, however, he showed that it is not from necessity but from choice that the wise possess no riches. For when his friends reproached him for his poverty, he answered them : Do you wish me to show that I can also acquire that which I consider unworthy of my labour, but which you seek so greedily ? And when they had said yes to this he hired all the presses throughout Greece : for, being a great expert in the course of the stars, he had seen that there would be that year a great superfluity of olives, of which there had been a great scarcity in the preceding years ; and then he hired out at a high price those presses which he had hired for little money, for they had to use them in order to press the oil out of the olives. In this way he acquired in one year great wealth, which he afterwards distributed with as much kindness as he had acquired it with cleverness.

I conclude by assuring you that I am, etc.

THE HAGUE, 17 *Feb.* 1671.

LETTER XLV   GOTTFRIED LEIBNIZ

TO THE ILLUSTRIOUS AND VERY FAMOUS MR. B. D. S.

ILLUSTRIOUS AND MOST HONOURABLE SIR,
      Among the other praises of you which fame has bruited abroad, I understand is your great skill in optics. This has made me wish to submit my essay,

* From the Latin version.

such as it is, to you, than whom I shall not easily find a better judge in this kind of study. This paper which I send you, and which I have called *A Note on Advanced Optics*, I have published so that I may be able to communicate more conveniently with my friends or with those who are interested. I hear that the most Honourable Hudde is also distinguished in this kind of study, and I do not doubt that he is very well known to you. You will, therefore, greatly add to your kindness if you will also obtain for me his judgment and approbation.

The paper itself sufficiently explains its object.

I believe you have received the *Prodromus* of Francis Lana, a Jesuit, a work written in Italian, in which he makes some notable remarks on Dioptrics. But Johannes Oltius, a young Swiss, very learned in these matters, has also published *Physico-Mechanical Reflections on Vision*, in which he promises some kind of very simple and universal machine for polishing all kinds of glasses, and also says that he has found some method of collecting *all* the rays, coming from *all* the points of an object, into as many other corresponding points. But this only in the case of an object at a certain distance and of a certain shape.

For the rest my proposal comes to this, not that all the rays from *all* the points should be collected again, which, as far as our present knowledge goes, is impossible in the case of every object at any distance or of any shape, but that the rays should be collected equally from the points outside the optic axis and on the optic axis, so that the apertures of the glasses may be of any size and yet the vision remain distinct. But these things will await your very penetrating judgment.

Farewell Honoured Sir, and favour your
  sincere admirer
   GOTTFRIED WILLIAM LEIBNIZ,
   Doctor of Laws and Councillor of Mainz.

FRANKFURT, 5 *October* 1671, *New Style.*

P.S.—If you will honour me with an answer, the most noble Diemerbroeck, Lawyer, will, I hope not unwillingly, take charge of it. I think you have seen my new Physical Hypothesis ; if not, I will send it.

To Mr. Spinosa,
   The very celebrated Doctor
   and very profound Philosopher,
               at Amsterdam.

par couvert.

LETTER XLVI   B. D. S.

To the Very Learned and Noble Mr. GOTTFRIED LEIBNIZ, Doctor of Laws and Councillor of Mainz.

Reply to the Preceding.

Most learned and Noble Sir,

I have read the paper which you were kind enough to send me ; and I thank you very much for communicating it to me. I regret that I have not been able fully to follow your meaning, which, however, I believe you have explained clearly enough. Therefore, I beg you not to mind answering me these few questions. Namely, do you think that there is any other reason why the aperture of glasses ought to be small than because the rays which come from a single point are not collected exactly in another point but over a small space (which we are wont to call a mechanical point) which is larger or smaller in proportion to the size of the aperture ? Further, I ask whether those lenses which you call *pandochal* correct this error, that is, whether the Mechanical point, or the small space, in which the rays coming from the same point are collected after refraction, remains the same in size, whether the aperture is great or small ? For if the lenses achieve this, it will be possible to enlarge their aperture as much as one likes, and they will, therefore, be far superior to those of any other shapes known to me; otherwise I do not see why you commend them so much more than the ordinary lenses. For circular lenses have everywhere the same axis; and therefore, when we employ them, all the points of an object must be considered as if placed in the optic axis; and although all the points of the object are not at the same distance, yet the difference which arises from this cannot be perceptible when the objects are very distant, because then the rays which come from the same point are regarded as if they entered the glass in parallel lines. This much, however, I believe, namely, that when we wish to apprehend several objects in one glance (as happens when we employ very large convex eye-lenses) your lenses can be of help to represent the whole ensemble of things more distinctly. But I shall suspend judgment on all these points until you explain to me your meaning more clearly, as I earnestly beg you to do.

I sent the other copy to Mr. Hudde, as you bade me. He replies that at present he has not time, but he hopes to be free to examine it in a week or two.

The *Prodromus* of Francis Lana has not yet come into my hands, nor the *Physico-Mechanical Reflections* of Johannes Oltius, and, what I regret more, I have not even been able to see your Physical Hypothesis. Here at the Hague at least it is not on sale. Therefore, if you will send it to me you will be doing me a very great kindness, and if in any other matter I can be of service to you, I shall not fail to show that I am, Most Honourable Sir,

Yours entirely

B. DESPINOZA.

THE HAGUE, 9 *November* 1671.

Mr. Dimerbruck does not live here. I am, therefore, compelled to give this to the ordinary letter-carrier.

I have no doubt that you know someone here at the Hague who would be willing to take charge of our letters, and I should like to know who it is, in order that our letters might be despatched more conveniently, and more safely. If the *Tractatus Theologico-Politicus* has not yet reached you, I will send you a copy if you do not mind. Farewell.

To THE VERY NOBLE AND HONOURABLE
  MR. GOTTFRIED WILLIAM LEIBNIZ
  DOCTOR OF LAWS AND COUNCILLOR
  OF MAINTZ.

  [FRANCO BIS   [MAINTZ]
    CÖLN]   <FRANKFORT>
      [2]
Port.

[DESPATCHED THE 8TH DECEMBER 1671.]

LETTER XLVII   J. LOUIS FABRITIUS

TO THE VERY ACUTE AND RENOWNED PHILOSOPHER B. D. S.

MOST RENOWNED SIR,

His Serene Highness the Elector Palatine, my most gracious Master, has commanded me to write to you, who are as yet unknown to me, but most highly commended to his Serene Highness the Prince, and to ask you whether you are willing to accept an ordinary Professorship of Philosophy in his Illustrious University. You will be paid the annual salary which the ordinary Professors enjoy to-day. You will not find elsewhere a Prince more favourable to distinguished geniuses, among whom he reckons you. You will have the utmost freedom of philosophizing, which he believes you will not misuse to disturb the publicly established Religion. I could not but comply with the request of the most wise Prince. Therefore I most earnestly beg you to answer me as soon as possible, and to entrust your answer to me to the care of Mr. Grotius, his Serene Highness the Elector's Resident at the Hague, or to Mr. Gilles van der Hek, to be forwarded in the packet of letters which they are wont to send to the court, or to make use of any other convenient means that may seem to you most suitable. I will add only this, that if you come here you will live pleasantly a life worthy of a Philosopher, unless everything turns out contrary to our hope and expectation. So Farewell and Hail to you, Most honoured Sir,

From your most devoted

J. LOUIS FABRITIUS,

*Professor in the University of Heidelberg, and
Councillor to the Elector Palatine.*

HEIDELBERG, 16 *February* 1673.

LETTER XLVIII   B. D. S.

To the Very Honourable and Noble Mr. J. LOUIS FABRITIUS, Professor in the University of Heidelberg, and Councillor to the Elector Palatine.

Reply to the Preceding.

MOST HONOURABLE SIR,

If I had ever entertained a wish to take on a Professorship in any faculty, I could have desired no other than that which is offered me through you by His Serene Highness the Elector Palatine, particularly on account of that freedom of philosophizing which the Most Gracious Prince is pleased to offer, to say nothing of my long-felt desire to live under the rule of a Prince whose wisdom all admire. Since, however, it was never my intention to give public instruction,

I cannot be induced to embrace this glorious opportunity, although I have debated the matter with myself
so long. For, first, I think that if I want to find time
for instructing youth, then I must desist from develop-
ing my philosophy. Secondly, I think that I do not
know within what limits that freedom of philosophizing
ought to be confined in order to avoid the appearance
of wishing to disturb the publicly established Religion.
For Schisms arise not so much from an ardent love of
religion as from men's various dispositions, or the love
of contradiction, through which they are wont to distort
and to condemn all things, even those that have been
correctly stated. I have already experienced these things
while leading a private and solitary life, much more then
are they to be feared after I shall have risen to this degree
of dignity. Thus you see, Most Honoured Sir, that I
am not holding back in the hope of some better fortune,
but from love of peace, which I believe I can obtain to a
certain extent, merely by refraining from public lectures.
Therefore I most earnestly beg you to pray his Most
Serene Highness the Elector to allow me to give the
matter further consideration, and also to win the favour
of the most gracious Prince for his most devoted admirer.
Thereby you will oblige all the more,

Most Honourable and Noble Sir,

Yours entirely

B. D. S.

THE HAGUE, 30 *March* 1673.

LETTER XLVIIIA   B. D. S.

To MR. JARIG JELLES.

[*Fragments reported by* (1) *Hallmann, and* (2) *Bayle.*]

(1) The date of the letter was 19 April 1673. It was
written at the Hague, and addressed to Jarig Jelles, who

had sent him his *Confession of the Universal Christian Faith*, and asked him his opinion of it. Spinoza, in his reply, paid him no compliments, but stated that it was open to this criticism. On page 5 of the said manuscript he stated that by Nature man inclines to evil, but, through the Grace of God and the Spirit of Christ, he becomes indifferent to Good and Evil. This, however, is unsound, because he who has the spirit of Christ, must necessarily feel impelled to Good only. In this letter Spinoza also referred to Mr. Kerckring, a medical man, whom he had consulted about some anatomical questions. Near the end of the letter he wrote to Jelles : I will send to you the Known Truth as soon as Mr. Vallon returns to me my copy ; but if he delays too long, I shall arrange for you to get it through Mr. Bronckhorst. The conclusion was : I remain, with cordial greeting,

Your devoted servant
B. SPINOZA.

(2) SIR AND MOST ILLUSTRIOUS FRIEND,
 Your writings, which have been sent to me, I have read through with pleasure, and found them such that I can change nothing in them.

LETTER XLIX B. D. S.

TO THE VERY ILLUSTRIOUS
MR. JOHN GEORGE GRAEVIUS.

MOST ILLUSTRIOUS SIR,
 I beg you to send me as soon as you can the letter concerning the death of Descartes, which I believe you have copied long ago. For Mr. de V. has several times asked me to return it. If it were mine I should

not be in any hurry. Farewell, most honoured Sir, and remember your friend who is

> Yours in all love and devotion,
>> BENEDICTUS DESPINOZA.

THE HAGUE, 14 *December* 1673.

> MR. JOHN GEORGE GRAEVIUS,
>> ORDINARY PROFESSOR OF RHETORIC
>>> AT UTRECHT.

Post.

(Hague night post.)

LETTER L   B. D. S.

TO THE VERY COURTEOUS AND PRUDENT MR. JARIG JELLES.

WORTHY FRIEND,

With regard to Politics, the difference between Hobbes and me, about which you inquire, consists in this that I ever preserve the natural right intact so that the Supreme Power in a State has no more right over a subject than is proportionate to the power by which it is superior to the subject. This is what always takes place in the state of Nature.

Further as regards the proof which I establish in the *Appendix to my Geometrical Proof of Descartes' Principles*, namely, that God can only very improperly be called one or single; I reply to this that a thing can only be said to be one or single in respect of its existence and not of its essence : for we do not conceive things under numbers until they have been subsumed under a common class. For example, he who holds in his hand a penny and a dollar will not think of the number two, unless he can call the penny and the dollar by one and the same name, such as pieces of money or coins : for then he can say that he has two pieces of money or two coins, because he calls the penny as well as the dollar a piece of money or a coin. Hence it seems clear that nothing can be called one or single unless some other thing has first been conceived which (as has been said) agrees with it. But since the existence of God is His essence itself, and since we can form no general idea of His essence, it is certain that he who calls God one or single has no true idea of God, or is speaking of Him inappropriately.

As regards this, that figure is a negation, and not something positive, it is clearly evident that the totality of matter, considered without limitation, can have no figure and that figure has a place only in finite and limited bodies. For he who says that he apprehends a figure wants to express thereby nothing else than that he is apprehending a limited thing, and how it is limited. The limitation, therefore, does not belong to the thing in virtue of its being, but, on the contrary, it is its not-being. Since, then, figure is nothing but limitation and limitation is negation, therefore, as has been said, it can be nothing but negation.

The book written against mine by the Professor of Utrecht, and published after his death, I have seen in a bookseller's window. From the little I then read of it I judged that it was not worth reading through, much less worth answering. Therefore I left the book lying there, and I left its author such as he was. I reflected with a smile how the ignorant are always the boldest and the most ready to write. It seemed to me that the . . . put up their wares for sale as do the shop-keepers who always show first what is worst. They say the devil is a crafty fellow, but I think their spirit far surpasses his in craftiness. Farewell.

THE HAGUE, 2 *June* 1674.

LETTER LI   HUGO BOXEL

TO THE VERY ACUTE PHILOSOPHER, B. D. S.

MOST ILLUSTRIOUS SIR,

The reason why I am writing this to you is that I desire to know your opinion about apparitions and spectres, or ghosts, and if they exist, what you think about them, and how long they live; for some think they are immortal, and others think they are mortal. Since I am in doubt whether you think that they exist, I will proceed no further. Meanwhile, it is certain that the Ancients believed in their existence. Modern Theologians and Philosophers still believe in the existence of creatures of this kind, although they are not agreed about their essence. Some say they are composed of a very thin and fine matter, others that they are spiritual. But (as I began by saying) we differ very much from each other, since I am doubtful whether you admit that they exist, although, as cannot have escaped you, there are found so many instances and stories [of them] throughout Antiquity, that it would really be difficult to deny them or to throw doubt upon them. This is certain, namely, that even if you admit that they exist, still you do not believe that some of them are the souls of the dead as the defenders of the Roman faith will have it.

Here I will end, and await your reply. I will say nothing about the war, nothing about the rumours, for our life is cast in these times, etc. Farewell.

14 *September* 1674.

LETTER LII   B. D. S.

To the Very Honourable and Prudent
Mr. HUGO BOXEL.

Reply to the Preceding.

Sir,

Your letter, which I received yesterday, was very acceptable to me, both because of my desire for some news of you and because I see that you have not yet entirely forgotten me. And although others, perhaps, might think it a bad omen that ghosts or spirits should have been the reason for your writing to me, I, on the contrary, find in it something that is more important; for I realize that not only real things but also trifles and fancies can turn to my advantage.

Let us, however, set aside this question whether ghosts are phantoms and fancies; since it seems extraordinary to you not only to deny that there are such things, but even to doubt them; for you are convinced by the numerous stories which the ancients and the moderns relate about them. The great respect which I have always entertained for you, and still entertain for you, does not permit me to contradict you, much less to flatter you. The middle course which I propose to take between the two, is to ask you please to select out of the numerous stories which you have read about ghosts, one or two which are least open to doubt, and which most clearly prove that there are ghosts. For, to tell the truth, I have never read a reliable Author who clearly showed their existence. I still do not know what they are, and no one has ever been able to tell me anything about them. And yet it is certain that in the case of a thing which is so clearly shown by experience we ought to know what it is: otherwise we can hardly infer from any story that there are ghosts, but only this that there is something, although no one knows what it is. If Philosophers want to apply the name ghosts to things that we do not know, I shall not say No, since there are countless things of which I have no knowledge.

Lastly, Sir, before I explain my opinion on this subject further, I beg you to tell me what sort of things are these ghosts or spirits? Are they children, fools, or madmen? For what I have heard of them seems to be suggestive of fools rather than of intelligent people, and, at best, is most like child's play, or the pastime of silly people. Before I conclude, I still want to draw your attention to one thing, namely, that the desire which people commonly have, to relate things not as they really are, but as they want them to be, is better seen in the stories about spirits and ghosts than in others. The principal reason for this, as I believe, is that, since stories of this sort have no other witnesses than those who relate them, the inventor of them can add or remove circumstances according to his own pleasure, without having to fear that someone may contradict him, and especially does he invent things to justify the fear which seized him in his dreams and weird fancies, or else to confirm his courage, his faith, and his opinion. In addition to these, I have found yet other reasons which make me doubt, if not the stories themselves, at least the circumstantial details with which they are related and which mostly serve to support the conclusion which is meant to be drawn from these stories. I will leave it at this now, until I know what are those stories about which you are so convinced that you think it absurd even to doubt them.

[THE HAGUE, *September* 1674.]

LETTER LIII   HUGO BOXEL

TO THE VERY ACUTE PHILOSOPHER B. D. S.

Reply to the Preceding.

[MOST ACUTE SIR,] *

I expected no other answer than the one which you have sent me, namely, the answer of a friend who holds different views. This last does not matter : for friends can differ over unimportant matters, as was always allowed, without their friendship suffering in any way.

Before you explain yourself you ask me to say what

* From the Latin version.

kind of things ghosts are, whether they are children, fools or madmen, etc., and you add that all you have heard about them looks like the work of fools rather than of the intelligent. The old proverb is true, that a preconceived opinion hinders the search for truth.

I say that I believe that there are ghosts. The reasons are these. First, because it adds to the beauty and the perfection of the universe that they should exist. Secondly, it is probable that the Creator has created them because they resemble Him more closely than do corporeal creatures. Thirdly, because just as there is a body without a soul, so there is a soul without a body. Fourthly and lastly, because I think that in the uppermost air, place, or space, there is no dark body which has not inhabitants of its own, and therefore that the immeasurable space which lies between us and the stars is not empty, but is full of inhabitants who are spirits, the highest and uppermost being true spirits whereas the lowest in the lowest atmosphere are possibly creatures of very fine and thin substance, and also invisible. I think therefore that there are spirits of all kinds, except that possibly there are no female spirits.

This argument will not convince those who perversely think that the world was made by chance. Apart from these arguments, experience daily shows that there are spirits, of whom there are many stories, old as well as modern, and even present-day stories. They have been related by Plutarch in the Treatise on *Famous Men*, and in other parts of his works; by Suetonius in the *Lives of the Caesars*; by Wierus in his books on ghosts, also by Lavater, who fully discuss this subject, for which they have drawn on all writers. Also Cardanus, who is so celebrated for his learning, speaks of them in his book *De Subtilitate* and in *De Varietate* and in his *Autobiography*, in which he recounts his own experiences and those of his relations and friends to whom ghosts had appeared. Melanthon, a lover of truth and an intelligent man, and many others, bear witness from their own experiences. A Burgomaster of Sc., a learned and wise man, who is still alive, once told me that in his mother's brewery work was heard going on at night just as it went on by day when they brewed, and he swore to me that this had happened several times. Such things have also happened to me personally, and not once only, so that I shall never forget it ; therefore, and for the said reasons, I am convinced that there are ghosts.

As regards devils, who torment poor people in this life and after it, that is another question, as is also everything connected with magic. I think that the stories told of these things are fables. Sir, in the Treatises on Ghosts you will find a superabundance of circumstantial details. Besides these you can look up the younger Pliny, Book VII, in his letter to Sura, also Suetonius, in the Life of Julius Caesar, Chapter 32, Valerius Maximus, Book I, Chapter VIII, § 8, and also § 7 in the *Dies Geniales* of Alexander ab Alexandro. For I believe that you have these authors at hand. I am not speaking of Monks and Clerics, who report so many apparitions, spirits and devils, and so many stories, or, as I should say, fables of spectres, that they tire one and one loathes reading them. Thyraeus, a Jesuit, in a book which he calls *Apparitions of Spirits*, deals with these things. But these people do these things simply for the sake of gain, and to prove the existence of purgatory, which is a mine from which they extract so much silver and gold. This, however, is not found to be the case with the above-mentioned authors and other modern writers, who are without partizanship and should therefore be all the more believed.

You say at the end of your letter that to commend me to God is something which you cannot do without smiling. But, if you still remember the conversation which we had once, you will see that there is no ground for alarm in the conclusion which I drew at the time in my letter, etc.

In reply to your letter, since you speak of fools and lunatics I will state the conclusion of the learned Lavater with which he ends his first book on Night Ghosts. It reads as follows: *He who is bold enough to repudiate so many unanimous witnesses Ancient as well as modern, seems in my judgment unworthy of belief as regards anything he asserts, for just as it is the sign of rashness immediately to believe all who say they have seen Night ghosts, so, on the other hand it must be a very great shamelessness rashly and impudently to contradict so many trustworthy Historians, the Fathers, and many others who have great authority, etc.*

21 *September* 1674.

LETTER LIV   B. D. S.

To the Very Honourable and Prudent
Mr. HUGO BOXEL.

Reply to the Preceding.

MOST HONOURABLE SIR,
        Relying on what you say in your letter of the 21st of last month, namely, that friends can differ about what is unimportant and yet their friendship remain unimpaired, I will say clearly what I think of the reasons and stories from which you conclude *that there are ghosts of all kinds but possibly none of the female sex.* The reason why I did not reply sooner is that the books you cite are not at hand, nor could I find any but Pliny and Suetonius. But these two have saved me the trouble of consulting the others, since I am sure that they all rave after the same fashion, and love stories of uncommon things, which astonish men, and win their admira-

tion. I confess that I was not a little amazed, not at the stories which are told, but at those who write them. I am surprised that men who are endowed with ability and judgment, should expend their eloquence and mis-use it in order to persuade us of such trifles.

Let us, however, dismiss the authors and attack the question itself. And first my discussion will turn for a little on your conclusion. Let us see whether I, who deny the existence of Spectres or Spirits, therefore under-stand less the writers who treat of this matter; or whether you, who state that they exist, do not esteem these writers more highly than they deserve.

On the one hand, you do not doubt the existence of spirits of the male sex, but, on the other hand, you doubt whether there are any of the female sex. This seems to me more like a fancy than a doubt. For if this really were your opinion it would resemble rather the popular imagination which makes God masculine and not feminine. I am surprised that those who have seen naked spirits did not turn their eyes to the genital parts, perhaps from fear or from ignorance of this difference.

You may reply, this is mockery, not argument; and hence I see that you think your reasons are so sound and well-founded that no one (at least in your opinion) can contradict them unless it be some-one who out of perversity thinks that the world was made by chance. This already impels me, before I examine your fore-going reasons, briefly to explain my opinion on the question whether the world was created by chance. My answer is that, as it is certain that *Fortuitous* and *Necessary* are two contrary terms, it is also clear that he who asserts that the world is the necessary effect of the divine Nature also absolutely denies that the world was made by chance; he, however, who asserts that God could have refrained from creating the world is affirming, albeit in other words, that it was made by chance; since it proceeded from an act of will which need not have been. Since, however, this opinion and this view are thoroughly absurd, it is admitted universally and unanimously, that the will of God is eternal and has never been indifferent; therefore they must also admit (mark this well) that the world is the necessary effect of the Divine Nature. Let them call it will, understanding, or by any name they please, they will eventually arrive at the conclusion that they express one and the same thing by various names. For if you ask them whether the Divine will does not differ from the human will, they will reply that the former has nothing in common with the latter except the name; moreover they mostly admit that God's Will, Understanding, Essence or Nature are one and the same thing; I too, in order not to confuse the Divine with human nature, do not assign to God human attributes, such as Will, Understanding, attention, hearing, etc. Therefore, I say, as I have said just now, that the world is a necessary effect of the Divine Nature, and was not made by chance.

This, I think, will be sufficient to persuade you that the opinion of those (if indeed there are such persons) who say that the world was made by chance, is entirely opposed to my opinion. Relying on this foundation, I proceed to inquire into those reasons from which you conclude that all kinds of Spectres exist. What I can say of them in general is that they seem to be conjectures rather than reasons, and that I find it difficult to believe that you hold them to be conclusive reasons. Let us see, however, whether they are conjectures or reasons, and whether we can accept them as established.

Your first reason is that the existence of Spectres is required for the beauty and perfection of the Universe. Beauty, most honoured Sir, is not so much a quality of the object which is perceived as an effect in him who perceives it. If our eyes were more long-sighted or more short-sighted, or if our temperament were other than it is, things which now appear to us beautiful would appear to be ugly and things which now appear to be ugly would appear to us beautiful. The most beautiful hand when seen through a microscope will appear horrible. Some things seen at a distance are beautiful, but seen at closer range are ugly. Therefore things regarded in themselves, or in relation to God, may be neither beautiful nor ugly. He, then, who says that God created the world to be beautiful must necessarily assert one of two alternatives, namely, either that God has made the world to suit the desire and the eyes of men, or the desire and the eyes of men to suit the world. Now, whether we assert the former or the latter, I do not see why God had to create Spectres and Spirits in order that one of these alternatives should result. Perfection and imperfection are designations which are not very different from those of beauty and ugliness. Therefore, not to be too diffuse, I only ask what will contribute more to the beauty and perfection of the world, is it the existence of Spectres, or that of numerous monsters, such as Centaurs, Hydras, Harpies, Satyrs, Griffins, Arguses, and more absurdities of this kind? The world would indeed have been well adorned had God for the pleasure of our Phantasy adorned and equipped it with these things which each man can easily imagine and dream for himself, but no one can ever understand.

Your second reason is that since Spirits express the image of God more than do other, corporeal creatures, it is also probable that God has created them. I confess that I still do not really know wherein Spirits express God more than do other creatures. This I know, that between the finite and the infinite there is no proportion : so that the difference between the greatest and most excellent creature and God is the same as the difference which exists between God and the least creature. This argument therefore is not to the point. Had I as clear an idea of Spectres as I have of a triangle or a circle, I should in no way hesitate to assert that they were created by God : but inasmuch as the idea which I have of them corresponds entirely to the idea of Harpies, Griffins, Hydras, etc., which I apprehend in my imagination, I can only consider them as dreams, which are as different from God as Being is from Not-Being.

Your third reason (which is, that just as body exists without soul, so should soul exist without body) seems to me equally absurd. Tell me, I pray you, whether it is also likely that memory, hearing, sight, etc., exist without bodies, because bodies are found without memory, hearing, sight, etc. ? Or a sphere without a circle, because a circle exists without a sphere ?

Your fourth and last reason is the same as the first, and I refer to my answer to that. Here I shall merely note that I do not know what are the highest and lowest places which you conceive in infinite matter, unless you think that the Earth is the centre of the universe. For if the Sun or Saturn is the centre of the Universe, the Sun or Saturn and not the earth will be the lowest. Therefore, putting aside this argument and the rest, I conclude that these and similar reasons will convince no one that there are Spectres and Ghosts of every kind, except those who close their ears to the understanding, and allow themselves to be led astray by Superstition, which is so hostile to right Reason that, in order to lower the prestige of Philosophers, it will put its faith in old women.

As regards these stories, I have already said in my first letter, that I do not deny them entirely but only the conclusion which is inferred from them. You may add that I do not think them so trustworthy as not to be dubious about many circumstantial details, which they too often add more for adornment than in order the better to prove the truth of the story, or the conclusion which they desire to draw from it. I had hoped that out of so many stories you would produce at least one or two which would be least open to doubt, and which would most clearly show that Spectres and Ghosts exist. That the said Mayor wants to conclude that Spectres exist because he heard them working by night in his mother's brewery, as he was wont to hear men work by day, seems to me ludicrous. Similarly, it would seem too long to examine here all the stories which have been written about these absurdities. To be brief, I refer to Julius Caesar who, as Suetonius bears witness, laughed at these things, and yet was fortunate, according to what Suetonius narrates about this Prince, in his biography, chapter 59. And in the same way, all who consider the effects of mortal imaginings and feelings must laugh at such things, whatever Lavater and others who dream with him about this business may adduce to the contrary.

[THE HAGUE, *September* 1674.]

LETTER LV   HUGO BOXEL

To the Very Acute Philosopher B. d. S.

Reply to the Preceding.

MOST ACUTE SIR,

I answer your letter later than I expected, because a slight illness has deprived me of the pleasure of study and reflection, and has prevented me from writing to you. Now, thank God, I am restored to health. In my answer I shall follow in the steps of your letter, and shall skip your declamations against those who have written on Spectres.

I say, then, that I think that there are no Spectres of the female sex, because I deny that there is any birth-giving among them. I omit the question of their precise shape and composition because it does not concern me.

A thing is said to have been made fortuitously when it is produced without regard to the aim of its author. When we dig the earth to plant a vine, or to make a pit or a grave, and find a treasure of which we never had a thought, this is said to happen by chance. But he who, of his own free will acts in such a way that he can either do so or not, is never said to act by chance, when he does act. For in that case all human acts would happen by chance, which would be absurd. Necessary and Free are contraries, but not Necessary and Fortuitous. Granted that God's will is eternal, it does not yet follow that the world is eternal, because God could from eternity determine that He would create the world at an appointed time.

Further, you deny that God's will has ever been indifferent. On this I disagree. Nor is it necessary to pay such careful attention to this as you think. Nor do all say that God's will is necessary. For this involves necessity; since he who attributes a will to some-one means thereby that he can act or not, according to his will. But if we ascribe necessity to him, then he must act necessarily.

Lastly, you say that you ascribe no human attributes to God in order not to confuse the Divine with human nature. So far I agree—for we do not perceive in what way God acts or in what way He wills, understands, considers, sees, or hears, etc. But if you altogether deny of God these activities and our highest reflections, and assert that they do not exist eminently and in a metaphysical sense in God, then I do not know your God, nor what you mean by the term *God*. That which is not apprehended should not be denied. Mind, which is spirit and incorporeal, can only act with the finest bodies, namely with the humours. And what is the relation between the Mind and the Body? In what way does Mind act with Bodies? For without these the Mind is quiescent, and when they are agitated the Mind does the contrary of what it ought to do. Show me how this happens. You will not be able to do so, nor shall I; nevertheless we see and feel that Mind is active, which remains true although we do not apprehend in what way the action takes place. Similarly although we do not grasp in what manner God acts, and we do not want to ascribe to Him human actions, yet we must not deny that His actions do eminently and incomprehensibly accord with ours, such as willing, understanding, seeing, hearing, though not with eyes or with ears, but with the intellect; just as the wind and air can without the aid of hands or other instruments destroy and even overthrow regions and mountains, which men cannot do without hands and engines. If you attribute necessity to God, and deprive Him of will and free choice, then it may be doubted whether you do not depict and represent as a monster Him who is an infinitely perfect Being. To attain your end, you will need other reasons on which to lay your foundation; for, in my opinion, there is no validity in those you have brought forward. And even if you prove them, there are still others which are possibly as weighty as yours. But, dismissing these questions, let us proceed.

You demand conclusive proofs that there are spirits in the world. There are few such proofs in the world, and none except those of Mathematics are found as certain as we wish. We are, in fact, satisfied with conjectures which are probable, and likely to be true. If the arguments by which things are proved were conclusive, none would be found to contradict them except the foolish and obstinate. But, my dear Friend, we are not so fortunate. In the world we are less exacting, we make a conjecture to a certain extent, and in our reasonings we accept the probable in the absence of proofs. This is evident from all the sciences, divine as well as human, which are full of controversies and disputes, the great number of which is the reason why there are so many different opinions found among all. Therefore, as you know, there have been in the past Philosophers, called Sceptics, who doubted everything. They debated both for and against a point in order that they might follow what was only probable in default of true reasons, and each of them believed what seemed to him more probable. The Moon is situated directly below the Sun ; and therefore the Sun will be obscured for a certain part of the earth ; and if the Sun is not obscured, while it is yet day, then the Moon is not situated directly below the Sun. This is a conclusive proof, from the cause to the effect, and from the effect to the cause. There are proofs of this kind, but very few, which if they are once perceived can be contradicted by nobody.

As to beauty, there are things whose parts are proportionate in relation to the others, and are better put together than others. God has granted to the understanding and judgment of man agreement and harmony with that which is proportionate, but not with that which has no proportion. Thus in sounds which are harmonious and dissonant the hearing can easily distinguish between harmony and dissonance, because the former brings pleasure but the latter displeasure. The perfection of a thing is also beautiful in so far as there is nothing lacking to it. Of this there are many examples, which I omit so as not to be too lengthy. Let us only consider the world to which the name of Whole or Universe is given. If this is true, as it really is, then it cannot be disfigured or degraded by incorporeal things What you say of Centaurs, Hydras, Harpies, etc., is out of place here : for we are speaking of the most universal kinds of things, and of their first grades, which comprehend under them various and innumerable species, we are speaking, that is, of the eternal and the temporal, of cause and effect, of the finite and the infinite, of the animate and the inanimate, of substance and accident, or mode, of the corporeal and the spiritual, etc.

I say that spirits are like God because He is also a spirit. You demand as clear an idea of spirits as of a triangle, which is impossible. Tell me, I adjure you, what idea you have of God, and whether it is as clear to your understanding as the idea of a triangle. I know that you have no such idea, and I have said that we are not so fortunate as to grasp things through conclusive proofs, and that, for the most part, the probable is predominant in this world. Nevertheless, I assert that just as body exists without memory etc. so also memory etc. exists without body, and that as a circle exists without a sphere, so does a sphere exist without a circle. But this is to descend from the most universal genera to particular species, for which this argument is not intended.

I say that the Sun is the centre of the world, and that the fixed stars are further from the earth than is Saturn, that Saturn is more remote than Jupiter, and Jupiter than Mars ; and so, in the unlimited air some bodies are more remote from us, and some are nearer to us, and these we call higher or lower.

It is not those who defend the existence of spirits who discredit Philosophers, but those who deny their existence, since all Philosophers, ancient as well as modern, think themselves convinced of the existence of spirits. Plutarch bears witness to this in his Treatises on the opinions of Philosophers, and on the dæmon of Socrates ; also all the Stoics, Pythagoreans, Platonists, Peripatetics,

Empedocles, Maximus Tyrius, Apuleius and others bear witness to it. Of modern philosophers none denies spectres. Reject then so many wise witnesses, who have themselves seen or have heard [spectres], so many Philosophers, so many Historians who relate such stories; assert that they are all foolish like the multitude, and mad. Your answers cannot persuade one but are even absurd, they do not anywhere touch the main point of our controversy, and you put forward no proof to confirm your opinion. Caesar, like Cicero and Cato, does not laugh at spectres, but at omens and presentiments; however, if, on the day on which he died, he had not laughed at Spurina, his enemies would not have stabbed him with so many wounds. But let these suffice on this occasion, etc.

[*September* 1674.]

LETTER LVI

B. D. S.

To the Very Honourable and Prudent
Mr. HUGO BOXEL.

Reply to the Preceding.

MOST HONOURABLE SIR,

I hasten to answer your letter, which I received yesterday, because if I go on delaying longer I shall be compelled to postpone my reply longer than I should wish. Your health would cause me anxiety if I had not heard that you are better, and I hope you are now entirely recovered.

How difficult it is for two persons who follow different principles to meet one another and agree on a subject which depends on many others, would be clear from this question alone, even if no argument demonstrated it. Tell me, I pray, whether you have seen or read any Philosophers who hold the opinion that the world was made by chance, that is, in the sense in which you understand it, namely, that God, when creating the world had set Himself a definite aim, and yet transgressed His own decree. I do not know that such a thing even occurred to any man's thought. Similarly, I am in the dark about the arguments by which you endeavour to persuade me to believe that *Fortuitous* and *Necessary* are not contraries. As soon as I realize that the three angles of a triangle are necessarily equal to two right angles, I also deny that this is the result of chance. Similarly as soon as I realize that heat is the necessary effect of fire, I also deny that it occurs by chance. It seems no less absurd and opposed to reason to suppose that *Necessary* and *Free* are contraries. For no one can deny that God knows Himself and everything else freely, and yet all are agreed in admitting that God knows Himself necessarily. Thus you seem to me to make no distinction between coercion or force, and Necessity. That man desires to live, to love, etc., is not a compulsory activity, but it is none the less necessary, and much more so is God's will to be, and to know, and to act. If, apart from these remarks, you turn over in your mind the fact that indifference is nothing but ignorance or doubt, and that a will ever constant and determined in all things is a virtue, and a necessary property of the intellect, then you will see that my words are thoroughly in accord with the truth. If we assert that God had it in His power not to will a thing, and did not have it in His power not to understand it, then we attribute to God two different kinds of freedom, one being that of necessity, the other that of indifference, and consequently we shall conceive the will of God as differing from His essence and His intellect, and in that case we shall fall into one absurdity after another.

The attention which I requested in my former letter

did not seem to you necessary, and this was the reason why you did not fix your thoughts on the principal point, and neglected what was of the utmost importance to the subject.

Further, when you say that if I deny to God the acts of seeing, of hearing, of attending and of willing, etc., and their occurrence in Him in an eminent degree, then you do not know what kind of God I have, I suspect therefrom that you believe that there is no perfection greater than that which is unfolded in the said attributes. I do not wonder at this, since I believe that a triangle, if only it had the power of speech, would say in like manner that God is eminently triangular, and a circle would say that the Divine Nature is eminently circular, and in this way each thing would ascribe its own attributes to God, and make itself like unto God, while all else would appear to it deformed.

The small compass of a letter, and limitation of time, do not permit me to explain in detail my opinion about the Divine Nature, or the other Questions which you put forward, to say nothing of the fact that to raise difficulties is not the same as to advance reasons. It is true that in the world we often act on conjecture; but it is false that our reflections are based on conjecture. In ordinary life we must follow what is most probable, but in philosophical speculations, the truth. Man would perish of thirst and hunger if he would not eat or drink until he had obtained a perfect proof that food and drink would do him good. But in contemplation this has no place. On the contrary, we must be cautious not to admit as true something which is merely probable. For when we admit one falsity, countless others follow.

Further, from the fact that divine and human sciences are full of disputes and controversies it cannot be inferred that all the things which are treated therein are uncertain: for there have been very many people who were so possessed by the love of contradiction that they laughed even at Geometrical proofs.   Sextus Empiricus and other Sceptics whom you cite say that it is not true that the whole is greater than its part, and they have the same view of the other axioms.

But, putting aside and admitting the fact that in default of proofs we must be satisfied with probabilities, I say that a probable Proof ought to be such that, although we can doubt it, yet we cannot contradict it ; because that which be contradicted is not likely to be true, but likely to be false.   If, for instance, I say that Peter is alive, because I saw him in good health yesterday, this is indeed likely to be true so long as no one can contradict me ; but if someone else says that yesterday he saw Peter suffering from loss of consciousness, and that he believes that Peter died from it, he makes my words seem false. That your conjecture about spectres and ghosts seems false and not even probable, I have so clearly shown that I find nothing worthy of consideration in your answer.

To your question whether I have as clear an idea of God as I have of a triangle, I answer in the affirmative. But if you ask me whether I have as clear a mental image of God as I have of a triangle, I shall answer No.   For we cannot imagine God, but we can, indeed, conceive Him. Here also it should be noted that I do not say that I know God entirely, but only that I understand some of His attributes, though not all, nor even the greater part of them, and it is certain that our ignorance of the majority of them does not hinder our having a know-ledge of some of them.   When I learnt Euclid's elements I first understood that the three angles of a triangle are equal to two right angles, and I clearly perceived this property of a triangle although I was ignorant of many others.

As regards spectres, or ghosts, I have never yet heard of an intelligible property of theirs, but only of

Phantasies which no-one can grasp. When you say that spectres, or ghosts, here in this lower region (I follow your form of expression, although I do not know that the matter here in this lower region is less valuable than that above) consist of the finest, thinnest, and most subtle substance, you seem to be speaking of spiders' webs, of air, or of vapours. To say that they are invisible means for me as much as if you said what they are not, but not what they are ; unless perhaps you want to indicate that, according as they please, they make themselves now visible, now invisible, and that in these as in other impossibilities, the imagination will find no difficulty.

The authority of Plato, Aristotle, and Socrates has not much weight with me. I should have been surprised had you mentioned Epicurus, Democritus, Lucretius or any one of the Atomists, or defenders of the atoms. It is not surprising that those who invented occult Qualities, intentional Species, substantial Forms, and a thousand other trifles, should have devised spectres and ghosts, and put their faith in old women, in order to weaken the authority of Democritus, of whose good repute they were so envious that they burnt all his books, which he had published amidst so much praise. If you have a mind to put faith in them, what reasons have you for denying the miracles of the Holy Virgin, and of all the Saints, which have been described by so many very famous Philosophers, Theologians, and Historians that I can produce an hundred of them to scarcely one of the others ?

Lastly, most honoured Sir, I have gone further than I intended. I do not wish to annoy you further with things which (I know) you will not admit, since you follow other principles which differ widely from my own, etc.

[THE HAGUE, *October* 1674.]

LETTER LVII

EHRENFRIED WALTER VON TSCHIRNHAUS

To the Very Distinguished and Acute Philosopher
B. d. S.

Excellent Sir,

I am surprised, at all events, that in the same way that Philosophers prove that something is false they also show its truth. For Descartes, at the beginning of his *Method*, thinks that the certainty of the understanding is the same for all : he proves it, moreover, in the *Meditations*. This is also approved by those who think that in this way they can prove something which is certain, in such a way that it is accepted as indubitable by individual men.

But, dismissing these things, I appeal to experience, and I humbly beg you to attend carefully to the following points. For thus it will be understood that if one of two men affirms something, but the other denies it, and they both speak as they think, then although they appear to contradict one another in words, yet when their thoughts are considered, they both (each according to his own thought) speak the truth. This I mention because it is of immense use in common life, and countless controversies, and the disputes which follow them, could be averted by the observation of this one fact, although this truth in thought is not always absolutely true, but only in so far as we grant what is assumed as true of the understanding. This Rule is so universal that it is found among all men, not excepting even those who are mad or asleep : for whatever they say that they see (although it may not appear so to us) or have seen, it is most certain that it really is so.

This is also very clearly seen in the case under consideration, namely, that of Free Will. For both, he who argues for, as well as he who argues against it, seem to me to speak the truth, namely each in accordance with his conception of Freedom. For Descartes calls that free which is compelled by no cause ; you, on the other hand, that which is not determined to something by a cause. Therefore I agree with you in saying that we are in everything determined towards something by a definite cause, and so we have no free will. On the other hand, however, I also think with Descartes that in certain things (as I shall soon show) we suffer no sort of compulsion, and thus we have free will. I will take an example from the present.

The state of the question is threefold. *First,* have we absolutely power over things which are outside us ? This is denied. For instance, my writing this letter now is not absolutely in my power, because I would certainly have written before now if I had not been hindered either by my absence or by the presence of friends. *Secondly,* have we absolutely power over the motions of our body, which follow when the will determines them thereto ? I answer with the reservation, if we are in sound physical health. For if I am well I can always set myself to write, or refrain from it. *Thirdly,* when I can take control over my reason, can I exercise it with complete freedom, that is, absolutely ? To this I answer in the affirmative. For, without contradicting his own consciousness, who would deny that I can in my thoughts think that I want to write or not to write ? And in so far as the operation itself is concerned, since external causes permit (this concerns the second point) that I should have the power alike of writing or of not writing, I agree with you that there are causes which determine me to write now, namely because you first wrote to me, and by that act requested me to answer at the first opportunity, and because there is now an opportunity which I would not willingly miss. I certainly assert, on the evidence of consciousness, and in agreement with Descartes, that such things do not therefore force me, and that I nevertheless really can (as it seems impossible to deny) refrain from writing, notwithstanding these reasons. Also if we were forced by external things, who could acquire a habit of virtue? Indeed, if this were granted, all wickedness would be excusable. But how often does it not happen that when we are determined to something by things outside us, we do nevertheless resist it with a firm and constant spirit?

To give a clearer explanation of the above Rule: You both indeed tell the truth, each according to your conception; but if we look for absolute truth, then it is only found in the view of Descartes. For in your thought you presuppose as something certain that the essence of Freedom consists in the fact that we are not determined by anything. If this is granted, both will be right. Although the essence of anything consists in that without which it cannot really be conceived, yet liberty can surely be clearly conceived, even if in our actions we are determined towards something by external causes, or even if there are always causes which are an incitement to us to direct our actions in a certain way, yet clearly do not produce the whole result; but freedom can not be conceived at all if it is supposed that we are forced. See further Descartes, Volume I, *Letters* 8 and 9, also Volume II, page 4. But these will be enough. I pray you to answer these difficulties, and you will find me not only grateful but, health permitting, also

Your most devoted
N. N.

ᵃ *October* 1674.

To the Very Learned and Expert
Mr. G. H. SCHULLER.

Reply to the Preceding.

Most Expert Sir,

Our friend J. R. has sent me the letter which
you were good enough to write to me, together with
your friend's criticism of Descartes' and my opinion
about free will, which were most acceptable to me.
And although just now besides being unwell, I am very
much distracted by other matters, nevertheless your
exceptional kindliness, or, what I consider most important, the love of truth which possesses you, compels me
to satisfy your wish to the best of my slender capacity.
I do not indeed know what your friend means, before
he appeals to experience and asks for careful attention.
He then adds, *If one of two men affirms something of a
thing but the other denies it, etc.* This is true if he means
that the two, although they use the same words, are yet
thinking of different things. Of this I once sent some
examples to our friend J. R., and I am now writing to
ask him to communicate them to you.

I therefore pass on to that definition of Freedom which
he says is mine ; but I do not know whence he has taken
it. I say that that thing is free which exists and acts
solely from the necessity of its own nature ; but that
that thing is under compulsion which is determined by
something else to exist, and to act in a definite and determined manner. For example, God, although He exists
necessarily, nevertheless exists freely, since He exists
solely from the necessity of His own nature. So also
God freely understands Himself and absolutely all things,
since it follows solely from the necessity of His own
nature that He should understand everything. You see,

therefore, that I do not place Freedom in free decision, but in free necessity.

Let us, however, descend to created things, which are all determined by external causes to exist, and to act in a definite and determined manner. In order that this may be clearly understood, let us think of a very simple thing. For instance, a stone receives from an external cause, which impels it, a certain quantity of motion, with which it will afterwards necessarily continue to move when the impact of the external cause has ceased. This continuance of the stone in its motion is compelled, not because it is necessary, but because it must be defined by the impact of an external cause. What is here said of the stone must be understood of each individual thing, however composite and however adapted to various ends it may be thought to be : that is, that each thing is necessarily determined by an external cause to exist and to act in a definite and determinate manner.

Next, conceive, if you please, that the stone while it continues in motion thinks, and knows that it is striving as much as possible to continue in motion. Surely this stone, inasmuch as it is conscious only of its own effort, and is far from indifferent, will believe that it is completely free, and that it continues in motion for no other reason than because it wants to. And such is the human freedom which all men boast that they possess, and which consists solely in this, that men are conscious of their desire, and ignorant of the causes by which they are determined. So the infant believes that it freely wants milk ; the boy when he is angry that he freely wants revenge ; the timid that he wants to escape. Then too the drunkard believes that, by the free decision of his mind, he says those things which afterwards when sober he would prefer to have left unsaid. So the delirious, the garrulous and many others of the same sort, believe that they are acting in accordance with the free decision of their mind, and not that they are carried away by impulse. Since this preconception is innate in all men, they are not so easily freed from it. For, although experience teaches sufficiently and more than sufficiently that the last thing that men can do is to moderate their appetites, and that often, when they are tormented by conflicting feelings, they see the better and follow the worse, yet they believe themselves to be free, because they desire some things slightly, and their appetites for these can easily be repressed by the memory of some other thing, which we frequently call to mind.

With these remarks, unless I am mistaken, I have sufficiently explained what my view is about free and compelled necessity, and about imaginary human freedom : and from this it will be easy to answer the objections of your friend. For, when he says with Descartes, that he is free who is compelled by no external cause, if by a man who is compelled he means one who acts against his will, I admit that in certain matters we are in no way compelled, and that in this respect we have a free will. But if by compelled he means one who, although he does not act against his will, yet acts necessarily (as I explained above), then I deny that we are free in anything.

Your friend, on the contrary, asserts that *we can exercise our reason with complete freedom, that is, absolutely.* He persists in this opinion with sufficient, not to say too much, confidence. *For who*, he says, *without contradicting his own consciousness, would deny that in my thoughts I can think that I want to write, and that I do not want to do so.* I should very much like to know of what consciousness he speaks, other than that which I explained above in my example of the stone. Indeed, in order not to contradict my consciousness, that is, my reason and experience, and in order not to foster preconceived ideas and ignorance, I deny that I can, by any absolute power of thought, think that I want, and that I do not want to write. But I appeal to his own consciousness, for he has doubtless experienced the fact that in dreams he has not the power of thinking that he wants, and does not want to write; and that when he dreams that he wants to write he has not the power of not dreaming that he wants to write. I believe he has had no less experience of the fact that the mind is not always equally capable of thinking about the same subject; but that according as the body is more fit for the excitation of the image of this or that object, so the mind is more capable of contemplating this or that object.

When he adds, further, that the causes of his applying himself to writing have stimulated him to write, but have not compelled him, he means nothing else (if you will examine the matter fairly) than that his mind was at that time so constituted that the causes which on other occasions, that is, when they were in conflict with some powerful feeling, could not influence him, could now influence him easily, that is, that causes which on other occasions could not compel him, have now compelled him, not to write against his will, but necessarily to desire to write.

Again, as to his statement that *if we were compelled by external causes then no one would be able to acquire the habit of virtue*, I do not know who has told him that we cannot be of a firm and constant disposition as a result of fatalistic necessity, but only from the free decision of the Mind.

As to his last addition, that *if this were granted all wickedness would be excusable*; what then? For wicked men are no less to be feared, and no less pernicious, when they are necessarily wicked. But on these things, look up, if you please, Part II, Chapter VIII, of my *Appendix to Descartes' Principles, Books I and II, geometrically demonstrated*.

Lastly, I should like your friend, who makes these objections to my theory, to tell me how he conceives human virtue, which he says arises from the free decision of the mind, together with the preordination of God. For if, with Descartes, he admits that he does not know how to reconcile them, then he is endeavouring to hurl against me the weapon by which he has already been pierced. But in vain. For if you will attentively examine my view, you will see that it is entirely consistent, etc.

[THE HAGUE, *October* 1674.]

LETTER LIX

EHRENFRIED WALTER VON TSCHIRNHAUS

To the Very Distinguished and Acute Philosopher
B. D. S.

MOST DISTINGUISHED SIR,

When are we to have your Method of rightly controlling the Reason in acquiring knowledge of unknown truths, as also your General Physics ? I know that you have recently made great advances in these subjects. The first was already known to me, the second is known to me from the lemmas added to the second part of the *Ethics*, by means of which many difficulties in Physics are easily solved. If you have the leisure and the opportunity, I humbly ask you to give me the true Definition of Motion, and the explanation of it, and also to tell me in what way, since Extension considered in itself is indivisible, immutable, etc., we are able to infer a priori that so many figures and such manifold varieties of them can arise, and consequently, the existence of figure in the particles of a body which constitute the form of another body. When we were together you pointed out to me the method which you employ in searching for truths as yet unknown. I find from experience that this method is most excellent, and yet very easy, as far as I understand it ; and I can assert that, with the help of this one observation of yours, I have made great advances in Mathematics. I therefore wish that you would communicate to me the true definition of an adequate, a true, a false, a fictitious and a doubtful idea. I have sought for the difference between a true and an adequate idea. So far, however, I have been able to discover nothing except that when I have investigated a thing and a certain concept or idea, then, I say, (in order to discover further whether this true idea was also the adequate idea of something) I asked myself what is the cause of this idea or concept ; when I discovered this, I again asked what is the cause of this concept, and so I pushed on my inquiry into the causes of the causes of ideas, until I at length obtained such a cause for which, in turn, I could see no other cause except that among all the possible ideas which I possess this one also exists. If, for example, we ask, wherein consists the true origin of our Errors, Descartes will answer, in the fact that we give assent to things not yet clearly perceived. But even if this is a true idea of this matter, I shall not yet be able to determine all that it is necessary to know about it, unless I have also an adequate idea of this thing. In order to attain to this I again inquire into the cause of this concept, that is, how it comes about that we give our assent to things not clearly understood, and I answer that this happens through lack of knowledge. Here, however, one cannot ask again, what is the cause why we are ignorant of some things, and from this I see that I have discovered an adequate idea of our errors.

Here, by the way, I ask you whether, since it is established that many things which are expressed in infinite modes have an adequate idea of themselves, and that from any adequate idea all that can be known of the thing can be derived, though it may be elicited more easily from one idea than from another, whether, I say, there is any means of knowing which idea should be used rather than another. Thus, for example, an adequate idea of a circle is one based on the equality of the radii, so also is one that is based on its infinite mutually equal right angles made by the intersection of two lines, and so, moreover, it has innumerable expressions each of which explains adequately the nature of a circle; and although from each of these expressions all other things which can be known about a circle may be deduced, yet the deduction is easier from one of them than from another. So also he who considers the applicates of curves will deduce many things concerning their measurement, but we discover them with greater ease if we consider their Tangents, etc. Thus I wished to show you how far I have progressed in this investigation: I await its completion, or, if I have anywhere made a mistake, its correction, and also the desired Definition. Farewell.

5 *January* 1675.

LETTER LX   B. D. S.

To the Very Noble and Learned
Mr. EHRENFRIED WALTER VON TSCHIRNHAUS.

Reply to the Preceding.

Most Noble Sir,
            I recognize no other difference between a true and an adequate idea than that the word true refers only to the agreement of the idea with its ideatum, while the word adequate refers to the nature of the idea in itself; so that there is really no difference between a true and an adequate idea except this extrinsic relation.
            But in order that I may know from which idea of a

thing, out of many, all the properties of the object may be deduced, I observe one thing only, that the idea or definition of the thing should express its efficient cause. For example, in order to investigate the properties of a circle, I ask whether from this idea of a circle, namely, that it is composed of innumerable right angles, I can deduce all its properties : I inquire, I say, whether this idea involves the efficient cause of a circle. Since this is not so, I seek another, namely that a circle is the space which is described by a line of which one point is fixed and the other moveable. Since this Definition expresses the efficient cause, I know that I can deduce from it all the properties of a circle, etc. So also, when I define God as the supremely perfect Being, since this definition does not express the efficient cause (for I conceive that an efficient cause can be internal as well as external) I shall not be able to discover all the properties of God from it ; but when I define God as *a Being*, etc. (see Definition VI, Part I, of the *Ethics*).

As for your other problems, namely those about Motion and those which concern Method, since my views have not yet been written out in proper order, I reserve them for another occasion.

As to your assertion that he who considers the applicates of curves will deduce many things about their measurement, but that this can be done with greater ease by considering Tangents, etc., I think, on the contrary, that even by considering Tangents many other things will be deduced with more difficulty than by considering the co-ordinates of curves ; and I absolutely assert that from certain qualities of a thing (whatever the given idea) some things will be discovered more easily, others with greater difficulty (although they all concern the nature of that thing). But this only, I think, must be kept in view, that the idea to be sought is such that all the properties may be elicited from it, as has been said above. For if one is to deduce from anything all the possible properties, it necessarily follows that the last ones will be more difficult than the prior ones, etc.

[The Hague, *January* 1675.]

LETTER LXI   HENRY OLDENBURG

To the Very Illustrious Mr. B. d. S.

Many greetings.

I was unwilling to miss this convenient opportunity which the very learned Mr. Bourgeois, a Doctor of Medicine of Caen, and an adherent of the Reformed Religion, who is just going to Holland, offers me, of informing you that some weeks ago I expressed to you my gratitude for sending me your Treatise, though it was never delivered, but that I doubt whether my letter duly came to your hands. *In it I indicated my opinion of that Treatise: this opinion, indeed, after having examined and weighed the matter more closely, I now think was very premature.* Certain things in it seemed to me, at the time, to tend to harm religion, when I measured it by the standard furnished by the crowd of Theologians, and the accepted Formulae of the Creeds (which seem to be too much inspired by partizanship). But, on reconsidering the whole matter more closely, many considerations occur to me which go to persuade me that you are so far from intending any harm to true Religion and sound Philosophy that, on the contrary, you labour to commend and establish the true object of the Christian Religion, and the divine sublimity and excellence of a fruitful philosophy. Since, therefore, I now believe that this is what is really in your mind, I do most earnestly beg you to be kind enough to explain what you are now preparing and considering to this end, in frequent letters to your old and sincere friend, who whole-heartedly wishes the happiest issue of so divine an enterprise. I give you my sacred promise that I will divulge no part of them to any mortal, if you enjoin silence; I will merely endeavour to do this, namely, gradually to prepare the minds of good and wise men to embrace those truths which you will some time bring to light more fully, and to remove the prejudices which have been conceived against your Thoughts.

If I am not mistaken, you seem to me to have a very deep insight into the nature and powers of the human mind, and its union with our body. I earnestly beg you to be willing to tell me your thoughts on this subject. Farewell, most distinguished Sir, and continue to favour the most devoted admirer of your Teaching and virtue

HENRY OLDENBURG.

LONDON, 8 *June* 1675.

LETTER LXII   HENRY OLDENBURG

TO THE VERY ILLUSTRIOUS MR. B. D. S.

Now that our literary intercourse has been so happily renewed, most illustrious Sir, I do not wish to fail in the duty of friendship by allowing an interruption of our correspondence. Since I understand from your answer to me, dated 5 July, that you intend to publish your Five-Part Treatise, allow me, I pray, to advise you out of your sincere affection for me not to include anything which may appear to undermine the practice of Religious virtue. Especially so since there is nothing for which this degenerate and wicked age seeks more eagerly than the kind of doctrines whose conclusions seem to give encouragement to flagrant vices.

For the rest, I shall not refuse to receive some copies

of the said Treatise. I would only ask you that, when the time comes, they should be addressed to a certain Dutch merchant, settled in London, who will then see to it that they are delivered to me. There will be no need to mention that such books have been forwarded to me. For, if only they come safely into my possession, I have no doubt that it will be easy for me to distribute them among my friends here and there, and to obtain a fair price for them. Farewell, and when you have time, write to

Your most devoted
HENRY OLDENBURG.

LONDON, 22 *July* 1675.

LETTER LXIII   G. H. SCHULLER

To the Very Distinguished and Acute Philosopher
B. D. S.

Most noble and distinguished Sir,

I should blush for my long silence, for which I could be accused of ingratitude for the favour which you of your kindness have shown to me though I did not deserve it, if I did not reflect that your generous kindliness is inclined to excuse rather than to accuse, and if I did not know that, for the common good of your friends, it makes you find time for such serious reflections as it would be culpable and wrong to disturb without special cause. For this reason, then, I kept silence, and was content, in the meantime, to hear from friends of your good health. But with the present letter I want to inform you that our most noble friend Mr. von Tschirnhausen is still in England and, like us, enjoys good health, and that in his letters (which he has sent to me) he has three times bidden me to convey his dutiful regards, and respectful greeting to you, Sir. He repeatedly begs me to ask you for the solution of the following difficulties, and at the same time to beg you to send the desired answer to them.

These are, whether you, Sir, will please convince us by some direct proof,* and not by a reduction to impossibility, that we cannot know more attributes of God than thought and extension? Further, whether it follows from this that creatures consisting of other attributes, cannot on the contrary conceive any extension, and that thus it would seem that there must be constituted as many worlds as there are attributes of God. For instance, our world of extension, so to say, has so much amplitude; worlds consisting of other attributes would also have as much amplitude. And just as we perceive nothing besides extension except thought, so the creatures of those worlds must perceive nothing but the attributes of their own world and thought.

Secondly, since the understanding of God differs from our understanding in essence as well as in existence, it will, therefore, have nothing in common with our understanding, and consequently (according to Book I, Proposition III) God's understanding cannot be the cause of our understanding.

Thirdly, in the Scholium to Proposition X, you say that nothing in Nature is clearer than that each Being must be conceived under some attribute (this I fully understand) ánd that the more reality or being it has, the more attributes belong to it. Hence it would seem to follow that there exist Beings which have three, four, or more Attributes, whereas from what has been proved it could be inferred that each Being consists of two attributes only, namely a certain attribute of God and the idea of that attribute.

Fourthly, I should like examples of those things which

* I beg you earnestly please to solve the doubts which are raised here, and to send me your answer to them.

are immediately produced by God, and of those which are produced by some infinite mediate modification. Thought and Extension seem to me to be of the first kind; of the second, Understanding in the case of thought, and Motion in the case of extension, etc.*

These are the questions which our above-mentioned Tschirnhausen desires with me to have elucidated by you, Sir, if your spare time permits. Moreover, he says that Mr. Boyle and Oldenburg had formed a strange conception of your person. Not only has he removed this, but he has added reasons which induced them not only to consider you again in a most worthy and favourable manner, but also to value very highly your *Tractatus Theologico-Politicus*. In obedience to your instructions, I dared not inform you of this. Be assured that I am at your service in every way, and that I remain,

Most noble Sir,

Your very devoted Servant

G. H. SCHULLER.

AMSTERDAM, 25 *July* 1675.

Mr. a. Gent and J. Riew. dutifully greet you.

LETTER LXIV   B. D. S.

TO THE VERY LEARNED AND EXPERT MR. G. H. SCHULLER.

Reply to the Preceding.

MOST EXPERT SIR,

I rejoice that at last an opportunity has presented itself to you to refresh me with one of your letters, which are always most welcome to me. I earnestly beg you to do so frequently, etc.

I turn to your doubts; and in reply to the first, I

* The face of the whole of Nature which, although it varies in infinite ways remains always the same. See Scholium to Proposition XIII, Part II.

say that the human mind can only get to know those things which the idea of an actually existing body involves, or what can be inferred from this idea. For the power of each thing is defined only by its essence (according to *Ethics*, Proposition VII, Part III). But the essence of the Mind (Proposition XIII, Part II) consists only in this, that it is the idea of a Body actually existing. Therefore the mind's power of understanding only extends to those things which this idea of the Body contains in itself, or which follow from the same. But this idea of the Body neither involves nor expresses any other attributes of God than Extension and Thought. For its ideatum, namely, the Body (by Proposition VI, Part II) has God as its cause, in so far as He is considered under the attribute of Extension and not in so far as He is regarded under any other attribute. Therefore (by Axiom 6, Part I) this idea of the Body involves the knowledge of God in so far only as He is considered under the attribute of Extension. Then, this idea, in so far as it is a mode of Thought, also (by the same Proposition) has God for its cause in so far as He is a thinking thing, and not in so far as He is considered under another attribute. Therefore (by the same Axiom) the idea of this idea involves the knowledge of God, in so far as He is considered under the attribute of Thought, and not in so far as He is considered under any other attribute. Thus it is clear that the human Mind, or the idea of the human Body, neither involves nor expresses any other attribute of God besides these two. Moreover (by Proposition X, Part I) no other attribute of God can be deduced or conceived from these two attributes or from their modifications. Therefore I conclude that the human mind cannot attain to knowledge of any attribute of God except these two, as has been asserted.

As to your additional question, whether for this reason there must be constituted as many worlds as there are attributes, see *Ethics*, Scholium to Proposition VII, Part II. This proposition could also be more easily proved by reduction to absurdity. This kind of proof I am accustomed to prefer to the other, when the Proposition is negative, because it is more in accordance with the nature of such propositions. But since you demand only a positive proof, I pass on to the other, that is, whether a thing can be produced by another whose essence and existence are different : for things which are so different from one another appear to have nothing in common. But since all individual things, except those which are produced by things like themselves, differ from their causes in essence as well as in existence, I see here no reason for doubt.

In what sense I understand that God is the efficient cause of things, of their essence as well as of their existence, I believe I have sufficiently explained in the *Ethics*, Scholium and Corollary to Proposition XXV, Part I.

The axiom of the Scholium to Proposition X, Part I, as I suggested at the end of that Scholium, we form from the idea which we have of an absolutely infinite Being, and not from the fact that there are, or may be, beings which have three, four, or more attributes.

Lastly, the examples for which you ask are, of the first kind, in Thought, absolutely infinite understanding, but in Extension, motion and rest ; of the second kind, the face of the whole Universe, which, although it varies in infinite modes, yet remains always the same ; on this subject see Scholium 7 to the Lemma before Proposition XIV, Part II.

With these remarks, most distinguished Sir, I believe I have answered your objections and those of our friend. If, however, you consider that any doubt still remains, I beg you not to mind telling me so, in order that I may, if possible, remove it.

Farewell, etc.

THE HAGUE, 29 *July* 1675.

LETTER LXV

EHRENFRIED WALTER VON TSCHIRNHAUS

To the Very Acute and Learned Philosopher B. d. S.

Most illustrious Sir,

I should like from you a proof of your assertion that the soul cannot apprehend more attributes of God than Extension and Thought. Although I clearly see this, yet it seems to me that the contrary can be deduced from the Scholium to Proposition VII, Part II of the *Ethics*, perhaps only because I do not sufficiently correctly understand the meaning of this Scholium. I, therefore, decided to explain in what way I deduce this, begging you most earnestly, most illustrious Sir, to be willing to assist me with your usual kindliness whenever I do not rightly follow your meaning.

Now my arguments are in this plight. Although I gather from them that the world is certainly one, yet it is also no less clear from them that it is expressed in infinite modes, and, therefore, that every individual thing is expressed in infinite modes. Hence it seems to follow that that Modification which constitutes my Mind, and that Modification which expresses my Body, although it is one and the same Modification, is yet expressed in infinite modes, in one mode through Thought, in another through Extension, in a third through an attribute of God unknown to me, and so on to infinity, because there are infinite Attributes of God, and the Order and Connection of the Modifications seems to be the same in all. Hence there now arises the question, why the Mind which represents a certain Modification, which same Modification is expressed not only in Extension, but in infinite other modes, why, I say, it perceives only that Modification expressed through

Extension, that is, the human Body, and no other expression through other attributes.

But time does not allow me to pursue these questions at greater length. Perhaps all these doubts will be removed by continued reflection.

LONDON, 12 *August* 1675.

LETTER LXVI B. D. S.

To THE VERY NOBLE AND LEARNED
MR. EHRENFRIED WALTER VON TSCHIRNHAUS.

Reply to the Preceding.

MOST NOBLE SIR,

In answer to your objection I say that although each thing is expressed in infinite modes in the infinite understanding of God, yet the infinite ideas by which it is expressed cannot constitute one and the same mind of an individual thing, but an infinity of minds : seeing that each of these infinite ideas has no connection with the others, as I explained in the same Scholium to Proposition VII, Part II of the *Ethics*, and as is evident from Proposition X, Part I. If you will pay a little attention to these, you will see that no difficulty remains, etc.

THE HAGUE, 18 *August* 1675.

LETTER LXVII ALBERT BURGH

To THE VERY LEARNED AND ACUTE MR. B. D. S.

Many greetings.

When leaving my country, I promised to write to you if anything noteworthy occurred during my journey. Since, now, an occasion has presented itself, and one, indeed, of the greatest importance, I discharge my debt, and write to inform you that, through the infinite Mercy of God, I have been restored to the Catholic Church, and have been made a member thereof. How this came to pass you will be able to learn in greater detail from the letter that I wrote to the most illustrious and experienced Mr. D. Craenen, Professor at Leyden. I will, therefore, now only add some brief remarks, which concern your own advantage.

The more I formerly admired you for your penetration and acuteness of mind, the more do I now weep for you and deplore you ; for although you are a very talented man, and have received a mind adorned by God with brilliant gifts, and are a lover of truth, indeed eager for it, yet you suffer yourself to be led astray and deceived by the wretched and most haughty Prince of evil Spirits. For, all your philosophy, what is it but a mere illusion and a Chimera ? Yet you stake on it not only your peace of mind in this life, but also the eternal salvation of your soul. See on what a miserable foundation all your interests rest. You presume to have at length discovered the true philosophy. How do you know that your Philosophy is the best among all those which have ever been taught in the world, or are actually taught now, or ever will be taught in the future ? And, to say nothing about the thought of the future, have you examined all those philosophies, ancient as well as modern, which are taught here and in India and everywhere throughout the world ? And, even if you have duly examined them, how do you know that you have chosen the best ? You will say : my philosophy is in accord with right reason, the others are opposed to it. But all the other philosophers except your disciples differ from you, and, with the same right, they declare each about himself and his philosophy what you do about yours, and they accuse you, as you accuse them, of falsity and error. It is clear, therefore, that, in order that the truth of your philosophy may become manifest, you must put forward arguments which are not common to the other philosophies, but which can be applied to yours alone. Otherwise it must be confessed that your philosophy is as uncertain and as worthless as the rest.

However, confining myself now to your book, to which you have given that impious title, and taking your Philosophy together with your Theology, for you yourself really blend them, although, with diabolical cunning, you pretend to show that the one is distinct from the other, and that they have different principles, I proceed thus—

Perhaps you will say: Others have not read Holy Scripture as frequently as I have, and it is from Holy Scripture itself, the recognition of whose authority constitutes the difference between Christians and the remaining peoples of the whole world, that I prove my views. But how? I explain Holy Scripture by applying the clear texts to the more obscure, and from this interpretation of mine I form my Doctrines, or confirm those which are already produced in my brain.

But I adjure you seriously to consider what you say. For how do you know that you make the said application correctly, and, next, that the application, even if made correctly, is sufficient for the interpretation of Holy Scripture, and that you are thus putting the interpretation of Holy Scripture on a sound basis? Especially since Catholics say, and it is very true, that the whole Word of God is not given in writing, so that Holy Scripture cannot be explained through Holy Scripture alone, I will not say, by one man but not even by the Church itself, which is the sole interpreter of Holy Scripture. For the Apostolic traditions must also be consulted. This is proved from Holy Scripture itself, and by the testimony of the Holy Fathers, and it is in accord not only with right reason but also with experience. Since, therefore, your principle is most false, and leads to perdition, where will your whole teaching remain, which is founded and built upon this false foundation ?

So then, if you believe in Christ crucified, acknowledge your most evil heresy, recover from the perversion of your nature, and be reconciled with the Church.

For do you prove your views in a way which is different from that in which all the Heretics who have left God's Church in the past, or are leaving it now, or will leave it in the future, have done, do, or will do ? For they all employ the same principle as you do, that is, they make use of Holy Scripture alone for the formation and confirmation of their dogmas.

Do not flatter yourself because, perhaps, the Calvinists or the so-called Reformers, or the Lutherans, or the Mennonites, or the Socinians etc. cannot refute your doctrine : for all these, as has already been said, are as wretched as you are, and, like you, sit in the shadow of death.

If, however, you do not believe in Christ, you are more wretched than I can say. But the remedy is easy : return from your sins, and realize the fatal arrogance of your wretched and insane reasoning. You do not believe in Christ. Why ? You will say : Because the teaching and life of Christ are not consistent with my principles, nor is the doctrine of Christians about Christ consistent with my doctrine. But I repeat, do you then dare to think yourself greater than all those who have ever arisen in the State or Church of God, than the Patriarchs, Prophets, Apostles, Martyrs, Doctors, Confessors and Virgins, Saints without number, and, in your blasphemy, even than Our Lord Jesus Christ Himself ? Do you alone surpass these in doctrine, in your manner of life, and in every other respect ? Will you, you wretched little man, vile worm of the earth, ay, ashes, food for worms, dare, in your unspeakable blasphemy, to put yourself above the Incarnate, Infinite

Wisdom of the Eternal Father ? Will you alone consider yourself wiser, and greater than all those who, from the beginning of the world, have belonged to the Church of God, and have believed or still believe that Christ will come, or already has come ? On what foundation does your bold, mad, pitiable and execrable arrogance rest ?

You deny that Christ is the son of the living God, the Word of the eternal wisdom of the Father, made manifest in the flesh, who suffered and was crucified for the human race. Why ? Because all this does not correspond to your principles. But, besides the fact that it has now been proved that you have not the true principles but false, rash, and absurd ones, I will now say more, namely, that, even if you had relied on true principles, and based all your views on them, you would not be more able to explain, by means of them, all things which exist, or have happened, or happen in the world, nor ought you to assert boldly that something is really impossible, or false, when it seems to be opposed to these principles. For there are very many, indeed innumerable, things which you will not be able to explain, even if there is some sure knowledge of natural things ; you will not even be able to remove the manifest contradiction between such phenomena and your explanations of the rest, which are regarded by you as quite certain. From your principles you will not explain thoroughly even one of those things which are achieved in witchcraft and in enchantments by the mere pronunciation of certain words, or simply by carrying about the words, or characters, traced on some material, nor will you be able to explain any of the stupendous phenomena among those who are possessed by dæmons, of all of which I have myself seen various instances, and I have heard most certain evidence of innumerable happenings of the kind from very many most trustworthy persons, who spoke with one voice.

How will you be able to judge of the essences of all things, even if it be granted that certain ideas which you have in your mind, adequately conform to the essences of those things of which they are the ideas ? For you can never be sure whether the ideas of all created things exist naturally in the human mind, or whether many, if not all, can be produced in it, and actually are produced in it, by external objects, and even through the suggestion of good or evil spirits, and through a clear divine revelation. How, then, without considering the testimony of other men, and experience of things, to say nothing now of submitting your judgment to the Divine omnipotence, will you be able, from your principles, to define precisely and to establish for certain the actual existence, or non-existence, the possibility, or the impossibility, of the existence of, for instance, the following things (that is, whether they actually exist, or do not exist, or can exist, or cannot exist, in Nature), such as divining rods for detecting metal and underground waters ; the stone which the Alchemists seek, the power of words and characters ; the apparitions of various spirits both good and evil, and their power, knowledge and occupation ; the restoration of plants and flowers in a glass phial after they have been burnt ; Syrens ; pygmies very frequently showing themselves, according to report, in mines ; the Antipathies and Sympathies of very many things ; the impenetrability of the human body, etc. ? Even if you were possessed of a mind a thousand times more subtle and more acute than you do possess, you would not be able, my Philosopher, to determine even one of the said things. If in judging these and similar matters you put your trust in your understanding alone, you no doubt already think in this way about things of which you have no knowledge and no experience, and which you, therefore, consider impossible, but which in reality should seem only uncertain until you have been convinced by the testimony of very many trustworthy witnesses. Thus, I imagine, would Julius Caesar have thought, if some one had told him that a certain powder could be made up, and would become common in subsequent ages, the strength of which would be so effective that it would blow up into the air castles, whole cities, even the very mountains, and such too that wherever it is confined, when ignited, it would expand suddenly to a surprising extent, and shatter everything that impeded its action. Julius Caesar would in no wise have believed this; but he would have derided this man with loud jeers as one who wanted to persuade him of something contrary to his own judgment and experience and the highest military knowledge.

But let us return to the point. If you do not know the aforementioned things, and are unable to pronounce on them, why will you, unhappy man swollen with diabolical pride, rashly judge of the awful mysteries of the life and Passion of Christ, which Catholic teachers themselves pronounce incomprehensible? Why, moreover, will you rave, chattering foolishly and idly about the innumerable miracles, and signs, which, after Christ, his Apostles and Disciples and later many thousands of Saints performed in evidence and confirmation of the truth of the Catholic Faith, through the omnipotent power of God, and innumerable instances of which, through the same omnipotent Mercy and lovingkindness of God, are happening even now in our days, throughout the whole world? If you cannot contradict these, as you certainly cannot, why do you object any longer? Give in, turn away from your errors and your sins; put on humility and be born again.

But let us also descend to truth of fact, as it really is the foundation of the Christian religion. How, if you give the matter due consideration, will you dare to deny

the efficacy of the consensus of so many myriads of
men, of whom some thousands have been, and are,
many miles ahead of you in doctrine, in learning, in
true and rare importance, and in perfection of life ? All
these unanimously and with one voice declare that
Christ, the incarnate son of the living God, suffered, and
was crucified, and died for the sins of the human race,
and rose again, was transfigured, and reigns in heaven
as God, together with the eternal Father in the Unity
of the Holy Spirit, and the remaining doctrines which
belong here ; and also that through the Divine power
and omnipotence there were performed in the Church
of God by this same Lord Jesus, and afterwards, in his
name, by the Apostles and the other Saints, innumerable
miracles, which not only exceeded human comprehension but were even opposed to common sense (and of
these there remain even to this day countless material
indications, and visible signs scattered far and wide
throughout the world) and that such miracles still
happen. Might I not in like manner deny that the
ancient Romans ever existed in the world, or that the
Emperor Julius Caesar, having suppressed the Liberty
of the Republic, changed their form of government to a
monarchy, if I disregarded the many monuments evident
to all, which time has left us of the power of the Romans ;
if I disregarded the testimony of the most weighty
authors who have ever written the histories of the
Roman Republic and Monarchy, wherein they particularly
treat of Julius Caesar ; and if I disregarded the judgment
of so many thousands of men who have either themselves
seen the said monuments, or have put, and still put,
their trust in them (seeing that their existence is confirmed by countless witnesses) as well as in the said
histories, on the ground that I dreamed last night that
the monuments, which have come down from the
Romans, are not real things, but mere illusions ; and

similarly, that those stories which are told of the Romans are just like the stories which the books called Romances relate, puerile stories about Amadis de Gaula and similar Heroes ; also that Julius Caesar either never existed in the world, or if he existed was a melancholic man, who did not really crush the liberty of the Romans, and raise himself to the Throne of the Imperial Power, but was induced to believe that he had performed these achievements, either by his own foolish imagination or by the persuasion of friends who flattered him. Might I not further, in like manner, deny that the kingdom of China was taken by the Tartars, or that Constantinople is the seat of the Empire of the Turks, and innumerable similar things ? But would anyone think me sane if I denied these things, or absolve me from deplorable madness ? For all these things rest on the consensus of opinion of some thousands of men, and therefore their certitude is most evident, since it is impossible that all who assert such things and indeed very many others, should have deceived themselves, or should have wished to deceive others during so many centuries, indeed in all the centuries in succession from the earliest years of the world to this day.

Consider, secondly, that God's Church, continued in uninterrupted succession from the beginning of the world until this day, remains unmoved and solid, whereas all other Religions, Pagan and Heretic, have had a later beginning at least, if they have not also already had their end. The same too must be said of the Dynasties of Kingdoms, and of the opinions of all Philosophers.

Consider, thirdly, that, by the advent of Christ in the flesh, the Church of God was led from the religion of the Old to the religion of the New Testament, and was founded by Christ himself, the Son of the living God, and was afterwards extended by the Apostles, and by their disciples and successors, men who, according to the world, were untaught, but who, nevertheless, put all the Philosophers to confusion, although they taught Christian doctrine which is opposed to common sense, and exceeds and transcends all human reasoning; men who, in the estimation of the world, were abject, vile, ignoble, who received no help from the power of earthly Kings or Princes, but who, on the contrary, were persecuted by them with every tribulation, and suffered all the other adversities of the world. But their work gained the more in growth, the more the most powerful Emperors strove to hinder it, or rather to suppress it by killing as many Christians as they could, with every kind of martyrdom. Consider that thus in a short time the Church of Christ was extended over the whole world, and at length, when the Roman Emperor himself, and the Kings and the Princes of Europe were converted to the Christian faith, the Ecclesiastical Hierarchy grew to such vast power as may be admired to-day. All this was brought to pass by means of charity, gentleness, patience, trust in God, and the other Christian virtues (not by the clash of arms, the violence of many armies, and the devastation of countries, as happens when worldly Princes extend their borders), and, according to the promise of Christ, the gates of Hell did not prevail against the Church. Here, too, consider the terrible, and unspeakably severe punishment by which the Jews were reduced to the last stage of misery and calamity, because they were the authors of Christ's crucifixion. Read through, consider, and reconsider the histories of all times, and you will find there that nothing similar has ever happened in any other society, not even in a dream.

Consider, fourthly, that in the essential character of the Catholic Church there are included, and are, in fact, inseparable from that Church, the following characteristics, namely, *Antiquity*, for, taking the place of the Jewish Religion, which was then true, it reckons its foundation by Christ sixteen and a half centuries ago, and throughout this antiquity it traces the line of its Shepherds in unbroken succession, wherefore, too, it comes to pass that the Church alone possesses the sacred and divine books in a pure and incorrupt state, together with the equally certain and immaculate tradition of the unwritten word of God; *Immutability*, for its Doctrine and its administration of the sacraments are preserved inviolate as ordained by Christ himself and the Apostles, and, as is fitting, are maintained in their vigour; *Infallibility*, for it determines and pronounces on all matters pertaining to faith with the highest authority, security and truth, according to the power bestowed on it by Christ for this purpose, and the direction of the Holy Ghost, whose Bride the Church is; *Absence of Reform*, of which, since it cannot be corrupted, or be deceived, or deceive, it is clear that it never has any need; *Unity*, for all its members hold the same beliefs, teach the same things about faith, and have one and the same altar, and have all the Sacraments in common, and at length in mutual obedience to one another, cooperate for the same end; *Inseparability of any soul from the Church*, on any pretext whatsoever, on pain of incurring eternal damnation thereby, unless before death, it is again united with it through penitence; whence it is clear that all heresies have departed from it, while it always remains self-consistent, and immovably firm, as built on a Rock; its *Very Vast Extension*, for it has spread itself throughout the world, and visibly so, as can be affirmed of no other society, Schismatic, or Heretic, or Pagan, nor of any Political Government, or Philosophical Doctrine, just as none of the said characteristics of the Catholic Church belongs, or can belong, to any other Society; and, lastly, *its*

Continuous Duration to the end of the world, of which the
very Way, the Truth and the Life assured it, and which
the experience of all the said characteristics, likewise
promised and given to it by Christ himself, through
the Holy Ghost, proves clearly.

Consider, fifthly, that the admirable order, by which
the Church, such a massive body, is directed and
governed, clearly shows that it depends to a special
extent on the Providence of God, and that its administration is marvellously arranged, protected and directed
by the Holy Ghost, just as the harmony, which is perceived in all the things of this universe, indicates the
Omnipotence, Wisdom and Infinite Providence which
has created and still preserves all things. For in no
other society is there maintained such order, so beautiful,
so strict and so unbroken.

Consider, sixthly, not only that innumerable Catholics
of both sexes (of whom many still survive to-day, and
some I have myself seen and known) have lived admirable
and holy lives, and through the omnipotent power of God
have performed many miracles in the revered name of
Jesus Christ, while there still take place daily instan-
taneous conversions of very many persons from a very
bad mode of life to a better, really Christian, and holy
life, but that Catholics in general the holier and more
perfect they are, the more humble they are, and the
more do they consider themselves unworthy and cede
to others the praise of a Holier life ; and that even the
greatest sinners do none the less retain a due regard for
Holy things, confess their own wickedness, inveigh
against their own vices and imperfections, and wish to
be freed from them, and so become better : so that it
may be said that the most perfect Heretic, or Philosopher,
who ever lived, is scarcely worthy to be considered among
the most imperfect Catholics. From all this it is also clear
and very evidently follows that the Catholic doctrine

is most wise and admirable in its profundity, in a word, surpasses all the other doctrines of this world, since, indeed, it makes men better than all the rest of any society, and teaches and gives them a safe way to peace of mind in this life, and to eternal salvation of the soul in the life which is to follow this.

In the seventh place, consider earnestly the public confession of many Heretics, hardened in their obstinacy, and of the most weighty Philosophers, namely that after adopting the Catholic faith they at length perceived and knew that they had been wretched, blind, ignorant, indeed foolish, and insane before, when, swollen with pride, and puffed up with the wind of arrogance, they falsely persuaded themselves that they far surpassed all the rest in perfection of doctrine, learning and life. Of these some afterwards lived a most holy life, and left behind them the memory of innumerable miracles, others went to meet martyrdom with alacrity and with the greatest joy; some, among whom was the Divine Augustine, even became the most subtle, the most profound, the wisest and therefore the most useful Doctors of the Church, indeed its pillars as it were.

Lastly, reflect on the very wretched and restless life of Atheists, although they sometimes make a display of great cheerfulness of mind, and wish to seem to spend their life joyfully, and with the greatest internal peace of mind. More especially consider their most unhappy and horrible death, of which I have myself seen some instances and know with equal certainty of many more, or rather of countless cases, from the report of others, and from History. Learn from their example to be wise in time.

Thus you see, or at least I hope you see, how rashly you entrust yourself to the opinions of your brain; (for if Christ is the true God, and at the same time man, as is most certain, see to what you are reduced: for by persevering in your abominable errors, and most grave sins, what else can you expect but eternal damnation? How horrible this is, you may ponder for yourself) how little reason you have for laughing at the whole world with the exception of your wretched adorers; how foolishly proud and puffed up you become with the knowledge of the excellence of your talents, and with admiration for your very vain, indeed quite false, and impious doctrine; how shamefully you make yourself more wretched than the very beasts, by depriving yourself of the freedom of the will; nevertheless, even if you do not actually experience and recognize this, how can you deceive yourself by thinking that your works are worthy of the highest praise, and even of the closest imitation?

If you do not wish (which I will not think) that God or your neighbour should have pity on you, do you yourself at least take pity on your own misery, whereby you endeavour to make yourself more unhappy than you are now, or less unhappy than you will be, if you continue in this manner.

Come to your senses, you Philosopher, and realize the folly of your wisdom, the madness of your wisdom; put aside your pride and become humble, and you will be healed. Pray to Christ in the Most Holy Trinity, that he may deign to commiserate your misery, and receive you. Read the Holy Fathers, and the Doctors of the Church, and let them instruct you in what you must do that you may not perish, but have eternal life. Consult Catholics profoundly learned in their faith and living a good life, and they will tell you many things which you have never known and whereat you will be amazed.

I, for my part, have written this letter to you with truly Christian intention, first that you may know the great love that I bear you although a Gentile; and secondly to beg you not to continue to pervert others also.

I will therefore conclude thus : God is willing to snatch your soul from eternal damnation, if only you are willing. Do not hesitate to obey the Lord, who has so often called you through others, and now calls you again, and perhaps for the last time, through me, who, having obtained this grace through the ineffable Mercy of God Himself, pray for the same for you with my whole heart. Do not refuse : for if you will not hear God now when He calls you, the anger of the Lord Himself will be kindled against you, and there is the danger that you may be abandoned by His Infinite Mercy, and become the unhappy victim of the divine Justice which consumes all things in its anger. May the omnipotent God avert this fate to the greater glory of His name, and to the salvation of your soul, and also as a salutary and imitable example for your most unfortunate Idolaters, through our Lord and Saviour, Jesus Christ, who with the Eternal Father lives and reigns in the Unity of the Holy Ghost as God for all eternity. Amen.

FLORENCE, 3 *September* 1675.

LETTER LXVIIa

A LETTER OF NICHOLAS STENO TO THE REFORMER OF THE NEW PHILOSOPHY, CONCERNING TRUE PHILOSOPHY.

I OBSERVE that in the book of which others have told me and I myself for various reasons suspect that you are the author, you refer all things to the public safety, or rather, which, according to you, is the aim of the public safety, to your own safety, although your have embraced means contrary to the desired safety, and have altogether neglected that part of yourself the safety of which was especially to be studied. It is clear that you have chosen means contrary to the desired safety because while you seek public peace you upset everything, and you expose yourself unnecessarily to the greatest danger while you study to free yourself from all dangers. That you have indeed altogether neglected that part of yourself whose safety was especially to be studied is clear because you grant to all men the liberty of thinking and speaking about God, each what he thinks fit, so long as this shall not be such as to destroy the obedience which, according to you, is due not so much to God as to men : which is the same thing as to confine the whole good of man to the goods of the civil government, that is, of the body. And it is nothing in your favour if you say that you reserve the care of your soul for philosophy, both because your philosophy and your mind work on a system formed from supposition and because you leave those who are incapable of your philosophy in such a state of life as if they were automata destitute of soul, and born with a body only.

Since I see a man in this darkness who was once very friendly to me and who, I hope, is not now unfriendly (for I am persuaded that the memory of an old companionship still preserves a mutual love) and since I remember that I too was stuck fast if not in altogether the same, yet in the gravest, errors, the more the magnitude of the danger from which I have been set free makes evident God's mercy towards me, the greater the commiseration for you by which I am moved to pray for the same heavenly grace for you which I have obtained not through any merit of my own, but solely through Christ's benevolence ; and, in order that I may add deeds to my prayers, I offer myself as most ready to examine with you all those arguments which it shall please you to examine concerning the true way of true security which is to be found and followed. And, although your writings show that you are very far removed from the truth, yet the love of peace and truth which I formerly perceived in you and which even in this darkness is not extinct, makes me hope that you will give a ready ear to our Church, if only it has been sufficiently explained to you what it promises to all, and what it shows shall happen to those who are willing.

As to the first, the Church promises to all true security, eternal security, or abiding peace united with infallible truth, and at the same time offers the necessary means for obtaining so great a good; first, sure forgiveness for what has been done amiss; secondly, the most perfect pattern for right actions; thirdly, a true practical perfection of all occupations according to this pattern; and these it offers not to the learned alone or to those who are endowed with a subtle mind and are free from the vicissitudes of business, but without distinction to all persons of every age, sex and condition: and that this may not move you to wonder, you must know that there is indeed required the cooperation besides the non-resistance of the penitent, yet these things come to pass through the internal operation of Him who pronounces the outward word through the visible members of the Church. And although He says to the penitent that he must bewail his sins in the eyes of God and that works worthy of this sorrow must be displayed to the eyes of men, and that such things must be believed of God, the soul and the body etc., yet here it is not as though He meant that the penitent must undertake these things by his own strength: for no more is required than that he should not deny his assent and cooperation to those who do and believe these things, which alone is in his power, since to will these things and, when you have willed them, to do them, depend on the Spirit of Christ preventing, accompanying and perfecting our cooperation. If you have not yet understood this, I am not surprised, and I shall not now act, nor indeed is it within my power to act so that you may understand these things : lest, however, they should seem to you altogether alien from reason, I shall briefly sketch the form of the Christian rule, in so far as this can be done by a new citizen of that state, or rather by a stranger who even now lags in the lowest seats.

The aim of this government is that man should direct not only his external actions but also his most secret thoughts according to the order established by the author of the universe, or, what is the same thing, that the soul should in every action look to God, its author and judge. With respect to this the life of any man tainted by sins is divided into four stages. The first stage is that in which the man performs all his actions as if his thoughts had not to be submitted to any judge, and this is the state of men either not yet purified by baptism or hardened by sin after baptism, and this stage is now called blindness because the soul does not take note of God who sees it, as when it is said, Wisdom 2, *For their wickedness blinded them* : now death because the soul lies hidden, as it were buried by the pleasures that are made to perish, in which sense Christ said, *Let the dead bury their dead*, and more things of the same kind. And it is not inconsistent with this state to speak much and often truly about God and the soul, but since he treats of these as of objects that are remote or external hence there are perpetual doubts about them, many contradictions, and frequent faults, if not of external actions, at least of thoughts, and this because the soul, destitute of the spirit that gives life to actions, like one that is dead, is moved by every wind of desire. The second stage is when man does not resist either the external or the internal word of God and begins to hear Him call, when recognizing by the ray of this super-natural light much that is false in his opinions and much that is vicious in his actions, he surrenders his whole self to God, who, administering to him His Sacraments through His servants, bestows on him an invisible grace under visible signs. This stage is the infancy of those who are born again, and is called childhood, and the word of God which is preached to them is compared to milk. The third stage is when through the continual exercise of virtue in taming the desires the spirit is prepared for the due understanding of the mysteries in the sacred letters, which are not grasped by the soul except when with a heart which is now pure it has attained the fourth stage when it begins to see God and obtains the wisdom of the perfect. And this is a perpetual union of the will and sometimes a mystic one, of which there are still examples among us to-day.

And so the whole ordering of Christianity is so directed that the soul may be transferred from a state of death to a state of life, that is, that that which at first had the eyes of the mind turned away from God and fixed on error, should then turn them away from every error and direct them always towards God in all the actions both of the body and of the mind, willing and not willing that which the author of it and of the whole order wills or does not will. And so if you will duly examine all things, you will find in Christianity alone a true philosophy, teaching things about God worthy of God, and things about man that are suitable to man, and leading its followers to true perfection in all their actions.

As to the second point, it alone fulfils all that it promises to those who do not resist, for the Catholic Church alone in every century has given perfect examples of virtues, and even now to-day is preparing for posterity examples to be venerated in persons of every age, sex, and condition. And one may not doubt of the good faith with which it promises eternal security, if it assures the means subordinate to this end, even to

a miracle, all with the greatest fidelity. I have not yet
come to the end of my fourth year in the Church, and
yet I have already seen such great examples of sanctity
that I am truly compelled to say with David : *Thy
testimonies are very sure.* I say nothing of Bishops,
nothing of Priests whose words, heard by me in ordinary
conversation, as I would testify even with my own blood,
were the human symbols of a divine spirit, such is the
blamelessness of their life and their eloquence ; nor
shall I name many who have embraced a strict rule of
life, about whom I would say the same thing : I shall
only adduce examples of two kinds, one of persons
converted from the worst life to the most holy, the other
of the ignorant, so-called in your way of speaking, but
who obtained sublime notions of God, without any
study, at the feet of the crucified. Of this kind I know
those who are occupied with mechanical arts or bound
to servile tasks, both men and women, who, through
the exercise of divine virtues, have been carried to the
praise of God and the understanding of the soul, whose
life was holy, their words divine, and their works
not seldom miraculous, such as the prediction of future
events, and other things, which I pass over for the sake
of brevity.

I know what objection you will be able to raise against
miracles : and we do not trust in miracles alone but
when we see that the effect of a miracle is the perfect
conversion of the soul of someone from vices to virtues
we shall rightly ascribe this to the author of all virtues.
For I hold it the greatest of all miracles that those who
have spent thirty or forty years or more in every license
of their desires should as it were in a moment of time
turn away from their wickedness and become the most
holy examples of the virtues, examples such as I have
seen with these eyes and clasped for joy with these hands,
and which have often moved me to tears for myself

and others. There is no God like our God. Surely, if you consider the history of the times, if you consider the present state of the Church, not in the books of our adversaries, not in the writings of those among us who are either dead or who, at least, have not yet put off their infancy, but, as is commonly done in the case of any other doctrine which is to be learnt, in the writings of those who, by the admission of our own people, are held to be true Catholics, you will see that the Church has always stood by its promises and is even now daily standing by them, and you will find there that evidence of credibility which will satisfy you, especially since you have much more kindly feelings for the Pope of Rome than the rest of our adversaries, and you admit the necessity of good works : but I beg you to examine ours in our writings, as your own teachings about the strength of prejudices will also easily persuade you to do.

I would gladly have produced the passages of Scripture which assign authority to the Pope, which you deny him for no other reason than because you do not find it in Scripture, and because you do not admit that the Christian commonwealth is similar to the commonwealth of the Jews. But since on the question of the interpretation of Scripture you hold views differing from our teaching, which admits only the interpretation of the Church, I pass over this argument on this occasion and say secondly, that the Christian rule, which seeks only unity of Faith, of Sacraments, and of Charity, admits of but one head, whose authority consists not in arbitrarily making any kind of innovations, which is the calumny of our adversaries, but in the fact that the things that belong to divine right, or necessary things, remain always immutable, but things that belong to human right, or indifferent things, are changed according as the Church judges it expedient for just causes, for instance, if it sees that the wicked are misusing indifferent things for the overthrow of those that are necessary. Hence in interpreting Holy Scripture and in determining the doctrines of the Faith it so acts that the doctrines and the interpretations handed down by God through the Apostles may be preserved, and new and human doctrines may be proscribed. I shall not speak of other things which are subject to his authority since it is sufficient to make this monarchy probable to you that there should be the unity of beliefs and actions which was so often taught by Christ.

And so if you are led by the true love of virtue, if you delight in perfection of actions, seek out all the societies in the world and you will not find elsewhere that the pursuit of perfection is undertaken with such fervour or carried out with such joy as among us, which argument alone may serve you instead of a proof, for verily *this is the finger of God*.

But in order that you may know this more easily descend first within yourself and examine your soul, for if you duly examine all things you will find it dead ; you move amidst matter in motion as though the moving cause were absent or were non-existent, for it is the religion of bodies not of souls that you introduce, and in the love of one's neighbour you see actions which are necessary for the preservation of the individual and for the propagation of the species. But you have little or almost no care for those actions by which we acquire the knowledge and love of our author. And you believe that all men are dead with you, who deny the light of grace to all men, since you have not experienced it yourself, and since you do not think that there exists any certainty but demonstrative certainty, and are ignorant of the certainty of a faith which is above all demonstration. But within what narrow limits is this demonstrative certainty of yours confined ! Examine, I beg of you, all your demonstrations and bring me even one about the way in which the thinking thing and the extended thing are united, in which the moving principle is united with the body which is moved. But why do I ask you for demonstrations on these points, who will not be able even to explain to me their probable ways? Hence it comes about that you cannot explain the sense of pleasure or of pain apart from suppositions, and the stirring of love or of hate, and likewise the whole Philosophy of Descartes, however diligently examined and reformed by you, cannot demonstratively explain to me this one phenomenon, namely, how the impact of matter on matter is perceived by a soul that is united to matter. But of matter itself, do you, I ask, give us any other knowledge beyond a mathematical examination of quantity relating to figures not yet proved of any kind of particles except hypothetically? What is more alien from reason than to deny His divine words whose divine works are obvious to the senses, because they are inconsistent with the demonstrations of men made by means of an hypothesis? and, although you do not understand even that condition of the body through the mediation of which the mind perceives corporeal objects, to offer an opinion concerning that condition of it which, glorified by the change of the corruptible into the incorruptible, is again to be united to the soul?

I am sure that to discover new principles explaining the nature of God, of the soul and the body is the same thing as to discover fictitious principles, since even reason teaches that it is inconsistent with the divine providence that the true principles about these things should have been hidden from the most holy men for so many thousands of years, to be first discovered in this century by men who have not even attained the perfection of moral virtues : for I should believe that only those principles about God, the soul, and the body, are true, which are preserved from the beginning of created things until this day always in one and the same society, the state of God. Among the first teachers of these principles that famous old man, who caused S. Justin to change from a worldly philosophy to the Christian philosophy, said that there *have been philosophers, ancient, blessed, just, beloved of God, who spoke under the inspiration of the Divine Spirit and prophesied that those things would come to pass which now do come to pass.* Principles put forward by such Philosophers and transmitted to us without interruption in the succession by successors like themselves, and even now to-day obvious through philosophers of the same kind to him who seeks them with a right reason, I should believe to be the only true principles, where the sanctity of life proves the truth of doctrine.

Examine the principles and the doctrines of this philosophy not in the writings of its enemies or in the writings of those who are its hangers-on, whom wickedness allies with the dead or ignorance allies with children, but in those of the masters thereof, perfect in all wisdom, dear to God and probably already sharing in eternal life, and you will acknowledge that the perfect Christian is the perfect philosopher, even if it were only an old woman, or a slave intent on servile tasks, or an ignorant man, in the world's judgment, seeking a living by washing rags. And you will exclaim with S. Justin, *I find this the one, and safe, and useful philosophy.*

If you wish, I shall willingly take upon myself the task of showing you partly the contradiction partly the uncertainty wherein your teachings are behind ours, although I should wish that you, recognizing one or two of the errors in your teachings in comparison with the evidence of credibility which stands out in ours, would make yourself a disciple of the said teachers, and among the first fruits of your penitence would offer to God a refutation of your own errors, acknowledged by yourself through the illumination of the Divine light, in order that if your first writings have turned aside a thousand souls from the true knowledge of God, the recantation of them reinforced by your own example may lead back to Him a thousand thousand with you as with another Augustine. I pray with all my heart that this grace may be yours. Farewell.

[FLORENCE, 1675.]

LETTER LXVIII

B. D. S.

To the Very Noble and Learned
Mr. HENRY OLDENBURG.

Reply to Letter LXII.

MOST NOBLE AND ILLUSTRIOUS SIR,

At the time when I received your letter of 22 July, I was setting out for Amsterdam with the intention of getting printed the work about which I had written to you. While I was engaged on this matter, a rumour was spread everywhere that a book of mine about God was in the press, and that in it I endeavoured to show that there is no God. This rumour was believed by many. Therefore certain Theologians (perhaps the authors of this rumour) seized the opportunity of bringing complaints against me before the Prince and the Magistrates ; moreover the dull-witted Cartesians, because they are believed to be in my favour, and in order to free themselves from this suspicion, continued and even now continue to denounce my opinions and writings everywhere. When I heard all this from certain trustworthy men, who also said that the Theologians were intriguing against me everywhere, I decided to postpone the publication I was preparing, until I saw how the matter turned out, and I also intended to inform you what plan I would then follow. But the business seems to grow daily worse, and I am yet uncertain what to do.

Meanwhile I do not want to delay my answer to your letter any longer. First, I thank you very much for your most friendly warning, of which, however, I should like a fuller explanation, so that I may know which you think are the doctrines that seem to undermine religious virtue. For I believe that the doctrines which seem to me to be in accord with reason are also most useful to virtue. Next, unless it cause you too much inconvenience, I should like you to point out to me the passages in the *Tractatus Theologico-Politicus* which have caused uneasiness to learned men. For I wish to elucidate this Treatise with some notes, and, if possible, to remove the prejudices which have been conceived against it. Farewell.

[THE HAGUE, *September* 1675.]

LETTER LXIX   B. D. S.

To the Very Learned
Mr. LAMBERT VAN VELTHUYSEN.

MOST DISTINGUISHED AND ILLUSTRIOUS SIR,

I am surprised that our friend Nieuwstad should have said that I was revolving in my mind a refutation of those writings which, for some time past, have been published against my treatise, and that among them I proposed to refute your manuscript. For I know that I never had it in my mind to refute any of my opponents, so unworthy did they seem to me of a reply. Nor do I remember having said to Mr. Nieuwstad anything except that I proposed to elucidate some of the more obscure passages of the said treatise with notes, and to add to these both your manuscript and my reply, if this could be done with your kind permission. This I asked him to seek from you, adding that, if perhaps you were unwilling to grant such permission, on the ground that some things in my answer were too harshly expressed, you should have complete power to correct or to delete them. Meanwhile, however, I feel no anger against Mr. Nieuwstad. I only wanted to show you how the matter stands, so that, if I cannot obtain the consent which I seek from you, I may at least show that I did not want to publish your manuscript against your wish. Although I believe that this can be done without any risk to your reputation, if only your name is not put to it, yet I will do nothing unless you give me permission to publish it.

But, to confess the truth, you would do me a far greater favour, if you would write down the arguments which you think you can bring against my treatise, and add them to your manuscript, and this I most earnestly beg you to do. For there is no one whose arguments I should more gladly consider, for I know that you are possessed only by the love of truth, and I know the singular fairness of your mind. Therefore, I beg you again and again not to mind undertaking this work, and to believe me

Your most respectful

B. DE SPINOZA.

MR. LAMBERT VELTHUYSEN,
DOCTOR OF MEDICINE,
DE NIEWE GRAGT,
UYTREGT.

[THE HAGUE, *Autumn* 1675.]

LETTER LXX   G. H. SCHULLER, MED. DR.

TO THE VERY EMINENT AND ACUTE PHILOSOPHER B. D. S.

AMSTERDAM, 14 *November* 1675.

MOST LEARNED AND EXCELLENT SIR, MOST HONOURED
    PATRON,
        I hope that my last letter, together with the *Process* of an anonymous writer, has been duly delivered

to you, and also that you are now very well, even as I am very well. I had, however, received no letter from our friend Tschirnhaus for a space of three months, whence I had made the sad conjecture that his journey from England to France was ill-starred. But now, having received a letter, I am full of joy, and in accordance with his request it is my duty to communicate it to you, Sir, to convey to you his most dutiful greetings, to inform you that he has reached Paris safely, that he has met there Mr. Huygens, as we had advised him to do, and that for the same reason he has in every way adapted himself to his way of thinking so as to be highly esteemed by him. He mentioned that you, Sir, had advised him to associate with him (Huygens), and that you esteem his person very highly. This greatly pleased him, so that he replied that he likewise esteems your person greatly, and that he had lately obtained from you the *Tractatus Theologico-Politicus*. This is esteemed by very many there, and inquiries are eagerly made whether any other works of the same author are published. To this Mr. Tschirnhaus replied that he knew of none save the *Proofs of the First and Second Part of Descartes' Principles*. Otherwise he related nothing else about you, Sir, than the remarks just reported; hence he hopes that this will not displease you.

Huygens has recently had our Tschirnhaus summoned to him and informed him that Mr. Colbert desired some one to instruct his son in mathematics, and that if a position of this kind pleased him, he would arrange it. To this our friend replied by asking for some delay, and eventually declared that he was ready to accept. Huygens returned with the answer that the proposal pleased Mr. Colbert very much, especially as, owing to his ignorance of French, he will be compelled to speak to his son in Latin.

To the objection made most recently, he replies that

the few words which I had written by your instruction, Sir, have revealed to him your meaning more deeply, and that he had already entertained these thoughts (since they chiefly admit of an explanation in these two ways) but that he has been led to follow that which was lately contained in his objection by the two following reasons. The first is that otherwise Propositions V and VII of Book II would seem to be opposed. In the former of these it is stated that the Ideata are the efficient causes of ideas, whereas the contrary seems to be shown by the proof of the latter, on account of the cited Axiom, 4, Part I. Maybe (as I rather persuade myself) I do not rightly apply the axiom in accordance with the Author's intention, which I would most willingly learn from him, if his affairs permit. The second cause which hindered me from following the given explanation was that in this way the Attribute Thought is made much more extensive than the other attributes; but since each of the Attributes constitutes the Essence of God, I certainly do not see how the one does not contradict the other. I will only add that if I may judge the minds of others by my own, then Propositions VII and VIII of Book II will be exceedingly difficult to understand, and this for no other reason than that it has pleased the Author (since I have no doubt that they seemed so clear to him) to explain the proofs added to them in such brief and sparing explanations.

He relates, moreover, that he has met in Paris a man called Leibniz, of uncommon learning, well versed in many Sciences, and free from the vulgar prejudices of Theology. He has formed an intimate friendship with him because it happens that like himself he is working at the problem of the continued perfecting of the understanding, than which, indeed, he thinks there is nothing better, and considers nothing more useful. In Morals, he says that he is perfectly disciplined, and speaks from the mere dictates of reason, without any influence of the feelings. In Physics and especially in Metaphysical studies about God and the soul, he continues, he is very expert. Lastly, he concludes that he is most worthy of having communicated to him your writings, Sir, if consent has been first obtained, since he believes that thus great advantage will come to the Author, as he promises to show more fully if it please you, Sir. But if not, then let it cause no uneasiness lest he may not keep them secret conscientiously according to the promise he gave, as he has not made the slightest mention of them. This same Leibniz thinks very highly of the *Tractatus Theologico-Politicus*, on which subject, if you remember, he once wrote a letter to you, Sir.

I would therefore pray you, Sir, unless there is some special reason against it, not to mind giving this permission, in your generous kindliness. If possible, tell me your decision as soon as you can, for as soon as I have received your reply, I shall be able to answer our friend Tschirnhaus, which I am anxious to do on Tuesday evening, unless rather weighty grounds for delay compel you, Sir, to put the matter off.

Mr. Bresser has returned from Cleves, and has sent hither a large quantity of the beer of his country. I advised him to let you, Sir, have half a barrel, which he promised to do with his most friendly greeting.

Lastly, I pray you to forgive the roughness of my style, and the haste of my pen, and to command me to do you some service, so that I may have a real opportunity of proving that I am,

Most distinguished sir,
Your most devoted servant
G. H. SCHULLER.

LETTER LXXI   HENRY OLDENBURG

To the Very Illustrious Mr. B. d. S.

Many greetings.

As far as I can see from your most recent letter, the issue of the book which you intended for publication is in danger. I cannot refrain from approving your communication, in which you say that you want to elucidate and to simplify the passages in the *Tractatus Theologico-Politicus* which have tormented its readers. Such are, first of all, I should think, those which seem to speak ambiguously about God and Nature; many are of opinion that you have confused these two. Moreover you appear to many to take away the authority and value of miracles, on which alone nearly all Christians are persuaded that the certainty of Divine Revelation can be based. Moreover they say that you conceal your opinion of Jesus Christ, the Redeemer of the world, and the only Mediator for mankind, and of his Incarnation and Atonement; and they want you to open your mind clearly on these three heads. If you do this, and therein please judicious and intelligent Christians, I think your interests will be safe.

These things I, who am your most devoted friend, wanted to tell you in a few words. Farewell.

15 *November* 1675.

P.S.—Let me know shortly, I pray, that these few lines have been duly delivered to you.

LETTER LXXII   B. d. S.

To the Very Learned and Expert Mr. G. H. SCHULLER.

[*Reply to Letter LXX.*]

Most experienced Sir, most honoured Friend,

       I was much pleased to understand from your letter received to-day that you are well, and that our friend Tschirnhaus has happily accomplished his journey to France. In the conversations which he had with Huygens about me he bore himself, in my opinion, very prudently. Moreover, I greatly rejoice that he has found such a fortunate opportunity for the end which he had set himself.

I do not see what he finds in Axiom 4, Part I, to contradict Proposition V, Part II. For in this proposition it is asserted that the essence of every idea has God for its cause in so far as He is considered as a thinking thing; whereas, in that axiom, it is asserted that the knowledge or the idea of the effect depends on the knowledge or the idea of the cause. But to confess the truth, I do not sufficiently follow the meaning of your letter on this point, and I believe that either in your letter, or in the original letter, there is an error due to haste in writing. For you write that it is asserted in Proposition V that the ideata are the efficient causes of ideas, whereas this very thing is expressly denied in this proposition. Hence, I now think, arises the whole confusion, and therefore any endeavour to write more fully on this matter would be vain, and I must therefore wait until you explain to me his meaning more clearly, and I know whether the original letter is sufficiently correct.

I think I know the Leibniz of whom he writes, through his letters, but I do not know why he has gone to France, when he was a Councillor of Frankfurt. As far as I could surmise from his letters, he seemed to me a man of liberal mind, and versed in every science. But still I consider it imprudent to entrust my writings to him so soon. I should like to know first what he is doing in France, and to hear the opinion of our friend Tschirnhaus, after he has associated with him longer, and knows his character more intimately. However, greet that friend of ours most dutifully in my name, and if I can be of service to him in anything, let him say what he wants, and he will find me most ready to comply with all his wishes.

I congratulate Mr. Bresser, my most honoured friend, on his arrival or return. For the promised beer I am very grateful, and I will repay in whatever way I may.

Lastly, I have not yet attempted to make trial of the process of your kinsman, nor do I believe that I shall be able to apply my mind to the attempt. For the more I consider the thing itself, the more I am persuaded that you have not made gold, but had not sufficiently separated what was latent in the antimony. But more of this on another occasion ; now I am prevented for want of time.

Meanwhile, if I can be of service to you in anything, here I am whom you will always find,

Most distinguished Sir,

Your most friendly and devoted servant

B. DESPINOZA.

THE HAGUE, 18 *November* 1675.

MR. G. H. SCHULLER,
DOCTOR OF MEDICINE,
IN DE KORTSTEEGH IN DE GESTOFEERDE HOET,
T'AMSTERDAM.

LETTER LXXIII   B. D. S.

TO THE VERY NOBLE AND LEARNED
MR. HENRY OLDENBURG.

Reply to Letter LXXI.

MOST NOBLE SIR,
I received your very brief letter to me, dated 15 November, last Saturday. In it you only indicate those passages in the *Tractatus Theologico-Politicus* which have tormented its readers. I, however, had hoped

also to learn from it which were the opinions which seemed to undermine the practice of religious virtue, of which you had previously warned me.

But in order to open to you my mind on the three heads you mention, I say, in the first place, that I hold an opinion about God and Nature very different from that which Modern Christians are wont to defend. For I maintain that God is, as they say, the immanent cause of all things, but not the transeunt cause. Like Paul, and perhaps also like all ancient philosophers, though in another way, I assert that all things live and move in God; and I would dare to say that I agree also with all the ancient Hebrews as far as it is possible to surmise from their traditions, even if these have become corrupt in many ways. However, those who think that the *Tractatus Theologico-Politicus* rests on this, namely, that God and Nature (by which they mean a certain mass, or corporeal matter) are one and the same, are entirely mistaken.

Then, as regards miracles, I am, on the contrary, persuaded that the certainty of divine revelation can be based only on the wisdom of the doctrine, and not on miracles, that is, on ignorance; this I have shown at sufficient length in Chapter VI, On Miracles. Here I will only add this, that I regard it as the chief difference between Religion and Superstition, that the latter has ignorance, the former has wisdom, for its foundation. This, I believe, is the reason why Christians are distinguished from the rest of mankind, not by faith, or charity, or the other fruits of the Holy Spirit, but simply by their opinion. For, like all others, they make a stand on miracles alone, that is, on ignorance, which is the source of all wickedness; and so they turn their faith, even if it is true, into a superstition. I very much doubt whether Kings will ever allow the application of a remedy for this evil.

Lastly, to open my mind more clearly on the third head, I say, that it is not entirely necessary to salvation to know Christ according to the flesh; but we must think far otherwise of the eternal son of God, that is, the eternal wisdom of God, which has manifested itself in all things, more especially in the human mind, and most of all in Christ Jesus. For without this wisdom no one can attain to a state of blessedness, inasmuch as it alone teaches what is true and what is false, what is good and what is evil. And since, as I have said, this wisdom was most manifest through Jesus Christ, his disciples, in so far as he had revealed it to them, preached it, and showed that they were able above others to glory in that Spirit of Christ. For the rest, as to the doctrine which certain Churches add to these, namely, that God assumed human nature, I expressly warned them that I do not understand what they say. Indeed, to confess the truth, they seem to me to speak no less absurdly than if some one were to tell me that a circle assumed the nature of a square.

This, I think, is enough to explain what I think on these three heads. Whether this opinion will please the Christians whom you know, you will be able to judge better than I can. Farewell.

[THE HAGUE, *November or December* 1675.]

LETTER LXXIV   HENRY OLDENBURG

TO THE VERY ILLUSTRIOUS AND LEARNED MR. B. D. S.

Many greetings.

Reply to the Preceding.

Since you seem to accuse me of excessive brevity, I will clear myself of the charge by excessive lengthiness on this occasion. You expected, as I see, an enumeration of those opinions in your writings which seemed to your readers to overthrow the practice of religious virtue. I will tell you what it is that causes them most distress. You seem to assert the fatalistic necessity of all things and actions : and they say that if this is admitted and affirmed, then the nerves of all laws, of all virtue and religion, are cut through, and all rewards and punishments are empty. They think that whatever compels, or involves necessity, also excuses ; and so, they think, no one would be inexcusable in the sight of God. For if we are driven by fate, and all things, turned by a strong hand, follow a definite and inevitable course, then they cannot see what place there is for blame or punishments. What wedge can be applied to this knot, it is extremely difficult to say. I should very much like to know and to learn what help you can supply for the problem.

As to your opinion on the three heads I noted, which you were kind enough to disclose to me, these questions arise. First, in what sense do you consider *Miracles and Ignorance* as synonyms and equivalent terms, as you seem to think in your last letter; since the raising of Lazarus from the dead and the resurrection of Jesus Christ from death, seem to exceed all the power of created Nature, and to belong to the divine power alone ; and it does not argue any culpable ignorance that it necessarily exceeds the limits of an intelligence that is finite, and confined within definite boundaries. Or do you not consider it proper for a created mind and for science to recognize such knowledge and power on the part of the uncreated Mind and supreme Deity that it can understand and do all things, the reason and manner of which cannot be given and explained by us petty men ? We are men, it seems that nothing human should be considered foreign to us.

Then, since you confess that you cannot grasp the thought that God has actually assumed human nature, it may be right to ask you in what sense you understand the words of our Gospel, and the passages in the Epistle written to the Hebrews, the former of which says, *the word was made flesh*; and the latter, *the Son of God took not on him the nature of angels; but he took on him the seed of Abraham*. I should think too, that the trend of the whole Gospel implies that the only-begotten Son of God, the Word, (who both was God, and was with God) showed himself in human nature, and by his passion and death paid the ransom for us sinners, the price for our redemption. I should much like to be informed what one ought to say about these and similar things, in order to maintain the truth of the Gospel and of the Christian Religion, to which, I think, you are favourably disposed.

I had intended to write more, but I am interrupted by the visit of friends, to whom I consider it wrong to refuse the duties of courtesy. But even those things which I have put together in this letter will be sufficient, perhaps will even weary you when you consider them as a philosopher. Farewell, then, and believe me ever to be an admirer of your learning and knowledge.

LONDON, 16 *December* 1675.

LETTER LXXV   B. D. S.

To the Very Noble and Learned
Mr. HENRY OLDENBURG.

Reply to the Preceding.

MOST NOBLE SIR,

At last I see what it was that you asked me not to publish. Since, however, this very thing is the principal basis of all those which are contained in the Treatise I had intended to publish, I want to explain here briefly in what sense I maintain the fatalistic necessity of all things and of all actions.

For in no way do I subject God to fate, but I conceive that everything follows with inevitable necessity from the nature of God, just as all conceive that it follows from the nature of God Himself that He should understand Himself. Certainly no one denies that this follows necessarily from the divine nature, and yet no one conceives that God is compelled by any fate to understand Himself, but that He does so absolutely freely, although necessarily.

Next, this inevitable necessity of things does not do away with either divine or human laws. For moral precepts, whether they do or do not receive the form of law, from God Himself, are nevertheless divine and salutary; and whether we receive the good, which follows from virtue and the love of God, from God as a Judge, or whether it proceeds from the necessity of the Divine nature, it will not, on that account, be either more or less desirable, just as, on the other hand, the evils which follow on wicked actions and feelings will not be less to be feared merely because they follow from them necessarily. Lastly, whether we do what we do necessarily or contingently, we are nevertheless led by hope and fear.

Further, men are inexcusable before God for no other reason than that they are in the power of God Himself as clay in the hand of the potter, who from the same lump makes vessels, some unto honour, others unto dishonour. If you will consider these few words, I do not doubt that you will be able to answer, with very little trouble, all the arguments which are usually advanced against this opinion, as I and many others have already discovered.

I assume that miracles and ignorance are equivalent terms, because those who endeavour to base the existence of God and of Religion on miracles, wish to explain what is obscure by something else which is

more obscure, and of which they are utterly ignorant,
and so they bring forward a new kind of argument,
namely, a reduction, not to the impossible, as they say,
but to ignorance. However, unless I am mistaken I
have explained my opinion about miracles sufficiently
in the *Tractatus Theologico-Politicus*. Here I will only
add this, that if you will consider these things, namely,
that Christ did not appear to the Senate, or to Pilate,
or to any one of the unbelievers, but only to the Saints,
and that God has neither right nor left, nor is in any
one place, but is everywhere according to His essence,
and that matter is the same everywhere, and that God
does not manifest Himself outside the world in some
imaginary space which they invent, and, lastly, that the
structure of the human body is only held together within
due limits by the pressure of the air, you will easily see
that this appearance of Christ is not unlike that with
which God appeared to Abraham, when he saw three
men whom he invited to eat with him. But you will
say that all the Apostles believed absolutely that Christ
rose again after death, and that he actually ascended
into heaven ; this I do not deny. For Abraham himself
also believed that God did eat with him, and all the
Israelites believed that God descended from heaven to
Mount Sinai, surrounded by fire, and spoke directly
with them, whereas, however, these and many other
things of this kind were apparitions, or revelations,
adapted to the comprehension and to the opinions of
these men, whereby God wished to reveal to them His
meaning. I conclude, therefore, that the resurrection
of Christ from the dead was really spiritual, and was
revealed only to the faithful in a way adapted to their
thought, namely, that Christ had been endowed with
eternity, and rose from the dead (here I understand
the dead in the sense in which Christ did when he said :
Let the dead bury their dead), and also by his life and death

gave an example of extraordinary holiness, and that he raises his disciples from the dead in so far as they follow the example of his life and death. And it would not be difficult to explain the whole teaching of the Gospel in accordance with this hypothesis.

Nay more, Chapter 15 of the First Epistle to the Corinthians can only be explained on this hypothesis, and only so can Paul's arguments be understood, since, otherwise, when we follow the ordinary hypothesis, they seem unsound, and can easily be refuted, to say nothing about the fact that all that the Jews interpreted according to the flesh the Christians interpreted spiritually.

I recognize with you the weakness of man. But on the other hand let me ask you whether we petty men have so great a knowledge of Nature that we can determine how far its force and power extends, and what is beyond its power? Since no one can presume this without arrogance, therefore one may, without boasting, explain miracles by natural causes as far as possible, and as to those which we can neither explain nor prove, because they are absurd, it will be better to suspend judgment about them, and, as I said, to base Religion solely on the wisdom of its teaching.

Lastly, you believe that the passages in the Gospel of John and in the Epistle to the Hebrews are opposed to what I have said, because you measure the phrases of oriental languages by European modes of speech, and although John wrote his Gospel in Greek, he Hebraized all the same.

However this may be, do you believe that when Scripture says that God manifested Himself as a cloud, or that He dwelt in a Tabernacle, or in a Temple, that God Himself assumed the nature of a cloud, of a Tabernacle or of a Temple? But this is the most that Christ said about himself, namely that he is the temple of God, because, undoubtedly, as I said in my previous letter, God manifested Himself most fully in Christ, and John, in order to express this more effectively, said that the word was made flesh. But enough of these things.

[THE HAGUE, *December* 1675.]

LETTER LXXVI

B. D. S.

SENDS GREETINGS TO THE VERY NOBLE YOUNG MAN ALBERT BURGH.

Reply to Letter LXVII.

What I could scarcely believe when it was related to me by others, I at last understand from your letter; that is, that not only have you become a member of the Roman Church, as you say, but that you are a very keen champion of it and have already learned to curse and rage petulantly against your opponents. I had not intended to reply to your letter, being sure that what you need is time rather than argument, to be restored to yourself, and to your family, to say nothing of other grounds which you once approved when we spoke of Stenonius (in whose footsteps you are now following). But certain friends who with me had formed great hopes for you from your excellent natural talent, earnestly prayed me not to fail in the duty of a friend, and to think of what you recently were rather than of what you now are, and similar things. I have been induced by these arguments to write to you these few words, earnestly begging you to be kind enough to read them with a calm mind.

I will not here recount the vices of Priests and Popes in order to turn you away from them, as the opponents of the Roman Church are wont to do. For they are wont to publish these things from ill-feeling, and to adduce them in order to annoy rather than to instruct. Indeed, I will admit that there are found more men of great learning, and of an upright life, in the Roman than in any other Christian Church; for since there are more men who are members of this Church, there will also be found within it more men of every condition. You will, however, be unable to deny, unless perhaps you have lost your memory together with your reason, that in every Church there are many very honest men who worship God with justice and charity; for we have known many men of this kind among the Lutherans, the Reformers, the Mennonites, and the Enthusiasts, and, to say nothing of others, you know of your own ancestors who in the time of the Duke of Alva suffered for the sake of their Religion every kind of torture with both firmness and freedom of mind. Therefore you must allow that holiness of life is not peculiar to the Roman Church, but is common to all. And since we know through this (to speak with the Apostle John, *The First Epistle*, Chapter 4, verse 13) that we dwell in God and God dwells in us, it follows that whatever it is that distinguishes the Roman Church from the others, it is something superfluous, and therefore based merely on superstition. For, as I said with John, justice and charity are the only and the surest sign of the true Catholic faith, and the true fruits of the Holy Spirit, and wherever these are found, there Christ really is, and where they are lacking, there Christ also is not. For by the Spirit of Christ alone can we be led to the love of justice and of charity. If you had been willing duly to ponder these facts within yourself, you would not have been lost, nor would you have caused bitter sorrow to your parents who sorrowfully lament your lot.

But I return to your letter in which you first bewail the fact that I suffer myself to be deceived by the Prince of evil Spirits. But I beg you to be of good cheer, and to come to yourself. When you were sane, if I am not mistaken, you used to worship an infinite God, by whose power all things absolutely come into being, and are preserved : but now you dream of a Prince, an enemy of God, who, against the will of God, misleads and deceives most men (for good men are rare), whom God consequently delivers up to this master of vices to be tortured for all eternity. Thus divine justice permits the Devil to deceive men with impunity, but does not permit the men who have been miserably deceived and misled by this same Devil to go unpunished.

These absurdities might still be tolerated if you worshipped a God infinite and eternal, and not one whom Chastillon in the town of Tienen, as it is called by the Dutch, gave with impunity to the horses to eat. And do you, unhappy one, weep for me ? And do you call my Philosophy, which you have never seen, a chimaera ? O brainless youth, who has bewitched you, so that you believe that you swallow the highest and the eternal, and that you hold it in your intestines ?

Yet you seem to want to use your reason, and you ask me, *how I know that my philosophy is the best among all those which have ever been taught in the world, or are taught now, or will be taught in the future?* This, indeed, I can ask you with far better right. For I do not presume that I have found the best Philosophy, but I know that I think the true one. If you ask me how I know this, I shall answer, in the same way that you know that the three angles of a triangle are equal to two right angles. That this is enough no one will deny whose brain is sound, and who does not dream of unclean spirits who inspire us with false ideas which are like true ones : for the truth reveals itself and the false.

But you who presume that you have at last found the best religion, or rather the best men, to whom you have given over your credulity, *how do you know that*

they are the best among all those who have taught other Religions,
or are teaching them now, or will teach them in the future?
Have you examined all those religions, both ancient and modern,
which are taught here and in India and everywhere throughout the
world? And even if you have duly examined them how do you
know that you have chosen the best? For you can give
no reason for your faith. But you will say that you
assent to the inward testimony of the Spirit of God,
while the others are cheated and misled by the Prince
of evil Spirits. But all those outside the Roman Church
make the same claims with the same right for their
Churches as you do for yours.

As to what you add about the common consent of
myriads of men, and of the uninterrupted succession
of the Church, etc., this is the same old song of the
Pharisees. For these also, with no less confidence than
the adherents of the Roman Church, produce their
myriads of witnesses, who relate what they have heard
about, with as much pertinacity as do the witnesses of
the Romans, just as if they themselves had experienced
it. They trace back their lineage to Adam. They boast
with equal arrogance that their Church maintains its
growth, stability, and solidity to this very day, in spite
of the hostility of the Heathen and the Christians.
Most of all do they take their stand on their antiquity.
They declare with one voice that they have received
their traditions from God Himself, and that they alone
preserve the written and unwritten word of God. No
one can deny that all heresies have left them, but
that they have remained constant for some thousands of years, without any imperial compulsion, but
through the mere power of superstition. The miracles
which they relate are enough to weary a thousand
gossips. But what they chiefly pride themselves on
is that they number far more martyrs than any other
nation and daily increase the number of those who with

extraordinary constancy of mind have suffered for the faith which they profess. And this is not untrue. I myself know, among others, of a certain Judah, whom they call the Faithful, who in the midst of the flames, when he was believed to be dead already, began to sing the hymn which begins *To thee, O God, I commit my soul*, and died in the middle of the hymn.

The order of the Roman Church, which you so greatly praise, I confess, is politic and lucrative to many. I should think that there was none more suited to deceive the people and to constrain the minds of men, were there not the order of the Mahomedan Church which far surpasses it. For from the time that this superstition began there have arisen no schisms in their Church.

If, therefore, you calculate correctly, you will see that only what you note in the third place, is in favour of the Christians, namely, that unlearned and common men were able to convert almost the whole world to the faith of Christ. But this argument militates not only for the Roman Church, but for all who acknowledge the name of Christ.

But suppose that all the arguments which you adduce, are in favour of the Roman Church alone. Do you think that you can thereby mathematically prove the authority of the Church? Since this is far from being the case, why then do you want me to believe that my proofs are inspired by the Prince of evil Spirits, but yours by God? Especially so, as I see and your letter clearly shows that you have become a slave of this Church, under the influence not so much of the love of God as of the fear of hell, which is the sole cause of superstition. Is this your humility, to put no faith in yourself, but only in others, who are condemned by very many? Do you regard it as arrogance and pride because I use my reason, and acquiesce in that true Word of God which is in the mind and can never be depraved or corrupted? Away with this deadly superstition, acknowledge the reason which God has given you, and cultivate it, if you would not be numbered among the brutes. Cease, I say, to call absurd errors mysteries, and do not shamefully confuse those things which are unknown to us, or as yet undiscovered, with those which are shown to be absurd, as are the horrible secrets of this Church, which, the more they oppose right reason, the more you believe they transcend the understanding.

For the rest, the basis of the *Tractatus Theologico-Politicus*, namely, that Scripture must only be explained through Scripture, which you so boldly and withou any reason proclaim to be false, is not merely assumed, but apodictically proved to be true or well-established, chiefly in Chapter 7, where the opinions of opponents are also refuted. Add to this what is proved at the end of chapter 15.

If you will consider these carefully, and also examine the Histories of the Church (of which I see you are most ignorant), in order to see how false are many of the Pontifical traditions, and by what fate and with what arts the Roman Pontiff, six hundred years after the birth of Christ, obtained sovereignty over the Church, I doubt not that you will at last come to your senses. That this may be so, I wish you from my heart. Farewell, etc.

[THE HAGUE, *December* 1675.]

LETTER LXXVII HENRY OLDENBURG

To the Very Illustrious Mr. B. d. S.

εὖ πράττειν.

Reply to Letter LXXV.

You hit the mark exactly when you perceive the reason why I do not wish the fatalistic necessity of all things to be published, that is, lest the practice of virtue be hindered thereby, and rewards and punishments become of no account. The suggestions on this subject contained in your last letter do not yet seem to settle this matter, or to calm the human mind. For if we human beings are in all our actions, moral as well as natural, as much in the power of God as clay in the hand of the potter, with what right, I pray, can any one of us be blamed for acting in this or that way, when it was absolutely impossible for him to act otherwise? Shall we not all to a man be able to retort to God: Your inflexible fate, and your irresistible power have compelled us to act thus, and we could not act otherwise; why, therefore, and with what right will you hand us over to such dire punishments, which we could in no way avoid, seeing that you do and direct everything through supreme necessity in accordance with your will and pleasure? When you say, men are inexcusable before God for no other reason than because they are in the power of God, I should certainly reverse that argument and say, apparently with more reason, that men are so evidently excusable because they are in the power of God. For it is easy for everybody to plead: Your power, O God, is inevitable; therefore it appears that I must deservedly be excused that I did not act otherwise.

Moreover in that you still take miracles and ignorance to be equivalent terms, you seem to confine the power of God and the knowledge of men, even of the wisest men, within the same limits, as if God were unable to do or to produce anything for which men cannot render a reason, if they exert the whole strength of their mind. Further, the history of Christ's Passion, Death, Burial and Resurrection seems to be described in such vivid and natural colours that I am even emboldened to appeal to your conscience whether you believe that it should be taken allegorically rather than literally, if you are really persuaded of the truth of the History? The circumstances which are so lucidly recorded about it by the Evangelists seem to urge profoundly that the story must be taken literally. This much I wanted to say in a few words in reply to that argument. This I earnestly beg you to forgive, and to answer with your usual candour and friendliness.

Mr. Boyle greets you dutifully. What the Royal Society is now doing I will explain on another occasion. Farewell and continue to love me.

HENRY OLDENBURG.

LONDON, 14 *January* 1676.

LETTER LXXVIII B. D. S.

To the Very Noble and Learned
Mr. HENRY OLDENBURG.

Reply to the Preceding.

MOST NOBLE SIR,

What I said in my previous letter, that we are inexcusable because we are in the power of God as clay in the hand of the potter, I wanted to be understood in this sense, namely, that no one can blame God because He has given him an infirm nature or an impotent mind. For it would be just as absurd for a circle to complain that God has not given it the properties of a sphere, or a child who is tortured by a stone, that He has not given him a healthy body, as for a weak-minded man to complain that God has denied him strength and the true knowledge and love of God, and that He has given him a nature so weak that he cannot restrain or moderate his desires. For to the nature of each thing there belongs no more than necessarily follows from its given cause. But that it does not belong to the nature of each man to be strong-minded and that it is no more in our power to have a sound body than a sound Mind, no-one can deny, unless he wishes to contradict both experience and reason. But you will insist that if men sin from the necessity of their nature, they are excusable : but you do not explain what you want to conclude from this, whether, namely, you want to conclude that God is unable to be angry with them or that they are worthy of blessedness, that is, of the knowledge and love of God. Now if you mean the former, I fully admit that God is not angry, and that all things come to pass according to His decision ; but I deny that they ought therefore all to be blessed : for men can be excusable and nevertheless lack blessedness, and be tormented in many ways. For a horse is excusable for being a horse and not a man ; nevertheless it must be a horse and not a man. He who goes mad from the bite of a dog is, indeed, to be excused, and yet is rightly suffocated, and, lastly, he who is unable to control his desires, and to restrain them through fear of the laws, although he must be excused for his weakness, is nevertheless unable to enjoy peace of mind, and the knowledge and love of God, but necessarily perishes.

I do not think it necessary to warn you here that when Scripture says that God is angry with sinners, and that He is a judge who takes cognizance of the actions of men, judges, and passes sentence, it is speaking in human fashion, and in accordance with the received opinions of the people, since its intention is not to teach Philosophy, nor to make men learned, but obedient.

Again, I do not see how, because I assume that miracles and ignorance are equivalent, I appear to confine the power of God and the knowledge of men within the same limits.

Further, I accept Christ's passion, death and burial literally, as you do, but his resurrection, allegorically.

I do indeed acknowledge that this is also related by the Evangelists with so many circumstantial details that we cannot deny that the Evangelists themselves believed that Christ's body rose again, and ascended into heaven to sit at the right hand of God ; and that he could also have been seen even by unbelievers if they had also been present in the places in which Christ himself appeared to his disciples ; in this, however, without harm to the teaching of the gospel, they could have been deceived, as happened also to other Prophets. I gave examples of this in my previous letter. But Paul, to whom also Christ afterwards appeared, glories that he knew Christ not according to the flesh but according to the Spirit.

I thank you very much for the Catalogue of the books of the very noble Mr. Boyle. Lastly, I wait to hear from you, when you have an opportunity, about the present proceedings of the Royal Society.

Farewell, most honoured sir, and believe me yours in all love and devotion.

[THE HAGUE, 7 *February* 1676.]

LETTER LXXIX   HENRY OLDENBURG

To THE VERY ILLUSTRIOUS MR. BENEDICT DE SPINOSA.

Many greetings.

[*Reply to the Preceding.*]

In your last letter, written to me on the 7th of February, there remain some things which seem to deserve closer examination. You say that a man cannot complain because God has denied him a true knowledge of Himself, or sufficient strength to avoid sins, since there belongs to the nature of anything no more than necessarily follows from its essence. But I say that inasmuch as God, the creator of men, formed them after His own image, which seems to include in its conception wisdom and goodness and power, it seems by all means to follow that it is more within the power of man to have a sound Mind than a sound body, since the physical health of the body depends on mechanical principles, but soundness of mind, on choice and purpose. You add that men may be excusable and yet be tormented in many ways. This seems hard at first sight; and what you add in place of proof, that a dog who is mad from a bite is indeed excusable, but is nevertheless rightly killed, does not seem to settle the matter: for the slaughter of such a dog would argue cruelty if it were not necessary for the protection of dogs, or other animals, and even men, from a bite of this kind which infects with madness. But if God had implanted a sound mind in men as He is able to do, there would be no contagion of vices to be feared. And certainly it seems exceedingly cruel that God should give men over to eternal torments, or to torments which are terrible at least for a time, on account of sins which could in no way be avoided by them. Moreover, the trend of the whole of Holy Scripture seems to suppose and to imply that man can refrain from sins: for it is full of curses and promises, of proclamations of rewards and of penalties, which all seem to militate against the necessity of sinning, and to imply the possibility of avoiding punishments. If this is denied then the human mind will have to be said to act no less mechanically than the human body.

Further, your continued assumption that Miracles and Ignorance are equivalent seems to rest on this basis, that a creature can and must have an insight into the infinite power and wisdom of the Creator: I am still very strongly convinced that it is certainly otherwise.

Lastly, your assertion that Christ's passion, death

and burial must be taken literally, but his Resurrection allegorically, is not supported by you, it appears to me, by any argument. In the Gospels, Christ's resurrection seems to be related as literally as the other events. And the whole Christian Religion, and its truth, rest on this article of the Resurrection, and if it is taken away, the mission of Christ and his heavenly Teaching collapse. It cannot be unknown to you how much Christ, when he had been raised from the dead, endeavoured to convince his disciples of the truth of the Resurrection, properly so called. To want to turn all these things into allegories is the same as if some-one tried hard to overthrow the whole truth of the Gospel History.

These few points I again wished to submit, in accordance with my liberty of philosophizing, and I earnestly beg you to take them in good part.

LONDON, 11 *February* 1676.

I will deal very fully with the present studies and investigations of the Royal Society if God grant life and health.

LETTER LXXX

EHRENFRIED WALTER VON TSCHIRNHAUS

To the Very Acute and Learned Philosopher B. d. S.

MOST ILLUSTRIOUS SIR,

First I find it exceedingly difficult to conceive how the existence of bodies having motion and figure can be proved a priori, since there is nothing of this kind in Extension when we consider it absolutely. Secondly, I should like to be informed by you in what sense is to be understood what you state in your letter on the Infinite in these words : *But they do not conclude that such things exceed every number because of the multitude*

361

of their parts. For in fact all Mathematicians seem to me always to show with regard to such infinities that the number of the parts is so great as to exceed any assignable number, and in the example about the two circles, which is adduced there, you do not seem to prove this point, although you had undertaken to do so. For there you merely show that they do not infer this from the excessive greatness of the intervening space, and *because we do not know its maximum and minimum*; but you do not show, as you wanted to do, that they do not infer it from the multitude of the parts.

Further, I gathered from Mr. Leibniz, that the tutor of the Dauphin of France, Huet by name, a man of extraordinary learning, is going to write about the truth of human Religion, and to refute your *Tractatus Theologico-Politicus.* Farewell.

2 *May* 1676.

LETTER LXXXI   B. D. S.

To the Very Noble and Learned
MR. EHRENFRIED WALTER VON TSCHIRNHAUS.

Reply to the Preceding.

MOST NOBLE SIR,

What I said in my letter about the Infinite, that they do not infer the infinity of the parts from the multitude of parts, is clear from the fact that, if it were inferred from their multitude, we should not be able to conceive a greater multitude of parts, but their multitude ought to be greater than any given one, which is untrue : for in the whole space between two circles having different centres we conceive twice as many parts as in half that space, and yet the number of the parts, of the half as well as of the whole of the space, exceeds every assignable number.

Next, from extension as Descartes conceives it, that is, as a quiescent mass, it is not only, as you say, difficult to prove the existence of bodies, but absolutely impossible. For matter at rest will continue at rest as much as possible, and will not be set in motion except by some stronger external cause. For this reason I did not hesitate to say once that Descartes' principles of natural things are useless, not to say absurd.

THE HAGUE, 5 *May* 1676.

LETTER LXXXII

EHRENFRIED WALTER VON TSCHIRNHAUS

To the Very Acute and Learned Philosopher B. D. S.

MOST LEARNED SIR,

I should like you to do me the favour of showing me how, according to your thoughts, the variety of things can be deduced a priori from the conception of Extension. For you remember the opinion of Descartes whereby he maintains that he can deduce this variety from Extension in no other way than by supposing that this was the effect produced in Extension by motion which was started by God. In my opinion, therefore, he does not deduce the existence of bodies from inert matter, unless perhaps you disregard the hypothesis of God as the mover; for you have not shown how that must necessarily follow a priori from the essence of God; a thing the demonstration of which Descartes believed to be beyond human comprehension. Therefore, I ask you about this subject, well knowing that you hold other views, unless perhaps there is some special reason why you did not hitherto want to make it public. That this may be so, I do not doubt, or it would not have been necessary to indicate such a thing obscurely. But you may certainly be sure that, whether you tell me something openly or whether you conceal it, my feeling for you will remain unchanged.

The reasons, however, why I should especially desire this, are these. In Mathematics I have always observed that from anything considered in itself, that is, from the definition of anything, we are able to deduce at least one property, but that if we desire more properties, then we must relate the thing defined to other things; then, if at all, from the combination of the definitions of these things new properties result. For instance, if I consider only the circumference of a circle, I shall not be able to infer anything except that it is alike at all points, or uniform, in which property it differs essentially from all other curves. But I shall never be able to deduce any other properties. If, however, I relate it to other things, say, to the radii drawn from the centre, or to two or also more intersecting lines, then I shall in this way be able to deduce some more properties. This seems to a certain extent to oppose Proposition XVI of the *Ethics*, which is almost the most important one in Book I of your Treatise. In this it is assumed as known that several properties can be deduced from the given definition of a thing. This seems to me impossible, unless we relate the defined thing to others. As a consequence of this I cannot see how from an Attribute, considered by itself, for instance from infinite Extension, there can arise a variety of bodies. If you think that this also cannot be concluded from a single attribute considered by itself, but only from all taken together, I should like to learn this from you, also how this should be conceived.

Farewell, etc.

PARIS, 23 *June* 1676.

LETTER LXXXIII   B. D. S.

To the Very Noble and Learned
Mr. EHRENFRIED WALTER VON TSCHIRNHAUS.
Reply to the Preceding.

Most Noble Sir,

You ask whether the variety of things can be proved a priori from the conception of Extension alone. I believe I have already shown sufficiently clearly that this is impossible, and that therefore matter is badly defined by Descartes as Extension, but that it must necessarily be defined by an attribute which expresses eternal and infinite essence. But perhaps, if life lasts, I will discuss this question with you some other time more clearly. For so far I have not been able to write anything about these things in proper order.

As to what you say in addition that from the definition of each thing considered in itself we can deduce one property only, this may be true in the case of the most simple things, or in the case of things of reason (under which I also include figures) but not in the case of real things. For from the mere fact that I define God as a Being to whose essence belongs existence I infer several of His properties, namely, that He exists necessarily, that He is unique, immutable, infinite, etc. And in this way I might adduce several other examples which I omit at present.

Lastly, I pray you to find out whether Mr. Huet's Treatise (namely, the one against the *Tractatus Theologico-Politicus*), of which you wrote before, has already been published, and whether you will be able to send me a copy, and also whether you already know what it is that has recently been discovered about Refraction.

And so, farewell, most Noble Sir, and continue to love, etc.

Your B. D. S.

The Hague, 15 *July* 1676.

LETTER LXXXIV   B. D. S.

To a Friend.

On the Political Treatise.

Dear Friend,

Your welcome letter was delivered to me yesterday. I thank you from my heart for the great trouble which you take on my behalf. I would not miss this opportunity, etc., if I were not busy with something which I consider more useful, and which, as I believe, will please you more, namely, in composing a *Political Treatise*, which, at your instigation, I began some time ago. Of this Treatise six chapters are already finished. The *first* contains as it were an Introduction to the work itself; the *second* treats of Natural Right; the *third* of the Right of the Supreme Powers; the *fourth*, of what Political Business is within the control of the supreme Powers; the *fifth*, of what is the ultimate and highest end which a Society can consider; and the *sixth*, of the way in which a Monarchical Government ought to be constituted, so as not to sink into a Tyranny. At present I am doing the *seventh* chapter, in which I prove methodically all those parts of the preceding sixth chapter which concern the constitution of a well-ordered Monarchy. Then I shall pass on to *Aristocracy and Popular Government*, and finally to Laws and other Special Questions concerning Politics. And so, farewell, etc.

[The Hague, 1676.]

THE END.

ANNOTATIONS

LETTER I

P. 73. This letter is only known from the *Posthumous Works* * (Latin and Dutch editions, 1677), the original letter, written in Latin, having been lost.

Oldenburg's letter is a remarkable tribute to the personality of Spinoza. At the time of their meeting Spinoza was not yet twenty-nine, Oldenburg was about forty-six, yet the attitude of the older and more influential man is almost that of a disciple to a master. His attitude, it is true, changed considerably when, after a long lapse of time, the early impression faded, and old prejudices re-asserted themselves in an environment in which such prejudices were too habitual, and too deeply rooted, to be even remotely suspected of being prejudices. See *Introduction*, § 3.

P. 73, l. 6. *Rhynsburg* is a little village about six or seven miles north-west of Leyden. It is situated on the banks of the old Rhine, and is within easy walking distance of Endgeest, where Descartes had stayed a number of years. Its modest cottages, narrow lanes, quiet waterways, and quaint medieval church still give Rhynsburg an old-world appearance such as it had when Oldenburg visited Spinoza there. The cottage in which the two met is still in existence. It stands in what is now known as Spinoza Lane, and it is preserved as a Spinoza Museum under the name of *Spinozahuis*. The spirit of its early owner or occupier may be gathered from an inscription on a stone which was once in the cottage wall, and which is still preserved. The inscrip-

---

* In these Annotations the expression *Posthumous Works*, without any qualification, refers to *both* the Latin and the Dutch editions ; *Opera Posthuma* denotes the Latin edition only ; *Nagelate Schriften* denotes the Dutch edition only.

tion is taken from Kamphuyzen's *May Morning*, and may be rendered as follows :

> " Alas ! if all men were but wise,
>   And would be good as well,
> The Earth would be a Paradise,
>   Where now 'tis mostly Hell."

The spirit expressed is that of the Collegiants, a sect of Quaker-like dissenters who made Rhynsburg their headquarters, and who were consequently also known by the name of Rhynsburgers. Spinoza had friends among them, and in 1660 he left Amsterdam for Rhynsburg, where he stayed until 1663. These were fruitful years, in which he wrote the later parts of the *Short Treatise on God, Man and his Well-being*, the unfinished *Treatise on the Improvement of the Understanding*, part of his geometrical version of Descartes' *Principles*, and the appended *Metaphysical Thoughts*, and possibly the first part of his *Ethics*.

P. 74, l. 9. *Certain Physiological Essays*, by Robert Boyle, was published in 1661. A Latin version was published in London in 1665 and in Amsterdam in 1667. Spinoza must have received from Oldenburg an advance copy of the Latin version of some of the essays. The essays are not *physiological* in the present sense of the term, but *physical*—both terms literally mean " concerning Nature."

LETTER II

P. 74. This letter is contained in the *Posthumous Works*, but is not extant in any other form. To judge from the dates of the preceding letter and of the next letter, it must have been written about the middle of September 1661.

P. 76, l. 6. " Every substance must be infinite or supremely perfect of its kind." This definition does not yet distinguish between *substance* and *attribute*. According to Spinoza's subsequent use of these terms, this definition really defines *attribute*, and not *substance*, which is *absolutely* infinite or perfect, not only of its kind.

P. 76, l. 14. " Proofs after the manner of Geometry." The geometric exposition of the fundamental ideas of his philosophy which Spinoza enclosed in this letter has been lost. But it can be reconstructed with the help of this and the two following letters, Appendix I of the *Short Treatise*, and the *Ethics*. The editors of the *Posthumous Works* identified the contents of the lost document with the contents of the beginning of the *Ethics* up to Proposition IV. But the lost outline must have been different in some ways both from the geometrical first Appendix to the *Short Treatise* (pp. 153–156 of my translation) and from the opening passages of the *Ethics*. The lost sketch may be reconstructed approximately as follows :

Definition 1.—God is a Being consisting of infinite attributes, of which each is infinite, or supremely perfect of its kind.

> [See p. 75, l. 21, *Short Treatise*, Appendix I, corollary to Proposition IV, and *Ethics*, Part I, Definition VI.]

Definition 2.—By Attribute or Substance I understand that which is in itself, and is conceived through itself and in itself, so that the conception of it does not involve the conception of another thing.

> [See p. 75, l. 25, *Ethics*, Part I, Definition III.]

Definition 3.—By Modification or Accident I mean that which is in something else, and is conceived through that in which it is.

> [See p. 82, l. 29, *Ethics*, Part I, Definition V.]

Axiom 1.—Substance is by nature prior to its *accidents*.

[See p. 82, l. 32, *Short Treatise*, Appendix I, Axiom 1, and *Ethics*, Part I, Proposition I.]

Axiom 2.—Besides Substances and *Accidents* there exists nothing in reality, or outside the understanding.

[See p. 79, l. 13, p. 82, l. 35, *Ethics*, Part I, Proposition IV, Proof.]

Axiom 3.—Things which have different attributes have nothing in common between them.

[See p. 79, l. 15, p. 83, l. 4, *Short Treatise*, Appendix I, Axiom 4, and *Ethics*, Part I, Proposition II.]

Axiom 4.—Things which have nothing in common between them cannot be one the cause of the other.

[See p. 79, l. 21, p. 83, l. 8, *Short Treatise*, Appendix I, Axiom 5, and *Ethics*, Part I, Proposition III.]

Proposition 1.—In Nature there cannot be two substances having the same attribute.

[See p. 76, l. 2, p. 79, l. 35, *Short Treatise*, Appendix I, Proposition I, and *Ethics*, Part I, Proposition V.]

Proposition 2.—A Substance cannot be produced, not even by another substance, but existence pertains to the essence of a substance.

[See p. 76, l. 4, p. 80, l. 3, *Short Treatise*, Appendix I, Propositions II and IV, and *Ethics*, Part I, Propositions VI and VII.]

Proposition 3.—Every Substance is by nature infinite or supremely perfect of its kind.

[See p. 76, l. 5, also the *Short Treatise*, Appendix I, Proposition III, and *Ethics*, Part I, Proposition VIII.]

ANNOTATIONS

Scholium.—The existence of an Attribute or Substance follows from its definition. For every definition, or clear and distinct idea, is true.
[See p. 81, l. 23, and l. 33.]

P. 77, l. 1. "Bacon . . . supposes that . . . the human intellect is fallible." The reference is to *Novum Organum*, I, xli: "The Idols of the Tribe have their foundation in human nature itself, and in the tribe or race of men. For it is a false assertion that this sense of man is the measure of things. On the contrary, all perceptions, as well of the sense as of the mind, are according to the measure of the individual, and not according to the measure of the universe. And the human understanding is like a false mirror, which, receiving rays irregularly, distorts and discolours the nature of things by mingling its own nature with it."

P. 77 l. 8. "Prone to abstractions." *Novum Organum*, I, li: "The human understanding is of its own nature prone to abstractions, and gives a substance and reality to things which are fleeting" (Ellis and Spedding's more picturesque than accurate translation). The *Opera Posthuma* gives Bacon's term *fluxa*, but Dr. Gebhardt has adopted *fluida* from the Dutch edition. Why?

P. 77, l. 10. "Thirdly. . . ." *Novum Organum*, I, xlviii: "The human understanding is unquiet; it cannot stop or rest, and still presses onward, but in vain."

P. 77, l. 15. "Aphorism 49." *Novum Organum*, I, xlix: "The human understanding is no dry light, but receives an infusion from the will and affections, whence proceed sciences which may be called 'sciences as one would.'"

P. 77, l. 29. "A thing of reason" (*ens rationis*) is an aid to thought. In the system of Spinoza it appears to occupy a position between professed fictions or fancies, on the one hand, and adequate ideas, on the other. Adequate ideas are apprehensions of the very essence of reality ; fictitious ideas or mere fancies have no reference to reality ; " things of reason," or aids to thought, may be described as devices of the human mind for apprehending reality, but not as it really is in itself. It may be said that the conception of " things of reason " contains the gist of Kant's critical philosophy on its epistemological side. What Kant did, in effect, was to reduce *all* human ideas to such aids to thought, and to deny any direct apprehension of ultimate reality, such as Spinoza claimed for " adequate ideas." In Vaihinger's Philosophy of " As If " all human ideas are reduced to fictitious ideas. In the passage with which we are immediately concerned Spinoza contends that the popular conception of Will and its free agency is the result of the hypostasis of a general idea (or " thing of reason ") obtained by abstraction from particular acts of volition.

LETTER III

P. 78. This letter is only known from the *Posthumous Works*, the original letter, written in Latin, having been lost.

Oldenburg's difficulties arose from his utter failure to understand Spinoza's conception of Substance and Attribute, and his persistence in identifying *substance* with any *thing* (what Spinoza calls a *mode*), and *attribute* with any *quality*. His objection to inferring the existence of a thing from the definition of it was true but irrelevant, because Spinoza did not speak of *things* in the ordinary sense, but of the unconditioned Ground of all conditioned reality. Spinoza's main point was that the existence of finite, dependent or conditioned things implies the reality of an Absolute or Unconditioned Ground or (immanent) Cause. And by Attributes Spinoza meant, of course, only such ultimate infinite qualities, or rather Aspects of Substance, as Extension and Thought, not any kind of finite quality.

P. 79, l. 3. "What thought is . . ." Oldenburg's allusion, in the second question, to the possibility of thought being a corporeal activity may have reference to the views of his contemporary Hobbes or to the older views of the Epicureans and of the Stoics.

P. 79, l. 8. "The light of Nature" (*lux naturae*, also *lumen naturae* or *lumen naturale*) means a natural power by which truths are apprehended independently of supernatural revelations or even of ordinary experience. The term occurs already in the writings of Cicero and of St. Augustine, as well as in those of Thomas Aquinas (1225–1274). According to Descartes all ideas clearly and distinctly apprehended by "the light of nature" are certain and true.

P. 80, l. 22. "Our Philosophical Society," that is, what was soon known as the Royal Society. See *Introduction*, § 4.

P. 80, l. 25. "History of the Mechanical Arts." *History* here means "a study or a descriptive account." This was its usual meaning then and long before that time (e.g. Aristotle's *History of Animals*). In the name *Natural History* the word still retains its older meaning. The restriction of the name *History* to a *chronological* account is quite modern.

P. 80, l. 30. "Inexplicable forms and occult qualities." The distinction between the *form* or configuration of a thing and its *matter* is sufficiently familiar. Thus the same form of medal may be struck in different materials, such as bronze, silver, or gold, and vice versa. The distinction is also applied metaphorically to literature, thought, conduct, etc. The contemptuous use of the term *formalism* shows the tendency to condemn the exaggerated estimate of mere form at the cost of content, as when Pharisees, ancient or modern, stress the importance of " good form " in conduct without sufficient regard to its substantial motive and results. In the history of thought, however, there has always been a tendency to esteem the " form " of things very highly. This tendency appeared first in Pythagoras (sixth century B.C.), who proclaimed number to be the essence of things. Number at that time was equivalent to geometrical form, because numbers were usually expressed then as dots arranged in geometrical patterns, as they still are in the case of cards and dominoes. The conception was further developed by Plato in his doctrine of Ideas. But the distinction between form and matter became most explicit in Aristotle, according to whom matter is the undifferentiated primal matrix out of which things emerge by acquiring various forms, which thus constitute the essential character of things. The Aristotelian conception dominated the Middle Ages, and survived into modern times in one form or another. Even the anti-Aristotelian Francis Bacon insisted that the problem and aim of induction is to discover the *forms* of natural phenomena. Among the less scientific alchemists " forms " came to be treated like magic powers or spirits, with the help of which everything was at once explained and obscured. Similarly with occult qualities—that is, qualities which were supposed to be " hidden " from our senses (as distinguished from " sensible " qualities, or those which can be apprehended by our senses). They were employed liberally to explain and to mystify. It was Boyle's greatest service to the revival of science to war incessantly against this kind of pseudo-explanation, in his *Sceptical Chymist*, *Origine of Formes and Qualities*, etc.

LETTER IV

P. 81.   This letter is only known from the *Posthumous Works*. The original letter, written in Latin, cannot be traced.   To judge from the dates of Letters III and V, this one must have been written in October 1661.

P. 82, l. 21.   "Common Notions" (*Notiones communes*) is here used as the equivalent of what Oldenburg (Letter III) called "indemonstrable Principles," that is, ultimate assumptions or axioms.   It was the Stoics who first brought into vogue the idea of common notions (κοιναὶ ἔννοιαι, *communes notiones*).   These were held to be ideas implanted in all human beings by the Universal Spirit, and therefore true.   The argument from *consensus gentium* was based on this thought.   In the seventeenth century the term was extensively used by Herbert of Cherbury (1585–1648) and by Descartes, among others.   In his *De Veritate*, Herbert of Cherbury elaborated a theory of knowledge in which "common notions" (*notitiae communes*) occupied an important place as ideas which were innate, indisputable, and of divine origin.   Descartes at first applied the term to such ultimate ideas as those of Existence, Duration, Equality (hence also the names *primae notiones* or *notions primitives*), but eventually identified them with "axioms" or "eternal truths" (such, e.g., as "things equal to the same thing are equal to one another"), on the ground presumably that they are conveyed to us along with "common notions" in the other sense of the term, namely, ultimate ideas like Equality, etc.   Spinoza eventually used the term "adequate ideas" instead of the term "common notions," which he also employed sometimes.   It is worth noting that Plato seems to have applied the term "adequate" (τι ἱκανόν) to an assumption or postulate (ὑπόθεσις), which was admitted by, or common to, all the parties to a discussion. So that Spinoza had to some extent an historical precedent for substituting " adequate " for " common " notions.

P. 82, l. 25. " *Accident* " (*accidens*) was commonly used in Scholastic philosophy for any kind of quality, inasmuch as a quality is dependent upon a substance which it qualifies. " Mode " (*modus*) was used in the same sense more or less. And even Descartes used the two terms as synonyms (*modus sive accidens*). In the passage before us Spinoza also uses *accident* and *modification* (= *mode*) as equivalent terms. Both denote some modification (or state, or *affection*) of Substance, or of an Attribute (in Spinoza's sense). In Letters X, XII and XVII we meet again with these terms used in the same way. In his later writings, however, Spinoza dropped the term *accidens* almost entirely in favour of the terms *modus, modificatio* or *affectio*. Speaking generally the use of *accident* (in contrast to *Attribute* or *Substance*) corresponded to the modern philosophical use of *adjectival* to designate what is inherent in or dependent upon something else, as opposed to the *substantival*, or self-dependent, or self-existing.

P. 83, l. 19. " Men are not created but begotten." Spinoza wants to emphasize the difference between creation out of nothing and the mere transformation of already existing material.

P. 83, l. 24. " The second Proposition," etc. See Annotations to Letter II. Oldenburg's misconception of what Spinoza meant by *substance* naturally misled him to suppose that Spinoza was setting up as many gods as there were *things*, whereas Spinoza's real aim was to prove that there could only be *one* Substance, or self-existing Ground of Reality.

LETTER V

P. 83. This letter also is only known from the *Posthumous Works*, the original letter, written in Latin, having been lost.

P. 83, l. 32. "The little book," that is, an advance copy of the Latin translation of parts of *Certain Physiological Essays* by Boyle.

P. 84, l. 13. "In what manner things began to be," etc. Oldenburg cannot get away from the story of the Creation. For Spinoza, of course, things did not "begin to be," the universe or substance being eternal.

LETTER VI

P. 84. The original letter, written in Latin, is in the possession of the Royal Society, London. A facsimile of it is given in W. Meyer's edition of the extant autograph letters of Spinoza (1903). Spinoza's draft of the letter must have been used for the *Posthumous Works*, and the two texts have a number of variants of no great importance. The most important difference between the two texts consists in the omission from the text of the *Posthumous Works* of the last two paragraphs of the original letter.

The letter is not dated. But it must have been written early in 1662. This appears from Letter VII, in which Oldenburg, writing in July 1662, acknowledges the receipt of the present letter many weeks ago.

P. 85, l. 11. "On Nitre." The ultimate aim and general significance of Boyle's experiments have already been described briefly in the *Introduction*, § 4. But for the benefit of those readers who are interested in the history of science an account is added here of the nature and aim of his experiments with nitre (or saltpetre) as described in *Certain Physiological Essays* (edition 1661, pp. 107–135), and a few comments are interspersed.

Among the chemists and alchemists before, and in the time of, Boyle, it was commonly believed that complex natural objects consisted of certain elements or " principles " (see Annotations to Letter XIV), together with a certain " Form," which was different for each class of objects (each kind of complex substance having its own " substantial form "), and which gave to each class its characteristic nature. This " form " (the early history of which is sketched in the Annotations to Letter III) was frequently conceived after the analogy of a soul, or a spirit, which held together the elements and qualities in one complex whole (or " concrete," as it was commonly called), helped to maintain it and its character, and what not. Boyle tried to show that this kind of mysterious, wonder-working " form " was a gratuitous, useless assumption, and that the only kind of form it was legitimate to accept was that consisting in the various groupings of the more elementary components which go to make up a complex whole or " concrete." In support of his contention he tried to show that even artificial compounds (such as glass or vitriol), which presumably were not endowed with " substantial forms " by Nature, behaved in the same sort of way as, in the case of natural " concretes," was wont to be explained by reference to the mysterious " substantial forms " ; and that, moreover, a natural " concrete," like nitre, could be broken up into more elementary components, so that its alleged " substantial form " was destroyed, and yet, when redintegrated artificially, the product was the same kind of nitre as before. All this, according to Boyle, tended to show that what really mattered was the way in which the more elementary particles of matter were grouped together. This was the real " form " of things ; the other more mysterious " substantial forms " were only a device for enabling ignorance to masquerade as knowledge.

If Boyle could disprove (as he thought he could) the need of assuming the reality of more or less supernatural " forms " he would obviously be promoting the cause of a strictly naturalistic explanation of chemical phenomena, such as the mechanical, atomistic or " corpuscularian " philosophy aimed at. But Boyle went even further. He tried to show that the secondary qualities of things (taste, smell, temperature, etc.) were the results of their primary qualities, and could be derived from these, or explained by reference to them. This was a more positive contribution to the " mechanical philosophy." And both these points must be borne in mind when reading Boyle's accounts of his experiments. In both these respects Boyle may be said to have helped the cause of the Atomic Theory, and much of what he has said may justify the commonly accepted view that that was what he was really aiming at by these experiments. But strictly speaking that view goes a little too far. It would be more accurate to say that the experiments were primarily and immediately directed to establish the two above-mentioned points, namely, the elimination of the supernatural from Chemistry, and the reduction of secondary to primary qualities. After these preliminaries we may now proceed to describe Boyle's experiment with nitre (or saltpetre).

A weighed amount of nitre was melted in a crucible and, while the nitre was still molten, a small live coal was cast into it. This kindled the nitre " and made it boyl and hisse and flash for a pretty while." After the action had subsided, further live coals were added from time to time until kindling ceased. After this the mixture was strongly heated for a quarter of an hour so that if any volatile part should yet remain, it might be forced off. The residual " fixed Nitre " was then divided into two equal parts. One part was dissolved in water, and Spirit of Saltpetre was dropped on it until it no longer effervesced. The other portion was similarly treated except that it was not dissolved in water prior to the addition of acid. Both solutions were then set to evaporate in the air near an open window.

In a few hours there appeared in the glass containing the first mixture some saline particles which seemed to be saltpetre, to judge by the shape of the crystals and from their manner of burning. The second mixture was very slow in crystallizing. So water was added, and the solution was evaporated. This also gave a salt resembling saltpetre in the shape of its crystals, and in the manner of its burning on live coals. But it was slightly different in taste when first applied to the tongue.

Boyle did not weigh the nitre recovered at the end of the experiment. He also disregarded the weight of the " live coals." He had not grasped the rôle played by the coals. To him they merely kindled the nitre, and thus set free its volatile parts. Boyle only aimed at a real severance or analysis of the " differing parts " of the " concrete," nitre, and thought he had achieved his aim.

Boyle discusses the significance of the experiment at great length. He says that it " seems to afford us an instance, by which we may discern that Motion, Figure and Disposition of parts, and such like primary and mechanical Affections (if I may so call them) of Matter, may suffice to produce those more secondary Affections of Bodies which are wont to be called Sensible Qualities." Now, saltpetre had been regarded as a cold body, one of the coldest : it was given in fevers by physicians. " And yet the parts of this so cold Body, its Spirit and

Alkali (by the latter of which Chymists are wont to
mean any fix'd Salt produced by burning), put together,
do immediately agitate each other with great vehemency ;
and did in our Experiment produce such an heat, that
I could scarcely endure to hold in my hand the Vial,
wherein much lesse than an ounce of each was mix'd,
though but leisurely and almost by drops : as if Heat
were nothing but a various and nimble motion of the
minute particles of Bodies. For in our Experiments,
as long as that confus'd agitation lasted, so long the
heat endur'd, and with that agitation it encreas'd and
abated ; and at length when the motion ceas'd, the
heat also vanish'd."

The production of sound and the sudden disappear-
ance of the " blewish green colour " of the " fix'd
Petre " on the addition of acid are also adduced as
evidence for the modification of the " disposition of
parts." Again, the " Nitrous Spirit " has an unpleasant
smell, which is made even more so when it is poured
on its own fixed salt, a substance of languid odour.
Yet saltpetre, from which these bodies of varying odour
spring, " and which may again emerge from the coalition
of them," is itself odourless. The two bodies also
differed in taste : the spirit was very acid, " a strong and
sour ' Acetum Minerale,' " while the " fixt Nitre " had
an equally strong taste of " Salt of Tartar "—properties
not exhibited by the petre.

The experiment also called into question the principle
that inflammability in " mixt bodies " argued " a distinct
sulphureous ingredient." It shows us " that Salt-
Petre (which not onely is inflammable but burns very
fiercely and violently) may be produc'd by the coalition
of two bodies, which are neither of them inflammable ;
the one being a fix'd Salt, that to become such has
already suffer'd the loss of all that the fire could deprive
it of, and the other being a Spirit abounding with acid

particles, which kind of Salts have been observ'd to be more apt to quench than foment fire."

Boyle here emphasizes the great difference between the various " active parts " of a body, when they are bound up in the texture of a " Concrete," and when they are free to assemble like with like. He comments on the " unwarinesse " of those Chymists, who had ascribed to every one of the several " Principles " of a " Concrete " the properties of the entire body ; for, " we may observe, that when Salt-Petre is distill'd, the volatile liquor and fix'd Salt into which it is reduc'd by the fire are endow'd with properties exceeding different both from each other, and from those of the undissipated concrete."

He then proceeds : " And if upon further and exacter tryal it appears that the whole body of the Salt-Petre, after it's having been sever'd into very differing parts by distillation, may be adequately re-united into Salt-Petre equiponderant to its first self ; this experiment will afford us a noble and (for aught we have hitherto met with) single instance to make it probable that that which is commonly called the Form of a Concrete, which gives it it's being and denomination, and from whence all it's qualities are in the vulgar Philosophy, by I know not what inexplicable wayes, supposed to flow, may be in some bodies but a Modification of the matter they consist of, whose parts by being so and so disposed in relation to each other, constitute such a determinate kind of body, endowed with such and such properties ; whereas if the same parts were otherwise disposed, they would constitute other bodies of very differing natures from that of the Concrete whose parts they formerly were, and which may again result or be produc'd after it's dissipation and seeming destruction, by the re-union of the same component particles, associated according to their former disposition."

" The Redintegration of an analyz'd body, if it can be accurately and really perform'd, may give much light to many particulars in Philosophy, and would certainly be very welcome both to the embracers of the Atomical Hypothesis, and generally to those other Modern Naturalists, who aspire to such Explications of Nature's Phenomena as may at last be understood."

Boyle thought he had effected a separation, which showed that nitre was a " Concrete," formed from the " differing parts " called " fix't Salt " and " Spirit of Nitre," and therefore more complex than either of the latter—a conclusion we now know to be erroneous. Boyle also considered that, in the subsequent interaction of the " fix't Salt " and the " Spirit of Nitre " to reform the original nitre, there was a modification of the " disposition of parts" of the reactants and that this modification gave rise to nitre and to its properties. To him it was the mere union of two ingredients. He saw nothing vital in the effervescence that occurred when the " Spirit of Nitre " was added to the " fix't Salt "—it was mere commotion in the liquid. The correct interpretation of this was not given until Black appeared nearly a century later.

For Spinoza, as appears from Letter XIII, from *Metaphysical Thoughts*, Part II, Ch. I, etc., the question of " substantial forms " and " occult qualities " was not a live question. He simply ignored them, and did not consider it worth anybody's while to waste time in disproving them formally. Like other people after him, Spinoza read into Boyle's endeavours more ambitious aims, such as the elaboration of a mechanistic system of explanation of natural phenomena. The result of this was a certain amount of mutual misunderstanding and mutual irritation. To understand Letters VI, XI and XIII it must be remembered that Spinoza was thinking all the time of a mechanistic natural science, while Boyle was mainly thinking of banishing "substantial forms," etc., from the realm of serious science.

P. 91, l. 7. "Mathematical" was commonly used for "exact" or "scientific."

P. 91, l. 36. The footnote shows that Spinoza kept the drafts or copies of his more important letters, perhaps with a view to publication.

P. 93, l. 16. "Affections." This term was commonly used for *states* or *modifications*.

P. 97, l. 21. "Four hundred and thirty-two" ounces. So the Latin edition of 1667. But the English editions of 1661 and 1669 say "an hundred thirty two ounces." The Latin translator must have mixed this up with the four hundred ounces mentioned in connection with the next experiment.

P. 98, l. 14. The last two paragraphs of this letter are from the autograph original, and are not contained in the *Posthumous Works*.

P. 98, l. 22. The concluding paragraph must refer to the *Short Treatise* and to the *Treatise on the Improvement of the Understanding*. When writing the present letter, in 1662, Spinoza's plan was evidently to write one work combining the contents of both these treatises as we have them now. The *Short Treatise* has certainly undergone some revision with that end in view. Eventually, however, Spinoza appears to have put it aside, and to have made a new start, which ended in his *Ethics*.

P. 99, l. 12. *Spinoza's signature*. This is the first letter which contains his autograph signature. Altogether eleven autograph signatures of Spinoza are known. In these the first name is always either *Benedictus* or the initial B. The surname, however, appears in three different forms : (*a*) Spinoza, (*b*) de Spinoza, (*c*) despinoza. The first of these forms, (*a*), occurs twice in the eleven extant signatures, the second, (*b*), six times, and the third form, (*c*), three times. In one case the *p* and the *n* have some kind of phonetic symbol over them. Presumably the *n* was originally pronounced as in *new*. The significance of the sign over the *p* is not known. The prevailing custom is in favour of *Spinoza* simply, as against de Spinoza or Despinoza. And the usual pronunciation is *Spin-o-za*, not Spy-noza. All that can be said in favour of the latter pronunciation is that it has a good story to its credit.

The story is related by Coleridge in his *Biographia Literaria*, Ch. X, and was staged at the outbreak of the Great War with France, when, as in every Great War, he who was not a blatant jingo was liable to be regarded as a spy. Coleridge and Wordsworth were staying in Somersetshire, in a cottage at the foot of Quantock, where they struggled with the problem of reconciling personality with infinity. " Yet neither my retirement nor my utter abstraction from all the disputes of the day could secure me in those jealous times from suspicion and obloquy, which did not stop at me, but extended to my excellent friend [Wordsworth]." " The dark guesses of some *Quidnunc* met with so congenial a soil in the grave alarm of a titled Dogberry of our neighbourhood, that a spy was actually sent down from the Government *pour surveillance* of myself and friend. There must have been not only abundance, but variety of these ' honourable men ' at the disposal of Ministers : for this proved a very honest fellow. After three weeks' truly Indian perseverance in tracking us (for we were commonly together) during all which time seldom were we out of doors, but he contrived to be within hearing,—(and all the while utterly unsuspected ; how indeed, *could* such a suspicion enter our fancies ?)—he not only rejected Sir Dogberry's request that he would try yet a little longer, but declared to him his belief, that both my friend and myself were as good subjects, for aught he could discover to the contrary, as any in

His Majesty's dominions. He had repeatedly hid himself, he said, for hours together behind a bank at the sea-side (our favourite seat) and overheard our conversation. At first he fancied that we were aware of our danger; for he often heard me talk of one *Spy Nozy*, which he was inclined to interpret of himself, and of a remarkable feature belonging to him; but he was speedily convinced that it was the name of a man who had made a book and lived long ago. Our talk ran most upon books, and we were perpetually desiring each other to look at *this*, and to listen to *that*; but he could not catch a word about politics."

LETTER VII

P. 99. This letter is not dated, but it must have been written towards the end of July 1662. This is clear from Oldenburg's mode of reference to the granting of the Charter to the Royal Society, which took place on July 15, 1662. The letter is only known from the *Posthumous Works*, the original, written in Latin, having been lost.

P. 100, l. 3. Boyle's *New Experiments Physico-Mechanical touching the Spring of the Air and its Effects, made for the most part in a new Pneumatical Engine* appeared in 1660. The "pneumatical engine" to which the title refers was an air-pump (also known as *Machina Boyleana*) which Boyle, with the aid of Robert Hooke, had constructed in 1659 after he had read in 1657 of Guericke's air-pump. By means of the air-pump Boyle studied the elasticity, compressibility and weight of air, also its function in combustion, respiration, and in the conveyance of sound, and he exploded the legend of a *fuga* (or *horror*) *vacui*, Nature's alleged shunning (or abhorrence) of a vacuum. The book was criticized by

Thomas Hobbes and Franciscus Linus. (Franciscus Linus was born in London in 1595. He joined the Jesuits, and taught Hebrew and Mathematics at Lüttich.) Boyle's reply (printed as an Appendix to the second edition of the *New Experiments* in 1662) is famous for its experimental proof of what has since become known as Boyle's Law (that the pressure and the volume of a gas vary in inverse proportion).

P. 100, l. 10. "The Royal Society" received its Charter on July 15, 1662. See *Introduction*, § 4.

P. 100, l. 34. "Momus" is a character from classical mythology noted for his censoriousness, indeed, he is the embodiment of it.

LETTER VIII

P. 101. The original letter, written in Latin, belongs to the Orphanage of the Baptist Collegiants in Amsterdam, and is deposited in the Archives of the United Baptists there. The *Posthumous Works* give it in an abridged form.

P. 101, l. 23. Johannes Casearius was born in 1642 and was probably a pupil in Van den Enden's school in Amsterdam. In 1661 he entered the University of Leyden, and sometime afterwards went to live in Rhynsburg, where he stayed in the same cottage as Spinoza and received instruction from him in the new (i.e. Cartesian) philosophy. Some of the more enterprising undergraduates at Leyden used to visit Rhynsburg (which is near Leyden) to attend the Collegiant meetings there. Casearius may have met Spinoza in that way, or he may have known him from Van den Enden's school, where Spinoza had taught for a time. Casearius appears to have caused Spinoza some anxiety during those Rhynsburg days, being rather superficial, and addicted to novelty rather than devoted to truth; but Spinoza confidently expected better things of him when he matured (see Spinoza's reply to De Vries, Letter IX). In 1665 Casearius was ordained by the Reformed Church in Amsterdam. In 1668 he was appointed to a post in the Dutch East Indies. Eventually he ministered to the Christian souls in Malabar. Here he came into contact with Van Reede, the Governor, who took a deep interest in Botany, and published eventually his *Hortus Malabaricus*. The text of the first two folio volumes of this once famous work was written by Casearius. He died in June 1677 of dysentery. In his Preface to Vol. III of the *Hortus Malabaricus* (1682) Van Reede paid a warm tribute to the memory of Casearius, whose name has since been given to a certain family of plants, the *Casearia*. Such in brief is the story of the pupil who was the occasion of Spinoza's first published work.

P. 102, l. 18. Giovanni Alfonso Borelli (1608–1679) was born in Naples, and became Professor of Mathematics in Messina (1649) and in Pisa (1656). In 1658 he published an edition of Euclid (*Euclides Restitutus*) in Pisa, and subsequently many other books on mathematics, astronomy, physics, and biology. From 1674 till his death he lived in retirement in Rome, under the protection of Christina, Queen of Sweden.

P. 103, l. 3. Andreas Tacquet was born in Antwerp in 1611. In 1654 he published his *Elements of Plane and Solid Geometry*, in an Appendix to which occurs the passage referred to in this letter.

P. 103, l. 6. Christopher Clavius (1537–1612) was born in Bamberg and died in Rome. He was a noted mathematician, and helped with the Gregorian Calendar. In 1574 he published an edition of Euclid with a commentary. The passage referred to in this letter occurs on page 27 of this edition of Euclid.

P. 103, l. 35. " The third Definition." See *Ethics*, I, Definitions III and IV.

P. 104, l. 13. " The Third Scholium to Proposition 8." Compare *Ethics*, I, Prop. X., Scholium.

P. 104, l. 24. " The fifth Definition." See *Ethics*, I, Definition VI.

P. 104, l. 32. " P. Balling." See *Introduction*, § 6.

P. 104, l. 33. " The Scholium to Proposition 19 " is not known. Concerning Simon de Vries, see *Introduction*, § 6.

Pp. 101–104. This reference to the society of young men in Amsterdam, who met to read and to discuss communications sent to them in manuscript by Spinoza, is of great interest. It was no doubt to them that the *Short Treatise* and its concluding message were addressed (see page 403).

LETTER IX

P. 105. The original draft of this letter, written in Latin, is preserved in the Library of the United Baptists in Amsterdam. A facsimile of it is contained in W. Meyer's edition (1903). The *Posthumous Works* print an abridged form of it. The concluding paragraph is only found in the Dutch edition of the *Posthumous Works*. The letter is not dated, but was probably written about the end of February 1663.

P. 105, l. 24. " My night-work." This confirms the report of Kortholt (1700) that Spinoza " devoted himself to his studies far into the night, and for the most part toiled . . . by lamplight from the tenth evening hour until the third " (see *The Oldest Biography of Spinoza*, p. 166). Spinoza had to devote his days to the making of lenses, whereby he maintained himself.

P. 105, l. 27.   Concerning Casearius, see Annotations to Letter VIII.

P. 108, l. 3.   What Spinoza is trying to explain to de Vries about the relation between Thought and Concepts (or Ideas) may perhaps be best expressed in this way.   De Vries seemed to suppose that the nature of Thought can be arrived at by abstracting from all definite ideas or concepts, as though Thought (to use a current expression) were an *abstract* universal.   For Spinoza, however, Thought is essentially what Bosanquet would have called a *concrete* universal—it is the whole system of ideas.   Not Thought, but the separate ideas are obtained by abstraction, by quasi-detachment.   Thought, as Spinoza conceived it, is a live system of ideas or concepts.   If you think away the concepts, you remove, so to say, the members of the organism, and then, of course, there is no organism left.

P. 108, l. 12.   " Creating Nature " and " Created Nature " (*Natura naturans* and *Natura naturata*).   Spinoza adopted these Scholastic terms to express the antithesis between unconditioned Substance (or the Attributes Thought and Extension) on the one hand, and the system of conditioned or dependent realities which follow from the former, on the other hand.   Here he wants to point out that intellect or understanding (even the infinite understanding) is not the same as the Attribute Thought (which pertains to " creating Nature "), but is a *mode* or *modification* of it (and so pertains to " created Nature ").

P. 108, l. 17.   Compare *Ethics*, Part I, Definitions III and IV, also Letter VIII.

P. 108, l. 21.   " With respect to the intellect."   This must not be taken to imply that Attribute is something merely subjective.   According to Spinoza the Intellect or Understanding apprehends Reality as it is.   It is only the separation in thought of one Attribute from the others with which it is organically interconnected in

Substance that distinguishes Attribute from Substance. There is nothing subjective in Spinoza's illustration drawn from the names of the third Patriarch, even if the other illustration given by Spinoza does lend itself to this misinterpretation.

P. 108, l. 30. " Jacob . . . because he had seized his brother's heel." The Hebrew root of the name Jacob means " a heel." Hence the Biblical legend.

P. 108, l. 32. "Plane " and "White." The idea that a plane or smooth surface which reflects all the rays of light incident upon it is white, while a rough surface which reflects only a few of the rays is black, appears to have been put forward by Democritus. So at least Aristotle reports. The idea prevailed more or less up to the time of Spinoza. It is to be found in Boyle's *Experiments and Considerations touching Colours* (1664) with some modifications.

LETTER X

P. 109. This letter is only known from the *Posthumous Works*, the original letter, written in Latin, having been lost.

P. 109, l. 10. "The Definition of some Attribute." See Letters VIII and IX, and *Ethics*, Part I, Definitions III and IV.

P. 109, l. 26. " Eternal truths." Spinoza here explains that in a sense any truth (even a truth concerning finite things and events) is an eternal truth. Once true, always true, if due regard is paid to conditions of time and place. It is more usual, however (Spinoza goes on to explain), to reserve the name " eternal truths " for axioms or " common notions," such as *ex nihilo nihil fit*. See Annotations to Letter IV (on " common notions ").

LETTER XI

P. 110. This letter is only known from the *Posthumous Works*, the original letter, written in Latin, having been lost.

P. 110, l. 28. " The Common Doctrine of Substantial Forms and Qualities." See *Introduction*, § 4, and the Annotations to Letter VI.

P. 111, l. 30. " Descartes' theory of fire." According to Descartes the physical universe is composed of three kinds of matter or elements : (1) The swiftly moving, finely divided *first element*, forming the sun and the stars and the core of the earth ; (2) the transparent *second element*, forming the heavens and filling space ; (3) the dense *third element*, forming the crust of the earth. Particles of earthly bodies assume the form of *fire* when they are separated from one another and carried along by the motion of the first element. This motion must, however, be maintained with sufficient vigour to dispel the second element, which is always tending to close round the particles and so to extinguish the fire. For a substance to be set on fire some force is required to drive out the second element from its pores so as to admit of the entrance of the first element. See Descartes, *Principles of Philosophy*, Part IV, Principles LXXX–CXIX.

P. 112, l. 26. Pierre Gassendi (1592–1655) attempted to combine the doctrines of Theism with the mechanistic and atomistic doctrines of the Epicureans.

P. 112, l. 28. " Visible forms," that is visible arrangements of materials, not the invisible and mysterious " substantial forms " discussed in the Annotations to Letter VI.

P. 114, l. 14. " That very important essay," etc.

See the concluding paragraph of Letter VI and the annotation thereto.

P. 114, l. 33. " Other works " by Boyle referred to here are his *Considerations touching the Usefulness of Experimental Natural Philosophy* and his *Experiments and Considerations touching Colours,* which were published, in Latin translations as well as in English, in 1663 and 1664 respectively.

LETTER XII

P. 115. This letter is only known from the *Posthumous Works.* The original letter or, more likely, Spinoza's draft or copy of it, is said to have appeared in the sale-room when the library of J. J. van Voorst, of Amsterdam, was sold by auction in 1860, and to have been purchased by a Paris bookseller named Durand. But it cannot be traced now. A copy of the letter made by Leibniz is preserved in the former Royal Library at Hanover.

P. 115, l. 15. Concerning L. Meyer, see *Introduction,* § 6. P. M. Q. D. stands for *Philosophiae Medicinaeque Doctor.*

P. 115, l. 16. " On the Nature of the Infinite." The fact that the letter has a title, and the way in which it is referred to by that title in Letter LXXXI, show that copies of some of Spinoza's letters circulated among his friends. This is confirmed by the fact that Leibniz copied with his own hand not only this letter, but also several others.

P. 115, l. 19. " Friend N. N." was probably Pieter Balling (*Introduction,* § 6), who visited Spinoza early in 1663, and no doubt brought him some letters from Amsterdam, just as on his return he took letters from Spinoza to friends in Amsterdam (see Letter VIII).

P. 120, l. 18. " A B C D." The *Posthumous Works*

give "A B and C D." The correct expression is found in the copy of this letter made by Leibniz.

P. 120, l. 20. On the title-page of Spinoza's geometric version of Descartes' *Principles*, published about the same time as this letter was written, there is printed a device very like this diagram, presumably as a symbol of infinity.

P. 121, l. 5. "Corporeal Substance" here means the Attribute Extension.

P. 121, l. 15. "Abstractly" means "apart from the whole of which they are aspects."

P. 121, l. 36. "Rab Chasdai" is usually known as Chasdai Crescas ("Rab" is simply the Hebrew for "Mr." or *Magister*). Chasdai Crescas was a famous Jewish theologian. He was born in Barcelona about 1340, and died there about 1410. In his book called *The Light of the Lord* (written in Hebrew) he contested the Aristotelian proof of God's existence, which proof Maimonides (1135–1204), the most famous Jewish philosopher of the Middle Ages and one of the main sources of the thoughts of Thomas Aquinas, had adopted in his book called *The Guide of the Perplexed* (written in Arabic). The argument in question relied on the impossibility of an infinite regression from effects to their causes, and thence inferred the existence of a First Cause. Crescas challenged the alleged impossibility of such an infinite regression, and suggested a sounder proof of God's existence. His argument was based on the impossibility of conceiving a world entirely conditioned or dependent, without some unconditioned Ground, some uncaused or self-caused Cause to sustain it all. Crescas himself was interested in religious apologetics rather than in pure philosophy, and his ultimate object in opposing Aristotelianism was to vindicate Revelation as the sole arbiter of religious problems. But this does not do away with the fact that Spinoza did take over from Crescas this very important argument from the conditioned to the Unconditioned or the Absolute, which is fundamental for Spinozistic philosophy. In other respects the views of the two thinkers are very divergent.

In his *Metaphysical Thoughts* (II, x), published *after* the date of this letter, Spinoza himself employed the argument from the impossibility of an infinite regression. But then, as may be seen from Letter XV and from Meyer's Preface to Spinoza's geometric version of Descartes' *Principles* (to which the *Metaphysical Thoughts* were appended), Spinoza was not expounding his own views therein. For Spinoza the whole question of proving the existence of God did not turn on the terms finite and infinite, as was commonly conceived then, but on the antithesis *conditioned* and *unconditioned*. By merely tracing each effect to its cause, and that cause to its cause, indefinitely, no real solution can be arrived at. For, so long as the First Cause is conceived as itself a member within the series of causes and effects, it is always possible to ask, as children sometimes do ask, " Who made God? " What Spinoza did was to conceive God (or Nature, or Substance) not as merely a member and transeunt cause of the infinite process, but as the unconditioned ground or immanent cause which sustains the whole and expresses itself in the whole. And his insistence on the *eternity* of Substance is a correction of the tendency to regard Substance (or God or the First Cause) merely as a link (or first link) in the endless *duration* of causal processes (to say nothing of the palpable inconsistency between a *first* cause and an *endless* process). That was also the main reason for his insistence on the fundamental difference between *Infinity* (as he conceived it) and mere *endlessness* or indefiniteness. These misleading and troublesome tendencies Spinoza attributed to man's proneness to substitute imagination for thought or understanding which alone can apprehend the real character of Extension, Time, etc. (see Letter LVI).

P. 119, l. 20. The argument that if you once begin to divide and subdivide time indefinitely, it becomes incomprehensible how an hour can ever elapse is a form of Zeno's paradox. Compare Bergson's treatment of Time and Duration.

LETTER XIII

P. 122. This letter is only known from the *Posthumous Works*, the original letter, written in Latin, having been lost.

P. 123, l. 7. " A certain young man," namely, J. Casearius. See Annotations to Letter VIII.

P. 123, l. 22. " A certain friend of mine," namely, L. Meyer (see *Introduction*, § 6).

P. 123, l. 32. " Some who hold the first places in my country." Spinoza probably meant Jan de Witt and his colleagues. Since 1650 the party of Jan de Witt had displaced the Orange Party. Spinoza evidently realized, much better than did the more experienced and much older Oldenburg, that his only chance of securing a measure of freedom of self-expression in Holland at that time lay in obtaining the protection of Jan de Witt and his friends against the fanaticism of the dominant Calvinist clergy.*

* The question whether Spinoza and de Witt really came into personal contact cannot be answered categorically. There is some evidence in support of the view that they did. But the evidence is not beyond question, and Dr. N. Japikse, in his *Spinoza en de Witt* (The Hague, 1927), is very sceptical about it. In view of the evidence of the usually well-informed " oldest biographer of Spinoza " (Lucas), and of Spinoza's communication to Leibniz about his extreme agitation at the murder of the de Witts, it seems to me highly probable that Spinoza and de Witt had come into personal contact. But Dr. Japikse is probably right in maintaining that their relationship could not have been intimate.

In addition to the reason here given by Spinoza for the publication of his *René Descartes' Principles of Philosophy, Parts I and II, demonstrated according to the geometrical method* (1663, Dutch version 1664) two additional reasons are given elsewhere. In Meyer's Preface to the book we are told that Spinoza did so because his Amsterdam friends (including Meyer himself) had earnestly begged him to do so. It is known that they were all deeply interested in " the new philosophy " (i.e. Cartesianism), and that Jelles actually defrayed the cost of printing this manual of Cartesianism. Yet a third reason is stated by Lucas in his *Biography of Spinoza*—namely, that Spinoza's criticisms of Descartes had caused something like a storm among the Cartesians in Holland, and that, at the request of his friends, Spinoza published his version of Descartes' *Principles* to show that he could speak with authority about the Cartesian philosophy (*The Oldest Biography of Spinoza*, pp. 57 f. and 147 f.).

P. 126, l. 11. " Real *accidents*." The Scholastic philosophers (as already explained in the Annotation to Letter IV) applied the term *accident* to any quality. Some of them, however, distinguished some qualities of things (namely, those like colour, smell, etc., which stimulate the sense-organs) as having a reality even apart from the substances in which they normally inhere. These they called " real accidents " (*accidentia realia*). But Spinoza, like Descartes, would admit no such " real accidents." Everything real must be either self-existent (substance, attribute), or dependent on something else (accident, mode, etc.). There is no middle course.

P. 128, l. 12. " Nothing human was alien to them." A witty application of the familiar line from Terence : *Homo sum, humani nihil a me alienum puto*, interpreted in the light of the popular maxim *humanum errare est*.

LETTER XIV

P. 131. This letter is only known from the *Posthumous Works*, the Dutch version of which gives August 10th (new style) as its date. The Latin original has been lost. The second sentence in the last paragraph but one is from the Dutch translation; it is omitted from the text printed in the *Opera Posthuma*.

P. 131, l. 26. Peter Serrarius was a Belgian, born in 1636. He lived in Amsterdam, and visited London frequently, and so could deliver, or arrange for others to deliver, the letters which passed between Spinoza and Oldenburg. Very little is known about Serrarius, except that he believed in the second advent of Christ and in the coming of the Millennium, and that he saw signs and portents of the coming of these great events in various contemporary happenings. Lots of people entertained such views then. Even among the Jews of that time there were pious dreamers like Manasseh ben Israel, a teacher of Spinoza, and there were credulous dupes who believed in the Messianic character of Sabbatai Zevi. Of course those who did not share his views regarded Serrarius as an eccentric character.

In 1667 Serrarius published a *Reply* to L. Meyer's *Philosophy the Interpreter of Holy Scripture*. The title of the *Reply* was *Responsio ad Exercitationem Paradoxam* (Amsterdam: Typis Cunradi, 1667. 4°.)

P. 132, l. 12. Boyle's *Sceptical Chymist* and a Latin translation of it (*Chymista Scepticus*) were published in 1662.

P. 132, l. 15. "Hypostatical Principles of the Spagyrists." The Spagyrists were those who embraced the views of Paracelsus (1490–1541). Until the time of Paracelsus it was commonly supposed that all material bodies were composed of the four elements earth, air, fire and water. The doctrine of " the four elements " was first formulated by Empedocles (490–430 B.C.), but became widespread chiefly through the writings of Aristotle. Hence those who embraced the doctrine of the four elements were known as the Aristotelians or the Peripatetics. Paracelsus rejected this view, and substituted a theory of three ultimate principles, namely, salt, sulphur, mercury. (*Principle* is here used in the literal sense of anything *original* or *ultimate*, and is practically equivalent to *element*; in fact, Boyle used *element* and *principle* as synonyms.) These three hypostatical or constitutive principles could, of course, only be made to account for all things by an extremely elastic conception of each of them, as Boyle delighted in showing. Some chemists compromised by including in their list of elements not only the three principles of Paracelsus, but also some or all of the four elements of Empedocles. But Boyle rightly insisted that all such doctrines were mere guesses unsupported by experiment, and that the number of ultimate elements, indeed the very question if there existed separate elements, were still open questions to be determined, if at all, by experiment. Boyle did much to clear up the notion of an " element." But even he could do nothing to indicate how an element might be recognized. This task was not accomplished till the time of Lavoisier, a century later.

P. 132, l. 21. Boyle's *Defence* against the criticisms of Franciscus Linus was published in 1663 (see annotations to Letter VII). The full title of the book is *Defensio doctrinae de elatere et gravitate aeris, adversus Franc. Lini objectiones*. A copy of it was in Spinoza's library, as appears from the official inventory of his belongings taken immediately after his death.

P. 133, l. 33. " The Torricellian experiment." Torricelli (1608–1647), at one time assistant to Galilei, was the discoverer of the principle of the barometer. His experiment, made in 1643, showed that the pressure of the atmosphere can support a column of water about thirty-three feet high, or a column of mercury, or of any other liquid, of a length inversely proportional to its specific gravity.

P. 133, l. 35. "The water in the Phial does not descend." This puzzled Boyle and Oldenburg, as it naturally suggested that even in the presence of air the stability of the column of water, or of mercury, etc., in the Torricellian tube may not be due to air-pressure. In reality, however, the two cases are very different. In a vacuum "the water in the phial," or any other liquid under similar conditions, "does not descend" because of the tensile strength of the liquid. See Poynting and Thomson's *Properties of Matter* : "Liquids from which the air has been carefully expelled can sustain a considerable pull without rupture." It has been shown, in fact, that water can sustain a tension of about 72 lb. per square inch without rupture.

LETTER XV

P. 134. This letter was not printed in the *Posthumous Works*. It was discovered by Victor Cousin and published by him, in 1647, in his *Fragments Philosophiques*, vol. iii. The original letter is now in the Sorbonne, and a facsimile of it is in W. Meyer's edition of the extant autograph letters of Spinoza (1903). Sir F. Pollock published a translation of it, on p. 448 of his *Spinoza, His Life and Philosophy*, in 1880.

P. 134, l. 21. Concerning Meyer and De Vries, see *Introduction*, § 6.

P. 135, l. 9. What exactly the passage was to which Spinoza objected is not known, as Meyer omitted it from his Preface as it was finally printed, and substituted for it some words very like those which Spinoza suggested in this letter. The Preface concludes as follows : " Lastly (to bring the preface to an end), we wish the Readers to know that all these treatises are published for no other purpose than that of discovering and spreading the truth, and in order to persuade men to turn to the study of true and genuine Philosophy " (*The Oldest Biography of Spinoza*, pp. 153 f.). Compare the *Short Treatise* (last Chapter): " I would beg of you most earnestly to be very careful about the communication of these things to others. . . . If ever you wish to communicate them to anybody, then let no other aim prompt you except only the happiness of your neighbour " (pp. 149 f. of my translation).

P. 136, l. 3. The first edition of Spinoza's *Geometric Version of Descartes' Principles* (1663) shows clearly that eleven lines of small type were interpolated on pages 76 and 77 after they had been set up.

LETTER XVI

P. 136. This letter is only known from the *Posthumous Works*, the original letter, written in Latin, having been lost.

P. 136, l. 25. " Forms, qualities and trivial elements." See Annotations to Letters III, VI and XIV.

P. 138, l. 4. It is interesting to find Oldenburg characterizing the difference between Boyle and Spinoza in terms which might almost serve to distinguish generally English thought from continental thought of the time—the mainly empirical character of the former, and the more speculative tendencies of the latter.

P. 138, l. 19. Concerning Mr. Serrarius, see Annotations to Letter XIV.

LETTER XVII

P. 138. This letter must have been written in Dutch originally. But the original letter is lost, and the Dutch edition of the *Posthumous Works* gives what seems to be a translation of the letter as it appears in the Latin edition. In the margin of the Dutch edition are the Latin technical terms which are used in the Latin version of this letter. This suggests that the Latin version had probably been made by Spinoza himself, and that the editors therefore treated it as though it had been the original letter.

Concerning P. Balling, see *Introduction*, § 6. He was subjected to violent criticism because of his *Light on the Candlestick* (1662) and some subsequent writings in defence of the Mennonites.

P. 139, l. 24. Did Spinoza re-visit Rhynsburg during the winter 1663–1664? Or is he referring here to the winter 1662–1663? He removed from Rhynsburg to Voorburg in April 1663, according to Letter XIII.

P. 140, l. 30. The last paragraph but one shows an interesting and touching attempt on the part of Spinoza to meet Balling's sentiments as far as was possible consistently with his own philosophy. The remarks about the relations between the states of the body and the states of the soul have reference to the doctrine which Spinoza expresses in *Ethics* II, Proposition XVII.

LETTER XVIII

P. 141. The original letter was in Dutch, and is printed in the Dutch edition of the *Posthumous Works*. The Latin version is a translation of it.

ANNOTATIONS

Concerning Blyenbergh, see *Introduction*, § 7.

P. 141, l. 32. The Treatise referred to is Spinoza's geometric version of Descartes' *Principles of Philosophy*, to which Spinoza appended *Metaphysical Thoughts*. The full title is: *Renati Des Cartes Principiorum Philosophiae Pars I et II. More Geometrico demonstratae per Benedictum de Spinoza Amstelodamensem. Accesserunt ejusdem Cogitata Metaphysica. In quibus difficiliores, quae tam in parte Metaphysices generali, quam speciali occurrunt, quaestiones breviter explicantur. Amstelodami, apud Johannem Riewerts. 1663. 4°.*

A Dutch translation, by Pieter Balling, was published in 1664.

P. 143, l. 11. "The promise made in your Book," that is, by Meyer in the Preface to Spinoza's above-mentioned geometric version of Descartes' *Principles*.

P. 143, l. 20. "In several places . . .," namely, in the above *Principles*, Part I, Proposition XII, and in the *Metaphysical Thoughts*, Part II, Chapters VII, X and XI.

P. 144, l. 6. "As you usually assert . . .," namely, in the *Metaphysical Thoughts*, Part I, Chapter III, and Part II, Chapter XI.

P. 144, l. 23. "By saying that evil is something unreal. . . ." See *Metaphysical Thoughts*, Part II, Chapters VII, IX and XI.

P. 144, l. 24. "In which God does not concur." Here and in other places there is an implicit reference to the conception known as *concursus Dei* (also *assistentia Dei*), "the co-operation of God," by which Descartes and the Occasionalists tried to account for the seeming interaction between body and soul, in the execution of one's will, for instance. The conception was also employed by Descartes and others to account for the continuous existence of things.

P. 143, l. 15. "*The* . . . disease." Was it an epidemic?

LETTER XIX

P. 146. This letter was written in Dutch. The original was once in the possession of Frans Halma (best known as the translator into Dutch of Bayle's account of Spinoza, given in his famous *Dictionnaire* (1697, etc.)—*Het Leven van B. Spinoza*, etc., 1698), and published by him in the periodical *Boekzaal der Geleerde Werrelt*, in March 1705. But all trace of the original has been lost since then. The Latin version printed in the *Opera Posthuma* appears to have been made by Spinoza himself, and was re-translated into Dutch for the *Nagelate Schriften*. The last paragraph of the letter was omitted from the *Posthumous Works*.

P. 147, l. 3. In order to understand Spinoza's attitude towards the problems discussed in this letter and in Letters XXI and XXIII, it must be borne in mind that Spinoza rejects the ordinary conceptions of reward and punishment, and the closely connected conceptions of merit and demerit as commonly conceived. He thinks always in terms of natural consequences of actions, and of character as expressed in actions. One character is more perfect than another, inasmuch as it has greater powers or capacities, and so embodies more reality. But it is not, therefore, more " meritorious " in the sense of deserving special rewards. Nor does the less perfect character " merit " punishment. Less perfect characters are, indeed, less in harmony with their social environment than are more perfect characters, and society may in self-defence have to eliminate them in some way. But this is not, for Spinoza, a matter of reward and punishment. Spinoza, in short, looks at the whole problem like a doctor rather than like a policeman.

P. 148, l. 7. "Everyone observes with admiration and delight in animals. . . ." This passage throws some light on what Colerus (in his *Life of Spinoza*, Chapter IX) describes as a pastime of the philosopher, namely, to watch the activities of spiders and their capture of flies.

P. 151, l. 12. "The pious . . . become more perfect by their service." Compare *Short Treatise*, II, xviii, end.

P. 151, l. 22. "The language in which I was brought up," namely, Spanish. Spinoza did not feel quite at home with Dutch as a medium of literary expression. But one feels that his Dutch correspondents were in no better plight. Spinoza's remark need not be taken very seriously. His Dutch is awkward, but not more so than (or even as much as) that of his correspondent. Spinoza could express himself very well in Latin. But Latin was not the language in which he was brought up, and occasionally his spelling of Latin words betrays reminiscences of Spanish cognate terms.

LETTER XX

P. 152. This letter was written in Dutch. The original is in the possession of the United Baptists of Amsterdam. It was printed in the Dutch edition of the *Posthumous Works*, and translated into Latin for the *Opera Posthuma*.

P. 154, l. 9. "There is no absolute evil, as is self-evident." These are the only words actually quoted. What follows is Blyenbergh's summary of *Metaphysical Thoughts*, Part I, Chapter VI.

P. 164, l. 29. "Two miles." Probably two French miles are meant (equal to about seven English miles).

P. 165, l. 24. "(As Monsieur Descartes somewhere

teaches us)." See Descartes's *Principles of Philosophy*, Part I, Principles XXXI ff.

P. 171, l. 16. "Both," namely, (1) the publication of Spinoza's own views, and (2) an enlarged edition of the *Metaphysical Thoughts*.

LETTER XXI

P. 172. This letter was written in Dutch, but the original is lost. The Latin version in the *Opera Posthuma* appears to have been made by Spinoza himself; the published Dutch version is a re-translation from this Latin version. But parts of the original Dutch letter are quoted in Blyenbergh's reply (Letter XXII).

P. 173, l. 4. "If I were once to find untrue. . . ." Compare the remark of Lessing that if God were to offer him the choice between the possession of Truth and the mere pursuit of it, he would prefer the latter.

P. 173, l. 2. "In my *Appendix*," namely, *Metaphysical Thoughts*, Part II, Chapter VIII.

P. 176, l. 3. "L. M." is L. Meyer.

P. 176, l. 10. "In the Appendix," namely, *Metaphysical Thoughts*, Part I, Chapter III, and Part II, Chapter XI.

P. 176, l. 36. "The assertion that God exists. . . ." Spinoza means that the existence of dependent, conditioned beings, such as human beings are, necessarily implies the reality of that unconditioned Ground of Reality whom we call God.

P. 177, l. 6. "In my Appendix," namely, in *Metaphysical Thoughts*, Part I, Chapter III.

P. 177, l. 35. "I do not deny that prayers are very useful to us," namely, as a means of inspiration or spiritual invigoration, not as a means of influencing God.

Spinoza cannot think of God as subject to persuasion by means of tears and prayers. The highest relation between God and man is that of complete understanding. And the State, as a " City of God," should likewise be guided by laws based on the highest possible understanding, and not merely by feelings of pity or of vindictiveness. See *Ethics* IV, Proposition XXXVII, Scholium 2, and Appendix XVI.

P. 179, l. 5. " In my Appendix," namely, *Metaphysical Thoughts*, Part II, Chapters VII–IX.

P. 179, l. 24. " To your second point," etc. It is noteworthy that Spinoza attaches great importance to the fact that human volition is not kept within the bounds of human understanding. Man's attitude to life and reality is not one of intellectual insight merely, but also of adventure, of faith and hope.

P. 180, l. 15. " When Micah said to King Ahab," etc. See *I Kings*, Chapter XXII, verses 19 ff., and *II Chronicles*, Chapter XVIII, verses 18 ff.

P. 180, l. 27. " According to the word of Christ," etc. See *St. Matthew*, Chapter XXII, verses 37 ff.

P. 181, l. 23. " The work on Descartes," namely, the Dutch translation (by P. Balling) of Spinoza's geometric version of Descartes' *Principles of Philosophy* (1664).

LETTER XXII

P. 181. This letter was written in Dutch. The original is in the possession of the United Baptists of Amsterdam, and was printed in the Dutch edition of the *Posthumous Works*. The Latin version in the *Opera Posthuma* was made by the editors from the Dutch original.

It is noteworthy that quite a number of manuscript

letters written by or to Spinoza have been discovered in " De Oranjeappel," the Collegiant Orphanage on the Keizersgracht in Amsterdam. This Orphanage was built in 1675. It is known that Jarig Jelles contributed 300 *fl.* towards it, and took a great interest in it. It would appear that when, two years later, he and Dr. Schuller and Dr. Meyer edited the *Opera Posthuma* and saw them through the press, " De Oranjeappel " must have been used for the purpose. For some of the manuscript letters discovered bear editorial notes. Thus the first part of the postscript to Letter XXII has a line round it, and at the side of it there is the editorial instruction to the printer " dit niet te zetten " (" this is not to be set up in type "). Similarly Letter XXVIII bears the editorial note " is van geener waarde " (" is of no value ")—presumably because it was mainly of biographical interest. Moreover, it was in " De Oranjeappel " that a number of autograph letters have been found which were written by Dr. Schuller, one of the editors of the *Opera Posthuma*. " De Oranjeappel " is still in existence, but is no longer used as an orphanage, a house on the Heerengracht being used instead.

P. 186, l. 25. " Because they are repugnant to your special nature, but not because they involve vice." This is an ingenious distortion of Spinoza's attitude. Spinoza had said that he abstained from vice because vice as such was repugnant to his nature, and not (like Blyenbergh and his like) merely from the fear of punishment. Blyenbergh thereupon separates the repugnancy from the vice which as such causes it, and credits Spinoza with the aversion, but not with the aversion from vice as such! The cleverness of fools passes all understanding.

ANNOTATIONS

LETTER XXIII

P. 188.   This letter was written in Dutch, but appears to have been rendered into Latin by Spinoza himself, and so printed in the *Opera Posthuma*.   The original letter is in the State Library in Berlin.   A facsimile of it is included in W. Meyer's edition (1903).   The version in the Dutch edition of the *Posthumous Works* is a re-translation from the Latin version.   There are, however, no important differences between the original and these versions.

P. 190, l. 11.   " Form " means " essential character." How it came to mean this has already been explained in the Annotations to Letter III.

P. 192, l. 17.   " In my *Ethics*."   The precise reference is difficult to make out.   But see *Ethics*, IV, Proposition XXXVII, Schol. 2, and Proposition LXXII.

LETTER XXIV

P. 193.   This letter was written in Dutch.   The original is in the possession of the United Baptists in Amsterdam.   It was printed in the Dutch edition of the *Posthumous Works*, and translated into Latin for the Latin edition by the editors.

P. 194, l. 21.   The quotation is from P. Balling's Dutch translation of Spinoza's geometric version of Descartes' *Principles* and the appended *Metaphysical Thoughts*.   In his other letters Blyenbergh usually quoted the Latin edition.

LETTER XXV

P. 196. This letter is only known from the *Posthumous Works*, the original letter, written in Latin, having been lost.

P. 196, l. 31. Concerning Serrarius, see Annotations to Letter XIV.

P. 197, l. 5. "Domestic calamities." What the domestic trouble was, to which Oldenburg refers, is unknown; but we know that he experienced serious difficulties in earning a living.

P. 197, l. 19. Boyle published his *Experiments and Considerations touching Colours* in 1664, and *New Experiments and Observations upon Cold* in 1665.

P. 197, l. 22. "This unfortunate war." England declared war against the Netherlands in January 1665.

P. 197, l. 24. "Treatise on Sixty Observations with the Microscope," namely, Robert Hooke's *Micrographia*, which was published in 1665. Hooke (1635–1703) was at one time a research assistant to Boyle, and helped in the construction of his air-pump. When Oldenburg died, in 1677, Hooke succeeded him as Secretary of the Royal Society.

LETTER XXVI

P. 198. This letter is only known from the *Posthumous Works*, the original, written in Latin, having been lost. It is undated, but the opening sentence shows that it must have been written in May 1665.

P. 198, l. 9. "Ser." stands for Serrarius, concerning whom see the Annotations to Letter XIV.

P. 198, l. 13. "Z. D." stands for *Zeelhemi Dominum*,

" Squire of Zeelhem " (or Züylichem), where his father, Sir Constantyn Huygens, had an estate. In the *Philosophical Transactions* of the Royal Society the full name is usually given—" Chr. Huygens de Zulichem."

P. 198, l. 26. " Certain Telescopes constructed in Italy," namely, by Giuseppe Compani in Rome. Christian Huygens endeavoured to find out how these big lenses were made, but failed to do so. Huygens himself was also very secretive about his own work on lenses, and warned his brother not to impart any information about them to Spinoza or to Hudde. Spinoza was very different in this respect.

P. 198, l. 28. The satellites of Jupiter were first discovered by Galilei, who observed four of them. A fifth was discovered in 1892, and two more in 1904. The shadow cast on Jupiter by the passage of its satellites or moons (or the Medicean stars, as they are also called) was first observed, in Rome, by Dominico Cassini, in 1665.

P. 198, l. 29. The Ring of Saturn was first observed clearly by Huygens in 1656. Already Galilei had observed something peculiar about Saturn, but owing to the inadequacy of his telescope he mistook the Ring for projections or for satellites.

P. 198, l. 31. " The rashness of Descartes." See his *Principles of Philosophy*, III, Principle CLIV.

LETTER XXVII

P. 199. This letter was written in Dutch. The original is in the University Library at Leyden. It was first published by F. Halma, in 1705, in the *Boekzaal der Geleerte Werrelt*. A facsimile of it is included in Meyer's edition (1903). The Latin translation of it, printed in the *Opera Posthuma*, was probably made by Spinoza himself, and was re-translated into Dutch for the Dutch edition of the *Posthumous Works*. There are no important differences between the original letter and the versions in the *Posthumous Works*.

LETTER XXVIII

P. 200. This letter was not included in the *Posthumous Works*. The original (in Latin) is in the possession of the United Baptists in Amsterdam. It was first published by Van Vloten in his *Ad Benedicti de Spinoza Opera Supplementum* (1860). A facsimile of the original letter is included in W. Meyer's edition (1903). On the back of the original there is a note (presumably by one of the editors of the *Opera Posthuma*) to the effect that it " is of no value." Hence its omission from the *Posthumous Works*. The letter is undated, but it must have been written early in June 1665. For the reference to the Dutch fleet, in the last paragraph, shows that it was written before June 13, 1665, when the Dutch fleet was beaten off Lowestoft.

Concerning Bouwmeester, see *Introduction*, § 6.

P. 201, l. 36. " Some of that conserve of red roses." A conserve of red roses, consisting of one part of rose-buds and two parts of sugar boiled in a little water, was at that time a recognized remedy for catarrhal affections of the lungs. The present letter affords the earliest explicit evidence of Spinoza's pulmonary tuberculosis, of which he died eventually, after more than twenty years of suffering.

P. 202, l. 9. " The third part of my philosophy . . . up to about the eightieth proposition." Part III of Spinoza's *Ethics* contains only fifty-nine propositions. It would appear that in 1665 he still intended to let the *Ethics* consist of only three parts, instead of the plan of five parts which he finally adopted. In 1665 accordingly the propositions of what is now Part IV were still included in Part III.

Concerning De Vries, see *Introduction*, § 6.

P. 202, l. 18. " Why the fleet does not set sail." Spinoza here voices the impatience of the Dutch with the inactivity of their navy. Eventually the authorities ordered an attack on the English coast near Harwich. But the attack, which took place on June 13, 1665, ended in disaster for the Dutch.

LETTER XXIX

P. 202. This letter was not included in the *Posthumous Works*. The original (in Latin) is in the possession of the United Baptists in Amsterdam. It was first published by Van Vloten in his *Ad Benedicti de Spinoza Opera Supplementum* (1860).

P. 202, l. 30. The letter of Spinoza (dated 4th September, 1665) to which this is the answer has unfortunately been lost. From the fourth paragraph of the present letter it is clear that in the lost letter Spinoza had given an account, among other things, of his intentions with regard to the *Tractatus Theologico-Politicus*.

P. 203, l. 7. " The Treatise on Colours." See Annotations to Letter XXV.

P. 203, l. 20. Athanasius Kircher (1601–1680) was a German born at Geisa near Fulda. He was educated at the Jesuit College in Fulda, joined the Jesuit Order in Mainz, and became Professor of Philosophy, Mathematics and Oriental languages at Würzburg. In 1631, owing to the Thirty Years War, he fled to Avignon, and in 1635 he settled in Rome. His *Subterranean World*

(*Mundus Subterraneus*) was published in 1665. It deals with the forces and processes within the earth.

P. 203, l. 33. Boyle's *Origine of Formes and Qualities according to the Corpuscular Philosophy* was published in 1666. See Annotations to Letter III.

P. 204, l. 1. "You are not so much philosophizing as . . . theologizing." See above, annotations to page 202, line 30, and to Letter XXX.

P. 204, l. 10. "A second naval battle." The renovated Dutch fleet under the command of de Ruyter, and with de Witt on board, set out on August 14, 1665, to attack the English fleet off the Dutch coast. But, owing to unfavourable weather conditions, no action was fought.

P. 204, l. 21. Johann Hevelius (or Hevel, or Höwelcke) was born in Danzig in 1611, and died in 1687. He studied Jurisprudence in the University of Leyden, travelled in England and France, and then settled down in Danzig, where his father was a wealthy brewer. He took part in municipal affairs, but his chief interest was in astronomy. In 1641 he built a private observatory, equipped it with a telescope of 150 ft. focal length, and made many observations. He discovered the moon's libration in longitude, also four comets, and he suggested they had a parabolic orbit. In 1665 he published his *Prodromus Cometicus*, dealing with the comet observed in 1664. In 1668 he published his *Cometographia*, a book dealing with comets generally.

P. 204, l. 33. Christian Huygens (1629–1695). His *Horologium*, describing the pendulum clock which he invented, was published in 1658. He had invented it in 1656, and presented one to the States General in 1657.

His *Dioptrics* (begun in 1654) and his *De Motu Corporum* (begun in 1663) were published posthumously in 1700.

P. 204, l. 35. "Finding out longitudes at sea." The method of measuring longitudes at sea by means of pendulum clocks is described as follows in Huygens' *Brevis Institutio de usu Horologiorum ad Inveniendas Longitudines* (also in the *Philosophical Transactions* of the Royal Society, No. 47, May 10, 1669).

At least two, preferably three or four, new clocks should be taken aboard the outgoing ship. They should be hung up in an enclosed place free from moisture and dirt, preferably amidships, where the motion of the vessel is least noticeable. Before the voyage the clocks should be adjusted to keep the correct time, by raising or lowering the pendulum bobs, or else they must be *rated* by finding how much each gains or loses during twenty-four hours. In rating the clocks against the sun, account must be taken of the *equation of time*, which is the difference between the apparent (solar) time and the mean (clock) time. Huygens appends a table giving the equation of time for each day in the year.

To determine longitude at sea, the *local* time must be obtained by observations of the sun or stars (see below), and compared with the corrected *clock* time, which is the *local* time of the port where the clocks were set going. If there is no difference between the observed local time and the clock time, then the ship is upon the same meridian as the home port; if the local time is later than the clock time, the ship is east of the meridian of the home port; if it is earlier, west. One hour's difference in the times corresponds to 15° difference in the longitudes.

The accuracy of the determination of longitude depends, then, upon the accuracy with which the local time can be estimated. Now the meridian altitude of the sun can be determined fairly accurately, and may suitably be used for calculating the *latitude*, but the *precise instant* when the sun attains its meridian altitude is very difficult to determine accurately, and should *not* be used for fixing the local time. The altitude of the sun may be measured when it is in the east or west, for its altitude is then changing most rapidly, and the local time can be calculated from the known latitude and the declination of the sun.

Huygens, however, prefers the following method :—
Note the time shown by the clock when the sun's centre is (1) rising in the east, (2) setting in the west. Add half the difference to the time of rising to obtain the clock time at the moment when the sun was crossing the meridian. Correct for rate and equation of time. This method is independent of the latitude, of the sun's declination, and of refraction, nor is any instrument required; the alteration of longitude occasioned by the ship's travel during the day is to be regarded as negligible. The method may be varied somewhat by noting the times when the sun, or a known star, is at *equal altitudes* on the two sides of the meridian.

LETTER XXX

P. 205. This is part of a letter not contained in the *Posthumous Works*, and is only preserved as a (Latin) quotation in a letter which Oldenburg wrote to Boyle on October 10, 1665, and which was published in *The Works of Robert Boyle*, London, 1772, Vol. VI, pp. 200 f. Oldenburg's letter introduces the extract from Spinoza's letter as follows : " In the same letter to Sir Robert [Moray] I took notice to him of what a certain odd philosopher (whom you know better than he, it being Signior Spinoza) hath very lately written to me concerning Mr. Huygens' transmigration into France, his pendulums and his progress in dioptrics, etc. The same Spinoza expresses a very great respect for you, and presents you his most humble service, and is displeased that the Dutch stationers will, in spight of our teeth, sell off one of their own Latin impressions of their History of Colours, before the translation made here can be sent thither. To give you an extract of what he is thinking and doing, he writes thus." [Here follows the extract from Spinoza's letter, as given in Letter XXX.]

P. 205, l. 21. "That famous scoffer," namely, Democritus (460–370 B.C.), who is alleged to have spent his time in deriding the vanity and stupidity of mankind. This side of his personality did not appeal to Spinoza, who held that human nature was not a fit subject for either laughter or tears, but for study. This is evident from the very next sentence in this letter, and from *Ethics*, Part IV, Prop. L, Scholium.

P. 206, l. 4. "A Treatise about my interpretation of Scripture," namely, the *Tractatus Theologico-Politicus*, published anonymously in 1670.

P. 206, l. 17. "The excessive authority and impudence of the preachers." The clergy of the dominant Calvinist Church, anxious to obtain control of the State, attempted to exploit the misfortunes of the war between Holland and England in order to overthrow the de Witts and their party, who were the defenders of religious liberty. The *Tractatus Theologico-Politicus* was intended by Spinoza to be a contribution to this bitter struggle, and is one of the classics written in defence of freedom of thought and of speech.

P. 206, l. 19. "Descartes' hypothesis." Descartes regarded space as full of matter. God set this matter in motion, and so gave rise to an enormous number of vortices or whirlpools of material particles of all sizes and shapes. Their friction rubs off their corners, with the result that in each vortex there are two kinds of particles, some coarse and some fine. The coarser particles are small spheres or globules which move round the centre of motion, but tend to recede from it. The finer particles are like fine dust, and tend to settle at the centre, where they form suns or stars. Some particles, however, become channelled and twisted in the course of their career through the vortex. And when they settle and form a crust on the surface of a star, the expansive force of the star is diminished so that neighbouring vortices encroach upon it and eventually catch it up. If the velocity of the star is greater than that of any part of the vortex which has caught it up, it will pass on to another vortex, and from that to another, and so on. Such a star is known as a comet.

LETTER XXXI

P. 206. This letter is only known from the *Posthumous Works*, the original letter, written in Latin, having been lost.

P. 207, l. 13. Concerning Kircher see Annotations to Letter XXIX.

P. 207, l. 22. Concerning Huygens see Annotations to Letter XXIX.

P. 207, l. 31. "I remember that you pointed out somewhere," namely, in the Preface to the Geometric version of Descartes' *Principles of Philosophy*, Parts I and II.

P. 208, l. 13. Concerning Hevelius, see Annotations to Letter XXIX.

P. 208, l. 14. Adrien Auzout was born in Rouen, and died in Paris in 1691. He was a member of the Paris Academy. The controversy in question turned on the comet which was observed in 1664. Hevelius (see Annotations to Letter XXIX) reported that the comet had appeared near the First Star of the constellation Aries. Auzout maintained that it had appeared near the Bright Star in the Left Horn of Aries. The Royal Society took up the matter in dispute between " these two deservedly celebrated Philosophers." On the strength of the reports of astronomers at home and abroad the Royal Society decided in favour of Auzout, and very courteously expressed the hope that " M. Hevelius, who is well known for his Ingenuity and Learning, will joyn and acquiesce in that sentiment." (*Philosophical Transactions* of the Royal Society, No. IX, February 12, 1666.)

P. 208, l. 23. Concerning the Hypothesis of Descartes, see Annotations to Letter XXX.

P. 208, l. 28. Huygens' removal to France. Under the regime of Jean Baptiste Colbert (1619–1683), who was Controller-General in 1665, attempts were made to attract to Paris eminent scholars and men of science from abroad. Huygens received a call in 1665, and moved to Paris in 1666.

P. 208, l. 31. " The Swedish army." During the war between England and Holland attempts were made to persuade the Swedish Government to send an army to attack the Dutch. But the project did not materialize.

P. 208, l. 32. " The Bishop of Munster," namely, Christoph Bernhard von Galen (1606–1678), invaded Holland in 1665 in the interests of the English, with whom he was allied. See Annotations to Letter XXXII.

P. 209, l. 5. " The nature of sounds." The experiments on this problem are referred to in Oldenburg's letter to Boyle, of October 10, 1665 (already mentioned).

LETTER XXXII

P. 209.   The original letter (in Latin) is in the possession of the Royal Society, London.   A facsimile of it
is contained in W. Meyer's edition (1903).   The editors
of the *Opera Posthuma* made use of a somewhat altered
version kept by Spinoza.   But the differences are not
of much importance.

This letter on the Unity of Nature is referred to by
Oldenburg in his letter to Boyle, dated November 21,
1665 (o.s.).   The manner of his reference to it only
shows how unworthy Oldenburg was of the pearls
which Spinoza sent him.   But allowances must probably be made for Oldenburg's keen awareness of Boyle's
utter want of appreciation of all really philosophical
discussions that were not intended merely to defend
the dogmas of Christianity against pagans, Jews and
Mohammedans.   This is what Oldenburg wrote : " I
had lately another letter from Signior Spinoza, who is
very much your servant, and who entertains me with a
discourse of his, concerning the agreement and coherence
of the parts of the world with the whole ; which is
not unphilosophical in my opinion, though it would
perhaps be tedious to you to have a letter filled with it ;
and this makes me forbear to send it to you " (*The
Works of Robert Boyle*, ed. 1772, Vol. VI, p. 204).   Nevertheless he appears to have been sufficiently impressed
with it to think of publishing the letter in the *Philosophical
Transactions* of the Royal Society, for on December 5,
1665, Oldenburg wrote to Boyle : " I think it will be
most convenient in every way to remit Signior Spinoza's
discourse *de consensu partium* till our personal interview "
(*ibid.*, p. 205).   This seems to suggest something more
than a mere private discussion of the letter between

Boyle and Oldenburg ; it appears to refer to the question of its publication.

P. 212, l. 1. " Power " (*potentia*). Under the influence of the logico-mathematical interpretation of Spinoza (see *Introduction*, § 8) the term *potentia* is usually taken to mean " possibility." But it is a misconception, and a very radical one. In *Ethics*, III, Proposition VII, Spinoza uses the term *conatus* as the equivalent of *potentia*. But nobody in his senses will interpret *conatus* as " mathematical possibility." In line 13 the Attribute Thought is also described as a power.

P. 212, l. 7. " Corporeal substance " here means the Attribute Extension.

P. 212, l. 32. Descartes' sixth law of motion was formulated by him as follows : " If the body C was at rest and exactly equal in size to the body B which is moving towards it, then it must partly be pushed by B and partly make it rebound ; so that if B approached C with four degrees of speed, it must transfer one degree to it and with the other three degrees return in the direction from which it had come " (*Principia*, Part II, Principle LI).

P. 212, l. 35. Concerning Huygens' dynamic experiments before the Royal Society, London, see Annotations to Letter XXXIII.

P. 213, l. 3. Huygens' optical researches in connection with the making of lenses were conducted with such secrecy that even if Spinoza had been inquisitive he would not have learned much about them. Huygens frequently mentioned Spinoza in his letters from Paris addressed to his brother Constantyn, but warned him to give no information, while obtaining all the information he could. The letters in question are those dated September 9, 1667 ; October 14, 1667 ; November 4, 1667 ; December 2, 1667 ; April 6, 1668 ; and May 11, 1668 ; and they are printed in Vol. VI of *Œuvres Complètes de Christian Huygens* (The Hague, 1895).

P. 213, l. 5. "A machine in which he can turn tools." The Latin *patina* means a *dish* or *pan*, in fact *pan* is probably derived from *patina*. The "surfacing tool" for grinding and polishing convex lenses is shaped like a shallow dish, that is to say, it is concave. Of course the surfacing tool for making concave lenses is convex, and does not look at all like a dish. But the earliest lenses were convex, and so the earliest "tools" were all concave or dish-shaped, and the term *patina*, or *dish*, continued in use even when convex tools were employed. The process of grinding small lenses was as follows. A disk of glass about two inches in diameter was fixed with pitch on a flat metal holder (or "button") of about the same size and shape. A little sand or emery was strewn on the "tool" (which is more or less rough), and the glass was rubbed against it by movements to and fro until the glass acquired the curvature for which the "tool" had been constructed. Each kind of curvature required, of course, a special "tool" made to the required radius of curvature. The "tools" were made usually of copper or of cast brass, and had to be ground and polished on the lathe in a manner resembling the grinding of lenses. In Huygens' machine the "button" holding the disk of glass, instead of being moved to and fro by hand (a process involving hard work, especially in the case of large lenses) is moved indirectly by turning the handle of the machine. The following diagram gives the essentials.

A is the "tool," and B is the "button" or holder with the glass disk attached to it. The "tool" is crossed by a beam C C' to the middle of which is fixed a steel spike pressing down the apex of the conical metal "button" or holder. A bow-shaped piece of wood, D D', fastened to the floor at E, keeps the glass pressed down to the "tool" by means of a cord passing over the beam C C'. A beam L L', perpendicular to

C C′ is pegged down on the block H so as to be capable of moving only in the direction of its length. Fixed to this beam at L is a block M, into which the beam C C′ is loosely mortised. Over L L′ and at right angles to it is mounted a wooden roller N N′, whose iron axle ends in a handle P. At L and L′ are fixed the ends of cords which are wound, in opposite directions, about the

roller N N′, their other ends being fixed to the roller. As the handle P is turned, first one way and then the other, the beam L L′ oscillates, and the glass is moved to and fro upon the tool A. The glass and the tool have to be adjusted periodically, and the escapement to the left of the picture is a device for the automatic counting of the turns of the handle. This account is based on Robert Smith's *Compleat System of Opticks* (1738), from which the illustration is also taken. See Huygens, *Œuvres Complètes*, Vol. V (1893).

P. 213, l. 14. The Bishop of Munster, Christoph Bernhard von Galen, was an ally of England, and invaded Holland on September 23, 1665. He only escaped with difficulty from the marshes near Bourtang. After several battles fought with varying fortunes he was glad to make peace with the Dutch, on April 18, 1666, on the basis of the *status quo ante*. Spinoza very appropriately compares the Bishop's adventure, in invading the marshy region, with the adventure of Æsop's goat when, lured by the fox, it entered the well without first considering the question of ways and means of getting out again. (See the Fable of the Fox and the Goat, p. 15 of G. F. Townsend's Translation of Æsop's *Fables*, edition 1906.)

P. 213, l. 24. The "Dutch ambassador sent to France" was Van Gogh.

P. 213, l. 30. "The Prince of Orange." Two deputies of Overysel, Pallandt and Van Langen, conceived the scheme of sending the Prince of Orange to England in order to negotiate peace with the King of England, his grandfather. The States-General were not even consulted about this scheme, which came to nothing.

P. 213, l. 34. "The plans of the Swede." See Annotations to Letter XXXI.

P. 214, l. 21. "Kepler's hypothesis." Kepler (1571–1630), though he revolutionized astronomy, still clung to the ancient view that the fixed stars are parts of a solid sphere in the centre of which is the sun. The interior of this cosmic sphere he regarded as filled with an ether or ethereal air. Sometimes this ether condenses and so becomes opaque to solar and stellar light. Such an opaque ether-mass or ether-cloud is what is called a comet. The rays of the sun communicate an impulse to the comet, and make it move in a straight line, with a gradually increasing velocity, through the ether. In time the matter of the comet is destroyed by the light of the sun and is pushed away in the direction of the rays of the sun, forming a tail until it is dissolved.

P. 214, l. 25. Oldenburg's London address, to which this letter was sent, was that of Boyle's sister, Lady Ranelagh, to whose children Oldenburg acted as tutor.

LETTER XXXIII

P. 214. This letter is only known from the *Posthumous Works*, the original letter, written in Latin, having been lost.

P. 215, l. 18. Huygens' experiments before the Royal Society in London were made in the summer of 1663. They are mentioned in the *Philosophical Transactions*, No. 46 (April 12, 1669), p. 100.

P. 215, l. 27. "A certain distinguished man who had proposed many such experiments." This was probably Lord Brouncker (1620–1684).

P. 216, l. 10. "The windpipe both of sheep and of oxen filled with grass." The observations are recorded in the *Philosophical Transactions* of the Royal Society, No. 6 (November 6, 1665), and are there said to have been made by "two very ingenious men, Dr. Clark and Dr. Lower." The alleged fact is indeed described as "a pretty odde kind of Observation," but no suspicion is expressed about its accuracy. It seems, however, more than doubtful if so much grass could possibly find its way into the lungs at all; and it is certain that the ox could not have lived "two or three days" if its lungs had been choked up in that way. The most probable explanation is that the ox had an occluded œsophagus which was mistaken for the trachea. Such crude mistakes were not unknown in the seventeenth century.

P. 216. l. 8. "Certain distinguished Anatomists at Oxford"—namely, Josiah Clark (1639–1714) and Richard Lower (1631–1691). An account of them will be found in Dr. R. T. Gunther's *Early Science in Oxford*, Vol. III.

P. 216, l. 23. "A certain inquiring Doctor, also of Oxford." According to the *Philosophical Transactions*, No. 6, p. 117, it was Dr. Lower who also reported the following case to Boyle. But it seems that he reported it at second hand, and that the actual observation was made by Dr. Timothy Clarke, a Fellow of the Royal Society and Physician to the King. T. Clarke died in 1672.

P. 216, l. 27. "Was bled." Blood-letting was a very common remedy in the seventeenth century and long afterwards.

P. 216, l. 32. "This blood immediately took the form of a cake of milk. . . ." The *Philosophical Transactions*, No. 6, pp. 100 and 117, give an account of two cases of blood-letting in which "Milk" was found "instead of Blood." The first is a case reported from Paris, the second from Oxford. The "milk" or chyle is a whitish or grey plasma usually called the "buffy coat," which mixes with the blood. When blood-clots settle, the plasma rises to the top and forms a whitish layer or "buffy coat." In the case of people suffering from certain diseases the "buffy coat" may constitute a third or more of their blood. The rate of sedimentation also varies enormously with the condition of the person whose blood it is. It may have been rapid in the case reported. But it is impossible that "the blood which was collected in the saucer was all chyle." Its more whitish appearance in comparison with the other blood was probably due to the presence of more protein in it, and possibly also to the presence of a larger number of white corpuscles. But there must have been present red corpuscles as well.

P. 217, l. 8. " The Jews . . . are to return to their country." The reference is to a movement led by the false Messiah, Sabbatai Zevi (1626–1676). In a letter to Boyle (dated March 6, 1666) Oldenburg reports : " The last letters from Holland mention that now Christians as well as Jews write from Constantinople the confirmation of the reports concerning the nation of the Israelites, and the great hopes the Jews entertain of recovering their land very shortly " (*The Works of Robert Boyle*, ed. 1772, Vol. VI, p. 219). Like Serrarius (see Annotations to Letter XIV), many people in the seventeenth century were living in expectation of great things, and Jews were not exempt from this epidemic. Their long sufferings had made them especially prone to dreams of relief. Sabbatai Zevi began his short career as Messiah at Salonica in 1658, stayed several times in Cairo, where he gained great influence over a wealthy fellow-Jew, visited Gaza, which was to be the new Holy City, and Smyrna, his birthplace, and in 1666 also Constantinople, where he was imprisoned and forced to become a Moslem. The movement aroused general interest throughout Christendom, because many Christians had come to think of the return of the Jews to Palestine as the sign of the imminent end of all things.

Spinoza's reply to this letter of Oldenburg's is unfortunately lost. But we know that Spinoza did not regard the restoration of the Jews either as impossible or as undesirable. In his *Tractatus Theologico-Politicus* (published in 1670, that is long after the tragi-comedy of Sabbatai Zevi's failure) Spinoza wrote : " I would go so far as to believe that, if the foundations of their religion have not enfeebled their minds, they may, if the occasion presents itself amid the changes to which human affairs are so liable, even raise up their empire anew, and that God may yet elect them a second time " (Chapter III, near the end).

P. 217, l. 22. " The Swede and the Brandenburger." The reference is to the strained relations between Sweden and Brandenburg over the possession of Hither Pomerania. The Great Elector of Brandenburg consequently more than once joined in a coalition against Sweden.

*   *   *   *   *

After this letter there is a gap of ten years in the extant correspondence between Oldenburg and Spinoza. Partly, no doubt, the interruption was due to the continuation of the war between England and Holland (1665–1667), the Plague of London (1665), the Great Fire of London (1666), and Oldenburg's imprisonment in the Tower of London (June 30 till August 26, 1667).

LETTER XXXIV

P. 217. This letter was written in Dutch, but the original is lost. What is printed in the *Opera Posthuma* is probably Spinoza's own Latin version of the original letter ; and the version in the Dutch edition of the *Posthumous Works* is a re-translation from the Latin.

Concerning Hudde, see *Introduction*, § 5.

LETTER XXXV

P. 219. This letter was also written in Dutch, and probably translated into Latin by Spinoza himself for future use or publication. The original letter is lost.

The version in the Dutch edition of the *Posthumous Works* is a re-translation of Spinoza's Latin version printed in the *Opera Posthuma*.

P. 219, l. 33. "Your last letter." No letter from Hudde to Spinoza is extant now. The editors of the *Opera Posthuma* probably destroyed these and other letters for reasons already explained in the *Introduction*, § 9.

LETTER XXXVI

P. 222. This letter also was written in Dutch, but the original is lost. The *Opera Posthuma* contains what is probably Spinoza's own Latin rendering of it, and the Dutch edition gives a re-translation from the Latin.

P. 223, l. 16. "*Limited* denotes nothing positive." The Latin is *determinatum*, usually translated "determined," which term, as also the term "determination," in the familiar statement that "all determination is negation," must be understood to refer to the limiting or delimiting of finite objects within the unlimited or complete Attribute or Substance of which they are modes. For example, the marking of the boundaries of a finite portion of space within infinite Extension. In the expression "qualitative determination," the term determination has a very different meaning. It means "positive characterization," not negative delimitation. It is impertinent to apply the principle that "determination is negation" to such qualitative "determination" or characterization, especially to the Attributes as Spinoza conceived them. This confusion has been responsible for serious misinterpretations of Spinozism.

P. 225, l. 35. "The ratio of refraction" is the ratio which the sine of the angle of incidence of a ray bears to the sine of the angle of refraction.

P. 226, l. 3. Note the use of $x\,x$ for x^2. The now

familiar index notation was introduced by Descartes, but was not generally adopted till much later. The sign of equality used by Spinoza is ∞. The usual symbol is substituted in the translation for the sake of simplicity. The symbol = was actually introduced by Robert Recorde in 1540 already, but it did not come into common use till much later.

LETTER XXXVII

P. 227. This letter was written in Latin, but the original has been lost. There is, however, an old copy of it in the Library of the United Baptists in Amsterdam. This copy differs from that printed in the *Opera Posthuma* only in a few unimportant details. The concluding sentence is from this old copy of the letter.
Concerning Bouwmeester, see *Introduction*, § 6.
P. 227, l. 32. Spinoza's sketch of the rationalistic side of his method almost suggests the phenomenological method of Husserl. It is certainly very different from the Baconian method, which Spinoza criticized, in Letter II, just because it does not set out from clear ideas about the nature of the understanding and its laws. Yet Dr. Gebhardt holds that this letter shows Baconian influences in the method of Spinoza!

LETTER XXXVIII

P. 228. This letter was written in Dutch. The original has been lost, but was, no doubt, faithfully reproduced in the Dutch edition of the *Posthumous Works*, and translated into Latin for the *Opera Posthuma* by the editors.

Nothing is known about Mr. John van der Meer, to whom this letter was addressed.

P. 229, l. 1. The problem of the calculation of chances, or of the calculus of probability as applied to games of chance, seems to have attracted considerable interest in Holland in the time of Spinoza. Christian Huygens wrote on the subject, in 1656, and Jan de Witt and Johannes Hudde interested themselves in the problem. A tract on the subject first published in 1687 (*Reeckening van Kanssen*) is usually attributed to Spinoza, and included among his Works because it was bound together with an essay on the Rainbow (*Stelkonstige Reeckening van den Reegenboog*), which he is known to have written, although it was not included in his *Posthumous Works*, because the manuscript could not then be traced. Doubt has been expressed, by Freudenthal, whether Spinoza really did write the tract on *The Calculation of Chances*.

LETTER XXXIX

P. 231. The original letter, written in Dutch, has been lost. But as Jelles was one of the editors of the *Posthumous Works*, it may be assumed that the text of this letter in the Dutch edition of the *Posthumous Works* was true, or at least very close, to the original letter addressed to him. The Latin translation printed in the *Opera Posthuma* appears to have been made by Spinoza himself.

P. 231, l. 6. Descartes' *Dioptrics* is a very striking instance of the application of the " mechanical philosophy " to the problems of the reflection and refraction of light. The whole treatment of the phenomena of light is ingeniously worked out on the analogy of moving particles impinging on materials varying in hardness.

The part of the *Dioptrics* to which this letter refers more especially is Chapter VIII.

P. 231, l. 34. " All come together at the point B." This would not be true for a solid sphere of glass, as it implies that the angle of refraction is always half the angle of incidence.

LETTER XL

P. 232. This letter also was written in Dutch, but the original has been lost. We may assume, however, that the text given in the Dutch edition of the *Posthumous Works* was true to the original letter, as Jelles was one of the editors. The Latin translation printed in the *Opera Posthuma* seems to have been made by Spinoza himself.

P. 232, l. 26. Johannes Fridericus Helvetius was Physician to the Prince of Orange. Christian Huygens knew " this little doctor," and had no great faith in him. In 1680 Helvetius published a book called *Theological Philosophy* (*Philosophia theologica*) against Descartes and Spinoza.

P. 232, l. 27. Isaac Vossius (1618–1689) wrote on the Septuagint (1661), on Poetry (1673), etc. He became Canon of Windsor in 1673.

P. 233, l. 4. The belief in the possibility of producing gold out of baser metals was widespread in the seventeenth century; even modern chemists have not altogether abandoned the idea.

LETTER XLI

P. 236. This letter was written in Dutch. The original has been lost. But it is most probably reproduced in the Dutch edition of the *Posthumous Works*.

In this case (unlike Letters XXXIX and XL) the Latin terms are not given in the margin of the Dutch text, and we may assume that the Latin version given in the *Opera Posthuma* was not made by Spinoza.

This short letter is the only one that has survived of Spinoza's correspondence during the years 1667–1670. Reasons for the absence of other letters readily suggest themselves. These were busy years for Spinoza, and a very trying period both for him and his friends. Simon de Vries died in 1667. Pieter Balling died in 1669. Oldenburg was imprisoned in the Tower of London in 1667. Koerbagh, a warm friend of Spinoza and a too ardent apostle of Spinozism, was imprisoned, in Amsterdam, in 1668, and died in prison under gruesome circumstances. All who were suspected of being free-thinkers, or even liberal thinkers, were watched closely, and denounced to the civil authorities during these years. People were accordingly particularly cautious about writing letters to each other on philosophical or theological matters, and such letters as they did write were probably destroyed promptly by the recipients. Spinoza, moreover, was deeply occupied with the composition of his *Tractatus Theologico-Politicus*, the most effective reply to the theological zealots of his time, and of all times.

P. 237, l. 33. " The difference . . . takes place only at the beginning." The longer the tube, the greater the quantity of water that has to be set in motion by the head of pressure, and hence the longer the time required for the flow to reach its constant terminal velocity.

P. 238, l. 13. " Four degrees of speed." Spinoza must be thinking of the *distance traversed*. This is proportional to the *square* of the time. The actual velocity developed by a body under the action of a constant force is simply proportional to the time.

LETTER XLII

P. 239. This letter is only known from the *Opera Posthuma*. The original letter, written in Latin, has been lost.

Concerning Velthuysen and Ostens, see *Introduction*, § 7.

P. 239, l. 8. "*Discursus*" is, of course, a slip for *Tractatus*.

P. 239, l. 31. Marin Mersenne (1588–1648) was educated at a Jesuit College, and wrote various theological treatises. He was a friend of Descartes, and defended him and his orthodoxy against various clerical critics. In 1624 Mersenne published an attack on freethinkers of all kinds—*L'Impiété des Deistes, Athées et Libertins combattue et renversée*.

P. 243, l. 25. "The paradoxical theologian" is L. Meyer (see *Introduction*, § 6). He was the author of *Philosophia S. Scripturae Interpres. Exercitatio Paradoxa in qua unam Philosophiam infallibilem S. Literas interpretandi Normam esse, apodictice demonstratur* (Amsterdam, 1666). In this book Meyer contended that the Bible in its original form and meaning must have been true to objective fact. For God was the author of both the Bible and the facts of Nature. Consequently, whatever there is now in the Bible, as we have it, that does not correspond with objective facts, must be a human interpolation or falsification. So it is only by means of true (that is, rationalistic) philosophy that the Bible can be properly studied and interpreted. Such a philosophy, in other words, is the proper interpreter of Scripture.

P. 244, l. 34. Spinoza's Note. The reference is to Chapter VI (On Miracles) of the *Tractatus Theologico-Politicus*.

ANNOTATIONS

LETTER XLIII

P. 254. This letter was written in Latin. The original draft has been preserved. It belongs to the Orphanage of the Baptist Collegiants in Amsterdam, and is kept in the Archives of the United Baptists there. A facsimile of it is included in W. Meyer's edition (1903), and there is also a facsimile of a part of it in Van Vloten's *Ad Benedicti de Spinoza Opera Supplementum* (1860). The text printed in the *Opera Posthuma* has a number of unimportant variations from the original draft.

The date of the letter is not quite certain. It was probably written in 1671, but possibly after Letter XLIV. It is put immediately after Letter XLII mainly because the two letters obviously belong together.

P. 255, l. 10. " For Atheists are wont inordinately to desire honours and riches." This expresses the usual conception of an atheist in the seventeenth century. Hence Spinoza's resentment. See Letter XLIV and the Annotations to it.

P. 255, l. 25. Gysbertus Voetius, or Voet (1588–1676), was a Dutch theologian. He was born in Heusden and studied in Leyden. In 1611 he became Pastor of Blynen, and in 1619 he played an important part in the Synod of Dort. In 1634 he was appointed Professor of Theology and of Oriental Studies at the University of Utrecht. He was also Vicar of Utrecht from 1637 onwards. He was an extreme Calvinist. In 1642 he persuaded the University of Utrecht to condemn the philosophy of Descartes. In 1643 there appeared a pamphlet (either written by him or at his instigation) in which the new (that is the Cartesian) philosophy was violently attacked as the cause of contemporary irreligion and immorality. Descartes replied to this in his *Epistola ad celeberrimum virum D. Gisbertum Voetium.*

P. 255, l. 35. " The reward of virtue is virtue itself. . . . " Compare *Ethics*, Part V, Proposition XLI, Scholium, and Proposition XLII. For Spinoza moral laws were divine whether ordained by God or not. Morality is autonomous, needing no other authority or sanction.

P. 256, l. 33. " Descartes who states . . ." The reference is to *Principia Philosophiae*, Part I, Principles XXXIX ff.

P. 258, l. 23. " Rabbi Judah Alpakhar " was a distinguished Jew of Toledo, and Physician-in-ordinary to King Ferdinand III. He died in 1235. He was rather anti-philosophical, and opposed to Maimonides, who tried to harmonize Judaism and Philosophy. The maxim of Alpakhar (to which Spinoza refers in the *Tractatus Theologico-Politicus*, Chapter XV) was that " whatsoever Scripture teaches . . . must on its own sole authority be admitted as absolutely true." The title " Rabbi " or " Rab " means " Mr." or " Magister," not " Reverend," as is sometimes supposed.

LETTER XLIV

P. 260. This letter was written in Dutch, and the Dutch edition of the *Posthumous Works* appears to reproduce the original, which has itself been lost. The Latin version in the *Opera Posthuma* was translated by the editors from the Dutch original.

P. 260, l. 4. " Professor . . . . . ." Who this was is not known for certain. It may have been Professor Kranen, at that time Professor of Philosophy at the University of Leyden, and a Cartesian. There is a reference to him in Letter LXVII by Burgh. In the Dutch edition of the *Posthumous Works* there are six dots after " Professor " (the Latin has N. N.), and they may stand for the six letters in the name Kranen. But that is only a conjecture.

P. 260, l. 6. The *Tractatus Theologico-Politicus*, which was published anonymously in Latin in 1670, was promptly translated into Dutch by J. H. Glazemaker, probably at the instigation either of Jelles or of Rieuwertsz (the publisher). Owing to the present letter, however, the Dutch version was not published at the time. In fact, it was not published until 1693, when it appeared under this title of *De Rechtzinnige Theologant*.

P. 260, l. 16. *Homo Politicus* was published anonymously in 1664. Its full title is *Homo Politicus, hoc est : consiliarius novus, officiarius et aulicus secundum hodiernam praxin,* auctore Pacifico a Lapide. The author of it is alleged to have been Christophorus Rapp, Chancellor to the Great Elector of Brandenburg. The book is a kind of adaptation of Macchiavelli's *Prince* for the use of unprincely folk. The summary of its leading ideas given by Spinoza in this letter fairly conveys the conception that people had then of an atheist. Spinoza did not carry out his first intention of writing a book against it, but parts of his *Political Treatise*, notably Chapter X, §§ 4–8, appear to be directed against it.

P. 261, l. 2. Thales of Miletus (*circa* 600 B.C.). The story is related in the *Lives of the Philosophers* by Diogenes Laertes (I, 26), also by Cicero (*On Divination,* I, 111), and by Alexander ab Alexandro (*Genialium Dierum libri sex*), etc.

LETTER XLV

P. 261. The original letter, written in Latin, is in the possession of the Orphanage of the Baptist Collegiants in Amsterdam, and is in the Archives of the United

Baptists there. It was printed in the *Opera Posthuma* with the omission of Hudde's name and of the postscript, and with a few unimportant changes.

P. 262, l. 3. "A Note on Advanced Optics" (*Notitia Opticae promotae*) was published in Frankfurt a. M. in 1671. It is, of course, reprinted in the complete works of Leibniz (pp. 14 f. of Vol. III in the edition of 1768). It is also given in T. de Murr's *Benedicti de Spinoza Adnotationes ad Tractatum Theologico-Politicum* (1802), pp. 24 ff.

P. 262, l. 7. Concerning Hudde, see *Introduction*, § 5.

P. 262, l. 13. Franciscus Lana (1631–1687) was, at the time of this letter, Professor of Philosophy and of Mathematics in Rome. His *Prodromus* was published in 1670. Its full title is *Prodromo, overo Saggio di alcune inventioni nuove premesse all' Arte maestra* (Brescia).

P. 262, l. 15. Johannes Oltius. Unknown.

P. 263, l. 2. J. de Diemerbroeck was a lawyer of Utrecht.

P. 263, l. 6. "Doctor" (*Médecin*) was used in the sense of "a man of science."

LETTER XLVI

P. 263. The original of this letter, written in Latin, is in the former Royal Library in Hanover, where Leibniz was librarian at one time to the Duke. There is a facsimile of it in W. Meyer's edition (1903), and of a part of it in T. de Murr's *Benedicti de Spinoza Adnotationes ad Tractatum Theologico-Politicum* (1802). For the *Opera Posthuma* Spinoza's rough draft of the letter appears to have been used. The differences are not important.

P. 263, l. 29. "*Pandochal*" means "all-receptive," or "receiving all the rays," in this context.

P. 265, l. 7. An interesting feature of the original of this letter is the seal of Spinoza, an oval ring containing a rose, the initials B. D. S., and the word *caute* (beware). Presumably the whole idea of the seal was a pun on the name Spinoza (*Spinosa* means a thorn). See the front cover of this volume. Some people see in this seal a symbol of the Rosicrucians, the Freemasons of the seventeenth century.

LETTER XLVII

P. 265. This letter is only known from the *Opera Posthuma*. The original letter, written in Latin, has been lost.

Concerning Fabritius, see *Introduction*, § 7.

P. 265, l. 19. The Prince Palatine who sent the invitation to Spinoza was Karl Ludwig, brother of Christina, Queen of Sweden, the patroness of Descartes. According to Urbain Chevreau (1613–1701), a learned courtier who travelled a good deal and visited many European courts, it was he who had recommended Spinoza to the Prince Palatine. In his *Chevraeana* (Vol. II, p. 100, edition 1700) he writes : " At the court of the Prince I spoke very favourably about Spinoza, although I only knew of this protestant Jew from the *First and Second Parts of Descartes' Principles of Philosophy*, printed in Amsterdam, in 1663, by Jan Rieuwertsz. The Prince had this book, and after I had read out to him a few chapters from it, he decided to invite him to his University at Heidelberg, to teach Philosophy there, but with the condition that he should not dogmatize." Supposing that Chevreau did not grossly exaggerate his share in Spinoza's call to Heidelberg, it is possible that Chevreau's account was intended to exonerate him from the charge of having recommended a heretic to an important post. So he pretends not to have known the *Tractatus* then. There is, however, some reason to suppose that it was the author of the *Tractatus Theologico-Politicus* that the Prince Palatine wanted, and not merely the author of the geometric version of Descartes' *Principles of Philosophy*. The spirit of the *Tractatus* probably appealed to the Prince because he was anxious to bring about a Union of the Reformed Churches, and for this end there was needed something of the spirit of undogmatic toleration advocated in the *Tractatus*.

LETTER XLVIII

P. 266. This letter also is only known from the *Opera Posthuma*, the original letter, written in Latin, having been lost.

P. 267, l. 1. Of the wisdom of Spinoza's refusal of the Heidelberg Professorship there can be no doubt. No University was sufficiently mature then to permit the teaching of Spinozism. It was also fortunate, inasmuch as already in the following year the French seized Heidelberg and closed the University.

LETTER XLVIIIA

P. 267. The story of these fragments is told by Bayle and by Dr. Hallmann as follows. (*a*) *Bayle :* " A certain Jarig Jelles, his intimate friend, being suspected of some heresies, thought that he ought to justify himself by publishing a confession of his faith. Having drafted it he sent it to Spinoza, and asked him to write his opinion of it. Spinoza replied to him that he had read it with pleasure, and that he had not found anything in it which could be altered. ' Sir and very distinguished Friend, etc.' . . . This confession of faith is in Dutch and was printed in the year 1684." (*Historical and Critical Dictionary*, edition 1702, Vol. III, p. 2783, Note S. Translated in *The Oldest Biography of Spinoza*, p. 164.) Jelles' *Confession* is accompanied by a biographical sketch written probably by Rieuwertsz, the publisher. In this we are told that Jelles had sent his *Confession* to " a certain friend outside the city," no doubt Spinoza, and that the reply received was, " I have read, etc." (the same as the reply cited by Bayle, but in Dutch, whereas Bayle quotes the letter in Latin).

(*b*) *Dr. Hallmann* reports the following conversation with Rieuwertsz, junior, in 1703. " More letters had been found than had been printed ; but they were of no importance, and so were burned. But he had kept one letter, which was lying upstairs among his things. At last I persuaded him to fetch the letter and show it to me. It was a short letter written in Dutch on half a sheet of paper. The date was the 19 April, 1673," etc. (as in the text). (From Dr. Hallmann's *Journal of Travels*, in German, quoted in J. Freudenthal's *Die Lebensgeschichte Spinoza's*, 1899, pp. 231 ff.)

P. 268, l. 4. " On page 5 of the manuscript he stated," etc. This statement is not in the printed text of the *Confession*. Presumably Jelles omitted the passage in consequence of Spinoza's comment.

P. 268, l. 10. Dirck (or Theodor) Kerckrinck was born in Hamburg in 1639, and came with his parents to Amsterdam at an early age. At eighteen he suddenly decided to prepare for the University, and went to Van den Enden to learn Latin, etc., for the purpose. Two years later (1659) he entered the University of Leyden, and was still there when Spinoza came to Rhynsburg in 1660. Kerckrinck became a distinguished doctor, and some of his medical treatises are included in the inventory of Spinoza's books—no doubt gifts from an old friend whom he had met originally at Van den Enden's house. In 1671 Kerckrinck married Clara Maria, the eldest daughter of Van den Enden. Clara was twenty-seven then. Kerckrinck eventually settled in Hamburg, where he died in 1693.

P. 268, l. 13. " The Known Truth." This must be the title of a book. But no such treatise can be traced now. It may have circulated in manuscript only, as happened with many books in the seventeenth century, especially with unorthodox books. Spinoza's *Short Treatise*, and Lucas' *Life of Spinoza*, for instance, only existed in manuscript then.

P. 268, l. 14. " Mr. Vallon " (*D. Vallon*; usually D = Dominus = Mr.). Rieuwertsz, junior, described Mr. Vallon to Dr. Hallmann as a Professor in the University of Leyden, and a particular friend of Spinoza's (see J. Freudenthal's *Die Lebensgeschichte Spinoza's*, 1899, p. 231). But he cannot be traced. The name may be an error for De Vallan, who was at one time Professor in the University of Utrecht, or for De Volder (1643–1709), who was Professor of Physics and Mathematics in the University of Leyden. Other names which have been suggested are De Vries, who was at one time co-Rector of the Grammar School at The Hague, and De Versé, a Socinian. But all this is mere conjecture.

P. 268, l. 16. " Mr. Bronckhorst." Probably Hendrik van Bronckhorst is meant. He was a Mennonite and a Cartesian, and apparently a friend of Spinoza. He was the author of the laudatory verses which were prefixed to the Dutch translation of Spinoza's *Geometric Version of Descartes' Principle of Philosophy* published in 1664. The laudatory verses in the Latin original, published in 1663, were by Bouwmeester.

ANNOTATIONS

LETTER XLIX

P. 268. The original letter, written in Latin, is in the Royal Library at Copenhagen. A facsimile of it is contained in W. Meyer's edition (1903).

Concerning Graevius, see *Introduction*, § 7.

P. 268, l. 29. "The letter concerning the death of Descartes" had been written on $\frac{1}{11}$ February, 1650, by Johannes a Wullen, an Amsterdam doctor who lived in Sweden, to W. Piso, a medical man in Amsterdam. What Graevius had was a copy of the original, and this copy is now in the University Library at Leyden. The letter is printed in Van Vloten and Land's edition of Spinoza's Works. The main purport of the letter was to the effect that Descartes was wholly to blame for his death, because he did not consult a doctor when he first became ill, and would not accept Wullen's services when, at the request of the Queen of Sweden, he visited Descartes and offered to treat him. To crown it all. Descartes resorted to excessive blood-letting when he was too weak, in consequence of having taken no nourishment for several days.

P. 268, l. 30. "Mr. de V." It is not known who this was. It may be the same person who is called Mr. Vallon [D. Vallon] in Letter XLVIIIA. See Annotations to that letter.

LETTER L

P. 269. The original of this letter, written in Dutch, has been lost. The *Opera Posthuma* gives what appears to be Spinoza's own Latin rendering of it, which was re-translated into Dutch for the Dutch edition of the *Posthumous Works*.

Concerning Jelles, see *Introduction*, § 6.

P. 269, l. 15. Thomas Hobbes of Malmesbury (1588–1679), author of *Leviathan*, etc., was the favourite political philosopher among the political theorists of the party of the De Witts. Van Hove, who was their chief spokesman, simply refers his readers to the writings of Hobbes for all further explanations. The naturalism of Spinoza also inclined him to embrace some of the political theories of Hobbes. Nevertheless there are important differences between them, which must be reserved for discussion in connection with the *Political Treatise* of Spinoza. In the meantime reference may be made to C. E. Vaughan's *Studies in the History of Political Philosophy before and after Rousseau* (2 vols., Manchester, 1925).

P. 269, l. 22. "*In the Appendix to . . . Descartes' Principles*," namely, in the *Metaphysical Thoughts*, Part I, Chapter VI.

P. 269, l. 23. "God can only very improperly be called one." What Spinoza says here of God or Substance applies equally to Attributes. So that strictly speaking it is not altogether correct to speak of " two " or of " innumerable " Attributes. Spinoza usually speaks of them as " infinite " in the sense that they are " all " there are (besides, of course, being each infinite or complete of its kind).

P. 269, l. 24. " A thing can only be said to be one . . . . in respect of its existence and not of its essence." See Letter IX.

P. 270, l. 13. " The limitation (*determinatio*) . . . is its not-being." See Annotations to Letter XXXVI.

P. 270, l. 18. " A Professor of Utrecht." This was Regner van Mansvelt, who had succeeded Voetius (see Annotations to Letter XLIII) as Professor of Philosophy in the University of Utrecht. Mansvelt published an attack on Spinoza's *Tractatus Theologico-Politicus* in 1674. The title of the book was *Adversus Anonymum Theologico-Politicum, Liber Singularis* (Amsterdam).

LETTER LI

P. 270. The original letter, written in Dutch, has been lost. The *Opera Posthuma* appears to give a Latin translation of it made by Spinoza himself. The Dutch edition of the *Posthumous Works* gives a re-translation of the Latin version.

Concerning Boxel, see *Introduction*, § 5.

P. 271, l. 21. " The war," namely, between Holland and France. On August 11, 1674, an indecisive battle had been fought between the Dutch army, under the Prince of Orange, and the French army, under Condé, at Séneffe. In September the Prince of Orange made an unsuccessful attack on the French at Oudenarde.

LETTER LII

P. 271. The original letter, written in Dutch, has been lost. It is probable, however, that the text contained in the Dutch edition of the *Posthumous Works* is an exact reproduction of it, since no Latin terms. are given in the margin of the letter, as they usually are given when the Dutch text is a translation of the Latin.

P. 272, l. 18. Spinoza's views on ghosts and spirits, good and evil, were quite revolutionary for that period. Already in 1660, or earlier, Spinoza gave a humorous account of evil spirits in his *Short Treatise* (Book II, Chapter XXV, p. 143 of my translation), where he remarked that if the devil is as god-forsaken as he is commonly believed to be, he must be so wretched that we ought to pray for him.

LETTER LIII

P. 273. The original letter, written in Dutch, is preserved in the Orphanage De Oranjeappel, in Amsterdam. The Latin version in the *Opera Posthuma* seems to have been made by Spinoza himself. There are no important differences between the two versions. The original Dutch text is given in J. Freudenthal's *Die Lebensgeschichte Spinoza's*, 1899, pp. 196 ff.

P. 274, l. 30. Johannes Wierus, also called Wier, or Weyer, was born in Belgium in 1515 or 1516, studied medicine in Paris, and eventually settled in Düsseldorf as Physician to the Duke of Jülich. In 1563 he shocked the clergy by his book *On Daemon-Illusions* (*De Praestigiis Daemonum*), in which he denounced the folly and cruelty of prosecutions against witches, whom he regarded as mentally afflicted. The book was put on the Index, but was soon followed by two others, *On Ghosts* (*De Lamiis*), and *Pseudomonarchia Daemonum* on the Hierarchy of Hell. The original text gives the name as Wierius, which is corrected in the *Opera Posthuma*.

P. 274, l. 31. Ludwig Lavater (1527–1586) was a Protestant Minister in Zurich. His book on ghosts, etc., entitled *Tractatus de Spectris, Lemuribus, Fragoribus, variisque Praesagiis* was published in 1580 at Geneva.

P. 274, l. 32. Cardanus. Girolamo (or Hieronymus) Cardanus (or Cardan) was born at Pavia in 1501, and died in Rome in 1576. In 1547 he became Professor of Medicine in Pavia, but got into trouble through exposing the medical practices of his time. In 1551 he visited Scotland as medical adviser to Archbishop Hamilton.

In 1562 he was appointed Professor at Bologna, but was dismissed soon as a heretic, apparently because he cast the horologue of Christ, and attempted to give an astrological account of his life. After that he lived in Rome on a pension from the Pope. His *De Subtilitate Rerum* was published in 1551, and his *De Rerum Varietate* in 1557. In these two treatises Cardanus attempted to explain natural phenomena in a very speculative manner, but still in a manner that was highly creditable for that period, inasmuch as he insisted on the inviolability of the laws of Nature. That even he was not entirely free from superstition seems to be shown by his claim that, like Socrates, he had the assistance of a guardian dæmon.

P. 275, l. 1. Melanthon. Probably the German Reformer Philipp Melanchthon (1497–1560) is meant.

P. 275, l. 21. Alexander ab Alexandro (1461–1523). He was an Italian lawyer, who studied and practised at Naples (his birthplace) and at Rome (where he died). On receiving a sinecure appointment at Rome, under papal patronage, he abandoned legal practice and devoted himself to literary work. His *Genialium Dierum, libri sex* was published in 1522. It deals almost entireiy with Roman antiquities and problems of legal and classical scholarship. It is a bulky miscellaneous work modelled more or less on the *Saturnalia* of Macrobius (395–423), or on the *Noctes Atticae* of Aulus Gellius (130–180).

P. 275, l. 26. Petrus Thyraeus, or Tyraeus (1546–1601), was Professor at various times at Trier, Mainz and Würzburg. His *De Apparitionibus Spirituum* was published in 1600, at Cologne.

P. 275, l. 35. The concluding two paragraphs of the letter are only in the original, not in the *Posthumous Works*. The reference to the concluding part of Spinoza's letter (LII) is obscure because we do not know wha it really was.

LETTER LIV

P. 276. The original of this letter, written in Dutch, has been lost. The Latin version of it in the *Opera Posthuma* appears to have been prepared by Spinoza himself.

P. 276, l. 29. A copy of Pliny's *Letters* is mentioned in the inventory of Spinoza's books compiled immediately after his death.

P. 278, l. 35. " Beauty . . . is not so much a quality of the object which is perceived as an effect in him who perceives it." In an age in which the most eminent thinkers (Galilei, Descartes, Boyle, Newton, etc.) regarded even secondary qualities as subjective rather than as objective, it is not surprising to find Spinoza treating a tertiary quality like beauty in the same manner. At the same time, it is quite possible to reconcile Spinoza's view with an objective conception of tertiary (as well as of secondary) qualities, if we bear in mind that for Spinoza the percipient subject is as much a part of the objective order of Nature as any other part thereof, and that the qualities in question are consequently objective if we enlarge the sphere of reference so as to include the observer as well as the observed phenomenon within the field of fact of which the quality is properly predicated.

P. 280, l. 28. For Spinoza the belief in supernatural apparitions, like the belief in miracles, is the result of ignorance or of stupidity. Compare Letters LXXV and LXXVIII, and *Tractatus Theologico-Politicus*, Chapter VI.

LETTER LV

P. 281. The original letter, written in Dutch, has been lost. But the Latin rendering of it in the *Opera Posthuma* seems to have been made by Spinoza himself.

P. 285, l. 7. "Substance and accident." See Annotations to Letter IV.

P. 286, l. 13. Caesar and Spurina. The story is related in Suetonius' *Caesar*, chapter 81.

LETTER LVI

P. 286. This letter was written in Dutch, but the original has not been preserved. Spinoza himself appears to have prepared the Latin version of it that is printed in the *Opera Posthuma*, the Dutch edition of which contains simply a re-translation of the Latin version.

P. 287, l. 18. "Coercion or Force and Necessity." The confusion between external coercion and inner necessity is one against which Spinoza is always protesting, though mostly in vain. Human conduct is partly the result of external influence, and partly the result of an inner drive which is the expression of the individual's own nature. The external factor is the element of coercion, the inner factor is the factor of freedom— the more the latter predominates, the more free the individual is. The libertarian idea of a Freedom of indifference, which would make conduct independent of character (and of the inner necessity that this implies), really puts caprice in the place of free-will.

P. 288, l. 12. "A triangle, if only it had the power of speech, would say in like manner that God is eminently triangular. . . ." Compare the remarks of Xenophanes (sixth century B.C.):—"If oxen and horses or lions had hands, and could paint with their hands, and produce works of art as men do, horses would paint the forms of the gods like horses, and oxen like oxen." "The Ethiopians make their gods black and snub-nosed; the Thracians say theirs have blue eyes and red hair,"

(See J. Burnet : *Early Greek Philosophy*, 3rd ed., p. 119. Compare also Rupert Brooke's poem *Heaven*.)

P. 288, l. 16. "Make itself like unto God." The context requires "make God like unto itself." Was it a slip, or an attempt to avoid the appearance of blasphemy ?

P. 288, l. 23. "In the world we often act on conjecture. . . ." Spinoza, it is clear, would agree with the subsequent remark of Bishop Butler that "probability is the guide of life," so far as the practical contingencies of life are concerned. We are often called upon to act under circumstances which make it impossible for us to make sure of our ground. Spinoza himself has pointed out the element of adventure or of faith in our practical attitude to life. Without it we should perish of hunger and thirst (see the next sentence but one in this letter, and the Annotations to Letter XXI). But in the case of theoretical or scientific problems his attitude is that subsequently expressed by Huxley, who insisted on a sceptical scrutiny of the credentials of every suggestion or belief.

P. 288, l. 26. "Man would perish of thirst and hunger if he would not eat or drink until he had obtained a perfect proof that food and drink would do him good." See Letter XXI, and compare Schiller's poem *Die Weltweisen*, which may be rendered roughly as follows :

> Since what Professors teach
> Not unto all can reach,
> 'Tis Nature's maternal rôle
> To keep things sound and whole.

> And while Philosophy strives
> To learn to guide our lives,
> Nature prompts us from above
> Through hunger and through love.

ANNOTATIONS

P. 289, l. 20. " As clear an idea of God as . . . of a triangle. . . ." Spinoza insists that we cannot have a clear and true *presentation* or *image* of God, but that we can have a clear and true *idea* or *conception* of Him. The attempt to image God can only result in our treating Him as one finite link in the whole system or chain of causes and effects in the universe. The outcome is an idol of some sort, such as usurps the place of God in popular theologies. To *conceive* God correctly is to realize intellectually that the conditioned events or dependent objects which we observe presuppose or imply an Unconditioned Ground, Substance, or *Causa Sui* (in Spinoza's sense of these terms). Compare the Annotations to Letter XII.

P. 290, l. 14. " The authority of Plato, Aristotle, and Socrates." It was characteristic of the age of revolt to hold " authority " in low esteem, even at the cost of insufficient appreciation of great thinkers whom the Schoolmen had unfortunately exploited as " authorities " and obstructions to independent thought in a manner that those " authorities " would have been the first to denounce.

The inventory of Spinoza's books includes a Latin translation of the complete works of Aristotle, but nothing of Plato.

P. 290, l. 16. Epicurus (341–271 B.C.), Democritus (460–370 B.C.), Lucretius (99–55 B.C.) were all of them supporters of the atomic theory, and as such were much in favour among the men of science of the seventeenth century. Lucretius' *De Rerum Natura* (*On the Nature of Things*) gives a poetical and classical account of the atomic theory of the ancients.

P. 290, l. 19. " Occult Qualities, intentional species, substantial forms." Concerning " substantial forms " and " occult qualities " see the Annotations to Letter III.

By " sensible species " were meant certain minute pictures or films which were alleged to pass from seen objects to the seeing eye. This theory of vision, by means of " representative pictures," appears to have been suggested first by Democritus, who called them " idols " (εἴδωλα). It was probably based upon a more primitive conception based on dream experiences. In any case all sorts of " species " flourished in scholastic philosophy, and were only gradually laid to rest by the corpuscular and the undulatory theories of light.

Sometimes the term " intentional species " (or " intentional sensible species ") was used as the equivalent of " sensible species." Usually, however, in the epistemological discussions in Scholastic philosophy the term *species* was used for any representation of the *form* of an object, and the term " intentional species " was restricted to the *mental* representation of the *form*—the term " form " being here used in its Platonic or Aristotelian sense (see Annotations to Letter III).

P. 290, l. 23. " They burned all his [Democritus'] books." The story is told by Diogenes Laertes in his *Lives of the Philosophers*, also in various Humanist compilations of the type of Alexander ab Alexandro's *Genial Days*.

LETTER LVII

P. 291. This letter is only known from the *Posthumous Works*, the original, written in Latin, having been lost. It was not addressed to Spinoza, but to Schuller, who sent Spinoza a copy of the part that concerned him.

Concerning Tschirnhaus and Schuller, see *Introduction*, §§ 5 and 6.

P. 291, l. 8. " At the beginning of his *Method*." The Dutch version has instead " in the said paragraph " (or section). The opening part of this letter has obviously been omitted. In the omitted part reference must have been made to Descartes' *Method*, and the Dutch version no doubt gives a correct rendering of the original in this case, while the more careful editors of the *Opera Posthuma* made the small alteration that was made necessary by the omission of the beginning of the letter.

P. 291, l. 17. "If one of two men affirms something but the other denies it. . . ." The meaning of this sentence is not very clear. Tschirnhaus seems to be confusing (as people often do) *Truth* with *Truthfulness* (or Veracity). What he says applies to the veracity of a statement, not to its truth. Two people may honestly or truthfully make inconsistent assertions, but inconsistent assertions cannot both be true, except, perhaps, for a pragmatist, who is not really concerned with Truth, but with Utility.

P. 293, l. 30. "And you will find me . . . N. N." Only in the Dutch edition of the *Posthumous Works*.

LETTER LVIII

P. 294. This letter is only known from the *Posthumous Works*, the original, written in Latin, having been lost.

P. 294, l. 6. "Our friend J. R." This was Jan Rieuwertsz, bookseller and publisher, of Amsterdam. He was born in Amsterdam in 1617. He was a Collegiant, and his bookshop was a rallying centre of liberal thinkers. He published J. H. Glazemaker's Dutch translation of the Works of Descartes (in four volumes), and he published all the works of Spinoza, though the fact had to be concealed in every case except in that of the *Geometric Version of Descartes' Principles of Philosophy*.

P. 295, l. 22. "This stone," etc. The kind of freedom which Spinoza rejects, and which this illustration is meant to explain away, is the so-called "freedom of indifference," according to which an individual, it is alleged, is utterly free to do anything within his power (that is to say, in so far as he is not hindered or coerced by forces outside him) entirely uninfluenced by his own character and his past history. Compare *Ethics*, Part III, Proposition II, Scholium.

P. 296, l. 8. "They see the better and follow the worse." From Ovid's *Metamorphoses*, VII, 20. Spinoza cites it again in *Ethics*, III, Proposition II, Schol.

LETTER LIX

P. 298. This letter is only known from the *Posthumous Works*, the original letter, written in Latin, having been lost.

P. 300, l. 13. "Applicates to curves . . . their Tangents." The oldest method of measuring the perimeters and the areas of curves was that of *exhaustion*. Polygons were inscribed and circumscribed to the curve, and an attempt was made to evaluate the perimeter or the area of these polygons as the number of their sides was increased until a limiting value could be determined. Next came the method of *applicates*, or of ordinates—that

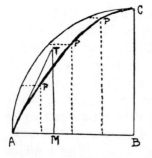

is, right lines drawn across the curves so as to be bisected by their diameters. This method developed into co-ordinate Geometry. Tschirnhaus discovered the method of *tangents*. This method might be illustrated with special reference to a quadrant, say A B C. The arc A C and the radius A B are divided into the same number of equal parts, and lines are drawn through the points of division of the arc parallel to A B, and through the points of division of the radius parallel to B C. Corresponding lines of the two sets meet in points P lying on a curve A P C. The tangent A T drawn to this curve at A (where $x = 0$) has a slope $\pi/2$. If from any point on this tangent a perpendicular T M is drawn to the radius, then T M is the length of the quadrant of the circle which has A M for radius. Hence, when A M = A B, then T M = perimeter of the quadrant. From this we can infer the perimeter and the quadrature of the circle.

LETTER LX

P. 300. This letter also is only known from the *Posthumous Works*, the original letter, written in Latin, having been lost.

P. 301, l. 8. " The efficient cause of a circle," etc. On the importance of this passage see *Introduction*, § 8. The vast majority of critics have been so prone to suppose that Geometry, as they understand or misunderstand it, has determined Spinoza's Metaphysics, that they never even considered the possibility that Spinoza's dynamic Metaphysics may have influenced his geometrical conceptions.

P. 300, l. 28. Spinoza's emphasis on the *adequacy* of ideas, as distinguished from their *truth*, and his identification of the two, may present some difficulty. The main point is this. A strict empiricist might say that a *true* idea is one derived from observed instances with which it agrees. Its truth would thus consist, as Spinoza says, in the agreement of the idea with its objects. But Spinoza is a rationalist primarily. As to the mere empiricist, who pretends to obtain his ideas as inductions from experience solely, Spinoza asks : " How can he possibly be sure that his experience of a few particulars can serve him as a rule for all ? " (*Short Treatise*, Book II, Chapter I, p. 68). Spinoza thinks of ideas as originating in thought (not as merely impressed on us by experience) and applied to the facts of experience in order to comprehend their interconnections. An idea is *adequate* in so far as it really does enable us to unify and interconnect a certain range of observations ; and if it is adequate it is also *true* because it then agrees with the observed facts. But for Spinoza the primacy is with the *adequacy* of the idea, because until we have the adequate idea the facts are not yet apprehended in such a way that the idea can be said to agree with them, that is, to be true. Spinoza's view of ideas anticipates to some extent the Kantian way of looking at thought. Although the two philosophies, the Spinozistic and the Kantian, are otherwise very different, Spinozism is very far from being so " uncritical " as Kant and others supposed. Epistemological criticism has its place in Spinozism, but is deliberately, and I think rightly, regarded as of secondary interest only. See the Annotations to Letter II (on " things of reason ").

P. 301, l. 14. " When I define God as the supremely perfect Being," etc. Spinoza's objection to this usual, Cartesian definition of God is due to the fact that it makes God merely a member in a series of more or less similar objects, whereas a good definition of anything should be causal or dynamic, and the correct conception of God is that of the unconditioned ground of the existence of the whole series of objects and events. Compare Annotation to Letter XII (on " Rab Chasdai ").

P. 301, l. 24. " Applicates to curves." See Annotations to Letter LIX.

ANNOTATIONS

LETTER LXI

P. 302. This letter is only known from the *Posthumous Works*, the original, written in Latin, having been lost. The date given in the *Opera Posthuma* is October 8, 1665 ; in the Dutch edition it is given correctly as June 8, 1675.

P. 302, l. 16. "My letter." There is no trace of this letter of Oldenburg's to Spinoza, written presumably in 1670, the year of publication of the *Tractatus Theologico-Politicus*, or later. Evidently Spinoza sent a copy to Oldenburg, which did not reach him, and possibly also a note which did, otherwise how did Oldenburg know that Spinoza had sent him a copy of the *Tractatus*, unless perhaps through some third person.

LETTER LXII

P. 303. This letter, too, is only known from the *Posthumous Works*, the original, written in Latin, having been lost.

P. 303, l. 25. "Your answer to me, dated 5 July." This letter cannot be traced.

P. 303, l. 26. "Your Five-Part Treatise," namely, the *Ethics*. See Annotations to Letter XXVIII.

P. 303, l. 33. Oldenburg had learned to be cautious and wary since he wrote Letters VII and XI, in which he urged Spinoza to publish his philosophical ideas in spite of the theologians, etc.

LETTER LXIII

P. 304. The original letter, written in Latin, is preserved in the Library of the United Baptists in Amsterdam. The *Opera Posthuma* contains an abridged and somewhat altered version of it. The complete text was first published by Van Vloten in his *Ad Benedicti de Spinoza Opera Supplementum* (1860).

P. 304, l. 30. Tschirnhaus visited London in April or May 1675, and there came into touch with various members of the Royal Society. That Oldenburg and Boyle should have formed " a strange conception " of Spinoza after reading his *Tractatus Theologico-Politicus* was to be expected, in view of their conventional orthodoxy. It is almost surprising that Tschirnhaus succeeded in disabusing their minds to the extent to which he did.

P. 305, l. 10. " As many worlds as there are Attributes of God." It is a common objection to Spinozism, or a common misinterpretation of it, that by describing each Attribute as being in itself, and being conceived through itself, it makes each Attribute really a substance, and so Spinozism is in effect a pluralistic philosophy in spite of Spinoza's intention and endeavour to make it monistic. The view was first expressed by Tschirnhaus in this very letter (which is mainly Schuller's copy of Tschirnhaus's letter), and has been repeated ever since. But it is a grave misconception all the same. It overlooks the fact that for Spinoza Substance was not merely the sum of distinct Attributes, but the organic unity of them. Just as each Attribute is not merely the sum of its modes, but the organic or systematic unity of them, so Substance, according to Spinoza, is the interconnected system of Attributes—interconnected just in so far as they are the forces or the expressions of the same and only Substance. The habit of speaking about the psycho-physical *parallelism* (which is usually but not quite correctly identified with Spinoza's conception of the relation between Thought and Extension), and the tendency to read Cartesianism into Spinozism are mainly responsible for the pluralistic misinterpretation of Spinozism. A plurality of Attributes is a very different thing from a plurality of Substances, and it is at once the most characteristic feature and a lasting merit of Spinozism that it holds tenaciously to the idea of the unity of the Unconditioned Ground and System of the Universe. In it, as in no other philosophy, the Universe really is a Universe—the All is One, and the One is All. In his reply Spinoza refers to *Ethics*, Part II, Proposition VII. Compare also his reply to Oldenburg, in Letter IV.

P. 306, l. 14. " In obedience to your instructions I dared not inform you of this." Of what ? Presumably the reference is to the changed views of Boyle and Oldenburg about the *Tractatus Theologico-Politicus*. It is probable that Spinoza had requested his friends not to mention, or in any way betray, in their letters his authorship of the *Tractatus*. For this there were good reasons. And so Schuller had not dared to mention the news until a specially favourable opportunity presented itself of transmitting a letter without risk of its being tampered with.

P. 306, l. 22. " Mr. a. Gent." It is not known who this was.

P. 306, l. 22. " J. Riew." is most probably Jan Rieuwertsz. See Annotations to Letter LVIII.

LETTER LXIV

P. 306. This letter is only known from the *Posthumous Works*, the original letter, written in Latin, having been lost.

P. 306, l. 31. " In reply to the first," etc. The question raised by Tschirnhaus about the number of Attributes expressed in each finite mode is closely connected with the question of the number of the Attributes of God or Substance. On the one hand, Spinoza usually speaks of their " infinite " number; on the other hand, he never speaks definitely of more than two, namely, Extension and Thought. Since for Spinoza " infinite " means " complete," it is possible that he did not seriously contemplate the reality of more than the two Attributes in question, although, of course, he had to leave open the possibility of other Attributes, since, according to Spinoza, man is certainly not the measure of reality. Commentators invariably speak of the " innumerable " Attributes of Substance according to Spinoza, and, of course, two cannot be equated with " innumerable." But Spinoza does not speak of " innumerable," only of " infinite " (i.e. the complete number or totality of) Attributes, and " two " may well be the complete or total number of them. If there were no more than two Attributes, then the problem raised by Tschirnhaus would not arise. But even the *possibility* of there being more Attributes than two, occasions the question why man is not aware of more than two of them. And Spinoza's answer is presumably suggested by the case of human experience, which shows us a mode of Thought conjoined with the mode of one other Attribute as its object. But difficulties have been urged against Spinoza's solution on the ground that it appears to give a privileged position to the Attribute Thought, which thus seems to be much more extensive than the other Attributes, inasmuch as it is coextensive, or parallel, not with *one* other Attribute only (say, Extension), but with *all* the other Attributes, since each mode of *every* other Attribute has its mode of Thought (see Letter LXX). This criticism, however, is based on an irrelevant spatial metaphor or analogy. Each Attribute is "infinite" (that is, complete) of its kind, and since each Attribute is entirely different from every other, there is no sense in comparing the "extensiveness" of one with that of another, whatever that may mean. (See A. Wolf: *Spinoza's Conception of the Attributes of Substance*, in *Proceedings of the Aristotelian Society*, 1927.)

P. 307, l. 36. "Whether . . . there must be constituted as many worlds as there are attributes." See Annotations to Letter LXIII.

P. 308, l. 21. "The idea which we have of an absolutely infinite Being. . . ." Spinoza may have suspected that Tschirnhaus was under the impression that the idea in question was regarded by Spinoza after the analogy of a "limiting case" in mathematics. There are beings with two attributes, three attributes, etc. So in the limit we can conceive a Being with infinite Attributes. But Spinoza was not thinking numerically in this case. As already explained, "infinite" meant for him "complete," "perfect" or "real in the highest sense." And he arrived at the conception of a substance having infinite Attributes, because such a Being was felt by him to be necessary as the Unconditioned Ground of all that is real but conditioned (or dependent).

P. 308, l. 24. "The examples" required were those of (*a*) an immediate infinite mode, and (*b*) a mediate infinite mode. Spinoza adduces "absolutely infinite understanding" as an instance of (*a*) in the Attribute Thought, and "motion and rest" as an instance of (*a*) in the Attribute Extension. Of (*b*) he only gives one instance, namely, "the face of the whole Universe" in the Attribute Extension.

LETTER LXV

P. 309. This letter is only known from the *Posthumous Works*, the original, written in Latin, having been lost.

LETTER LXVI

P. 310. This letter also is only known from the *Posthumous Works*, the original, written in Latin, having been lost.

LETTER LXVII

P. 310. Also this letter is only known from the *Posthumous Works*, the original letter, written in Latin, having been lost.

Concerning Burgh see *Introduction*, §§ 1 and 5.

P. 311, l. 5. "Mr. D. Craenen." See Annotations to Letter XLIV (on Professor Kranen).

P. 312, l. 5. "Your book," that is the *Tractatus Theologico-Politicus*.

P. 315, l. 20. "The stone which the Alchemists seek." The so-called "Philosopher's Stone," which would help to transmute base metals into gold.

P. 317, l. 1. "The consensus of so many myriads of men." On the argument from the *consensus gentium* see Annotations to Letter IV (on "Common Notions").

P. 321, l. 2. "The very Way, the Truth and the Life." *St. John*, Chapter XIV, verse 6.

P. 324, l. 22. Concerning the approximate coincidence of this letter with that of Steno see Annotations to Letter LXVIIA.

LETTER LXVIIᴀ

P. 324. This letter was printed, in Florence, in 1675. The original letter cannot be traced. There is no evidence that it ever reached Spinoza, and no reply from him is extant. Spinoza's name is not mentioned, nor is any one of his books referred to by its title. Yet there can be little doubt that it was addressed to Spinoza. The description of the addressee, " the reformer of the new philosophy," is hardly applicable to anybody else at that time. " The Book " to which Steno refers is obviously the *Tractatus Theologico-Politicus*, which by 1675 was well known in all centres of learning throughout Europe. Moreover, Spinoza makes explicit mention of Steno in his reply to Burgh (see Letter LXXVI), and mentions him in such a way as can leave no doubt that it is the same Steno who wrote this letter. Spinoza also possessed a copy of Steno's *Prodromus de Solido* (1669), presumably a gift from his old friend, the author. (See J. Freudenthal's *Die Lebensgeschichte Spinoza's*, p. 161.)

The fact that both Burgh and Steno wrote to Spinoza from Florence, in the same year, perhaps about the same time, and to the same purpose, may have some significance. It may be a mere coincidence, but more likely it was the result of mutual agreement, or of a suggestion made to both by some Roman Catholic authority.

In spite of general similarity of contents, the two letters are markedly different in tone. Burgh becomes ill-mannered, as well as stupid, in his fanaticism, whereas Steno remains the friendly scholar and gentleman.

The first edition of this letter is very scarce, but it has been reproduced in facsimile and edited by W. Meyer in the *Chronicon Spinozanum*, Vol. I (The Hague, 1921).

P. 324, l. 26. "The book," namely the *Tractatus Theologico-Politicus.*

P. 326, l. 34. "The Spirit of Christ preventing." *Preventing* is, of course, used here in its original meaning of "coming or going before," not in the sense of hindering. Compare *Psalm* XCV, 2 : *Let us prevent his face with thanksgiving* (Marginal Version).

P. 327, l. 21. "*For their wickedness blinded them.*" *The Wisdom of Solomon,* Chapter II, verse 21.

P. 327, l. 24. "*Let the dead bury their dead.*" *St. Matthew,* Chapter VIII, verse 22 (*Leave the dead to bury their own dead*).

P. 329, l. 5. "*Thy testimonies are very sure.*" *Psalm* XCIII, verse 5.

P. 331, l. 17. "*This is the finger of God.*" *Exodus,* Chapter VIII, verse 19.

P. 333, l. 3. St. Justin : *Dialogue with Trypho,* Chapter VII. The quotation is not quite accurate.

P. 333, l. 27. St. Justin : *Dialogue with Trypho,* Chapter VIII. The quotation is not quite accurate.

LETTER LXVIII

P. 334. This letter is only known from the *Posthumous Works,* the original letter, written in Latin, having been lost.

P. 334, l. 16. " The work about which I had written to you," that is the *Ethics.* See Letter LXII and the Annotations to it.

P. 334, l. 21. "Certain Theologians," etc. Of the fanaticism of the Dutch theologians and churches in relation to Spinoza there is ample evidence. J. Freudenthal has printed a considerable number of amiable resolutions passed by various Church councils and synods throughout Holland from the year in which

the *Tractatus Theologico-Politicus* appeared (1670) until
1676 (*Die Lebensgeschichte Spinoza's*, pp. 121–154). He
has also adduced evidence of what was happening at the
time of this letter of complaint (see his *Spinoza*, vol. I,
pp. 238 ff.). And no sooner did the *Posthumous Works*
appear than these good Christians resumed their amiable
occupation (see *Die Lebensgeschichte Spinoza's*, pp. 169–
189).

P. 334, l. 23. "The Prince," that is the Prince of
Orange, who owed much to the clerical zealots who
had helped to bring about the downfall of the De Witts
and their more liberal regime.

P. 335, l. 12. Notes to the *Tractatus Theologico-
Politicus* were added by Spinoza with his own hand in
some copies of this work. These notes were first
published in the French translation of the *Tractatus*,
1678. The original notes, in Latin, were first published,
in 1802, by C. T. de Murr—*Benedicti de Spinoza Adnotationes ad Tractatum Theologico-Politicum*. This was printed
from a copy of the *Tractatus* (once in the possession
of J. Rieuwertsz, the publisher) which contained the
notes in Spinoza's own writing. Another copy of the
Tractatus with these notes in Spinoza's handwriting is in
Königsberg.

LETTER LXIX

P. 335. This letter was not included in the *Posthumous
Works*. The original letter, written in Latin, somehow
came into the possession of Professor H. W. Tydeman
(1778–1863), of Leyden, who announced the fact in
1842, and published the letter, together with a litho-
graphic facsimile of it, in 1844, in the *Utrechtsche Volks-
Almanak* for that year. In 1865 the original was sold
at the sale of Tydeman's books, but it cannot be

traced now. A copy of the facsimile is contained in W. Meyer's edition (1903).

Concerning Velthuysen, see *Introduction*, § 7.

P. 335, l. 20. " Nieuwstad." Joachim Nieuwstad was Secretary of the city Utrecht from 1662 till 1674. According to K. O. Meinsma (*Spinoza en zijn Kring*, 1896, p. 376) Spinoza must have visited Nieuwstad during his stay in the French camp in Utrecht in 1673.

P. 335, l. 24. " Manuscript," that is Velthuysen's letter to Ostens. See Letter XLII.

P. 335, l. 30. Notes to the *Tractatus Theologico-Politicus*. See Annotations to Letter LXVIII.

P. 336, l. 16. " I know that you are possessed only by the love of truth," etc. Spinoza had evidently entirely changed his view of Velthuysen since he wrote Letter XLIII. This was the result of personal acquaintance with him during Spinoza's stay in Utrecht in 1673. Velthuysen, in the Preface to his own Works (published in 1680), relates that he had many conversations with Spinoza. Whether Velthuysen gave Spinoza the permission asked for, is not known. In any case Spinoza had no opportunity of preparing an enlarged edition of the *Tractatus Theologico-Politicus*.

LETTER LXX

P. 336. This letter is not contained in the *Posthumous Works*. The original letter, written in Latin, is in the possession of the Orphanage of the United Baptists in Amsterdam, and was first published by Van Vloten in his *Ad Benedicti de Spinoza Opera Supplementum* (1860).

P. 337, l. 27. " Mr. Colbert," that is Jean Baptiste Colbert, Chancellor of the Exchequer under Louis XIV. See Annotations to Letter XXXI.

P. 338, l. 17. " The Attribute Thought is much more extensive than the other Attributes."   See Annotations to Letter LXIV.

P. 338, l. 29.   Leibniz stayed in Paris from 1672 till 1676 in order to try to persuade Louis XIV to turn his attention to Egypt, and to leave Europe in peace.   See *Introduction*, § 5.

P. 339, l. 12.   " Leibniz . . . the *Tractatus Theo-logico-Politicus*."   Leibniz was a diplomat, and so acquired the habit of professing whatever views were likely to suit his interlocutors.   When addressing orthodox people Leibniz described the same *Tractatus* as " intolerably impudent " and " shocking," or " monstrous " (see his *Philosophische Schriften*, edition 1875, Vol. I, pp. 16, 34, 39, 70).

P. 339, l. 14.   A letter on this subject.   This letter of Leibniz to Spinoza on the subject of the *Tractatus Theologico-Politicus* cannot be traced.

P. 339, l. 24.   " Mr. Bresser."   Who this was is not known.

LETTER LXXI

P. 340.   This letter is only known from the *Posthumous Works*, the original letter, written in Latin, having been lost.

P. 340, l. 21.   To judge from this naïve letter, Oldenburg must have been under the impression that Spinoza had left orthodox Judaism because it did not prescribe a sufficiently large number of articles of faith.   What he wanted Spinoza to do was simply to explain away his philosophy, and to show what a good conventional Christian he really was !

LETTER LXXII

P. 340. This letter was not printed in the *Posthumous Works*, but the original was found in the collection of autograph letters owned by J. J. van Voorst, and was published soon afterwards in Van Vloten's *Ad Benedicti de Spinoza Opera Supplementum* (1860). The original letter has appeared at various sales, and has changed hands several times since then. It is believed still to be in existence, but the name of its present owner has not been divulged. A facsimile of it is included in W. Meyer's edition (1903).

P. 341, l. 32. "I should like to know first what he is doing in France." Concerning Spinoza's suspicion of Leibniz, see *Introduction*, § 5.

P. 342, l. 11. "Gold . . . latent in the antimony." The normal amount would be imperceptible.

LETTER LXXIII

P. 342. This letter is printed in the *Posthumous Works*. The original letter, written in Latin, has been lost; but a copy of it made by Leibniz (and with notes by him) is in the Library at Hanover. The Heidelberg edition of Spinoza's Works (1926) gives both texts. The differences are of no great importance.

P. 343, l. 9. "Like Paul," namely, in *Acts*, Chapter XVII, verse 28 : *For in him we live, and move, and have our being.*

P. 343, l. 17. "Nature" for Spinoza is identical with God or Substance. The common use of the term for the *material* world only was a constant source of misunderstanding among his early readers and critics.

P. 343, l. 23. "Miracles" for Spinoza spell ignorance.

For miracles are alleged to be supernatural interferences
with the order of Nature. For Spinoza there is nothing
outside Nature or the Universe, and so there is nothing
Super-natural. Moreover, Nature is thoroughly nomistic
or orderly. The so-called miraculous, or the alleged
supernatural interference with Nature, and the so-called
" accidental " or contingent (that is mere chance occur-
rences) are simply the result of our failure, through
ignorance, to place certain phenomena (in so far as they
are real and not merely imaginary) in their proper place
in the order of Nature. Spinoza protests against the
tendency of the Churches to base their claims on miracles
instead of on " the fruits of the Holy Spirit." The
tendency, moreover, encourages obtuseness to the
wonders of the natural and the orderly. Lessing, a
great admirer of Spinoza, and himself a great genius,
saw in this proneness to miracles and miraculous deliver-
ances not only an expression of ignorance, but also an
expression of conceit and pride. In his dramatic poem
Nathan the Wise, one of the greatest gospels of eighteenth-
century Humanism, he said *apropos* of a claim to a
miraculous deliverance from fire :

> " Pride ! and nought but pride ! The pot
> Of iron would feign be lifted from the fire
> With tongs of silver, just to deem itself
> A pot of precious silver."
>
> > (*Act I, Scene* 2.)

It is the same conceit which at once inclines the Churches
to lay stress on miracles, and makes them centres of
sectarian friction instead of gardens for " the fruits of
the Holy Spirit."

P. 343, l. 35. " Whether kings will ever allow. . . ."
Spinoza was too good a republican to repose great faith
in autocratic monarchs. The intrigues of the Prince of

Orange with the fanatical Calvinist preachers were not at all encouraging in this respect.

P. 343, l. 13. " The ancient Hebrews." Spinoza was thinking, no doubt, of the many passages in the Old Testament in which God's omnipresence is emphasized, and especially, perhaps, of what may be called the nature-poetry of the Bible.

LETTER LXXIV

P. 344. This letter is only known from the *Posthumous Works*, the original letter, written in Latin, having been lost.

P. 345, l. 10. " If we are driven by Fate," etc. Allusion to Seneca's *Œdipus*, 980, 986 f. Oldenburg cannot grasp Spinoza's distinction between Necessity and Coercion. See Annotations to Letter LVI.

P. 346, l. 4. " *The Word became flesh.*" *St. John*, Chapter I, verse 14. " *The Son of God took not on him the nature of angels. . . .*" See *Hebrews*, Chapter II, verse 16.

P. 346, l. 7. " The only-begotten Son of God . . . paid the ransom for us sinners. . . ." See *I Timothy*, Chapter II, verses 5, 6 ; and *St. Matthew*, Chapter XX, verse 27.

LETTER LXXV

P. 346. This letter was included in the *Posthumous Works*. The original letter, written in Latin, has been lost ; but a copy of it made by Leibniz (and with notes by him) is preserved in the Library at Hanover. The Heidelberg edition of Spinoza's Works (1926) prints both texts. The differences are of no great importance.

P. 347, l. 10. " This inevitable necessity of things,"
etc. This paragraph is repeated from Letter XLIII,
fifth paragraph. J. Martineau (*A Study of Spinoza*,
1882, p. 98) held that Letter XLIII was written after this
letter, in 1675. But a comparison of Letters XLIII
and LXIX shows a radical change in Spinoza's views
about Velthuysen. Letter XLIII must therefore have
been written before Letter LXIX, and therefore before
Letter LXXV. Moreover, there is no reason whatever
for supposing that Spinoza waited four years or more
before replying to the Letter (XLII) which Velthuysen
wrote to Ostens in January 1671, and which Ostens
presumably forwarded to Spinoza with little, if any,
delay.

P. 347, l. 26. " As clay in the hand of the potter."
See *Romans*, Chapter IX, verses 20, 21, also Hebrew
Liturgy.

P. 348, l. 18. " God appeared unto Abraham, when
he saw three men. . . ." See *Genesis*, Chapter XVIII,
verses 1 ff.

P. 348, l. 36. " *Leave the dead to bury their own dead.*"
St. Matthew, Chapter VIII, verse 22 ; *St. Luke*, Chapter
IX, verse 60.

LETTER LXXVI

P. 350. This letter is contained in the *Posthumous
Works*. The original letter, written in Latin, has not
been preserved. At least it cannot be traced. But
there exists a copy of it made by Leibniz himself, and
having notes on it written by him. This copy is in the
former Royal Library at Hanover. The Heidelberg
edition of Spinoza's Works (1926) gives both texts.
The differences in the two texts are not important.
Concerning Burgh, see *Introduction*, § 5.

P. 350, l. 20. Concerning Steno, see *Introduction*, § 7, Letter LXVIIa, and the Annotations to it.

P. 351, l. 19. *I John*, Chapter IV, verse 13. Spinoza put this verse as a motto on the very title-page of his *Tractatus Theologico-Politicus*.

P. 351, l. 23. " As I said with John," namely, in the *Tractatus Theologico-Politicus*, Chapter XIV. The reference is to *I John*, Chapter IV, verses 7 and 8 : *Love is of God ; and every one that loveth is begotten of God, and knoweth God. He that loveth not knoweth not God ; for God is love.*

P. 352, l. 13. " Not one whom Chastillon in the town of Tienen . . . gave with impunity to the horses to eat." This seems to refer to an unsavoury incident which occurred in May 1635 when a Franco-Dutch army attacked the Spanish army in Tienen (or Tirlemont), Belgium. The French general Gaspard de Coligny, Maréchal de Châtillon, was a Huguenot, and when the town was sacked he appears to have had the " hosts " thrown to the horses, as an expression of his disgust with what he regarded as Catholic idolatry.

P. 352, l. 25. " Not . . . the best Philosophy, but . . . the true one." What Spinoza claims is that his philosophy is true as far as it goes, although it is not the whole truth (" the best "). This claim must not be interpreted in a spirit of conceit. It must be remembered that for Spinoza the *true* idea is primarily the *adequate* idea (see the Annotations to Letter LX), and the adequate idea is that which helps one to grasp the interconnectedness of the facts to which it is applied. And Spinoza had a perfect right to say, and to say in all modesty, whether his ideas or his philosophy had this adequacy for him.

P. 352, l. 33. " The true reveals itself and the false." The ultimate test of knowledge is more knowledge, or the coherence of all that is known ; and the false is betrayed by its incoherence or disharmony with what is already known.

P. 353, l. 16. " The Pharisees." Spinoza uses this term to designate and to condemn also the post-Talmudic exponents of an over-ritualistic Judaism. This use of the term appears to have been introduced by Gabriel da Costa, commonly known as Uriel Acosta. Da Costa was born in Portugal in 1585, of Marrano parents, escaped to Holland about 1618 in order to live as a Jew, but came into conflict with the Jewish authorities, was twice excommunicated, and eventually committed suicide in 1640. In his revolt against the narrow Judaism of the Amsterdam Rabbinical authorities, and in his excommunication, as well as in certain other respects, Da Costa was a forerunner of Spinoza, who had probably seen him when he was still a little boy, and who no doubt remembered the time when Da Costa shot himself. The bitterness with which Spinoza speaks of " the Pharisees," especially in his *Tractatus Theologico-Politicus*, is to be explained by reference to his experiences with Amsterdam Jewish orthodoxy. He speaks more respectfully of " the ancient Hebrews," and even indicates his intellectual kinship with them (Letter LXXIII). By " the ancient Hebrews " he meant chiefly the Prophets and the Psalmists. And it is noteworthy that nearly all Jewish " Reform " movements in modern times profess to go " back to the Prophets and the Psalmists." Incidentally it may be pointed out that " the Pharisees " have really been much maligned (see R. Travers Herford : *The Pharisees*).

P. 354, l. 3. " Judah . . . the Faithful." The tragedy referred to appears to have occurred in Valladolid (Spain), on July 25, 1644. The victim was Don Lope de Vera y Alarcon, of San Clementi. By birth he was a Christian nobleman. But the study of Hebrew literature led him to embrace Judaism, and he adopted the name *Juda el fido*. He was imprisoned by the Inquisition, and eventually burned at the stake. An account of these events is contained in Manasseh ben Israel's *Esperanza de Israel* (The Hope of Israel), which was published in 1650, and was dedicated to the Wardens of the Amsterdam Synagogue when Spinoza's father was one of its Wardens. Spinoza had a copy of the book in his library, as we know from the official inventory of his estate. According to Manasseh ben Israel, " Judah the Faithful " suffered martyrdom in 1649 (not in 1644), and was twenty-five years old at the time.

P. 354, l. 6. " To thee, O God, I commit my soul." *Psalm* XXXI, verse 5 : *Into thine hand I commend my spirit.*

P. 354, l. 12. " The Mohammedan Church. . . ." Spinoza was, of course, mistaken in supposing that there were no sects in Islam.

LETTER LXXVII

P. 355. This letter is only known from the *Posthumous Works*, the original letter, written in Latin, having been lost.

P. 355, l. 30. εὖ πράττειν means " to prosper " or " do well," and is used as a greeting, like *Vale*.

P. 356, l. 14. Oldenburg, like Blyenbergh, of course, cannot escape from the traditional way of regarding human life as a drama of deserts and retributions. For Spinoza's view see Letters XIX, XXI, XXIII, and the Annotations to them, also Letter LXXVIII.

LETTER LXXVIII

P. 357. This letter is included in the *Posthumous Works*. The original letter, written in Latin, has not been preserved. But there is a copy of it made by

Leibniz (with his notes on it) in the Library at Hanover. Both texts are printed in the Heidelberg edition of Spinoza's Works (1926). The differences are not important.

P. 357, l. 19. " My previous letter," namely, Letter LXXV.

P. 357, l. 27. " Stone," that is, gall-stone.

P. 359, l. 15. " The Catalogue of the books of the Noble Mr. Boyle." Already in 1665 Oldenburg appears to have begun the compilation of a chronological list of Boyle's works (see *The Works of Robert Boyle*, edition 1772, Vol. VI, p. 68). In 1677 Oldenburg published such a catalogue in the *Philosophical Transactions* of the Royal Society (No. CXXX, pp. 766 f.). Presumably Oldenburg had sent Spinoza an advance copy of this catalogue.

LETTER LXXIX

P. 359. This letter is not printed in the *Posthumous Works*. Nor is the original letter, written in Latin, preserved. But there is an old copy of it (apparently intended for the printers of the *Opera Posthuma*, but not used) in the possession of the Orphanage of the United Baptists in Amsterdam. It was first published by Van Vloten in his *Ad Benedicti de Spinoza Opera Supplementum* (1860).

P. 360, l. 31. " Miracles and ignorance." See Annotations to Letter LXXIII. Oldenburg does not see the difference between failing to see the precise place of an event in the order of Nature while believing that it has such a place, and turning such ignorance into a ground for regarding the event in question as miraculous or supernatural.

*   *   *   *   *

This letter closes the extant correspondence between Oldenburg and Spinoza. As a matter of fact, Oldenburg wrote again to Spinoza in October 1676, and entrusted the letter to Leibniz for transmission. But for some reason or other this letter was never delivered. In a letter written on the very day after Spinoza's death, Oldenburg informed Leibniz of his surprise at the non-delivery of his letter to Spinoza.

LETTER LXXX.

P. 361.　This letter is only known from the *Posthumous Works*, the original letter, written in Latin, having been lost. The last paragraph of the letter is not contained in the Latin edition, only in the Dutch edition.

P. 361, l. 30.　"Your letter on the Infinite," that is, Letter XII.

P. 361, l. 31.　"But they do not conclude. . . ." This is quoted from page 120, line 14.

P. 362, l. 13.　Huet.　Pierre Daniel Huet (1630–1721) was born in Caen. In 1651 he went to Paris. In 1652 he visited the Swedish Court, and various Universities, and discovered and edited some fragments of Origen's commentary on *St. Matthew*. In 1670 he was appointed assistant tutor to the Dauphin, and edited the "Delphin Classics." He was admitted to the Academy in 1674, took Holy Orders in 1676, and was created a Bishop in 1685. He was, of course, a defender of revealed religion against free philosophy. The book to which Leibniz referred is probably the *Demonstratio Evangelica*, which Huet published in 1679. Another book in which Huet attacked the *Tractatus Theologico-Politicus* is the one called *Quaestiones Aletnanae de Concordia Rationis et Fidei*, published in 1690.

LETTER LXXXI

P. 362. This letter, originally written in Latin, is only known from the *Posthumous Works*, the original having been lost.

P. 362, l. 23. " In my letter on the Infinite," namely, Letter XII. The Dutch edition has " in my letter to L. M.," that is, to L. Meyer. The editors of the *Opera Posthuma* naturally wished to omit the name of the correspondent ; but there seems to have been an oversight in the Dutch edition.

P. 363, l. 1. On the Cartesian and the Spinozistic conceptions of Extension see *Introduction*, § 8.

LETTER LXXXII

P. 363. This letter is only known from the *Posthumous Works*, the original letter, written in Latin, having been lost.

P. 363, l. 17. Tschirnhaus points out that Descartes did not explain natural or material phenomena by reference to Extension alone, but that he supposed that God had imparted motion to extension. Tschirnhaus does not seem to realize that such supernatural interference is entirely contrary to the strict Naturalism of Spinoza's philosophy. See *Introduction*, §§ 2 and 8.

P. 364, l. 19. " Proposition 16 of the *Ethics* " (Part I), namely, " From the necessity of the divine nature infinite things must follow in infinite ways (that is, all things which come within the infinite understanding)."

LETTER LXXXIII

P. 365. This letter, too, is only known from the *Posthumous Works*, the original letter, written in Latin, having been lost. The Latin edition gives no signature at all. The signature given in the text is from the Dutch edition.

P. 365, l. 12. " If life lasts." Spinoza died seven months after writing this letter.

P. 365, l. 9. " Matter is badly defined by Descartes. . . ." See *Introduction*, §§ 2 and 8, on the difference between Spinoza's and Descartes' conception of Matter or Extension.

P. 365, l. 32. " What . . . has recently been discovered about Refraction." The allusion is probably to one or both of the following discoveries :—

(*a*) Newton discovered, about 1670, that the prism resolves a beam of white light into coloured beams of various refrangibilities. He communicated his discovery in a paper to Oldenburg, Secretary of the Royal Society, dated February 6, 1672, and the resulting discussion continued for some years.

(*b*) Erasmus Bartholinus, in his *Experimenta crystalli islandici disdiaclastici* (Copenhagen 1669), gives an account of his discovery of *double refraction*. A ray of light, upon passing into a crystal of Iceland spar, gives rise to two refracted rays, one having a direction given by Snell's law of refraction (discovered 1621), and the other obeying a more complicated law which was first correctly represented by Huygens in his *Traité de la Lumière* (composed 1678).

ANNOTATIONS

LETTER LXXXIV

P. 366. This letter is contained in the *Posthumous Works*, but not among the Correspondence. It is given in lieu of a Preface to the *Political Treatise* printed in the same volume. The original letter cannot be traced, and it is not known to whom it was addressed. Nor is the precise date of it known. But it was probably written in the latter part of 1676. For the *Tractatus Politicus*, as Spinoza eventually left it, contained the chapter on Aristocratic Government, and part of the chapter on Democratic Government, which had not yet been written when Spinoza wrote this letter, as is evident from its concluding sentence. As Spinoza died on February 21, 1677, he must have written this letter still in 1676, to leave time for the above-mentioned additions.

SUGGESTED EMENDATIONS

IN THE HEIDELBERG EDITION OF THE CORRE-
SPONDENCE (SPINOZA, OPERA TOM. IV., 1926) AND
IN THE TEXTS ON WHICH IT IS BASED.

Page 49   line 18   ' illum ' should be ' illam '.

Page 61   line 18   ' Ghasdai ' should probably be ' Chasdai '.

Page 75   line 12   ' eandem ' should be ' eadem '.

Page 76   line 17   ' hanc ' should be ' hunc '.

Page 77   line 21   ' quae ' should be ' qui '.

Page 79   line 13   ' nie ' should be ' niet '.

Page 81   line 2   ' niet ' should probably be inserted before ' soude '.

Page 83   line 13   The bracket should probably be inserted after ' aenmerckt ' instead of after ' Ziel '.

Page 99   line 2   ', maer ' should probably be '. Maer '.

Page 102   line 1   . after ' noemt ' should be , .

Page 110   line 20   ' evenveel ' should probably be ' evenwel '.

Page 117   line 6   ' sich ' should be omitted.

Page 118   line 37   ' ni ' should be ' in '.

Page 120   line 13   ' niet ' might better be omitted.

Page 133   lines 9, 10   The bracket should be inserted after ' fecisse ' instead of after ' contraria '.

Page 133   line 14   ' sed non ' should not be in italics.

Page 137   line 28   ' tum ' should probably be ' tam '.

Page 153   lines 16–19   These lines have been displaced. 'Vragen' should be followed by 'waer in ick . . . hadden. Ick wenschte . . . geven'.

Page 180   line 1   'hauc' should be 'hanc'.

Page 193   line 22   'te' should be 'de'.

Page 194   lines 1, 2   'quam' should be 'quem'.

Page 208   headline   LXII should be XLII.

Page 216   line 15   'enarrataram' should be 'enarratarum'.

Page 218   line 27   'Turca' should be 'Turcae'.

Page 220   line 8   'si' should be 'sic'.

Page 274   line 16   The bracket should be inserted after 'dedit' instead of after 'literis'.

Page 286   line 19   'Amadiis' should be 'Amadis'.

Page 288   line 15   ? should be ; .

Page 295   line 25   'rato' should be 'raro'.

Page 305   line 32   'te' should be perhaps 'eum'.

Page 306   Heading   'ad praecedentem' should be 'ad Epistolam LXXII'.

Page 318   line 5   'omnium' should probably be 'omnia'.

Page 329   line 23   '$\pi\rho\sigma$ . . .' should be '$\pi\rho o$ . . .'.

INDEX

INDEX

487

INDEX

INDEX

INDEX

INDEX

INDEX

INDEX